Tactics and Procurement in the Habsburg Military, 1866–1918

John A. Dredger

Tactics and Procurement in the Habsburg Military, 1866–1918

Offensive Spending

palgrave
macmillan

John A. Dredger
Assumption Academy
Walton, KY
USA

ISBN 978-3-319-57677-0 ISBN 978-3-319-57678-7 (eBook)
DOI 10.1007/978-3-319-57678-7

Library of Congress Control Number: 2017939559

Cover credit: Group photograph: © The Protected Art Archive/Alamy Stock Photo.
Coin: © Christoph Rueegg/Alamy Stock Photo.

Printed on acid-free paper

This Palgrave Macmillan imprint is published by Springer Nature
The registered company is Springer International Publishing AG
The registered company address is: Gewerbestrasse 11, 6330 Cham, Switzerland

To my wife Vanessa

Acknowledgements

Many individuals deserve my gratitude for the various ways in which they have made this book possible. I must first thank the late Mr Mark Chapman for funding this present work and my 4 years as a full-time student at Kansas State University. Without his generosity through the Chapman Fellowship, my writing may never have been completed. I must also thank the Kansas State University History Department for awarding me the Colonel Peter Cullen Military History Fellowship, which supported my research trip to Vienna. I am also grateful to my recently departed father, Oliver Dredger, who generously helped me financially with my Viennese sojourn.

The members of my committee proved of inestimable value during my writing. All showed unending willingness to provide answers covering the spectrum of academic queries. Professor Brent Maner constantly offered helpful criticism, while trying to keep me on track as I wandered off into the details. Similarly, Professor David Stone repeatedly guided me to see the forest when I was lost in the trees. Professor Marsha Frey's continually positive and amazingly quick feedback encouraged me during the arduous writing and revising process. Professor Derek Hillard inspired me to improve my German skills, a most useful and necessary ability as I learned in Vienna while poring over the cryptic scribblings of Austro-Hungarian officers.

In Vienna, the staff at the *Kriegsarchiv* performed the impossible by supplying me with inaccessible boxes during remodeling of the archive holdings. I must especially thank the late Dr Jerko, who offered his help when I was lost and led me to sources that I had no idea existed. In addition, I wish to thank Miha Simac for befriending me and alleviating the tedium of leafing through seemingly endless documents. My thanks must also go to my brother William Dredger, my friend Patrick Maguire, and my niece Pauline Dredger for always expressing interest in my writing while reading, discussing, and commenting on each chapter.

My gratitude would not be complete without an immense thank-you to my wife Vanessa and our children Margaret, Kathleen, Patricia, Cecilia, Anthony, Elizabeth, and Raymond. Vanessa endured the long hours of loneliness and boredom that a writer's spouse must tolerate in addition to keeping the household in a state of relative quiet for me to work. Supporting me with words of encouragement, while putting up with my fits of frustration, she continued to supply me with the consolation of her presence and her mouth-watering brownies. Our children suffered through days, weeks, and months of Daddy being too busy to spend much time with them as they often heard such words as "Not right now" and "Just wait until I'm done with this chapter."

Finally, I must thank others no longer here, especially Brother Sidonius Lepsi, OCSC, for the inspiration of his immense historical knowledge, Mr Eugene Dinet, for his friendship and linguistic skills, and my mother, Elizabeth Dredger, who helped me more than anyone could know.

Contents

1 Introduction 1

2 The Problems of 1866: Tactics, Weapons, and Money 13

3 1866–1876: First Steps Toward Progress 49

4 Adapting in Bosnia-Hercegovina 99

5 From Progress to Reversion 133

6 Financial Shock: Conradian Tactics and Wasteful Spending 175

7 The Catastrophe of the Offensive 235

8 Conclusion 281

Bibliography 289

Index 299

CHAPTER 1

Introduction

In 1866, Habsburg staff officer Lieutenant-Colonel Eduard Bartels commented in his book, *Österreich und sein Heer*, on the dismal results suffered by the Austrian military whenever it confronted a major power: "The history of the Austrian army is a history of defeats. Every time it fights alone against another European great power, it loses. This permanent misfortune must have its reasons."[1] This comment came in the wake of the disastrous defeat of the Habsburg army against the Prussians at Königgrätz in the Austro-Prussian War, also called the Seven Weeks' War, denoting how quickly the Austrian army collapsed in the face of an aggressive enemy.

In 1914, the Austro-Hungarian army embarked on its final failure, World War I. Although this time Habsburg forces held out for over 4 years, the result resembled previous losses except for the finality of 1918 for the monarchy and the Habsburg Empire. As in 1866, poorly trained troops led by incompetent commanders, who refused to adapt to the effects of new technology on the battlefield, met disaster. Surely, a state as large and populated as the Austro-Hungarian Empire could have provided the means of military victory more successfully than history relates.

The causes for these failures stemmed primarily from flawed offensive strategies and tactics, as well as imprudent spending decisions that resulted from the desire to maintain great power status and restore the prestige of the Habsburg Empire. During both the Austro-Prussian War and the First World War Habsburg troops charged headlong into enemies bearing superior weaponry, the Dreyse breech-loading needle

J.A. Dredger, *Tactics and Procurement in the Habsburg Military, 1866–1918*, DOI 10.1007/978-3-319-57678-7_1

gun in 1866 and modern Russian and Serbian artillery in 1914. Austro-Hungarian forces did not suffer from numerical inferiority in the Bohemian campaign of 1866, but attacked the far larger Russian army in Galicia in 1914 while simultaneously assaulting equal numbers of Serbian troops in the Balkans. During the 48 years between the Austro-Prussian War and the Great War, the Habsburg high command had seemingly learned nothing. Repeating the same mistakes, using the same offensive tactics, Austro-Hungarian armies garnered the same debilitating results.

Scholars have voiced various reasons for Habsburg defeat. American historian Gunther E. Rothenberg in *The Army of Francis Joseph* discusses backwardness and conservative rejection of technology, as well as nationalistic problems within the empire, that led to parliamentary delegates refusing to fund military budget requests adequately. Rothenberg also points to the linguistic difficulties of an army that recruited speakers of ten major languages into its ranks as an essential reason for poor performance on the battlefield.[2] In *The Habsburg Empire 1790–1918*, British historian C.A. Macartney speaks of parliamentary stinginess as a primary cause of Austro-Hungarian defeats.[3] The Austrian historians Walter Wagner and Johann Christoph Allmayer-Beck in their contributions to *Die Habsburgermonarchie 1848–1918*, Vol. 5 *Die Bewaffnete Macht* emphasize the paucity of funds available to the Habsburg military during the mid to late nineteenth and early twentieth centuries.[4] Apologists for the Austro-Hungarian army, especially former Habsburg officers such as Hugo Kerchnawe in *Die Vorgeschichte von 1866 und 19??* and Oskar Regele in *Feldzeugmeister Benedek und der Weg nach Königgrätz* and *Feldmarschall Conrad*, as well as the official history of 1866, *Österreichs Kämpfe im Jahre 1866*, and the official history of the Great War, *Österreich-Ungarns letzter Krieg 1914–1918* (*ÖULK*), also prefer to blame members of the *Reichsrat* for failing to provide sufficient money to enlarge the Dual Monarchy's military and procure modern weaponry.[5] Other historians focus more on the general backwardness of Austria-Hungary as the main cause for military failure. Jonathan E. Gumz in *The Resurrection and Collapse of Empire in Habsburg Serbia* sees the Habsburg army as a backward-looking preserver of the old order.[6] A.J.P. Taylor in *The Habsburg Monarchy 1809–1918* also portrays the Austro-Hungarian Empire as politically, economically, and socially anachronistic, falling behind the other powers in every way throughout the nineteenth century.[7] More recently, American historian John R. Schindler validly makes the point that ethnic differences, especially Slavic sympathy for

Russia and Serbia, did not result in the collapse of the Habsburg military in the First World War. Schindler cites the obstruction of politicians, primarily Hungarians, to fund the Habsburg military as the main cause of Austro-Hungarian disaster.[8]

These explanations fall short of a full analysis of Habsburg defeat. The presence of ten major languages and ethnicities did create communication problems within the Austro-Hungary military, as Rothenberg ably argues. Similarly, Macartney, Wagner, Allmayer-Beck, Schindler, and apologists for the army make the valid point that internal political and economic conditions, including a smaller industrial base, hampered the Habsburg army from receiving as much funding as other European military powers such as Germany, France, and Russia. In 1868, Russia spent 34% of its state income on the military, the North German Confederation spent 28%, and France 20.8% whereas Austria-Hungary expended only 18% on its army, less than any other major power.[9] In 1911, the Dual Monarchy's military spending amounted to 420 million Kronen compared with Germany's 1786 million, Russia's 1650 million, Great Britain's 1514 million, France's 1185 million, and Italy's 528 million.[10]

Not only did the Austro-Hungarian military receive less funding than the other major powers but also, more importantly, the spending decisions of the Habsburg high command reflected poor judgment in recognizing how to use funding most effectively. Although artillery had proven the most effective part of the Austro-Hungarian army in 1866, Habsburg military leaders did not ensure that the artillery branch continued to possess an adequate quantity of field pieces nor sufficient quality to match the major powers. Instead, the Dual Monarchy's high command decided to upgrade old fortresses and build new permanent fortifications costing millions of florins and Kronen. Officers argued that Austria-Hungary would most probably engage in a future war on multiple fronts while suffering from an inferiority in numbers. Therefore, to fend off one enemy in part of the empire while fighting another on a different front, permanent fortresses would supposedly provide advantages to offset the numerical deficiencies of the Habsburg army. Even worse, during the decade preceding the First World War, Austro-Hungarian military leaders embarked on a grand plan of naval construction that included four Dreadnought battleships, which consumed hundreds of millions of Kronen. Rather than wasting hundreds of millions on fortresses and Dreadnoughts that had little impact on the war, the Habsburg high command could have procured modern artillery to replace the outdated steel-bronze cannon that weighed more and possessed a far shorter range than the field pieces of the enemy.

Permanent fortresses appealed to the desire to defend the borders of the empire against multiple enemies, and a large fleet attracted the support of politicians and officers who wanted to restore the great power status of the Dual Monarchy by establishing an overseas empire and fostering commerce. Thus, prestige played a major role in determining both parliamentary funding and spending decisions for the Austro-Hungarian army, especially in naval matters. Historians such as A.J.P. Taylor in *The Habsburg Monarchy 1809–1918*, Edward Crankshaw in *The Fall of the House of Habsburg*, Steven Beller in *Francis Joseph*, and Alan Sked in *The Decline and Fall of the Habsburg Empire, 1815–1918* have rightly argued that prestige played a large role in guiding the policy of the Dual Monarchy, both during the latter half of the nineteenth century and especially when entering war in 1914.[11] These discussions, however, involved politicians more than army officers. Günther Kronenbitter in *"Krieg im Frieden." Die Führung der k.u.k. Armee und die Großmacht politik Österreich-Ungarns 1906–1914* asserted that both Dual Monarchy politicians and military men considered restoration of Austro-Hungarian prestige to be the main motive for crushing Serbia and entering World War I.[12] As the main support of the Habsburg dynasty in a multi-ethnic state, the army had wanted to restore the great power status of Austria-Hungary since the debacle of 1866. With little opportunity for this restoration before the First World War, the Habsburg high command welcomed the chance to prove the worth of Habsburg arms by invading Serbia in 1914. This desire to restore the fallen prestige of the Dual Monarchy resulted in poor spending decisions that wasted hundreds of millions on useless battleships. Thus, the predilection for maintaining prestige prevailed against a more prudent approach to war and spending.

Like the discussions of ethnic and linguistic problems and of parliamentary stinginess, arguments attempting to prove Austro-Hungarian military backwardness and conservatism fail to divulge the whole story of the history of the Habsburg army between 1866 and 1918. Some historians, such as Barbara Jelavich in *The Habsburg Empire in European Affairs*, David Good in *The Economic Rise of the Habsburg Empire 1750–1914*, and Sked, have pointed out the positive development of the Habsburg Empire in political and economic affairs. These historians make the important point that Austria-Hungary did not decline precipitously throughout the nineteenth century, nor did the fall of the empire appear inevitable.[13] This view also applies to the military. Although certain sections of the Dual Monarchy's officer corps, especially in the cavalry, tried to maintain older styles of warfare, such as mounted troops charging infantry, most officers recognized the changing landscape of the modern battlefield. The fast-paced progress of technology impacted weaponry immensely and Habsburg military thinkers took great interest in technological innovations. Austro-Hungarian officers debated the merits of new inventions and materials for rifles, field guns, bicycles, handguns, ships, and airplanes. Even members of the imperial house called for technical improvements in the Dual Monarchy's equipment. War ministers and general staff chiefs continually strove to upgrade the weaponry of the Habsburg army. These men, however, while striving to improve artillery and rifles, also poured money into field guns of inferior quality and unnecessary and expensive permanent fortresses and battleships. Poor choices about technology, not backwardness or conservative rejection of technology per se, hindered the Austro-Hungarian military from keeping pace with the rest of the European powers, especially in artillery.

This more complex portrait of a military leadership that willingly engaged in intellectual debate and took great interest in new technology and its effects on the modern battlefield emerges from the heated debates about strategy and tactics in the main Austro-Hungarian military journals, primarily the *Österreichische Militärische Zeitschrift* (*ÖMZ*) and the *Organ der militärwissenschaftlichen Vereine*. These discussions increasingly favored abandoning the offensive *à outrance* (to the last extremity) that had met disaster in the Austro-Prussian War and showed a readiness to employ defensive and advantageous use of terrain. Archduke Albrecht, the victor of Custozza in 1866, provided the foremost impetus toward this logical method of warfare that required the combined efforts of all branches of the military. Thus, throughout the 1870s and 1880s, the Habsburg high command made progress not only in procuring new weaponry but also in putting these innovations to good use. The Austro-Hungarian army even went beyond the measures of most European militaries by dedicating cavalry to security and reconnaissance missions instead of to shock tactics, and eliminating the lance from the weaponry of mounted troops. This progress failed to move completely from theory into practice as certain parts of the officer corps still believed in the old offensive methods, especially as the attacker had always appeared to win wars throughout history.

Articles from the Austro-Hungarian military journals reveal the active theoretical debates on technology, strategy, and tactics. Not only low-ranking officers but also colonels and generals, including members of the royal family, used these journals as mouthpieces for critiques and analyses of battles, weapons, and regulations. The war ministry also employed the periodicals as a means of distributing official proclamations and introducing new measures. These journals, as the voice of the Austro-Hungarian army, reached a great number of officers and their contents are indicative of the intellectual debates within the Dual Monarchy's military. They comprise a little-used, yet highly important, source for historical research on the Habsburg army.

The archival resources in the *Kriegsarchiv* (military archives) in Vienna, especially for the *Kriegsschule* (war college) and general staff, provide documents on the offensive strategic and tactical theory that directed staff officers during maneuvers and combat. Regulations manuals, strategic and tactical handbooks, war college study guides, memoranda from war ministers and general staff chiefs, and military budget requests reveal what the Habsburg high command thought about the issues of rifles, artillery, fortresses, battleships, and their effects on strategy and tactics. These sources display the penchant for attack, the importance of prestige in spending decisions, especially for the navy, and the proclivity for permanent fortresses that seemingly contradicted the offensive tactics of the Austro-Hungarian army. The minutes of the budget debates in the Delegations show the attitudes of parliamentary representatives toward army requests, particularly the more positive view of military expenditure after 1878, as well as the role of imperial prestige in parliamentary support of the Habsburg fleet. Memoirs of former officers offer vital insight into the events of 1866, 1914–1918, and the years between the Austro-Prussian War and the First World War. The writings of high-ranking officers, such as Anton von Mollinary and Daniel von Salis-Soglio, reveal the tactical thinking of *Feldzeugmeister* (*FZM*) Ludwig von Benedek, commander of the Austrian army in Bohemia in 1866, and explain why inferior artillery was chosen during the 1870s. The writings of Arthur Arz von Straussenburg, Moritz Auffenberg von Komarów, Anton von Pitreich, and Maximilian von Pitreich show the development of Austro-Hungarian offensive tactics and training before the Great War as well as the results of poor prewar decisions on the battlefield.

The present study shows how the Habsburg high command reached conclusions about tactics and military spending. As Geoffrey Wawro said in *The Austro-Prussian War: Austria's War with Prussia and Italy in 1866*, the fault for choosing the wrong tactics and mismanaging funding, and thus for military defeat in 1866, lay within the Austro-Hungarian high command, not in outside sources such as a stingy parliament or civilian government officials.[14] This assessment also applies to World War I. In *A Mad Catastrophe: The Outbreak of World War I and the Collapse of the Habsburg Empire*, Wawro blames the ineptitude and shortsightedness of Habsburg military leaders for the disastrous losses of 1914.[15] Basing decisions on the desire to maintain great power status and prestige, Austro-Hungarian military leaders again chose offensive tactics and mismanaged funding.

Like Isabel Hull's *Absolute Destruction: Military Culture and the Practices of War in Imperial Germany* and Bruce Menning's *Bayonets Before Bullets: the Imperial Russian Army, 1861–1914*, this work looks at a major European military power during the latter part of the nineteenth century until the outbreak of the First World War.[16] The following pages reveal how the Habsburg high command made the same crucial mistakes in 1914–1918 as in 1866, that is, use of offensive strategy and tactics against enemies possessing superior weaponry. These mistakes stemmed from the desire to raise the fallen prestige of the Dual Monarchy, which also caused poor spending decisions during the years between 1866 and 1914. The Austro-Hungarian army never adopted the military culture of absolute destruction of the enemy that Hull describes in Germany. Some Habsburg military leaders, such as Conrad von Hötzendorf, would have liked to adopt such an idea and spoke of annihilation of the opponent, emphasis on tactics rather than strategy, disregard of logistics, unrealistic views of war, focus on the offensive and *élan*, and pursuit of initiative and action. Military views, however, did not penetrate Austro-Hungarian society in the same way as in Germany, nor did the Habsburg army play a dominant political role. The Austro-Hungarian army resembled the Russian army (as described by Menning) far more than the German army, especially in its struggle to adapt to modern warfare by building railroads and procuring new weaponry, in failure of the high command to learn from past conflicts, and in the division between diplomats and soldiers.

Chapter 2 points out the primary causes of the disaster against Prussia in 1866: the abysmal leadership of Benedek, offensive tactics that failed to suit the Austrian rifle, and fiscal corruption within the Habsburg army. Chapter 3 underscores the attempts of the new Austro-Hungarian high command to reform the military in response to defeat in the Austro-Prussian War. During the late 1860s and 1870s, Archduke Albrecht, victor of the battle of Custozza against Italy in 1866, and other reformers strove to procure breech-loading rifles and implement reasonable regulations that combined the defensive with the offensive. Reforms also took place in officer training, though the problem of transferring theory into practice remained. Imprudent spending decisions continued to stunt military progress, while internal rivalry delayed the reform process.

Chapter 4 investigates the performance of the Habsburg army during the invasion of Bosnia-Hercegovina in 1878. Fighting a weak opponent, the Dual Monarchy's military achieved victory. This success resulted in renewal of popular acclaim for the Austro-Hungarian army within the empire as well as a more favorable attitude towards military funding by parliamentary representatives. Although problems still existed in spending decisions, tactics, and strategy, the Habsburg army showed progress in adapting to the requirements of the modern battlefield. Chapter 5 explains the continued progress of the Habsburg army toward the creation of a modern fighting force until the pivotal years in which a return to offensive tactics took place. During the 1880s, the high command continued attempts to improve weaponry with the purchase of repeating rifles and smokeless powder, but provided the artillery with the inferior Uchatius bronze-steel cannon. The war ministry retained the favor of parliamentary delegates by proving efficient and responsible, yet needlessly spent large sums on permanent fortresses because of the fear of fighting numerically superior opponents on multiple fronts. The early 1890s brought about a turning point in Austro-Hungarian military history with the appointment of Conrad, considered an innovative and progressive thinker, as tactical instructor at the war college in 1888 and the death of Albrecht in 1895. These changes resulted in a return to the errors of 1866.

Chapter 6 describes the reversion of the Dual Monarchy's army to the offensive *à outrance* (to excess) despite the lessons of the Boer War, the Russo-Japanese War, and the Balkan Wars, showing that modern weaponry gives the advantage to the defensive. With the selection of Conrad as chief of the general staff, the most important position in the Habsburg military, the offensive took even greater prominence among the high-ranking officers of Austria-Hungary. At the same time, the Dual Monarchy's high command spent millions on permanent fortifications and on the little-used navy to maintain prestige and great power status instead of upgrading the artillery. Chapter 7 describes the main reason for Habsburg defeat in the First World War as the offensive strategy and tactics of Conrad against enemies superior in numbers and weapons, especially artillery, in an effort to restore prestige. Conrad's methods resulted in catastrophe for the Austro-Hungarian army, which lost the majority of its trained officers and soldiers and had to rely on Germany for support. The Dual Monarchy's military, however, proved resilient as Habsburg industry began producing modern weaponry, in particular artillery, in greater quantities. After the accession of Charles to the throne in 1916 and the dismissal of Conrad the following year, the new Austro-Hungarian high command started enacting reforms to restore the Habsburg Empire as a major power with sufficient weaponry and intelligent spending. Despite these belated efforts, the war ended in the collapse of both the army and the Dual Monarchy.

In these chapters, I suggest that the Habsburg army would have had more success if military leaders had employed defensive strategy and tactics and/or chosen to spend more on modern artillery, or even tanks, rather than on permanent fortresses and Dreadnoughts. These suggestions imply the use of counterfactuals, but I do not contend that the Dual Monarchy would have won the First World War if the Austro-Hungarian military had made better spending or tactical decisions. While pointing out the mistakes of Habsburg military leaders, I felt obliged to offer alternatives to Austria-Hungary's military choices in the context of discussions within the army before World War I. Because humans make choices that affect the outcomes of wars, decisions to use better strategy, tactics, and weaponry prior to 1914 could have brought more favorable results.

All the primary sources reveal that the choice of offensive tactics did not suit the numerical inferiority of the Dual Monarchy's forces. In addition, poor spending decisions because of a misguided desire to restore Habsburg prestige resulted in inadequate and insufficient material. The ensuing combination, more than general backwardness or conservatism, or even parliamentary stinginess, doomed Austro-Hungarian troops to suffer catastrophe in the Great War.

Notes

1. Eduard Bartels, *Österreich und sein Heer* (Leipzig: Otto Wigand, 1866), 1, 28–29.
2. Gunther E. Rothenberg, *The Army of Francis Joseph* (West Lafayette, IN: Purdue University Press, 1976).

3. C.A. Macartney, *The Habsburg Empire 1790–1918* (London: Weidenfeld and Nicolson, 1969).
4. Walter Wagner, "Die k.(u.)k. Armee - Gliederung und Aufgabenstellung," and Johann Christoph Allmayer-Beck, "Die Bewaffnete Macht in Staat und Gesellschaft," in *Die Habsburgermonarchie 1848–1918*, Vol. 5 *Die Bewaffnete Macht* (Vienna: Verlag der Österreichischen Akademie der Wissenschaften, 1987).
5. Hugo Kerchnawe, *Die Vorgeschichte von 1866 und 19??* (Vienna: C.W. Stern Verlag, 1909); Oskar Regele, *Feldzeugmeister Benedek und der Weg nach Königgrätz* (Vienna: Verlag Herold, 1960), 10–11; Oskar Regele, *Feldmarschall Conrad* (Vienna: Verlag Herold, 1955); K.k. Generalstabs-Bureau für Kriegsgeschichte, *Österreichs Kämpfe im Jahre 1866* (Vienna: R.v.Waldheim, 1867–1869), vol. 1–5; Edmund Glaise-Horstenau, Josef Brauner, Eduard Czegka, Jaromir Diakow, Friedrich Franek, Walther Heydendorff, Rudolf Kiszling, Franz Mühlhofer, Ernst Wisshaupt, Georg Zobi, *Österreich-Ungarns letzter Krieg 1914–1918* (*ÖULK*) (Vienna: Verlag der Militärwissenschaftlichen Mitteilungen, 1930–1938).
6. Jonathan E. Gumz, *The Resurrection and Collapse of Empire in Habsburg Serbia, 1914–1918* (New York: Cambridge University Press, 2009).
7. A.J.P. Taylor, *The Habsburg Monarchy 1809–1918* (London: Hamish Hamilton, 1948).
8. John R. Schindler, *Fall of the Double Eagle: The Battle for Galicia and the Demise of Austria-Hungary* (Lincoln, Nebraska: Potomac Books, 2015).
9. Hauptmann Ernst Schmedes, "Die Kriegsmacht der europäischen Staaten im Vergleiche mit deren Bevolkerungs- u. Budget-Verhältnisse im Jänner 1868," *Österreichische Militärische Zeitschrift* 2 (1868), 54.
10. Macartney, *The Habsburg Empire 1790–1918*, 791.
11. Taylor, *The Habsburg Monarchy 1809–1918*; Edward Crankshaw, *The Fall of the House of Habsburg* (New York: Viking Press, 1963); Steven Beller, *Francis Joseph* (New York: Longman, 1996); Alan Sked, *The Decline and Fall of the Habsburg Empire, 1815–1918* (London: Longman, 1989).
12. Günther Kronenbitter, *"Krieg im Frieden." Die Führung der k.u.k. Armee und die Großmacht politik Österreich-Ungarns 1906–1914* (Munich: Oldenbourg, 2003), 9–10.
13. Sked, *The Decline and Fall of the Habsburg Empire, 1815–1918*; Barbara Jelavich, *The Habsburg Empire in European Affairs, 1814–1918* (Chicago: Rand McNally & Co., 1969); David Good, *The Economic Rise of the Habsburg Empire, 1750–1914* (Berkeley: University of California Press, 1984).
14. Geoffrey Wawro, *The Austro-Prussian War: Austria's War with Prussia and Italy in 1866* (Cambridge: Cambridge University Press, 1996), 2–5.

15. Geoffrey Wawro, *A Mad Catastrophe: The Outbreak of World War I and the Collapse of the Habsburg Empire* (New York: Basic Books, 2014).
16. Isabel V. Hull, *Absolute Destruction: Military Culture and the Practices of War in Imperial Germany* (Ithaca: Cornell University Press, 2005); Bruce W. Menning, *Bayonets Before Bullets: The Imperial Russian Army, 1861–1914* (Bloomington & Indianapolis: Indiana University Press, 1992).

Bibliography

Published Primary Sources

Bartels, Eduard. *Österreich und sein Heer.* Leipzig: Otto Wigand, 1866.

Glaise-Horstenau, Edmund, Josef Brauner, Eduard Czegka, Jaromir Diakow, Friedrich Franek, Walther Heydendorff, Rudolf Kiszling, Franz Mühlhofer, Ernst Wisshaupt and Georg Zobi, *Österreich-Ungarns letzter Krieg 1914–1918* (*ÖULK*). Wien: Verlag der Militärwissenschaftlichen Mitteilungen, 1930–1938.

Kerchnawe, Hugo. *Die Vorgeschichte von 1866 und 19??* Wien: C.W. Stern Verlag, 1909.

K.k. Generalstabs-Bureau für Kriegsgeschichte. *Österreichs Kämpfe im Jahre 1866.* Wien: R.v.Waldheim, 1867–1869, vol. 1–5.

Österreichische Militärische Zeitschrift (ÖMZ), 1866–1914.

Secondary Sources

Allmayer-Beck, Johann Christoph. "Die Bewaffnete Macht in Staat und Gesellschaft." in *Die Habsburgermonarchie 1848–1918*, Vol. 5 *Die Bewaffnete Macht.* Vienna: Verlag der Österreichischen Akademie der Wissenschaften, 1987.

Beller, Steven. *Francis Joseph.* New York: Longman, 1996.

Crankshaw, Edward. *The Fall of the House of Habsburg.* New York: The Viking Press, 1963.

Good, David. *The Economic Rise of the Habsburg Empire, 1750–1914.* Berkeley: University of California Press, 1984.

Gumz, Jonathan E. *The Resurrection and Collapse of Empire in Habsburg Serbia, 1914–1918.* New York: Cambridge University Press, 2009.

Hull, Isabel V. *Absolute Destruction: Military Culture and the Practices of War in Imperial Germany.* Ithaca: Cornell University Press, 2005.

Jelavich, Barbara. *The Habsburg Empire in European Affairs, 1814–1918.* Chicago: Rand McNally & Co., 1969.

Kronenbitter, Günther. *"Krieg im Frieden." Die Führung der k.u.k. Armee und die Großmachtpolitik Österreich-Ungarns 1906–1914.* Munich: Oldenbourg, 2003.

Macartney, C.A. *The Habsburg Empire 1790–1918.* London: Weidenfeld and Nicolson, 1969.

Menning, Bruce W. *Bayonets before Bullets: The Imperial Russian Army, 1861–1914.* Bloomington & Indianapolis: Indiana University Press, 1992.

Regele, Oskar. *Feldmarschall Conrad.* Wien: Verlag Herold, 1955.

Regele, Oskar. *Feldzeugmeister Benedek und der Weg nach Königgrätz.* Wien: Verlag Herold, 1960.

Rothenberg, Gunther E. *The Army of Francis Joseph.* West Lafayette, IN: Purdue University Press, 1976.

Schindler, John R. *Fall of the Double Eagle: The Battle for Galicia and the Demise of Austria-Hungary.* Lincoln, NE: Potomac Books, 2015.

Sked, Alan. *The Decline and Fall of the Habsburg Empire, 1815–1918.* London: Longman, 1989.

Taylor, A.J.P. *The Habsburg Monarchy 1809–1918.* London: Hamish Hamilton, 1948.

Wagner, Walter. "Die k.(u.)k. Armee - Gliederung und Aufgabenstellung." in *Die Habsburgermonarchie 1848–1918*, Vol. 5 *Die Bewaffnete Macht.* Vienna: Verlag der Österreichischen Akademie der Wissenschaften, 1987.

Wawro, Geoffrey. *A Mad Catastrophe: The Outbreak of World War I and the Collapse of the Habsburg Empire.* New York: Basic Books, 2014.

Wawro, Geoffrey. *The Austro-Prussian War: Austria's War with Prussia and Italy in 1866.* Cambridge: Cambridge University Press, 1996.

CHAPTER 2

The Problems of 1866: Tactics, Weapons, and Money

As visitors to the Military History Museum in Vienna enter Hall 4, they meet a sign with the title "Radetzkysaal: Field Marshal Radetzky and His Time (1848–1866)." The placard might not seem odd to those unfamiliar with the life of the undefeated Habsburg commander Johann Josef Wenzel Graf Radetzky von Radetz. However, the dates appear strange to those who know that the victor of Custozza and Novara died in 1858. Further investigation of the room reveals an emphasis on the feats of the Austrian military, especially Radetzky's Italian campaigns of 1848, whereas the defeats of 1859 and 1866 remain muted. Almost 150 years after the disastrous campaign against the Prussians in Bohemia, Austria (even though no longer under Habsburg rule) still attempts to conceal the low points of its military history and feature the highlights. According to the museum guidebook, "After a number of ill-fated skirmishes, the Austrian Army under *FZM* Ludwig von Benedek suffered a devastating defeat near Königgrätz (Hradec Králové, east of Prague; the battle is also called Battle of Sadová) on 3 July."[1] The key word "ill-fated" shows the intention to lay fault somewhere other than on the Habsburg army.

Despite the claims of contemporary army supporters and some later historians that parliamentary stinginess hindered the Austrian military from procuring the best weaponry, the Habsburg high command deserved the primary blame for the disaster of 1866. The choice of offensive tactics against an enemy possessing superior firepower condemned Austrian infantry and cavalry to horrendous losses while

J.A. Dredger, *Tactics and Procurement in the Habsburg Military, 1866–1918*, DOI 10.1007/978-3-319-57678-7_2

granting little hope of success. Poor prewar spending choices and wasteful financial practices eliminated any chance of facing the Prussians in Bohemia with equal weaponry. These causes, inherent within the Austrian military leadership, brought about defeat in 1866.

Casting Aside the Blame

The museum pieces pertaining to the Austro-Prussian War of 1866 consist mainly of rifles, official reports and proclamations from after the climactic battle, and two paintings. The rifle displays reveal the desire to blame the defeat on inferior weaponry. As the museum guidebook states, "With the needle-gun the Prussian army already possessed an efficient breech-loader in the Battle of Königgrätz (Hradec Králové) on 3 July, 1866. This weapon was clearly superior in rate of fire (cadence) to the Austrian muzzle-loaders of the Lorenz system."[2] Although this analysis contains truth, the guidebook does not explain why the Habsburg army relied on an inferior weapon. The museum's collection of official reports and proclamations from the aftermath of Königgrätz admit the gravity of the loss but focus more on the heroism of the Habsburg troops and call upon the people of the Austrian Empire to display their patriotism and courage in the face of disaster.

The two paintings strikingly reveal the devastation of the Austrian catastrophe in Bohemia, far more than the other exhibits. In *The Battery of the Dead*, the Czech artist Vaclav Sochor depicts the panic and confusion of the Habsburg army's attempt to retreat from the battlefield. Amid the carnage of human and equine cadavers of the Austrian 8th Field Artillery Regiment that dominates the center and foreground of the painting, a driverless team of horses leading a cannon and its caisson tries to plow through the bodies and becomes hopelessly entangled in the wreckage. On the left, another team with riders successfully avoids the central mass, while careening frantically down the rut-filled path. In the background, riderless horses rear and run in panic, while the Prussian troops in the distance advance to overrun the abandoned Austrian guns. Sochor not only reveals the horrors of war but also, and more pointedly, the utter confusion of the Habsburg army as it tries to avoid capture and total collapse.[3]

Rudolf Baron Otto von Ottenfeld's oil canvas *A Glorious Chapter of the Austrian Artillery. The Artillery Reserve Unit after the Battle of Königgrätz on 3 July, 1866* sets a stark contrast to *The Battery of the Dead*. Sochor's title could easily belong to von Ottenfeld's painting as it depicts an abandoned artillery reserve unit in a treeless landscape after the battle. A solitary horse stands as the only living creature in the midst of dead soldiers and animals lying near abandoned and broken artillery pieces. In the distance, under a gray sky, smoke rises from a village, perhaps Chlum. The serenity of the scene creates a very different impression from that of the chaos and panic of Sochor's painting, but the desolation of complete defeat hangs over the battlefield and portrays the hopelessness of the Austrian situation.[4] The title of the painting conveys the artist's view of the glory of the Habsburg military, even in catastrophe. The museum guidebook again attempts to elicit a positive message from the battle: "While suffering heavy losses, the artillery reserve covered the orderly retreat of the Austrian northern army across the river Elbe."[5]

This same attitude pervades the official Austrian general staff history of the Austro-Prussian War published in 1869. Its main editor, General Friedrich Fischer, attempted to portray the outcome of the fighting as almost inevitable because of the difficulties of waging a two-front war against enemies with a combined superiority in manpower and the technological advantages of Prussian weaponry, while having insufficient funding for the Habsburg military and only the weak support and campaign performance of Austria's small German allies. According to the official history, these problems stemmed from diplomacy and funding issues outside the control of the army. Thus, Fischer and his staff tried to shift blame away from the inner problems of the Habsburg military.[6] This view also exonerated *FZM* Ludwig von Benedek, the commander-in-chief of the Northern Army, who after the war attributed his defeat to "bad luck."[7]

One military source, *Sechzig Jahre Wehrmacht 1848–1908*, the anonymous work of several Austrian officers, carries the same spirit in its description of the heroic deeds of the Habsburg military: "The war against Prussia was also unlucky, but the fault lay thus, as indicated, not in the army, not in the leadership alone, not in the deficiency in ability, training, and valor." The officers fault the stinginess of the *Reichsrat* as the primary cause of Austrian defeat in Bohemia in the following passage: "In Austria the means for the development of the army were denied by parliament because of financial considerations, unconcerned about training, unconcerned about consequences, while even the army's status was diminished... Therefore, even if we had been victorious at Königgrätz, (and) possessed an equivalent tactical training and an evenly matched rifle (to the Prussian weapon), Austria would still finally have been defeated, because it was not capable of fighting through the war without an equivalent number of replacement troops."[8]

Other writers also blamed civilians for the disastrous outcome of 1866. In 1900, the Viennese Liberal Heinrich Friedjung accused reactionaries in the Habsburg government of forming an ultraconservative policy that opposed liberal attempts at reform and led the Austrian state, shackled by Catholicism, into an unwinnable war against the more liberal Prussia. Oskar Regele, an officer in the Austrian federal army, also tried to exonerate the military for the defeat of 1866 and blamed the timidity and parsimony of Habsburg civil officials for the debacle. Similarly, the German historian Emil Franzel, the American historian Gordon Craig, and the Austrian historian Adam Wandruszka, among others, agree with the contention that parliamentary deputies and bureaucrats ruined the Austrian military's chances to gain victory against Prussia in 1866.[9] The inevitability of Habsburg defeat comes out strongly in all of these works and many later historians took up the military cry of blaming others for the disaster rather than analyzing causes within the Austrian army. These attempts to cover up the true reasons for failure present an erroneous picture of reality and thus deserve to be refuted.

Recognizing Reality

The claim that parliamentary monetary restrictions and diplomatic bungling rendered final victory impossible tries to hide the grave shortcomings in the Austrian military. Although some attempted to lay blame on civilian errors, important voices spoke about the real situation in the military. On 21 August 1866, Archduke Albrecht, the oldest son of Archduke Charles (the revered Habsburg commander during the Napoleonic Wars) and cousin of Emperor Franz Joseph, submitted to the emperor a report containing his observations on the problems and causes of defeat in the northern campaign against Prussia. Juxtaposing the Austrian campaign in Bohemia with that in Venetia, where Albrecht had achieved victory over the Italians, Albrecht found numerous reasons for the catastrophe of Königgrätz. Starting with poor army organization and preparation for war by Benedek, Albrecht noted the weakness of the Austrian army at the beginning of the war, a point that "had been repeated several times already by the Military Commission." The Archduke accused the high command of exhibiting poor leadership in failing to enforce proper control and discipline over subordinates. Albrecht continued with a critique of the general staff and its officers, who did not have adequate knowledge of the Bohemian terrain and the enemy to the north because of a deficiency in training. Despite the presence of the best general staff officers in the Northern Army, the Austrian leadership did not know the theater of war because they had trained in Italy and, therefore, had no familiarity with the northern areas. As for the troops, Albrecht praised their bravery and especially commended the Habsburg artillery for its superior performance in the field. The cavalry, however, he claimed did not fare well in combat because of poor leadership, resulting in horsemen being deployed in unfavorable situations. The infantry did not fight with enough of the discipline that comes from drill, while the insufficient number of officers, both commissioned and non-commissioned, increased the branch's difficulties. Thus, the Austrian troops could not stand against the superior Prussian rifles and discipline. Albrecht made no attempt to exonerate the leadership of the Northern Army. Without naming anyone directly, he accused Benedek and his staff of the mistaken belief that "bravery is everything, but skillfulness in maneuver and knowledge of terrain are not necessary." The archduke criticized the field army's administrative apparatus for being too cumbersome and too removed from contact with the rest of the army, and concluded by blaming the leadership once again for the bleak results of the northern campaign.[10] Coming from the victor of Custozza in Venetia and new commander-in-chief of all Habsburg forces, this report and its criticisms carried great weight.

In 1867, Colonel Friedrich von Beck of the general staff, the special envoy of Franz Joseph to Benedek's headquarters in the Northern Army, wrote several reports about the poor state of the army, especially its morale. Beck pointed out that deficiencies in military administration were the main cause of poor campaign performance by Habsburg forces. Explaining the disadvantage of joining several important positions in one person, as was the case when Benedek both commanded the whole army and controlled the general staff during the previous years, Beck called for the simplification of army administration, better preparation of the general staff for war, and procurement of breech-loading rifles for the infantry.[11]

The general staff colonel elaborated on these issues and others in another document concerning the deflated morale of the army. Instead of blaming outside sources for the disaster in 1866, Beck said, "the fault for the failed campaign against the Prussians lay in the army and its institutions." Again, he advocated the simplification of army administration in addition to unity throughout the military leadership. Beck indicated the loss of trust in the army's high command on all sides as well as the propensity of the higher military positions, such as the war ministry, field command, and general staff, "to lose sight of important tasks because of too great attention to details."

Beck also discussed other difficulties that had appeared during the recent war. He claimed that the general staff did not play a prominent enough role in relation to the rest of the army, as the Prussian general staff did. Troop training failed to correspond to the requirements of modern warfare. The education of the officers and strength of the troops needed improvement. In addition, he bemoaned the high costs accrued by generals who enjoyed high living, especially during campaigns. To prevent unqualified officers or political appointees from rising to important positions of command, the general staff colonel advised a promotion system that would base advancement on merit and competence rather than on connections and influence.[12] Like Albrecht, Beck pointed to the high command as the primary reason for the catastrophe of Königgrätz. Neither the archduke nor the colonel tried to blame parsimonious parliamentary deputies or financial deficiencies for the defeat, but rather called for reforms within the military to revive the flagging martial spirit and deteriorating status of the Austrian forces.

Another military writer, most likely Major General Gideon Baron von Krismanić, the chief of the operations bureau for the Northern Army, also found fault with the Habsburg army's leadership and Benedek in particular. Krismanić expressed his views shortly after the war in an anonymous article in the *Österreichische Militärische Zeitschrift* (*ÖMZ*), the mouthpiece for many officers who wished to publish their ideas without attaching their names.[13] Krismanić accused the commander of the Northern Army of wasting the opportunity of beating the dispersed Prussian army's individual units as they entered Bohemia instead of fighting a major pitched battle at Königgrätz against superior numbers. For Krismanić, numerical superiority held greater importance than the advantage of the Prussian breech-loader over the muzzle-loading Austrian Lorenz rifle. Like Albrecht and Beck, he did not blame politicians for hindering the Habsburgs from putting an adequate military force in the field. Instead, Krismanić censured Benedek for employing massed shock tactics against the superior firepower of the Prussian needle gun and the ensuing loss of morale for the Austrian troops, who saw the heavy casualties resulting from their charges. Krismanić denied the invincibility of the Dreyse rifle and claimed that the Austrian army, especially the artillery, fought better than the Prussians and could have gained victory with a more intelligent field commander. The Habsburg forces possessed the means to succeed, but Benedek failed to prepare properly for war by practical training in maneuver and use of terrain.[14]

Once again, an Austrian military source had identified the problems within the army, especially the high command, as the primary causes of failure in 1866. These internal negative assessments of the Habsburg military contrasted sharply with the official history and other writings published by officers and supporters of the army, which diverted blame onto civilian leaders and influenced some later authors. Austrian military leaders realized that the problems stemmed from within the army but wished to maintain a more positive public view of the military. Some later writers also saw the complaints against the politicians as a façade.

The Austrian historian Johann Christoph Allmayer-Beck, writing in 1966, stated that the causes of the 1866 disaster in Bohemia came from within the Habsburg army itself. He refuted claims that a series of unlucky accidents culminated in the fateful battle of Königgrätz, or that inferior numbers or weaponry predetermined the outcome. Instead, Allmayer-Beck blamed the outdated Austrian theory of war, as Archduke Charles had instilled his version of Napoleonic warfare into the Habsburg military: "But the spirit, which should give everything direction and effect—which the victor of Amberg, Würzburg, and Aspern made it his business to kindle and keep alive—this spirit now after half a century had become rigid and lacked elasticity, and one of the proudest armies that Austria had ever put in the field broke to pieces on it."[15]

Twentieth century American historian, Gunther Rothenberg, also rejected the easy explanation of a miserly parliament unwilling to give necessary monetary resources to the Austrian military establishment. However, Rothenberg did not place the blame solely on Benedek. The Northern Army field commander made serious mistakes during the campaign, but prewar choices by the Austrian high command in weaponry and tactics put the Habsburg army at a great disadvantage.[16] According to Rothenberg, the explanation for defeat lies in both the battlefield command and the army administration that decided weapons procurement, tactics, strategy, and training, as Albrecht and Beck maintained in their reports.

Another American historian, Geoffrey Wawro, asserted in 1992 that blame for the catastrophe lay primarily with Benedek because the field commander's strategy and tactics did not suit the capabilities of the Austrian rifle. In addition, Wawro stated that the Habsburg war ministry had used funding carelessly by spending money on bureaucracy and high living rather than on training and weaponry.[17] Clearly, certain historians have seen that, even though the Austrian military preferred publicly to blame outside sources for defeat, the main causes came from within the army itself, as the postwar high command realized.

Breech-Loader Versus Shock Tactics

For those who wished to exonerate the military, such as Fischer, who directed writing of the official Austrian general staff history of the Austro-Prussian War, and the authors of *Sechzig Jahre Wehrmacht 1848–1908*, the claim of having to employ inferior weaponry and rely on poorly trained troops because of financial constraints imposed by a recalcitrant *Reichsrat* (Parliament) conveniently explained the defeat in Bohemia, and at the same time accounted for success against a similarly trained and equipped Italian army in Venetia.[18] Certainly, the Prussian breech-loader, the Dreyse needle gun, surpassed the Austrian Lorenz rifle in rate of fire. Not only did the breech-loading weapon shoot four to seven rounds per minute compared with the one to two rounds per minute of the Austrian muzzle-loader and its Minié bullets, but also soldiers using the needle gun could fire it when standing, kneeling, or prone. Thus, the Dreyse afforded the Prussian troops more flexibility, greater possibility to find cover, and increased firepower over the muzzle-loading weapons of the Habsburg army.[19] An *ÖMZ* author estimated the superiority of the breech-loader over the Lorenz as three to one, and claimed that the needle gun overpowered the courage and perseverance of the enemy.[20] This advantage led to a great discrepancy in casualties between the Prussian and Austrian forces. Habsburg losses amounted to roughly 48,000 men at the battle of Königgrätz, while their adversary lost less than 9000.[21] Not all Austrian casualties resulted from the Prussian breech-loader, but its superior firepower must account for a large proportion. The Dreyse rifle greatly impressed Albrecht. Even though he had not encountered it in Italy, the archduke commented after the Bohemian campaign that the needle gun had proven the theoretically established advantage of an easily and quickly loaded weapon against troops equipped with slower firing rifles.[22]

The superior rate of fire of the Prussian breech-loader over the Austrian muzzle-loader was not the only cause of the enormous discrepancy in casualties. The reliance of the Habsburg forces on *Stoßtaktik* (shock tactics) eliminated the advantages of the Lorenz rifle's greater range and muzzle velocity.[23] An *ÖMZ* review of an article in the *Revue des Deux Mondes* contended that the *Schnellfeuer* (rapid fire) of the breech-loader, together with the Prussians' greater capability for and use of maneuver, explained the Austrian catastrophe in Bohemia.[24] Another *ÖMZ* writer asserted after the war: "The Prussians knew most how to draw profit from dominating positions, how to use terrain positions for cover, how to bring the enemy into crossfire, etc.; the Austrians on the other hand held themselves more to formal mass tactics and the direct attack with bayonets and sabers, which, hindered by superior enemy fire, could scarcely come to execution and yet brought heavier and heavier losses with it."[25] Clearly, Habsburg military leaders recognized the advantages of the breech-loading rifle over the muzzle-loader as well as the mismatch between Austrian shock tactics and the Lorenz rifle used by Habsburg troops.

The Habsburg army had maintained an offensive spirit in its tactics for decades, like most other nineteenth-century powers. Ever since the great offensive victories of Napoleon I, the European armies had adopted the French emperor's style of emphasizing mobility, rapidity, and the decisive battle with shock tactics and concentration of artillery.[26] In keeping with the ideas of the two great theorists of the Napoleonic Age, Antoine Henri Jomini, who stressed the importance of bringing the greatest mass of troops to bear upon the decisive point of the battlefield, and Carl von Clausewitz, who signified the aim of warfare as the disarming of the enemy and the destruction of his forces, the great victories leading up to 1866 had all contained offensive assaults.[27] Napoleon defeated the Austrians at Ulm and Austerlitz in 1805, the Prussians at Jena and Auerstädt in 1806, and the Russians at Friedland in 1807, all with impressive assaults. Radetzky's famous victories over the Italians at Custozza and Novara as well as Habsburg gains in Hungary came from timely offensives. In the Crimean War, Sevastopol finally fell to a French attack after a long siege. In 1859, the Austrians succumbed to French storm columns at Magenta and Solferino. Even in the Danish War, the Prussian and Austrian frontal assaults appeared to bring decisive victory.

All these achievements were the result of employing the offensive tactics of Napoleon. However, military leaders who chose to continue emulating the Little Corporal's methods ignored the increasing number of casualties resulting from frontal assaults and the battles in which the tactical offensive failed. These battles included Waterloo, Balaclava, and Inkerman, as well as many engagements in the American Civil War, such as Fredericksburg, Gettysburg, and Cold Harbor.

Austrian officers, like the soldiers of most European armies, saw the successes of Napoleon and other generals who won with the tactical offensive. Habsburg leaders especially looked to Archduke Charles' victory at Aspern and Radetzky's feats in 1848 as belonging to a tradition of offensive battle, and hoped to imitate them with similar effect. With this view, most of the Habsburg officer corps did not even consider the tactical defensive as an effective option. Wawro also posits that the Austrian high command could not pit its troops against the superior Prussian forces except in assault formations: "Basically, in 1866, Austria had no choice but to employ storm columns. The poorly educated, poorly trained, largely non-German-speaking Austrian army could not shoot accurately or maneuver in open order. Shock tactics thus met the organizational needs of the unruly Austrian regiments; they massed large numbers of men in formations which could be literally driven into action."[28] With the offensive as the only consideration for the Habsburg high command, shock tactics fit the inferior Austrian soldiers. The defensive, however, would have provided better use of Austrian military resources, especially superior artillery and the Lorenz rifle, but still allowed officers to control their assortment of poorly trained troops. If the Habsburg leaders had understood Clausewitz properly and taken the time to train their units to shoot accurately, they would have realized the superiority of the defense. Instead, Benedek elected to do the opposite by sending his men directly into the *Schnellfeuer* of the Prussian needle gun.

Benedek had emphasized *Stoßtaktik* in his numerous instructions and orders, both before and during the early stages of the 1866 campaign.[29] As the only Austrian general who emerged from the Franco-Austrian War of 1859 with a good reputation, Benedek had received the command not only of the Army of Italy but also of the Austrian General Staff. Thus, he became the most powerful soldier in the Habsburg Empire. Disdainful of military science and intellectual pursuits in general, Benedek, like his emperor and many other Austrian officers, had concluded that shock tactics achieved the best results in battle. This idea stemmed from his experiences in Italy in 1859 where the French had stormed Habsburg positions and put the Austrian troops to flight, despite the superior rifle and maneuver capabilities of the Habsburg units. Austrian commanders, however, learned the wrong lessons from the war. As Wawro wrote, "Although the secret of French arms was *flexibility*, Austrian critics ignored that and focused instead on the intangible quality of *élan* supposedly conferred by bayonet charges into the breach."[30]

The commander of the North Army clung to these erroneous tactical ideas, even after the experiences of Habsburg forces in the Danish War of 1864 and publication of the writings of Helmuth von Moltke, chief of the Prussian general staff. Prussian units had inflicted devastating losses by rapid fire of the needle gun on the Danish troops, whereas the Austrian massed frontal assaults on entrenched Danish positions had endured heavy casualties.[31] In articles published both in a Prussian army journal and in the *ÖMZ*, which promoted dissemination of the views of foreign military thinkers, Moltke explained the advantages of the Prussian breech-loader and its superior employment in the Danish War.[32] Nevertheless, Benedek, in his devotion to *élan* (vigor) and the supposed merits of the offensive displayed by the French in 1859, insisted on closed formations and shock tactics to achieve decisive results with rapid bayonet charges.[33]

Benedek did not stand alone in his preference for *Stoßtaktik*. Other high-ranking officers in the Habsburg army agreed upon shock as the premier method of attack. Major General Anton von Mollinary praised the French offensive tactics during the 1859 campaign because of their emphasis on closed formations for concentration of the greatest power on decisive points. Even in defensive positions, they tried to maintain their offensive spirit through frequent counterattacks.[34] The 1865 Austrian tactical manual, written by Colonel Johann Waldstätten, stressed the bayonet as the most important weapon and the bayonet attack as the high point of battle.[35] Even Archduke Albrecht advocated bayonet attacks and a perpetual offensive before he realized the decimating effect of the Dreyse rifle.[36] Austrian frontal assaults had found success against the poorly trained Italian troops.[37] In Bohemia, against a highly competent enemy, a far different outcome had resulted.

The combination of shock tactics and the Prussian needle gun contributed heavily to the Austrian defeat in 1866. A defensive form of tactics could have taken advantage of the superior range and muzzle velocity of the Lorenz rifle without exposing soldiers as much to the devastating effect of the Dreyse's *Schnellfeuer*. The Bavarians, allies of the Habsburgs during the Austro-Prussian War, demonstrated the ability to adapt tactics to the rapidly changing battlefield of the nineteenth century by avoiding massed frontal assaults, and the offensive in general. Ludwig Tann, the Bavarian chief of staff, learned the devastating effect of the breech-loader by observing the Danish War of 1864. During this conflict, at the battle of Düppel, Prussian troops inflicted five times the number of casualties they received from the Danes. Tann interpreted this large differential as the effect of the needle gun and thus included defensive tactics, including lying prone behind cover, in the new Bavarian tactical manual. The Bavarian commander proved the possibility of successfully adapting to technological change on the battlefield during his own encounters with the Prussians in 1866.[38]

Although the Bavarians showed how to limit the advantages of the Dreyse rifle and changed their tactics to accommodate Prussia's style of warfare, Benedek, the chief architect of Austrian tactics, did not see the need to do the same until it was too late. Under the influence of the successful French assaults in 1859 and the Austrian offensive victories against the Danes in 1864, Benedek saw no reason to change tactics. Some members of the Austrian army, however, realized the superior firepower of the Prussian weapon. Beck warned Benedek about the danger of frontal assaults across open spaces in the spring of 1866, before war broke out. The North Army commander, nevertheless, disregarded Beck's advice, claiming that the Austrian attackers would run under the arc of the Prussian bullets, much as the French had done in 1859.[39] Such a plan required poor shooting from the enemy, an unfounded hope against the well-trained Prussians. Only after repeated defeats and heavy losses did Benedek consider changing his tactics. In an order of 28 June, he tried to adjust the offensive methods he had constantly employed up to that time. However, Benedek refused to give up the attack, especially the bayonet charge, commanding his officers to soften up the enemy with artillery fire before any assaults, not wishing to diminish the offensive spirit of his troops.[40]

The Austrian high command clung to the offensive during 1866 until the saner minds of Albrecht and his chief of staff, *Generalmajor* Franz Freiherr von John, ordered no more frontal assaults. In July, before the official end of the war, John began working on a new tactical manual, in which he mandated an emphasis on firepower, the defensive, use of terrain and cover, coordination with artillery, and open order advances.[41] Although immediate implementation of such a different set of tactics would have proved difficult for the poorly trained Habsburg forces, at least the new Austrian leadership had started to address the problems.

Strategic Failure and Permanent Fortifications

The North Army high command also erred in the realm of strategy. Wavering and tentative, Benedek originally wanted to await the Prussians in the fortified positions surrounding the fortress at Olmütz in Moravia. This plan not only gave the initiative to the enemy during the opening stages of the war, but also withdrew any hope of Austrian assistance for the Habsburg allies in the German Confederation, in particular Hanover, Hesse, and Saxony. Therefore, Franz Joseph sent Beck to prod Benedek into action, though the general complained that his army could not withstand the strain of an advance into Bohemia. Even under pressure from Vienna, Benedek did not act with enterprise and alacrity. Failing to take advantage of his interior lines to attack the three separate Prussian armies invading Bohemia, he wasted his men in isolated assaults against the needle gun. After heavy losses, the Austrian army drew back to Königgrätz, another fortress, where Benedek pleadingly requested Franz Joseph to make peace. Receiving a negative response from the emperor, the leader of the North Army fought the Prussians and lost disastrously.[42]

Strategy certainly played an integral role in Austrian defeat. In an article translated and published in the *ÖMZ*, Jomini, the famous French military writer and strategist, expressed his view that weaponry did not influence the Prussian victory as much as strategy. Although changes in armament affected tactics, they did not alter the immutable principles of war and the goal of great maneuvers. Weapons merely affected the execution of these principles: "As it always is with these secondary questions, one must search much higher for the causes of the extraordinary success of the Prussians in the war in Bohemia; the strategic calculations have certainly more share than the needle gun, if this even contributed to it."[43] Though the octogenarian Jomini denigrated the impact of the Dreyse rifle, he pointed to the superior strategy of concentration on a decisive point and the maneuverability of the Prussian army.

The North Army command received much criticism after the war for its indecisiveness and mishandling of the strategic operations against

Moltke's forces. *FZM* Ladislaus Baron Nagy von Alsó-Szopor, de facto chief of the Habsburg general staff from 1862 to 1864, wrote a report in September 1866 about the Königgrätz campaign and published it anonymously in the *ÖMZ*. Nagy took the view that nations engaging in a two-front war should fight defensively, especially when confronted by enemies who had a combined strength greater than the single nation. In the Austro-Prussian War, Italy and Prussia held an advantage of roughly 200,000 men over Austria and its allies. Lieutenant Colonel Eduard Bartels of the Austrian general staff similarly claimed the two-front war against Prussia and Italy as the primary cause of defeat, especially because of the inability of the Habsburg government and military to provide enough men for the army.[44] Likening the Habsburg Empire to a fencer facing two opponents, Nagy asserted that a strategic defense should have taken precedence over the offense in a war against a military power like Prussia, especially when being fought together with a simultaneous campaign against Italy. Instead of Benedek's idea of hiding behind the fortifications of Olmütz, Nagy favored the occupation of defensive positions in Bohemia not based on fortresses, claiming that defense of the province closer to Berlin would have afforded protection for the rest of the empire as well as the opportunity to take the offensive toward the Prussian capital if the occasion arose.[45] Although not blaming Benedek as much as Nagy, Albrecht, and Beck did, Bartels also criticized the North Army commander for not taking control of Bohemia to ward off any Prussian invasion attempts and to offer the possibility of beating enemy units individually as they crossed into Habsburg territory.[46]

Benedek's desire to stay in Moravia and defend against an enemy advance by holding a position based on permanent fortifications and abandoning most of Bohemia, coincided with the cordon defense strategy that Austrian generals had followed for years. Dating from the previous century, the Habsburg military had attempted to defend imperial lands by establishing a series of fortified outposts throughout the border areas. This strategy had succeeded against Frederick the Great during the Seven Years' War and the War of the Bavarian Succession, when the fortresses at Olmütz and Königgrätz had blocked the Prussian king's routes toward Habsburg possessions. However, the advent of larger armies and more destructive weaponry, especially rifled cannon, rendered these fortresses obsolete. During the Bohemian campaign of 1866, Königgrätz offered no protection for Habsburg forces despite the hopes of Austrian leaders who relied on outdated strategy. Instead, the fortress, which could hold only one brigade, impeded an orderly retreat from the battlefield across the Elbe and Adler rivers and resulted in a bottleneck that caused even more casualties.[47]

Although the Habsburg high command should have realized the problems that nineteenth-century warfare posed for the cordon system, the disastrous Bohemian campaign at least caused military leaders to start questioning the efficacy of permanent fortifications. Field Marshal Heinrich Hess had advocated permanent fortresses before 1866.[48] After the war, Hess decidedly changed his views: "Already before the application of steam as mobile power, the offensive had a decisive preponderance over the defensive, and since the death of Vauban, when all states began to multiply their great road networks, the cordon fortifications in the borders have almost completely lost their purpose."[49]

Lieutenant Colonel Bartels agreed with Hess that the fortresses in Bohemia no longer served any purpose for the army. Arguing more from a strategic than technical viewpoint, Bartels claimed that any Austrian wars in Germany must take an offensive stance to stop Prussia from swallowing the smaller German states. Such a war would negate the advantages of permanent fortifications. Russia alone presented an opportunity for a defensive war that could use fortresses to protect strategic railroad bridgeheads in Galicia and the Carpathian Mountains.[50]

Hess and other Habsburg leaders had ample precedents for underscoring the tactical obsolescence of relying on fortresses. The permanent fortifications of the Quadrilateral fortresses in Italy (Mantua, Peschiera, Verona, and Legnago) had provided little assistance to the Austrians against the French in 1859. During the Napoleonic wars, the French emperor had merely bypassed Habsburg strongholds, such as Ulm, on the way to finding and decisively defeating the main Austrian force. Archduke Karl, Napoleon's main adversary at the time, did not respond by adopting the new style of warfare. On the contrary, he advocated a return to the eighteenth-century method of fortifying strong positions to create a network of impregnable fortresses that would fend off any enemy who ventured to breach them. Despite losing to Napoleon and his greater strategic and tactical mobility, Karl failed to learn the right lessons. Instead, he adhered to the idea that whoever possessed certain decisive points would win.[51] This strategy resembled more the writings of Jomini and Bülow than those of Clausewitz.[52] According to Karl, "Strategy determines decisive points whose possession is necessary for one's planned purpose. It also marks the lines for their use. These points must be secured and claimed, and then mutually connected lines must be created. In a defensive war they are called defensive lines, and in an offensive war they are the base of operations."[53] Karl's status as victor at Aspern over Napoleon I and the recent publication of his military ideas greatly influenced Austrian officers to favor permanent fortresses.

However, this strategy did not garner positive results for the Austrian army because the permanent fortresses did not deter the Prussians from invading Habsburg territory. Captain Graf Geldern tried to defend their usefulness in the *ÖMZ*, but he had to admit that they could not withstand modern technology: "...in general the worth and advantages of the fortified points of the northern theater of war were not appreciated as perfectly as they deserved in reality; because the individual fortresses belonged to various time periods, they could not be considered or used as members of a state fortification system corresponding to modern demands; in addition, Josephstadt, Königgrätz, Theresienstadt were built according to the old system to produce no stonework protection and comparatively few bombproof areas, therefore they no longer possessed the resistance that they once had."[54] Even this proponent of fortresses, who continued to defend their merits throughout the rest of his article, had to admit how little the old permanent fortifications helped the Austrians in 1866.

Although a defensive strategy based on the cordon system proved ineffective during the nineteenth century, the strategic defensive in Bohemia could have produced better results than the halting, indecisive offensive waged by Benedek. An anonymous veteran of the Austrian army published an article in the *ÖMZ*, in which he maintained, like Nagy and Bartels, that the possession of Bohemia in a defensive posture with the goal of hindering the unification of the various Prussian armies would have benefitted the Habsburg forces far more than the North Army commander's plans. Although the author noted the impossibility of knowing Benedek's thoughts exactly, he censured the commander for his strategic indecision and for allowing the decisive battle to take place at a poor position near Königgrätz.[55]

Flawed Leadership and Unrealistic Training

Benedek made grave errors in both his strategic and tactical choices in 1866, and thus a large amount of the blame for the disaster fell upon him. His command structure resembled the overly bureaucratic Austrian government and army, with four different levels: *Kommandantur* (Benedek), *Präsidium* (Henikstein), *Operationskanzlei* (Krismanić), and *Detailkanzlei* (Kriz). As Wawro said, "Benedek erected a four-tier monstrosity of a headquarters that delayed the conception and transmission of orders for critical hours and even whole days."[56] As happens after many heavy defeats on the battlefield, the losing commander-in-chief must bear the brunt of the criticism. In the case of Benedek, he deserved the critical judgments that Albrecht, Beck, Nagy, and others gave him, even if they did not mention him by name in their reports and articles. Before the war, Benedek had earned a reputation as an opponent of intellectual views and anything resembling a scientific approach for the army. Boasting that he had never read a book since his graduation from the Habsburg war college and denigrating those who did study, he claimed that a strong stomach and good digestion were the only talents necessary for a chief of staff.[57] Regardless of Benedek's bravado, his ideas showed in his propensity for adherence to regulations and "iron discipline." He sought to instill obedience and the observance of rules in his troops, with the result that he produced within the army a *Formalismus*, an excessive attention to the details of outward form.[58] According to *FZM* Anton Baron von Mollinary, one of Benedek's subordinates in 1866, "This dashing field soldier held very little to tactical exercises and appeared content if in a parade review the divisions marched by straight and in closed order."[59] As one *ÖMZ* author wrote sarcastically, perhaps the time will come when a wandering traveler will see a faded statue of the goddess "Parade."[60]

Yet, the Austrian army needed more than discipline and obedience to gain victory over the Prussians. Good leadership requires intelligence as well as the so-called military virtues. One Austrian officer recognized this necessity in an *ÖMZ* article: "The mere acquiring of the purely formal part of tactics is more a matter of drill than understanding; it is clearly and distinctly standardized, therefore made very easy, by the exercise regulations, which are the code of the soldier. In the employment of this form for actual war conditions, in which one sees everything from the terrain, mere praxis and routine is not sufficient; a free development of intelligence, bound by neither blind obedience nor regulatory norms, is indispensable, praxis and the gaining of suitable routine should be made possible by utility."[61] The author continued by stating that the higher the officer's rank, the more necessary theoretical training becomes for him rather than formal handbooks and instruction manuals. He must know military geography and statistics, logistics and supply, and political and foreign relations. The commander-in-chief must use all this knowledge to plan a strategy based on the situation in which he finds himself and his army, rather than on preset rules that may or may not apply. Unfortunately for the Austrian army, Benedek adhered to his *Formalismus* and did not study the terrain or base his decisions on the nature of the battlefield and theater of war.[62]

The problems of Benedek's leadership indicated a deeper issue within the Habsburg military. Officers often received promotions because of family or political connections rather than worthiness and merit proven in battle. Although Benedek had exhibited quick and direct action in squelching a Galician uprising in 1846 and showed his courage on the battlefield at Curtatone in 1848 and Solferino in the Franco-Austrian War, he had never done anything to earn a reputation as a competent strategist or army commander. Popular as the "Lion of San Martino" in 1859 for his stalwart defense at Solferino, loved by his soldiers but suspect among his fellow officers, Benedek had attained the high positions of *FZM*, commander-in-chief of the Army of Italy in Verona, and chief of the general staff in Vienna.[63] In Wawro's words, "His promotion had been a political ploy by Emperor Franz Joseph to win popularity among Austria's newly enfranchised middle class, who revered Benedek for his colorful personality and common origins and tended to overlook the obvious shortcomings of the *FZM* as a staff officer."[64]

Benedek's successor as chief of the general staff in 1863, *Feldmarschalleutnant* (*FML*) Alfred Baron Henikstein, provided another egregious example of the faulty promotion system in the Austrian army. Even though he had less experience and fewer qualifications than Benedek, Henikstein received the position despite admitting his own incompetence.[65] Bartels looked on Henikstein's appointment as a political move by Benedek to obtain a representative in Vienna to counter his rivals.[66] Beck as well as *Generalmajor* Gideon Ritter von Krismanić, the assistant chief of staff for the North Army, considered Henikstein's appointment to be a concession to Benedek and not a beneficial move because of Henikstein's outmoded ideas about war and his amicable relationship with Benedek.[67]

Benedek and Henikstein were not the only officers who received positions for which they had no proper experience. Solm-Braunfels stated the situation accurately: "Besides the customary bestowal of infantry brigades on old cavalry officers, the brigade commanders had been chosen for the most part in rather unusual ways for the use of the army."[68] A serious problem existed in the promotion system of the Habsburg military, as Beck pointed out in his 1867 report on the poor morale of the army.[69] Bartels, however, exaggerated in claiming that the troops had no confidence in any of the Habsburg corps commanders.[70] Austrian leaders needed to find a solution so that competent and experienced generals, not political appointees, would make the critical decisions in future campaigns.

The Austrian rank and file did not perform well in battle, though this shortcoming stemmed more from poor training than an innate inability to fight. Although Albrecht noted the courage of the Habsburg forces, he lamented their insufficient discipline and cohesion.[71] Beck agreed that troop training required improvement to prepare Austrian soldiers for the practical exigencies of the battlefield.[72] Neither of these leaders cast aspersions on the men themselves or raised the issue of the willingness of the various peoples within the empire to fight for the Habsburg Empire.

Other officers also noted the deficiencies of the Austrian troops. Major General Zaitschek wrote to Albrecht, saying that the army lost the campaign in Bohemia because of the individual and tactical shortcomings of the infantry, who could not fight the Prussians on an equal level without better training.[73] Krismanić lauded the Austrian infantrymen for their indisputable superiority in hand to hand combat because of his supposed contempt for firepower and his strong fists, but castigated the officer corps for not leading the troops with enough intelligence.[74] Contempt for firepower, however, merely led to enormous casualties for both Habsburg officers and soldiers, whose strong fists did not even reach the enemy lines. Too many parades and not enough practical training with an emphasis on shooting had rendered Austrian soldiers inferior to the enemy.

Bartels attributed the poor battle performance and morale of Austrian troops to the failure of the Habsburg government and army to inspire them with love of the Austrian Empire as their country. According to the lieutenant colonel, the lack of discipline that led to the dissolution of certain units during the retreat stemmed from the poor morale of the army. In addition, Bartels claimed that Habsburg forces disintegrated even though casualties remained insignificant.[75] Although the Austrian loss of 48,000 men at Königgrätz hardly comprised an insignificant number, Bartels made the valid point of the difficulty involved in unifying an army composed of soldiers from so many ethnic and linguistic backgrounds.

For the most part, the various peoples of the Austrian Empire (Czechs, Slovaks, Slovenes, Hungarians, Ruthenians, Poles, Croats, Rumanians, and Austrians) remained loyal to the Habsburgs as long as their officers kept them in their units and they had sufficient supplies. Not surprisingly, certain Venetian units refused to fight against Prussia, Italy's ally.[76] In general, Austrian forces, whether German, Slavic, or any other ethnicity, tended to try to escape from danger in difficult situations, especially if no officers remained in the vicinity.[77] This behavior resulted from the Habsburg high command's failure to train the soldiers adequately, with too many parades and not enough realistic exercises in target practice and maneuvers, rather than insufficient love of the Austrian Empire. Confidence in commanders and familiarity with weaponry builds morale, no matter what ethnic background the soldiers represent.

Spending Unwisely

In addition to the wrong choice of tactics for Austrian weapons and poor leadership and training, the internal finances of the army presented a major problem for Habsburg military leaders. Although the official campaign history *Österreichs Kämpfe im Jahre 1866* tried to exonerate the Habsburg high command by finding fault in other areas, especially parliament and its stinginess, the Austrian high command did not critically examine their own handling of money. Instead, they continued to focus on civilian officials as the source of their financial problems, as asserted in *Sechzig Jahre Wehrmacht 1848–1908* as well as by later historians who favored the public military account of events.[78]

The army budget debates in the *Reichsrat*, however, reveal a different explanation. In an 1865 session of the *Abgeordnetenhaus* (House of Representatives), Dr. Čupr, a Liberal delegate from Bohemia, accused the Austrian war ministry of spending seven million florins more than it should have. Taking examples from the army's supply system, he showed how the military "supports the monopoly of profit-seeking, usurious purveyors and speculators, because it pays too much regard to class and party interests at the cost of the common good, because thereby not only the producers in general, but also the soldiers and the taxpayers themselves suffer." Instead of purchasing necessities from industries within the Habsburg Empire, the army did business with suppliers who procured provisions from foreign sources at higher prices. This system wasted money and, much worse in the eyes of Dr. Čupr, ruined homeland industries. He even went so far as to blame the losses of 1859 at Magenta and Solferino on the system: "Our sons had to starve on the battlefield while unscrupulous speculators sought to enrich themselves by this imperial calamity."[79] Aside from Dr. Čupr's exaggerations concerning the causes of defeat in 1859, he made a valid point in maintaining that the Austrian military could both save money and support Habsburg industry by procuring supplies within the Austrian Empire.

The Liberal party led parliamentary opposition to military overspending and corruption. Although not in the majority before the war, the Liberals became the strongest political group in the *Reichsrat* in 1867. This party, composed mainly of anticlerical Germans, represented the industrial and commercial interests of the empire. The Liberals advocated equality before the law and liberty of the press, religion, and association. As heirs of the Viennese bourgeois revolutionaries of 1848, the Liberals desired limitations on the Habsburg monarch's authority, particularly in finances. This combination of constitutionalism and emphasis on financial matters led Liberals to oppose the army as the primary support of imperial authority and, thus, to oppose military expenditure.[80] The Liberal party did not reject all army expenditures, only those expenses they considered unnecessary, including contracts from foreign producers, such as Čupr bemoaned. In many cases, such as pensions and permanent fortresses, these expenses constituted legitimate concerns.

The Liberal party leader, Dr. Karl Giskra, the mayor of Brno, Moravia, stated during the budget debate of 1863 that from 1850 to 1861 the military had cost over 2 billion florins, and that, as a result, the state debt had risen from 1.3 to 2.5 billion florins with a projected interest payment of 128 million florins, which was more than any other branch of the government.[81] This outlay on interest represented an enormous amount for a state with an overall budget of only 305 million florins in 1862, 138 million of which the army already took, leaving a mere 52 million florins for the rest of the government after the 115 million interest payment servicing the national debt.[82]

Apologists for the army within the *Reichsrat* argued in favor of military expenditure by emphasizing the importance of maintaining Austria's status as a first class power by means of a large military presence. These men stated that the state budget should be looked at as a whole rather than merely inspecting the army's share minutely. They also pointed out that parliament did not allow anyone representing the army to sit on its benches, thus disallowing true representation.[83] These arguments did not take into account whether the army wasted its funding on useless expenses or not, as Deputy Dreher from Lower Austria declared while underscoring "the contrast of this military luxury with the public emergency, with financial ruin."[84] In 1862, the Habsburg army received a budget of 138 million florins. According to Wawro's calculations, the high command spent only 76.7 million (55%) on regimental troops while the rest went to areas such as pensions, construction costs, army offices, general expenses, and "other expenses."[85]

Giskra continued the debate by accusing the military of shifting numbers within the amount requested for the army by the war ministry. The four million florins of savings the war minister claimed the army had achieved through natural price declines appeared in the 1863 extraordinary request for funding, rather than as a true subtraction from the budget segment designated as ordinary. In addition, the army moved six million florins for other expenses from the ordinary to the extraordinary so that the ten million it purported to save merely showed up in another part of the budget.[86] Aside from the war ministry's number games, Giskra pointed out the army's propensity for wasting money by employing higher ranking officers for positions that lesser officers could easily hold; for example, a colonel was employed as head of a stud farm rather than a major, or a major as riding instructor at a military academy instead of a lieutenant. This practice resulted in an overabundance of officers and administrative officials, who absorbed more funds because of the frequent promotions that the Habsburg high command felt necessary to raise the morale of the army. Thus, the Austrian military had 15,000 officers in 1863, more than in the larger prerevolutionary army of 1848. Earlier, when the army assigned an officer to an administrative position, no new officer replaced him. That policy no longer remained in effect and supernumeraries abounded, with a cost of over half a million florins. Compared with other branches of the Austrian state, such as the justice department, promotions took place far more often and thus raised the expenses of the military accordingly. Giskra said that parliamentary delegates would consider the army's budget requests seriously "as soon as it has happened that in peacetime all superfluous positions are eliminated, superfluous ranks removed, the administration expenses are compressed to a minimum, which is really necessary, all the luxury of the officer ranks and positions is withdrawn, and only what is necessary is introduced."[87]

The superabundant bureaucracy of the Austrian military continued unabated and parliamentary delegates continued to complain about these issues when they debated the army budget again in 1865. Once again, Giskra raised issues of monetary irresponsibility on the part of the military. Even though the number of soldiers and horses in the Austrian army had declined from the previous year, the costs for the military had increased because of the transfer of two lieutenant field marshals from corps commands to administrative boards and the subsequent creation of two new positions to replace them. These positions constituted part of the six new troop commands established within the past 2 years that had no tactical or administrative purpose and did not require men of such high rank to oversee them, as only major generals held similar positions in the rest of the army.[88] Overspending on superfluous officers marked a major source of financial mismanagement for the military. The army spent 8,124,044 florins on 8256 pensioned officers, not counting pensions for invalids and widows, more than half of the 14,954,570 florins it spent on 15,099 active officers. The situation among the generals and staff officers revealed the problem more distinctly because the pensioned outnumbered the active generals and staff officers by 2352 to 1252.[89] The cost of maintaining generals and pensioned officers at the imperial court, where they served as little more than advisors, alone amounted to 141,222 florins.[90] Compared with France and Prussia, Austria spent more on pensions and army administration and less on the rank and file, while consuming more of the state budget.[91]

Asking rhetorically what caused the great overload and ensuing monetary burden of the pensions, Giskra answered, “it is the existing promotion regulations and their management. It is this, and one can say against it what one wishes, because, as it is extremely well known, very frequent pensionings must occur because of the existing promotion regulations.”[92] After the Austro-Prussian War, Archduke Albrecht and *Generalmajor* John concurred that the promotions resulting from the large number of supernumerary officers brought about the high rate of pensioning, which only appeared to indicate savings for the active army while in reality burdening the budget with excessive amounts of pension payments.[93] Even *FML* August Count Degenfeld-Schonburg, the war minister, admitted the need for new rules regarding promotions.[94] Thus, the problem of promotions based on political connections and favoritism affected not only battlefield command performance but also the financial situation of the whole empire.

Giskra also attacked the exorbitant sums that the Habsburg army wasted on permanent fortifications. Whereas the Prussians spent a mere 370,000 thaler on their more numerous fortresses in 1865, Austrian expenses amounted to 1,244,000 florins.[95] The Liberal party leader questioned this enormous outlay for structures that would not serve any purpose in modern warfare: "I certainly ought to permit myself the remark, that it has come into question whether in recent time, when the cannon system has changed, the construction of fortification works should not be carried out with greater foresight, as, for example, it is a notorious concern, that fortresses, which were considered impregnable because of their territorial sites according to the old system—impregnable is actually not the right term—but difficult to take, now lie in the range of the new cannon, so that all the works can be bombarded and razed in a very short time."[96] Even though parliamentary delegates pointed out the uselessness of outdated permanent fortifications that held little strategic value, the Austrian high command insisted on spending large sums on upgrading old fortresses or building new ones.

With such imprudent decisions, the deficiency in funding for the procurement of breech-loading rifles, better material for the artillery, and more training and target practice for the rank and file stemmed from the mishandling of funds by the Habsburg high command. In 1865, the Austrian military spent a mere 42,500 florins on rifles, 20,000 on artillery shells, 8500 on new fortress cannon, and 317,000 on troop exercises.[97] Parliamentary stinginess did not hinder the improvement of Austrian military might, as a comparison of the army budgets of the major European powers shows. According to Wawro, "Austrian expenditures on the land army in 1862 were double Prussian expenditures, more than Italy's, nearly equal to France's and only 25% less than Russian appropriations.... In fact, the 1860s did not see a 'catastrophic decline' in Austrian spending, as apologists for the Austrian army have argued, but rather a return to barely sustainable, but still quite high levels of spending."[98] The financial problems for the Habsburg military stemmed not from insufficient funding but from budgetary mishandling on the part of the high command.

Conclusion

The catastrophic defeat in 1866 against the Prussians revealed many grave problems in the Habsburg army. Although the Austrian artillery surpassed their enemies' cannon in range and precision, the infantry definitely proved inferior in training and rifle firepower. The Habsburg high command failed to implement tactics suitable for the Lorenz. Instead of employing defensive tactics that would have taken advantage of the Austrian weapon's greater range and muzzle velocity, Benedek insisted on shock tactics and reliance on the bayonet for decisive action. This decision played directly into the strength of the Prussians, the *Schnellfeuer* of the Dreyse needle gun, which could fire much faster than the Lorenz but without as much range or impetus.[99] Combined with the indecisive semi-offensive strategy of the North Army commander, the offensive shock tactics resulted in heavy casualties and disaster at Königgrätz. In addition, the expensive permanent fortresses of the defensive cordon system had not stymied the Prussian advance into Bohemia nor afforded the Austrians sufficient protection to take up a favorable position using fortifications.

The abysmal performance of the Austrian army in Bohemia exposed deeper issues within the military than the battlefield actions of certain individuals. The high positions of Benedek and Henikstein revealed the corruption of relying on political and financial bases for promotion rather than a system valuing merit, experience, and ability. Training among the soldiers and officers, including general staff officers, proved deficient, especially in knowledge of the terrain of the northern theater. The troops generally displayed adequate courage but had communication issues with their officers because of language barriers and lack of trust in the high command. Their training proved insufficient in shooting, maneuver, and discipline. All these inadequacies resulted in little cohesion and poor morale.

Although many high ranking officers could see the purely military reasons for Austrian defeat in 1866, they failed to realize the true state of the army's financial situation. Too much bureaucracy, in addition to the waste of resources and corruption within the military, used up a large part of the military budget each year without providing for the procurement of sufficient new weaponry and proper training of troops for battle. Despite the warnings and castigations of the Liberal party, Habsburg military officials continued to excuse their actions and blame the supposed stinginess of parliamentary delegates for the fiscal shortcomings.

The Austrian high command was now confronted with the task of solving the problems that had become clear during the war with Prussia and Italy. Despite the desire to conceal these issues from unfavorable public opinion and to blame parliament, the new leadership recognized that the problems stemmed from within the military. To maintain its status as a world power, the Habsburg monarchy would have to procure the new weaponry that nineteenth-century technology had to offer, and adapt its tactics and strategy to employ it to full advantage. This endeavor would require a new way of thinking, different from the traditional views of the Austrian military since the time of Archduke Charles. The army would also have to improve its command structure and make sure its officers and soldiers received better training in modern warfare. Finally, the Habsburg army would have to eliminate the financial mismanagement within its ranks to prove itself deserving of further appropriations from the *Reichsrat*. How Austrian leaders would respond to these challenges would shape the status and success or failure of the army in the coming decades.

Notes

1. Manfried Rauchensteiner, *Heeresgeschichtliches Museum Vienna* (Vienna: Styria Verlag, 2000), 49.
2. Rauchensteiner, *Heeresgeschichtliches Museum Vienna*, 54.
3. Vaclav Sochor, *The Battery of the Dead*, 1901/7.
4. Rudolf Ritter Otto von Ottenfeld, *Ein Ruhmesblatt der österreichischen Artillerie. Die Armeegeschützreserve nach der Schlacht bei Königgrätz am 3. Juli 1866*, 1897.
5. Rauchensteiner, *Heeresgeschichtliches Museum Vienna*, 54.
6. K.k. Generalstabs-Bureau für Kriegsgeschichte, *Österreichs Kämpfe im Jahre 1866* (Vienna: R.v. Waldheim, 1867–1869), vol. 1–5; Geoffrey Wawro, "The Austro-Prussian War: Politics, Strategy and War in the Habsburg Monarchy, 1859–1866" (Ph.D. dissertation, Yale University, 1992), 12; Wawro, *The Austro-Prussian War: Austria's War with Prussia and Italy in 1866* (Cambridge: Cambridge University Press, 1996), 2–3.
7. Ludwig August Ritter von Benedek and Heinrich Friedjung, *Benedeks nachgelassene Papiere* (Leipzig: Grübel & Sommerlatte, 1901), 417.
8. *Sechzig Jahre Wehrmacht 1848–1908* (Vienna: k.u.k. Kriegsarchiv, 1908), 132–135.
9. Heinrich Friedjung, *Der Kampf um die Vorherrschaft in Deutschland 1859 bis 1866*, 2 vols. (Stuttgart: J.G. Cotta, 1900), vol. 1, 32; Oskar Regele, *Feldzeugmeister Benedek und der Weg nach Königgrätz* (Vienna: Herold, 1960); Regele, "Staatspolitische Geschichtsschreibung: erläutert an Königgrätz 1866," *Mitteilungen des österreichischen Staatsarchivs (MÖSA)* 3 (1950), 305; Emil Franzel, *1866. Il Mondo Casca. Das Ende des alten Europa* (Vienna: Verlag Herold, 1968); Gordon Craig,

The Battle of Königgrätz (Philadelphia: Lippincott Co., 1964); Adam Wandruszka, *Schicksalsjahr 1866* (Vienna: Styria Verlag, 1966). Wawro provides an in-depth account of the historiography of the Austro-Prussian War in both his book (pp. 2–4) and his dissertation (pp. 11–16). Johann C. Allmayer-Beck also provides an earlier overview of the historiography in "Der Feldzug der österreichischen Nordarmee nach Königgrätz," in *Entscheidung 1866: Der Krieg zwischen Österreich und Preußen*, eds. Wolfgang v. Groote and Ursula v. Gersdorff (Stuttgart: Deutsche Verlags-Anstalt, 1966), 106–110.

10. Feldmarschalleutnant (FML) Erzherzog Albrecht, No. 1017 "Allerunterthänigster Vortrag," 21 August 1866, Kriegsarchiv (KA) Militärkanzlei Seiner Majestät (MKSM) Sonderreihe, Karton Nr. 22, 1866.
11. Oberst Friedrich von Beck, "Promemoria über Armee-Verhältnisse," August 1867, KA MKSM Sonderreihe, Karton Nr. 66, Studien.
12. Beck, "Theilweise Ursachen des gegenwärtigen schlechten Armee-Geistes und Mittel, welche zur Hebung desselben beitragen dürften," 1867, KA MKSM Sonderreihe, Karton Nr. 66, Studien.
13. The *ÖMZ* appeared for the first time in 1808 as the official organ of the war ministry because of Archduke Karl's desire to raise the intellectual level of the Austrian officer corps and bring about unity of thought throughout the army. The journal took this Tacitean saying as its motto: *Omnia quae vetustissima creduntur, nova fuere et quod hodie tuemur exemplis, inter exempla erit.* (All things which are believed to be very old, were new at one time, and what today we preserve in examples, later will be among examples.) The *ÖMZ* lasted until 1849, at which time it ceased to publish its quarterly issues. After a hiatus until 1860, Karl's son Wilhelm, perceiving a declining intellectual level in the officer corps, revived the journal for the same reasons as his father. The journal, as an attempt to stimulate discussion and spread military knowledge from Habsburg as well as foreign sources among the officers, thus continued without interruption until the First World War. Oberleutnant Zitterhofer, *Streffleurs Militärische Zeitschrift 1808–1908: Eine Geschichte dieser Zeitschrift anlässlich ihres 100jährigen Bestehens* (Vienna: L.W. Seidel & Sohn, 1908), 1–25.
14. "Uber die Ursache der Mißerfolge bei der österreichischen Nordarmee im Kriege Preußens gegen Deutschland im Jahre 1866," *Österreichische Militärische Zeitschrift* 2 (1866): 341–361. The author of this article is most likely Generalmajor Gideon Ritter von Krismanić, the assistant chief of staff for the North Army, as it mirrors his report to the commission inquiring into the defeat in Bohemia. Krismanić to Untersuchungs-Commission, 24 August 1866, KA, Nachlässe, Nosinic. However, Zitterhoffer lists the article among the writings of Valentin Streffleur, the editor of the *ÖMZ*. Marginal notes by a reader of the *ÖMZ* express

a difference of opinion about the needle-gun, while claiming that the Dreyse weapon alone rendered the Prussian army numerically superior to the Austrians.

15. Johann Christoph Allmayer-Beck, "Der Feldzug der österreichischen Nord-Armee nach Königgrätz," in *Entscheidung 1866: Der Krieg zwischen Österreich und Preußen*, eds. Wolfgang v. Groote and Ursula v. Gersdorff (Stuttgart: Deutsche Verlags-Anstalt, 1966), 140–141.
16. Gunther E. Rothenberg, *The Army of Francis Joseph* (West Lafayette, IN: Purdue University Press, 1976), 72.
17. Wawro, "The Austro-Prussian War," 807–808, 811–812.
18. *Sechzig Jahre Wehrmacht*, 134–135.
19. Geoffrey Wawro, "An 'Army of Pigs': The Technical, Social, and Political Bases of Austrian Shock Tactics, 1859–1866," *The Journal of Military History* Vol. 59, No. 3 (July 1995), 413; Dennis E. Showalter, *Railroads and Rifles: Soldiers, Technology, and the Unification of Germany* (Hamden, CT: Archon Books, 1975), 112–113.
20. "Der Krieg im Jahre 1866. Im Auszuge nach einem Artikel von Xavier Raymond in der 'Revue des deux mondes'," *ÖMZ* 3 (1866): 101.
21. Wawro, "The Austro-Prussian War," 714.
22. Albrecht, No. 1086 Allerunterthänigster Vortrag, 27 August 1866, Karton Nr. 22, 1866, 1.
23. Walter Wagner, "Die k.(u.)k. Armee - Gliederung und Aufgabenstellung," in *Die Habsburgermonarchie 1848–1918*, vol. 5 *Die Bewaffnete Macht* (Wien: Verlag der Österreichischen Akademie der Wissenschaften, 1987), 349.
24. "Der Krieg im Jahre 1866. Im Auszuge nach einem Artikel von Xavier Raymond in der 'Revue des deux mondes'," *ÖMZ* 3 (1866), 101.
25. "Uber die Ursache der Mißerfolge bei der österreichischen Nordarmee im Kriege Preußens gegen Deutschland im Jahre 1866," *ÖMZ* 2 (1866), 353.
26. Azar Gat, *A History of Military Thought: From the Enlightenment to the Cold War* (New York: Oxford University Press, 2001); Robert Holtman, *The Napoleonic Revolution* (New York: J.B. Lippincott, 1967); Gunther Rothenberg, *The Art of Warfare in the Age of Napoleon* (Bloomington, IN: Indiana University Press, 1980); Geoffrey Wawro, *Warfare and Society in Europe, 1792–1914* (New York: Routledge, 2000).
27. Carl von Clausewitz, *On War*, edited and translated by Michael Howard and Peter Paret (Princeton, NJ: Princeton University Press, 1976); Antoine Henri Jomini, *The Art of War* (Westport, Connecticut: Greenwood Press, 1862).
28. Wawro, "The Austro-Prussian War," 813–814.

29. *Sammlung der Armeebefehle und speziellen Anordnungen des k.k. Feldzeugmeisters Benedek, Kommandanten der k.k. Nordarmee vom Jahre 1866* (Vienna: k.k. Staatsdruckerei, 1866); "Taktische-und Dienst Instruction für die k.k. Nord Armee," *ÖMZ* 1 (1866); Friedjung, *Der Kampf um die Vorherrschaft in Deutschland 1859 bis 1866*, vol. 1, 424; Rothenberg, *The Army of Francis Joseph*, 69.
30. Wawro, "An 'Army of Pigs'," 415; Wawro, *The Austro-Prussian War*, 26–27.
31. Johann Christoph Allmayer-Beck, "Die Bewaffnete Macht in Staat und Gesellschaft," in *Die Habsburgermonarchie 1848–1918*, Vol. 5 *Die Bewaffnete Macht* (Wien: Verlag der Österreichischen Akademie der Wissenschaften, 1987), 55; Wawro, "An 'Army of Pigs'," 424–431.
32. Helmuth von Moltke, "De l'influence des armes perfectionées sur le combat," *Militär Wochenblatt*, 8 July 1865; "Bemerkungen über den Einfluß der verbesserten Schußwaffen auf das Gefecht," *ÖMZ* 2 (1865).
33. Rothenberg, *The Army of Francis Joseph*, 69; Allmayer-Beck, "Die Bewaffnete Macht in Staat und Gesellschaft," 56.
34. Anton von Mollinary, *Studien über die Operationen und Tactique der Franzosen im Feldzuge 1859 in Italien* (Wien: Wilhelm Braumüller, 1864), 128–129.
35. Friedjung, *Der Kampf um die Vorherrschaft in Deutschland 1859 bis 1866*, vol. 1, 342.
36. Wawro, "An 'Army of Pigs'," 433.
37. Rothenberg, *The Army of Francis Joseph*, 69.
38. Wawro, "The Austro-Prussian War," 812–813; Wawro, "An 'Army of Pigs'," 430; Rolf Förster, "Die Leistungsfähigkeit der bayrischen Armee im Feldzuge 1866: Dargestellt an der militärische Ausbildung vor dem Krieg" (Ph.D. dissertation, Munich, 1987), 155–156.
39. Edmund von Glaise-Horstenau, *Franz Josephs Weggefährte* (Wien: Amalthea Verlag, 1930), 96.
40. Ludwig von Benedek, "Army Order No. 41," Josefstadt, 28 June 1866, KA MKSM Sonderreihe, Karton Nr. 26, Akten (1866); Showalter, *Railroads and Rifles*, 126–127.
41. Wawro, "The Austro-Prussian War," 770.
42. Rothenberg, *The Army of Francis Joseph*, 68–71; Wawro, *The Austro-Prussian War*, 124–273.
43. H., "Jomini über den Feldzug 1866 in Böhmen," *ÖMZ* 1 (1867), 154. The "H" most likely stands for Field Marshal (FML) Heinrich Hess, Chief of the General Staff from 1849 to 1860.
44. Eduard Bartels, *Östreich und sein Heer* (Leipzig: Otto Wigand: 1866), 15.
45. FZM Ladislaus Freiherr Nagy von Alsó-Szopor, "Bemerkungen über den Krieg zwischen Österreich und Preussen 1866, "September 1866, KA

MKSM Sonderreihe, Karton Nr. 22, 1866, 1; "Bemerkungen über den Feldzug der k.k. Nordarmee 1866, mit einem aphoristischen Anhange," *ÖMZ* 2 (1867), 158.

46. Bartels, *Österreich und sein Heer*, 16–17.
47. Wawro, *The Austro-Prussian War*, 264–265.
48. FML Heinrich Freiherr von Hess, "Strategische Grundsätze über die Verteidigung der österreichischen Monarchie," in *Schriften aus dem militärwissenschaftlichen Nachlass*, ed. Manfried Rauchensteiner (Osnaburg: Biblio Verlag, 1975). Sébastien Le Prestre de Vauban (1633–1707) was a French Marshal and the foremost military engineer of his time.
49. H., "Jomini über den Feldzug 1866 in Böhmen," *ÖMZ* 1 (1867), 150.
50. Bartels, *Östreich und sein Heer*, 30–31.
51. Archduke Karl, "Strategie und Taktik. (Geschrieben im Jahre 1845.) Aus dem hinterlassenen Papieren weiland Sr. kaiserlichen Hoheit des Erzherzogs Carl von Österreich," *ÖMZ* 1 (1866), 1.
52. The Prussian officer Dietrich Heinrich von Bülow, who published *Practical Rules of Strategy* in 1805, set the keys of strategy on geometrical formulae with converging lines coming from bases. Thus, possession of both bases and their corresponding lines would assure victory.
53. Milan N. Vego, *Joint Operational Warfare: Theory and Practice* (Newport, Rhode Island: Naval War College, 2009), I-37.
54. Graf Geldern, "Befestigungs-Vorschläge, basirt auf die Vertheidigung von Manövrirplätzen," *ÖMZ* 4 (1867), 299.
55. "Praxis und Routine. - Wissenschaft und Kunst. - Betrachtungen über den Kriegsschauplatz in Böhmen von 1866 und die auf demselben stattgehabten Kriegsereignisse dieses Jahres. (Aus den schriften eines Veteranen des österreichischen Heeres)," *ÖMZ* 4 (1866): 199–207.
56. Wawro, "The Austro-Prussian War," 807.
57. Rothenberg, *The Army of Francis Joseph*, 60; Wawro, *The Austro-Prussian War*, 25–27.
58. Allmayer-Beck, "Die bewaffnete Macht in Staat und Gesellschaft," 34.
59. FZM Anton Freiherr von Mollinary, *Sechsundvierzig Jahre im österreich-ungarischen Heere, 1833–1879*, 2 vols. (Zurich: Art. Institut Orell Füssli, 1905), II 106.
60. B.P.S., "Unsere Aufgabe," *ÖMZ* 4 (1866): 42. Scrawled under the article title is "Prince v. Solms-Braunfels," most likely the author (B[romfels] P[rinz] S[olms]). Friedrich Wilhelm Karl Ludwig Georg Alfred Alexander Prinz zu Solms-Braunfels (1812–1875), a German prince, served in the Austrian army as a major general in charge of a brigade during the Austro-Prussian War and retired as a lieutenant field marshal in 1868.
61. "Praxis und Routine. - Wissenschaft und Kunst. - Betrachtungen über den Kriegsschauplatz in Böhmen von 1866 und die auf demselben

stattgehabten Kriegsereignisse dieses Jahres. (Aus den schriften eines Veteranen des österreichischen Heeres)," *ÖMZ* 4 (1866): 192–193.

62. "Praxis und Routine," 194–195, 198–199.
63. Allmayer-Beck, "Die bewaffnete Macht in Staat und Gesellschaft," 32–33; Rothenberg, *The Army of Francis Joseph*, 57–60.
64. Wawro, *The Austro-Prussian War*, 25.
65. Rothenberg, *The Army of Francis Joseph*, 60; Wawro, *The Austro-Prussian War*, 27.
66. Eduard Bartels, *Kritische Beiträge zur Geschichte des Krieges im Jahre 1866* (Zurich: Cäsar Schmidt, 1901), 24.
67. Glaise-Horstenau, *Franz Josephs Weggefährte*, 96–97.
68. B.P.S., "Unsere Aufgabe," *ÖMZ* 4 (1866), 41.
69. Beck, "Theilweise Ursachen des gegenwärtigen schlechten Armee-Geistes und Mittel, welche zur Hebung desselben beitragen dürften,"1867, KA MKSM Sonderreihe, Karton Nr. 66, Studien.
70. Bartels, *Östreich und sein Heer*, 17.
71. Feldmarschalleutnant (FML) Erzherzog Albrecht, No. 1017 "Allerunterthänigster Vortrag,"21 August 1866, Kriegsarchiv (KA) Militärkanzlei Seiner Majestät (MKSM) Sonderreihe, Karton Nr. 22, 1866, 7–8.
72. Beck, "Theilweise Ursachen des gegenwärtigen schlechten Armee-Geistes und Mittel, welche zur Hebung desselben beitragen dürften,"1867, KA MKSM Sonderreihe, Karton Nr. 66, Studien.
73. Wawro, "The Austro-Prussian War," 813.
74. "Uber die Ursache der Mißerfolge bei der österreichischen Nordarmee im Kriege Preußens gegen Deutschland im Jahre 1866,"*ÖMZ* 2 (1866), 352–353.
75. Bartels, *Östreich und sein Heer*, 7–8, 10–11.
76. Wawro, *The Austro-Prussian War*, 138.
77. Wawro, "The Austro-Prussian War," 815.
78. See pages 3–4.
79. *Stenographische Protokolle des Hauses der Abgeordneten des Reichsrathes*, 55. Sitzung der 3. Session am 4. Mai 1865 (Vienna: k.k. Hof- und Staatsdruckerei, 1865), 1499–1500.
80. C.A. Macartney, *The Habsburg Empire 1790–1918* (London: Weidenfeld and Nicolson, 1968), 519–520; 571.
81. *Stenographische Protokolle des Hauses der Abgeordneten des Reichsrathes*, 61. Sitzung der 2. Session am 11. December 1863 (Vienna: k.k. Hof- und Staatsdruckerei, 1864), 1396.
82. Wawro, "The Austro-Prussian War," 171.
83. *Stenographische Protokolle des Hauses der Abgeordneten des Reichsrathes*, 61. Sitzung der 2. Session am 11. December 1863, 1405–1406.

84. *Stenographische Protokolle des Hauses der Abgeordneten des Reichsrathes*, 61. Sitzung der 2. Session am 11. December 1863, 1414. By public emergency Dreher meant the financial ruin that military expenditures were bringing the rest of the government and in particular lower officials and teachers who did not receive enough pay.
85. Wawro, "The Austro-Prussian War," 178.
86. *Stenographische Protokolle des Hauses der Abgeordneten des Reichsrathes*, 61. Sitzung der 2. Session am 11. December 1863, 1401–1402, 1416.
87. *Stenographische Protokolle des Hauses der Abgeordneten des Reichsrathes*, 61. Sitzung der 2. Session am 11. December 1863, 1417–1419. The Austrian army had 10,000 officers for a peacetime footing of 327,000 soldiers in 1848. By 1865, the peacetime footing had risen to 374,000 men.
88. *Stenographische Protokolle des Hauses der Abgeordneten des Reichsrathes*, 53. Sitzung der 3. Session am 2. Mai 1865, 1446–1447.
89. *Stenographische Protokolle des Hauses der Abgeordneten des Reichsrathes*, 54. Sitzung der 3. Session am 3. Mai 1865, 1481.
90. *Stenographische Protokolle des Hauses der Abgeordneten des Reichsrathes*, 54. Sitzung der 3. Session am 3. Mai 1865, 1469.
91. Antonio Schmidt-Brentano, *Die Armee in Österreich: Militär, Staat und Gesellschaft 1848–1867* (Boppard am Rhein: Harald Boldt, 1975), 146.
92. *Stenographische Protokolle des Hauses der Abgeordneten des Reichsrathes*, 54. Sitzung der 3. Session am 3. Mai 1865, 1482.
93. Albrecht and John, "Die Beförderungs-Vorschrift für die k.k. österreichische Landarmee vom 24. April 1867," *ÖMZ* 2 (1867), 138.
94. *Stenographische Protokolle des Hauses der Abgeordneten des Reichsrathes*, 54. Sitzung der 3. Session am 3. Mai 1865, 1482.
95. According to the Vienna Coinage Treaty of 1857, 1 thaler equaled 1.5 Austrian florin, which would make the Prussian fortress expenditure 555,000 Austrian florins. Steven P. Reti, *Silver and Gold: The Political Economy of International Monetary Conferences, 1867–1892* (Westport, CT: Greenwood Press, 1998), 52.
96. *Stenographische Protokolle des Hauses der Abgeordneten des Reichsrathes*, 54. Sitzung der 3. Session am 3. Mai 1865, 1461.
97. Wawro, "The Austro-Prussian War," 182.
98. Wawro, "The Austro-Prussian War," 174.
99. Showalter, *Railroads and Rifles*, 122. Showalter puts the Dreyse's normal effective range around 600 paces, whereas the Lorenz had a range of 900 paces.

Bibliography

Unpublished Documents

Kriegsarchiv (KA), Vienna.
Allerhöchster Oberbefehl (AhOB).
Militärkanzlei Seiner Majestät des Kaisers (MKSM) Sonderreihe 1866–1918.
Chef des Generalstabs (GSt) Operationsbüro 1866–1918.
Zentralstellen.
Kriegsministerium (KM) Präsidialbüro (Präsidium) 1866–1918.
Militärerziehungs- und Bildungsanstalten (MEB).
Kriegsschule Wien 1867–1914.

Published Primary Sources

Bartels, Eduard. *Kritische Beiträge zur Geschichte des Krieges im Jahre 1866.* Zurich: Cäsar Schmidt, 1901.

Bartels, Eduard. *Österreich und sein Heer.* Leipzig: Otto Wigand, 1866.

Benedek, Ludwig August Ritter von, and Heinrich Friedjung, *Benedeks nachgelassene Papiere.* Leipzig: Grübel & Sommerlatte, 1901.

Friedjung, Heinrich. *Der Kampf um die Vorherrschaft in Deutschland 1859 bis 1866*, 2 vols. Stuttgart: J.G. Cotta, 1900.

Hess, FML Heinrich Freiherr von. "Strategische Grundsätze über die Verteidigung der österreichischen Monarchie," in *Schriften aus dem militärwissenschaftlichen Nachlass*, ed. Manfried Rauchensteiner. Osnäbruck: Biblio Verlag, 1975.

Jomini, Antoine Henri. *The Art of War.* Westport, CT: Greenwood Press, 1862.

K.k. Generalstabs-Bureau für Kriegsgeschichte. *Österreichs Kämpfe im Jahre 1866.* Wien: R.v.Waldheim, 1867–1869, vol. 1–5.

Mollinary, FZM Anton Freiherr von. *Sechsundvierzig Jahre im österreich-ungarischen Heere, 1833–1879*, 2 vols. Zurich: Art. Institut Orell Füssli, 1905.

Mollinary, Anton von. *Studien über die Operationen und Tactique der Franzosen im Feldzuge 1859 in Italien.* Wien: Wilhelm Braumüller, 1864.

Österreichische Militärische Zeitschrift (ÖMZ), 1866–1914.

Ottenfeld, Rudolf Ritter Otto von. *Ein Ruhmesblatt der österreichischen Artillerie. Die Armeegeschützreserve nach der Schlacht bei Königgrätz am 3. Juli 1866*, oil on canvas, Heeresgeschichtliches Museum, Vienna, 1897.

Sammlung der Armeebefehle und speziellen Anordnungen des k.k. Feldzeugmeisters Benedek, Kommandanten der k.k. Nordarmee vom Jahre 1866. Vienna: k.k. Staatsdruckerei, 1866.

Sechzig Jahre Wehrmacht 1848–1908. Vienna: k.u.k. Kriegsarchiv, 1908.

Sochor, Vaclav. *The Battery of the Dead*, oil on canvas, Heeresgeschichtliches Museum, Vienna, 1901/7.

Stenographische Protokolle des Hauses der Abgeordneten des Reichsrathes. Vienna: k.k. Hof- und Staatsdruckerei, 1863–1871.

Zitterhofer, Oberleutnant. *Streffleurs Militärische Zeitschrift 1808–1908: Eine Geschichte dieser Zeitschrift anlässlich ihres 100jährigen Bestehens*. Vienna: L.W. Siedel & Sohn, 1908.

Secondary Sources

Allmayer-Beck, Johann Christoph. "Der Feldzug der österreichischen Nordarmee nach Königgrätz," in *Entscheidung 1866: Der Krieg zwischen Österreich und Preußen,* eds. Wolfgang v. Groote and Ursula v. Gersdorff. Stuttgart: Deutsche Verlags-Anstalt, 1966.

Allmayer-Beck, Johann Christoph. "Die Bewaffnete Macht in Staat und Gesellschaft." in *Die Habsburgermonarchie 1848–1918*, Vol. 5 *Die Bewaffnete Macht*. Vienna: Verlag der Österreichischen Akademie der Wissenschaften, 1987.

Clausewitz, Carl von. *On War*. Edited and translated by Michael Howard and Peter Paret. Princeton, NJ: Princeton University Press, 1976.

Craig, Gordon. *The Battle of Königgrätz*. Philadelphia: Lippincott Co., 1964.

Förster, Rolf. "Die Leistungsfähigkeit der bayrischen Armee im Feldzuge 1866: Dargestellt an der militärische Ausbildung vor dem Krieg." Ph.D. dissertation, Munich, 1987.

Franzel, Emil. *1866. Il Mondo Casca. Das Ende des alten Europa*. Vienna: Verlag Herold, 1968.

Gat, Azar. *A History of Military Thought: From the Enlightenment to the Cold War*. New York: Oxford University Press, 2001.

Glaise-Horstenau, Edmund von. *Franz Josephs Weggefährte*. Wien: Amalthea Verlag, 1930.

Holtman, Robert. *The Napoleonic Revolution*. New York: J.B. Lippincott, 1967.

Macartney, C.A. *The Habsburg Empire 1790–1918*. London: Weidenfeld and Nicolson, 1969.

Rauchensteiner, Manfried. *Heeresgeschichtliches Museum Vienna*. Vienna: Styria Verlag, 2000.

Regele, Oskar. *Feldzeugmeister Benedek und der Weg nach Königgrätz*. Wien: Verlag Herold, 1960.

Regele, Oskar. "Staatspolitische Geschichtsschreibung: erläutert an Königgrätz 1866." *Mitteilungen des österreichischen Staatsarchivs (MÖSA)* 3 (1950).

Reti, Steven P. *Silver and Gold: The Political Economy of International Monetary Conferences, 1867–1892*. Westport, CT: Greenwood Press, 1998.

Rothenberg, Gunther E. *The Army of Francis Joseph.* West Lafayette, IN: Purdue University Press, 1976.
Rothenberg, Gunther E. *The Art of Warfare in the Age of Napoleon.* Bloomington, IN: Indiana University Press, 1980.
Schmidt-Brentano, Antonio. *Die Armee in Österreich: Militär, Staat und Gesellschaft 1848–1867.* Boppard am Rhein: Harald Boldt, 1975.
Showalter, Dennis E. *Railroads and Rifles: Soldiers, Technology, and the Unification of Germany.* Hamden, CT: Archon Books, 1975.
Vego, Milan N. *Joint Operational Warfare: Theory and Practice.* Newport, Rhode Island: Naval War College, 2009.
Wagner, Walter. "Die k.(u.)k. Armee - Gliederung und Aufgabenstellung." in *Die Habsburgermonarchie 1848–1918*, Vol. 5 *Die Bewaffnete Macht.* Vienna: Verlag der Österreichischen Akademie der Wissenschaften, 1987.
Wandruszka, Adam. *Schicksalsjahr 1866.* Vienna: Styria Verlag, 1966.
Wawro, Geoffrey. "An 'Army of Pigs': The Technical, Social, and Political Bases of Austrian Shock Tactics, 1859–1866." *The Journal of Military History* Vol. 59, No. 3 (July 1995): 407–433.
Wawro, Geoffrey. *The Austro-Prussian War: Austria's War with Prussia and Italy in 1866.* Cambridge: Cambridge University Press, 1996.
Wawro, Geoffrey. "The Austro-Prussian War: Politics, Strategy and War in the Habsburg Monarchy, 1859–1866." Ph.D. dissertation, Yale University, 1992.
Wawro, Geoffrey. *Warfare and Society in Europe, 1792–1914.* New York: Routledge, 2000.

CHAPTER 3

1866–1876: First Steps Toward Progress

"We wish to utilize our experiences for the future!"[1] exclaimed Emperor Franz Joseph when commanding his military leaders to investigate the causes of defeat and ensure that such catastrophic losses would not happen again. These causes permeated the whole Habsburg army and made any superficial changes useless. As one officer later expressed it, "The cannon thunder of Königgrätz also became the funeral march of the old army, the army of Radetzky and Benedek. Vast upheavals awaited, which necessitated the introduction of an almost completely new foundation. The experiences in the last campaign compelled a deep running reform in head and members."[2] Only a full scale remodeling could remedy the problems of outdated weaponry, tactics, and strategy; promotions based on political connections and money; inadequate training of officers and enlisted men; inefficient organization; and financial waste and mismanagement. If the army could resolve these grave problems, Austria could return to great power status and play a prominent role in Europe. The decade following the disaster of 1866 brought improvements in weaponry and tactics, though the Habsburg high command retained the same faulty strategic ideas and failed to remedy the fiscal problems completely. Internal rivalry also hindered effective reforms.

J.A. Dredger, *Tactics and Procurement in the Habsburg Military, 1866–1918*, DOI 10.1007/978-3-319-57678-7_3

Early Measures and Self-Awareness

With the removal of the North Army commander-in-chief Benedek on 10 July 1866, the new leaders, Archduke Albrecht and his chief of staff *FML* Franz von John, made rapid changes to stabilize the army and enable it to continue the war. Almost immediately, Albrecht ordered an end to frontal attacks, while John set to work on a new tactical manual emphasizing firepower, defensive strategies, use of terrain and cover, coordination with artillery, and open order advances.[3] Later, as chief of the general staff and minister of war, positions he held simultaneously, *FML* John renewed the proposal he had made in 1859 that the Habsburg army should do away with the customary white coats, which it had used for centuries, and outfit its troops in a darker hue. Although no one attributed the catastrophe of Königgrätz to the color of Austrian uniforms, military leaders finally realized the disadvantage of using a uniform that the enemy could see from a distance. Habsburg soldiers had worn gray cloaks over their white uniforms to conceal themselves from the Prussians in Bohemia. After the war, they adopted a blue darker than "Prussian blue." As Austrian historian Allmayer-Beck noted, "Now finally the adaptation of the uniform for the requirements of battle appeared more important than for the needs of parade."[4]

The structure of the Habsburg high command contained several different components. The minister of war maintained the highest position within the army and was responsible directly to the emperor, who possessed supreme command. Other men also held powerful positions. The chief of the general staff, as the preparer of war plans and main advisor to field commanders, had a major role in army operations and was responsible to the war minister. The president of Franz Joseph's military chancellery, with direct access to the emperor, also held great influence over important military decisions, though without the rank or power to make final decisions. In addition, Archduke Albrecht, the victor of Custozza in 1866 and member of the royal house with personal access to the emperor, possessed the highest position at the end of the Austro-Prussian War as commander-in-chief and desired to maintain his power in the future.[5]

This situation created a rather complex structure that gave ample opportunities for friction to develop within the high command. Albrecht wished to hold power over reforming the army, but John, who became minister of war and chief of the general staff, positions which he perceived as superior to Albrecht's role, held responsibility for procuring funding from parliamentary representatives. The rivalry that ensued between the various members of the Habsburg military command prevented any one man from gaining too much power, yet delayed the implementation of reforms. The command structure also remained somewhat fluid over the following decades, with certain positions gaining more prominence than others. Under this indefinite arrangement, the Austrian army set out to remedy the problems of 1866.

Before anyone could institute major reforms, Franz Joseph considered his first priority to find out why Austria had lost the war in such a disastrous fashion. He convened a court of inquiry to investigate the conduct of Benedek, Henikstein, Krismanić, and other high ranking officers during the campaign. The court concluded that Benedek's incompetent leadership was the primary cause of defeat.[6] However, it did not choose to inspect more than the period of the war and did not look at issues such as weapons procurement that could implicate the whole military hierarchy, including members of the royal family. Thus, Benedek, Henikstein, and Krismanić retired on 1 November 1866, and the court dropped all charges of military irresponsibility and incompetence on 4 December.[7] The inquiry allowed Franz Joseph and his court to find someone to blame for the debacle as the accusations against Benedek and his staff contained accurate assessments of the North Army command's actions.

Austrian officers nevertheless realized that the war was not lost by Benedek alone. Problems existed within the military that would continue to exist after Benedek retired if army leaders did not institute necessary reforms. In the words of one veteran of 1866, "Self-knowledge is the first step towards improvement."[8] The theme of self-knowledge played an important part in the reform process, as Habsburg leaders could remedy only what they perceived as problematic. Opinions differed on the crucial issues, but they agreed that the dire situation required widespread changes. An *ÖMZ* writer quoted the new war minister John, "Frankly be assured before all that one has recognized the causes of the suffered misfortune not merely in superficial reasons and chance, but also in deep lying evils, and one is strongly determined to remove them thoroughly."[9] Friedrich von Beck of the general staff advocated sweeping reform in army administration, and in officer and troop training with an emphasis on better intelligence, weapons procurement, and improvement of the general staff.[10] Albrecht, while stressing the importance of discipline above all, argued strongly for the adoption of breech-loading rifles as well as improvements in organization, preparation for war, training, and leadership.[11] Clearly, the Habsburg high command had determined to remedy the problems of 1866, especially in officer education, tactics, and weaponry.

Procuring a Breech-Loader

The call for arming Habsburg troops with breech-loading rifles resounded throughout the whole army. Albrecht had appealed to Franz Joseph almost immediately after the conclusion of peace in 1866, stressing the necessity of obtaining breech-loaders so that Austria could defend itself against incursions from other European powers, who were all procuring weapons similar to the Prussian needle gun. The archduke emphasized the loss of trust in the Lorenz rifle and the ensuing fall in morale as the decisive reason for the emperor to order new breech-loaders for the infantry.[12] Beck concurred with Albrecht that raising the depressed morale in the Austrian army was a pressing argument for acquiring better weaponry.[13] Even officers such as Krismanić and Solm-Braunfels, who did not attribute the disaster of Königgrätz solely to the Dreyse rifle, advocated the purchase of breech-loaders to improve the fighting ability of the Austro-Hungarian army.[14]

The Austrian high command hastily assembled a commission for selecting the best breech-loader for the Habsburg army. Attempts to convert the Lorenz rifles into breech-loaders, the so-called Wänzl modification, failed because parts of the old Austrian weapons proved too worn. The commission finally decided on the weapon design of Josef Werndl, whose factory at Steyr in Upper Austria used American machine tools and industrial methods and could produce rifles faster than the Vienna arsenal.[15] John placed an order for 611,000 Werndl pieces in 1867, which was not enough for the wartime army after the 1868 introduction of universal conscription. By November 1870, the Steyr factory had delivered only 316,650 rifles, partially because of delays in production and more importantly because of insufficient funding from the Austro-Hungarian army. At a cost of 50 florins per rifle, the total cost of the order came to 30,550,000 florins, or 37.6% of the 81,200,000 florin budget for 1867. The first installment of 100,000 pieces cost 5 million florins.[16] Parliamentary delegations from Austria and Hungary were unwilling to grant such large amounts of money to a branch of the government that they felt spent far too much every year. Although the delegates had approved more than 14 million florins for the new Werndl rifles and ammunition, the parliamentary representatives did not wish to continue granting the same amount each year until the army had procured enough weapons. Thus, the special weapons funding dropped to less than 1 million florins in 1869.[17] Despite the Liberal party connections of *FML* Franz Baron Kuhn von Kuhnenfeld, minister of war from 1868 until 1874, the war minister reported that the army still needed another 370,000 Werndl rifles in 1873. The Habsburg army did not finish equipping itself with breech-loaders until the mid-1870s.[18] Until Austrian military leaders proved capable of making trustworthy decisions and showed success on the battlefield, parliamentary representatives did not wish to risk pouring large funds into a mismanaged army. The Habsburg military leadership showed great interest in technology and a willingness to test and procure new weaponry, in contrast to the conservatism and aversion to progress evident before the Austro-Prussian War. The inner workings of the Austrian government and its army delayed the achievement of military goals.

Tactical Debate: Infantry

To incorporate the Werndl rifles fully into the army and to implement the lessons of 1866, the Imperial-Royal (*kaiserlich königlich*; *k.k.*) high command had to develop new tactics. The 1870–1871 tactical manual of the *Kriegsschule* revealed the details of these tactics, though in many ways they resembled old ideas. The author, Colonel Wilhelm Reinländer, took a Clausewitzian approach to war. Echoing the Prussian theorist's definition of war as a continuation of political policy by other means,[19] Reinländer divided war into the positive side of attack and the negative side of defense. The colonel added to this concept Moltke's goal of a decisive defeat of the enemy by an enclosing movement, emphasizing the importance of mobilization and concentration of units toward a fixed point. Although Reinländer acknowledged the rarity of destruction of all enemy forces in one battle, he still maintained that the decisive battle was the ultimate goal of war. However, he believed that victory depended not on the old linear tactics but on firepower and mobility. The general staff colonel also adhered to the view of Archduke Charles that possession of vital points or places on the battlefield brought success. Reinländer in addition stressed the importance of both arms and morale for favorable results, especially emphasizing self-confidence and surprise as decisive means for achieving victory.[20]

In his discussion of attack and defense, the colonel asserted his preference for attack as positive and forward moving, thereby raising troop morale with feelings of superiority: "The attack is the form of the strong." Assault forces have the advantage of surprise over the defenders because the attackers can choose objective points, whereas the defense does not know where exactly the attack will come. In addition, the attacker can employ the demoralizing effects of "the roar of battle, the crackle of firing, the hurrah of the storming troops" against the defender so that the assault troops can find cover in the smoke of battle while the enemy sits unsure of where to fire: "Under these psychological influences favoring the attack it is certainly to be expected that despite the breech-loader, the direct attack will succeed." The attacker merely needs to use quick recognition of the terrain and weak points of the defender to overcome the advantages of the breech-loader's rapid fire.[21]

Reinländer then said that the effect of fire constitutes the greatest strength of the defense because the defender can employ terrain and firepower from a steady and secure position to deter the attacker. The colonel nevertheless maintained the disadvantage of defense as a passive form of battle that can only react to the aggressive moves of the enemy. The negative effect of this passivity weighs upon the morale of the defender and results in a feeling of weakness, with a corresponding reduction in courage and energy. Reinländer summed up his analysis of attack and defense thus, "A powerfully undertaken, well led attack strengthened by the raised moral element of the troops will finally overcome all difficulties, and, despite the murderous fire of the breech-loader, will break through the line of the defender."[22]

Reinländer also discussed the role of the bayonet attack. Although admitting the superiority of firepower on the modern battlefield and the ineffectiveness of using a bayonet to drive away an enemy armed with a breech-loader, he refused to admit the complete demise of shock with steel. In his opinion, after weakening the defender with artillery and infantry fire, the attacker will almost always achieve victory through an energetic bayonet assault, primarily because of the psychological advantage of attack. Reinländer also asserted that the bayonet can bring about a decisive outcome, which rifle fire cannot accomplish.[23]

To avoid heavy losses in the attack, the general staff colonel recommended the employment of open order tactics or swarms as skirmishers instead of closed lines. The developed line gives greater effect to the firepower of the defender, but the company column presents the most effective main assault formation because of its flexibility, greater cohesion, and morale as well as being easier to control by its commander. Thus, even though Reinländer saw the need for open order tactics, he advocated retaining the attack column to culminate the assault in a bayonet charge.[24]

Other members of the Austrian military had already voiced differing opinions. Immediately after taking charge in 1866, Albrecht and John ordered no more frontal assaults and a greater emphasis on defense, firepower, and open order tactics.[25] Debate took place in the *ÖMZ*. Captain Wendelin Boeheim, using examples from the Austro-Prussian War, expressed his view that the defensive offered far better opportunities for success than the offensive, especially considering the effects of new technology such as the breech-loading rifle: "The so beloved aggressive elementary tactics of the Austrian army are no longer useful in any way for modern times and should have been changed long ago, as also for the reason that this [the examples from the Bohemian campaign] demonstrates precisely the present power of the elementary defensive."[26] Boeheim assessed frontal attacks against the breech-loader as ineffective and dangerous and advocated two methods that had proved successful: first, the defensive in order to ruin the enemy's fighting power, induce him to attack prematurely, or seek a propitious moment for counterattack after weakening the enemy physically and morally; and second, aggressive moves against the enemy's flanks and rear, but always with a defensive reserve ready. Proving the worthiness of imitating Prussian ideas, Boeheim stated that linear formations rather than columns took better advantage of the benefits of increased firepower and that skirmishers in swarms should be used if the offensive became necessary or advisable.[27] The Habsburg high command demonstrated its conviction of the importance of firepower by raising the numbers of bullets issued for training, setting up shooting grounds, and releasing new instructions for artillery in 1869 and 1872.[28] Austrian military leaders realized the importance of firepower on the battlefield and the need to have trained soldiers firing breech-loading rifles.

Nonetheless, some officers claimed that the breech-loader offered equal advantages to both attacker and defender and continued to adhere to the offensive as the surest guarantee of martial success. Although these officers saw no need to change previous tactics, they at least admitted that defense was an option if the circumstances of battle did not allow attack.[29] Friedrich von Fischer, a general staff colonel who presided over writing of the official history of the Austro-Prussian War, took a more extreme view concerning the advantages of attack over defense, maintaining that Clausewitz erred in his belief of the superior strength of the defensive. Fischer claimed that, despite the firepower of the breech-loader, "positions can hardly be held at least against armies in which the spirit of the offensive enlivens the smallest divisions up to the individual common soldier." The reasons for the superiority of the defense, "as plausible as they may be, are supported in reality only with illusions and deceptions."[30] This analysis coincided with Fischer's view in the official history that the army had not caused the defeat of 1866: Austrian offensive tactics still maintained superiority over the defensive, which would not have achieved better results.

As *Kommandant* of the general staff war college from 1873 to 1874, Fischer influenced the views of prominent military leaders during the First World War, including Franz Conrad von Hötzendorf, chief of the general staff and de facto commander-in-chief of Austro-Hungarian forces for most of the Great War. As a student of the *Kriegsschule* from 1874 to 1876, Conrad studied under Fischer and absorbed the tactical principles of Reinländer while learning from the instructor of tactics Colonel Johann Baron Waldstätten, author of the pre-1866 tactical manual. With such men teaching at the war college, the curriculum failed to reflect the more reasonable tactics of Albrecht and John. Thus, even though reformers advocated a more reasonable defensive approach during debates in the military journals, the offensive still held sway in the *Kriegsschule*.

The war college had an immense influence over the Habsburg army. Founded in 1852, this institution educated general staff officers, who as chiefs of staff had responsibility for drawing up war plans and advising field generals. These officers learned both the technical and practical aspects of all branches of the military to become capable of joint planning for the infantry, cavalry, and artillery. Only lieutenants who had served with the troops for at least 3 years and passed competitive examinations gained entrance to the *Kriegsschule*. General staff officers received rapid promotions after graduation from the war college, with the result that by the early 1900s most Austro-Hungarian generals had graduated from the *Kriegsschule*.[31] Thus, the tactical ideas that general staff officers received at the war college dominated the higher ranks of the Habsburg officer corps.

During this crucial time of reform in the 1870s, the Franco-Prussian War afforded an opportunity for officers to debate tactics using recent examples. The Prussians, using offensive tactics, had defeated the French, who fought primarily defensive battles, leading one Habsburg general staff officer to reach the simplistic conclusion that the offensive always brought victory. According to this officer, troops employing the defensive, especially in entrenched positions, ruined their offensive spirit, which must culminate in the bayonet charge.[32] However, First Lieutenant Gustav Ratzenhofer, who later became the leading tactical writer for the Austro-Hungarian army during the 1870s and 1880s, provided a different viewpoint. Ratzenhofer stated that the defense has certain advantages over the offense because of the advent of breech-loading rifles. Thus, military leaders must choose the offensive or defensive depending on the battlefield situation.[33] Under the guidance of Ratzenhofer and Albrecht, a more reasonable view of tactics slowly spread throughout the Habsburg army.

Tactical Debate: Cavalry

Austrian military thinkers also debated the employment of cavalry during the decade following the defeat at Königgratz. The ineffectiveness of cavalry charges near the end of the battle and the insignificant effect of cavalry on the outcome led Habsburg officers to search for the best role for mounted troops. Solm-Braunfels asserted that the effect of increased firepower and the use of broken terrain on battlefields rendered cavalry attacks pointless. Therefore, commanders should employ their mounted forces for reconnaissance, security patrols, and harassing the operations lines of the enemy.[34] Other Austro-Hungarian officers concurred about the lesser role of cavalry in what they termed "small war," such as raids, patrols, and reconnoitering, but still maintained the overall importance of the branch for campaigning, especially in attacks on enemy mounted troops.[35]

Other officers insisted on the offensive quality of cavalry in massed formations.[36] Reinländer's tactical manual for the war college expressed this idea: "Shock is the most decisive part of attack, the touchstone of battle, the most important task of cavalry." Thus, commanders must inspire mounted troops with the spirit of the offensive and high morale in order to assault the enemy "with the sword in the fist."[37] Another officer shared this conviction of the decisive quality of mounted troops, lamenting the reduction from 40,000 mounted troops to 29,000 before the Austro-Prussian War as the cause of poor cavalry performance during the Bohemian campaign. An increase in mounted troops back to prewar numbers was imperative if the Habsburg army wished to compete with other European powers, who possessed at least 50,000 (the French) to 90,000 (the Russians) cavalry.[38] Archduke Albrecht, citing the significant advantage in cavalry forces that the Prussians held over the French in 1870, also favored an increase in the number of Austro-Hungarian cavalry.[39]

Many officers, however, realized that cavalry would play a diminished role on future battlefields because of the devastating firepower of defending infantry. One first lieutenant recommended a reduction in the number of mounted troops because of their excessive cost and their uselessness as a purely offensive weapon against infantry armed with breech-loading rifles.[40] Other officers suggested the adoption of breech-loaders for cavalry to enable the mounted branch to take advantage of the increase in firepower. Thus, cavalry could use its superior mobility to capture strategic positions and its new rifles to maintain possession. In this way, mounted troops would retain a significant role in warfare, possibly as mounted infantry like the Russian cavalry.[41] Franz Joseph also saw the need to reform the cavalry and ordered the arming of his cuirassiers with carbines so that they could fight like dragoons.[42]

Habsburg officers realized the necessity of adapting their tactics to modern war. Many, however, remained incapable of abandoning the traditional aggressive style of Austrian warfare. These men combined misinterpretation of Clausewitzian thought as favoring the offensive, the recent victories of Moltke, and their own defeats while employing the defensive, concluding that the offensive was still the stronger choice. Despite the obvious effect of the breech-loader, Austro-Hungarian officers attempted to find ways of assault that would allow them to bring the bayonet to bear. The emphasis on morale revealed how *élan* still held sway in the officer corps. The events of 1870 confirmed this view in the minds of Habsburg officers.[43] The wars of 1866 and 1870 remained a fixation for *k.k.* officers. This obsession would last for over four decades among officers who saw the offensive victories of the Prussians as proof of the success of Moltke's methods. They tried to solve the problem of retaining offensive tactics in an era of technological innovation and ever-increasing firepower. These attempts resulted in Reinländer's tactical manual that presaged the tactics of the First World War, with emphasis on the offensive using frontal assaults in swarms culminating in a bayonet attack.

At the same time, through the influence of Albrecht and John, many officers understood that defense would have to take a greater part in future wars. The devastating firepower of the breech-loader necessitated a more prudent style of warfare. Thus, there was at least debate within the Habsburg army concerning changes in tactics, with voices of reason advocating less emphasis on the offensive. Austro-Hungarian leaders began to recognize the need for change in the employment of cavalry. Nevertheless, reforms came slowly as gallant cavalry charges lasted in *k.k.* maneuvers until the First World War. The constant attempts to prove the worth of the mounted branch while simultaneously calling for limitations or alterations in its use revealed the attachment that some *k.k.* officers, especially from the cavalry, maintained for the battlefield importance of cavalry. This view came partially from Franz Joseph's desire to use the impressiveness of cavalry on parade to influence his subjects, the traditional Austrian supremacy in mounted forces, and a belief in officers as modern knights.[44] The cavalry charge against emplaced cannon at the 1876 maneuvers impressed Franz Joseph greatly, though some officers silently objected.[45] The 1866 cavalry attacks had never even reached the enemy, presenting large targets that the Prussian breech-loaders could hardly miss. Ten years later, the situation had not improved, but Franz Joseph and many of his cavalry officers believed that the prestige of the Habsburg cavalry and the Habsburg Empire would suffer without glorious charges into the fire of the enemy.

Cordon Strategy

Strategically, the Austro-Hungarian high command persisted in employing the cordon system of permanent fortifications to defend the empire, despite the meager part that fortresses played in 1866. Several officers saw the drawbacks of depending on the cordon system for defending the Dual Monarchy. *FML* Hess admitted that the fortress strategy had almost completely lost its purpose.[46] Colonel Fischer argued against the merits of the defensive and stated the disadvantages of weakening a strong army by having to garrison many forts, especially considering that modern artillery had gained "a truly irresistible power, so infinitely superior that it must certainly break through resistance with means far more insignificant and relatively very inexpensive, and the fall of bulwarks according to their interior strength and the means that stand at the disposal of the attack, becomes only a question of time."[47] Dr. Hermann Orges, a government councilor and captain in the *k.k. Landwehr*, agreed that permanent fortresses were useless in resisting new technology in the form of rifled breech-loading cannons. With examples from the wars of the eighteenth and nineteenth centuries, Orges showed how the cordon system represented an outmoded style of warfare for the age of steam power, railroads, and universal conscription.[48]

The majority of Habsburg officers still believed in the efficacy of permanent fortifications as deterrents to enemy invasions, especially in the case of a multifront war against enemies with superior numbers. Officers of the engineering staff proposed extension of the cordon system around the empire, plus a set of fortresses within the empire to provide fortified places for regrouping after retreat and to prepare for attacks from all sides. These men advocated continued use of the cordon system and permanent fortifications, assuming that their strength could withstand mortar shot and that they could be built inexpensively. Other officers recognized the expense of building or upgrading fortresses but trusted the Habsburg army to spread out the cost during times of peace. One contributor to the *ÖMZ* even recognized the tendency of nineteenth-century armies to grow in size and become less dependent on fortresses, which weakened military strength by absorbing too many men for garrison duty. Nevertheless, the author still preferred permanent fortifications because of their positive effect on morale and suggested a smaller number of forts but an extension of fortresses to create groups of forts (like the Quadrilateral in Lombardy) that would have a greater impact on warfare.[49]

Archduke Albrecht also lent his voice in favor of the cordon system of defense: "It has been called wishing to wash Moors white, if one has tried to convince someone who despite all the lessons of history denies the necessity of a well-ordered system of permanent fortifications as one of the most important conditions of the defense of every state. And thus the most recent history has just delivered the clearest proof."[50] The archduke believed that holding permanent fortresses in the key points of a potential theater of war was the first step in preparing for future campaigns. Albrecht advised against the construction of many small fortified locations that would absorb garrisons and weaken the army, but advocated the building of a few extensive fortresses in Carpathia, such as Krakau and Przemyśl, that would strategically control the whole area in case of war with Russia.[51] Numerous reports in the military chancellery and the general staff's operations bureau during the late 1860s and 1870s also advocated permanent fortifications to meet the requirements of modern warfare.[52]

None of the members of the Austro-Hungarian high command considered permanent fortifications to be a useless strategy or a waste of millions of florins that could benefit the army by procuring better weaponry. At a commission meeting for solving the problem of defending the Galician border against a possible Russian invasion, four members including John voted for the fortification of Przemyśl, three including Kuhn voted for Jaroslau, and two for both.[53] In adhering to the cordon system, whether in the form of upgrading old fortresses or building new expansive fortifications, Habsburg officers failed to recognize the changes taking place in modern warfare, especially in the presence of increasingly larger armies and more destructive artillery.

The Franco-Prussian War did nothing to alter this viewpoint, but instead confirmed *k.k.* convictions.[54] Even though some officers realized the reality of war in the latter half of the nineteenth century and published articles in the *ÖMZ* against the cordon system, the belief persisted among the majority of the military that the isolated political situation of the Habsburg Empire required in-depth fortification of every border to thwart invasion.[55] This attitude resulted in the building of the fortress at Przemyśl, where thousands of soldiers became surrounded and hundreds of thousands died during relief attempts in World War I. The only hindrance to erecting and remodeling the whole system of permanent fortresses throughout the Dual Monarchy arose from the deficiency of funding, a point on which almost all *k.k.* officers agreed.[56]

Budgetary Imprudence

The Austro-Hungarian army budget depended on parliamentary approval. From 1868 to 1877, military expenses varied between a low of 173,760,000 florins in 1869 and a high of 253,360,000 florins in 1871, with an average outlay of 228,795,000.[57] In 1868, the military requested only 80 million florins because of the unpopularity of the army with parliamentary representatives. Even the Liberal party leader, Dr. Carl Giskra, minister of the interior for the Austrian half of the Dual Monarchy from 1868 until 1870, who had opposed excessive army spending before 1866, advised representatives to approve this far lower request than the budgets of the 1860s.[58]

However, in 1871, Giskra as a representative of Lower Austria objected to War Minister Kuhn's request for parliamentary approval and funding to raise the number of cavalry by 7000 men and horses to 37,000. Arguing against the war minister's assertion that the effectiveness of Austro-Hungarian mounted troops depended on this increase to compete with other European military powers, Giskra pointed out that France had only 34,500 cavalry and Russia 33,600 without counting "the 100,000 Cossacks on paper, whom no European eye, which has not been in Russia, has seen." The ineffectiveness of Habsburg cavalry did not lie in the small number of sabers but rather in its employment: "The Austrian cavalry could not prove its excellent reputation in war against Prussia, because it was used worthlessly; one led the cavalry against infantry, one charged a Prussian cavalry division, which opened, and behind it stood infantry and artillery. The Austrian cavalry was thrown back."[59] This accurate assessment proved the need to limit the role of mounted troops on the battlefield and to limit spending on cavalry.

Giskra also mentioned the constant changes in how many cavalry the army leadership deemed necessary as an indication of the instability and untrustworthiness of the Habsburg military. Comparing Austrian defeats with the years and decades of success in war of other states, the parliamentary representative wondered how anyone could consider the war ministry as an authority, "where change and lack of stability is the rule."[60] The *k.k.* army could have acquired a more favorable assessment from the Liberal-dominated *Reichsrat* if its leaders had exhibited more constancy, less infighting, and greater responsibility with the funds granted by parliament. The Liberal majority leader, Dr. Anton Banhans, showed how the army asked for and received a grant of 1300,000 florins to maintain the battle readiness of the army for eight weeks until it could train new recruits. Several months later, the high command reported that all the money had gone to troops suppressing a revolt in Dalmatia and not gone to maintain battle readiness. Banhans asserted, "after a few months what was so earnestly repeated in the committee and public sessions of the delegation as absolutely unavoidably necessary for the battle readiness of the army, has at the same time again disappeared and been presented as not necessary."[61] Even Major General von Scholl, the minister for national defense, expressed his opinion that "so long as we labor with a deficit, I am not of the view that one spend more money on the cavalry."[62] Because of the instability and dishonesty that the Liberal majority perceived in the war ministry, most of the parliamentary representatives did not see the wisdom of granting the army the millions of florins requested by Kuhn.

During the 1869 budget debate in the Delegations of both halves of the Dual Monarchy, Dr. Carl Rechbauer observed how the price of the Werndl rifle rose every time the war ministry asked for funding: "Therefore I cannot help expressing my surprise that for us, the longer the order lasts, the more expensive the rifles become. The first cost 27 florins, then 29, consequently with the inclusion of all the attachments first 33 florins and then 35, and today they cost 40 florins. If we continue the order, rifles will soon come to cost us perhaps 100 florins per piece."[63] The delegates also objected to granting 1,800,000 florins for raising the pay of the 1982 supernumerary officers in the Habsburg army.[64] In addition, Dr. Johann Baron von Elswehr Demel believed that 400,000 florins to build two steamships in the *Monitor* style to patrol the Danube River for defense constituted a waste of resources. The *Monitor* style suited sea warfare more than river patrol and two ships would not suffice for proper defense. Their purchase merely signaled the prospect of far greater expenses in the future to build a larger fleet.[65]

Similarly, Friedrich Freiherr zu Weichs objected to granting 380,000 florins for the fortification of Komorn in Hungary. According to Colonel von Tunkler, who spoke for the war ministry, completion of the permanent fortress would require five million florins. The government had made only a small request for funds, which the Delegations should grant. Weichs, however, pointed out that, at 380,000 florins per year, by the time the army finished building the fortress, artillery technology would have developed cannon powerful enough to destroy the new construction. The five million florins for Komorn represented a fraction of the total cost of upgrading the cordon system of the whole empire, which would require at least 50 million by one reckoning and 350 million by another. Both sums amounted to impossible numbers considering the financial situation of the Dual Monarchy.[66]

Furthermore, Dr. Rechbauer found the rising cost of supplying a smaller army inexplicable. Even though the number of men in the *k.k.* military had decreased by over 15,000 from 1868 to 1870, the war ministry asked for three million florins more in 1870 than previously. Rechbauer also noted the significant increase in staff officers from 240 to 400, not including the burdensome number of pensionaries and their corresponding pay from 1868 to 1870, even though there were fewer soldiers to command. The delegate singled out the surprising demands for more cavalry funding, despite the lesser role that cavalry played on the battlefield. The war ministry requested 12,352,041 florins in 1870, 123,041 florins more than in 1868, though 4000 fewer mounted troops served in the army. This expense was in sharp contrast to the 3,559,009 florins spent on a far larger number of infantry.[67] Clearly, the Habsburg high command had not yet rid the army of the financial imprudence and overspending that had existed before the Austro-Prussian War.

Restructuring and Rivalry

On 9 September 1866, John sent a communication to Franz Joseph with his recommendations for restructuring the army leadership. Although echoing Albrecht's ideas concerning the primacy of discipline, John did not want to see the archduke take complete control of the Habsburg army. He suggested the creation of an *Armee-Ober-Kommando* (*AOK*), which would have authority over individual troop commanders in order to raise the morale of the army and enhance its sense of duty. The *AOK* would also decide personnel issues and choose capable leaders who would guarantee favorable results. John's own position, minister of war, "would find in an *Armee-Ober-Kommando* equipped with the indicated authority an essential support in maintaining the complete battle capability of the army."[68] Thus, John expressed his wish to possess overall control of the army through the war ministry, with the help of a commander in the *AOK* who would take care of all concerns other than material. The holders of both positions were responsible for communication with each other as well as with the various army inspectors and the chief of the general staff concerning all important questions.[69] In this way, the high command would achieve the unity that Beck had desired while avoiding the disadvantages of one man having total power.[70] This system resembled the Prussian arrangement, with the chief of the general staff controlling important decisions, except that John wanted the war minister to have the final say.

Franz Joseph put John's proposal into action when he appointed Albrecht as head of the *AOK* on 15 September.[71] This led to friction between Albrecht and John, whose roles suddenly became reversed, with John, at least in his own mind, superior to the archduke. Albrecht opposed this power arrangement and believed that the *AOK* should hold supreme command. He also clashed with John over who deserved credit for the victory of Custozza in 1866.[72] Civil-military officials, such as Foreign Minister *FML* Alexander Count Mensdorff-Pouilly, feared a revival of the 1850s neo-absolutist military control under the aegis of the *AOK*. Beck saw the *AOK*, even under the control of the war ministry, as an unwieldy body with too much power and a staff too large even to go on campaigns. Thus, with a great part of its apparatus remaining in Vienna, army operations would come to a standstill. According to Edmund von Glaise-Horstenau, an Austrian officer and Beck's earliest biographer, "Despite his personal good relations with Archduke Albrecht, he [Beck] resolutely set himself on the side of those who stood for the dissolution of an *Armeeoberkommando* growing to a gigantic position of command."[73] Although, in theory, the *AOK* and war ministry worked together, with the minister of war in charge, Beck believed that the new arrangement would not run smoothly according to his ideas of unity within the army, with dispersion of powers among several boards. Under the new arrangement, Beck feared too much control might come into the hands of either Albrecht or John.

All of these differing opinions revealed the difficulties inherent in establishing a new command hierarchy for the Habsburg military, as well as the rivalry endemic among its various members, who held very different opinions on how best to structure the possession of power within the high command. Beck's theories of unity within the army and dispersion of power made the most sense for smooth operation. In practice, ongoing rivalries limited effectiveness, to a greater or lesser degree, throughout the years leading up to the Great War, despite Beck's status, first as head of the imperial military chancellery (*Militärkanzlei*) with direct access to Franz Joseph and later as chief of the general staff. The antipathy between Albrecht and John, as well as Beck's opposition to John's elevation of the power of the war ministry and consequent decrease in the importance of the general staff and the *Militärkanzlei*, rendered the war minister's position barely tenable. Additional antagonism stemming from civil officials, including the new foreign minister, the Hungarian Julius Count Andrássy von Csik-Szent Király u. Kraszna-Horka, combined to force John to resign in January 1868, less than 2 years after his appointment.[74]

The removal of John from the war ministry did not solve the problem of rivalries within the Habsburg military. On the contrary, the appointment of his successor, *FML* Franz Baron Kuhn von Kuhnenfeld, caused even more antagonism, especially with Albrecht. Kuhn followed the ideas of his predecessor in desiring to make the war ministry supreme in all decisions affecting the military. This view obviously clashed with Albrecht's position in the *AOK*. Further antagonism between Kuhn and Albrecht occurred at the political level. Kuhn had a more progressive attitude toward the military, especially because of his connections to the Liberal party in the *Reichsrat*, in opposition to Albrecht's dynastic perception of the army as the sole guardian of the empire.[75] According to Colonel Valentin Streffleur, editor of the *ÖMZ*, Habsburg soldiers had to guard against nationalistic feelings and propaganda that threatened the empire. The paramount cultural-historical task of Austria and its army was the spread and inculcation of loyalty and devotion to the Habsburg monarch throughout the imperial lands, regardless of the ethnic background of the people.[76]

Both the conservative faction of Albrecht, Beck, and their supporters and the progressive party of Kuhn and the Liberals agreed on the need to improve the army's battlefield performance by raising the intellectual level of the officer corps and putting men who displayed the best abilities into leadership positions. Both sides saw education and promotion as the means to achieve these goals. In theory, the plans for attaining success appeared worthwhile. Albrecht's and John's prescriptions for basing promotions on battle records, academic examinations, physical fitness, and personal behavior (all measures of merit and ability) seemed the best solution without opening up the field to competitive examinations. The archduke's plan may have worked well in an era with frequent wars, a time through which the *k.k.* army had recently passed, but protracted peace limited the significance of battle performance and raised the issue of what to do with reserve officers.

Kuhn believed the inferior status of the Austrian military stemmed from the incompetence and backwardness of those who held to the old dynastic principle and neo-absolutism of the 1850s. To make progress toward transforming the army into a modern fighting force with a constitutional war minister responsible to the people, the high command needed to eliminate members holding on to what Kuhn called "feudal" values.[77] Instead of an absolute state ruled by an absolute monarch for his own good or for the benefit of certain vested interests, according to Kuhn's younger brother Colonel Franz Baron Kuhn von Kuhnenfeld, "the uppermost practical purpose of the state consists in the realization of a condition of human society corresponding to the principle of right, which the purpose of each individual—that is, the harmonic development of one's intellectual, moral, and material elements—promotes, the attainment of which is facilitated and thus the sum of the powers of all public society is led into an asymptote for ideal humanity."[78]

As part of Kuhn's attempt to control every aspect of the Habsburg army through the imperial war ministry, in 1868 he made the general staff a *Hilfsorgane*, or supporting organ, directly subordinate to the war minister.[79] Kuhn held a special dislike for the general staff, which he considered a "Jesuit caste" blocking liberal reforms. According to twentieth century American historian Scott Lackey, "The war minister aimed at nothing less than the complete elimination of the general staff corps and a scattering of its functions across the entire officer corps. Kuhn felt that this would engender a 'meritocracy' within the Habsburg officer corps and end advancement on the basis of birth, family connections, and sycophancy."[80]

Kuhn also convinced Franz Joseph to appoint Major General Josef Gallina as director of the general staff rather than chief. In this way, Kuhn reserved control over the general staff for himself and mirrored the command arrangement of Benedek before the Austro-Prussian War. The war minister also opened the general staff to any Austro-Hungarian officer who proved his abilities by competitive examinations. In this way, Kuhn eliminated the independent status of the general staff as he tried to create an officer corps whose promotions relied on talent.[81]

Kuhn's views, of course, led to friction with the archduke. The antipathy between the two men became bitterly hostile and personal, particularly on the part of Kuhn.[82] In his diary, he called Albrecht the proponent of "Spanish absolutism, bigotry, ultramontanism, falseness and jesuitness."[83] Certainly, Kuhn exaggerated in his estimation of Albrecht and his negative effect on the Austrian military. Nonetheless, the war minister's venom provides an excellent example of the crippling rivalry within the Habsburg army.

This rivalry led once again to an alteration of the command structure. A mere month after Kuhn's appointment, Franz Joseph dissolved the *AOK* and the following year appointed Albrecht as inspector general of the armed forces. This position gave the archduke less independence because he had to submit all his reports to the war ministry and enjoyed only limited access to the emperor.[84] Although Albrecht's influence on military decisions decreased, the antagonism between the archduke and the war minister did not abate and their quarrels even spilled over into the press. As Rothenberg stated, "The rift split the army into opposing 'court' and 'ministerial' factions which lambasted each other in their respective journals, the semi-official *ÖMZ* and the liberal-leaning *Österreichisch-ungarische Wehrzeitung*."[85]

Ausgleich and *Wehrgesetz*

Another issue that augmented the difficulty of reforming the organization of the Austrian army came from the *Ausgleich* (compromise) of 1867. This agreement between Franz Joseph and the Magyar leadership of Hungary led to the Dual Monarchy, in which German-speaking Austria and Hungary became the two main components of the Habsburg lands, with their own governments under the Habsburg monarch. The ministry of foreign affairs, the ministry of finance, and the ministry of war remained common to both parts of the empire. The two halves of the monarchy, however, handled the other state functions separately. Although no one particularly liked this new constitutional arrangement, especially the Slavic nationalities, who received no benefits from the *Ausgleich*, it lasted until the end of the empire in 1918.[86] Even the Hungarians, by far the greatest beneficiaries of the compromise, complained that they did not receive enough autonomy and worked incessantly to gain more and more concessions in their favor.

The *Ausgleich* created an increasingly difficult situation for the Habsburg army. Although military leaders succeeded in retaining the unity of the army, they conceded a national guard for Austria, the *Landwehr*, and one for Hungary, the *Honvédség*. Many officers, such as Albrecht, remembered the 1848 revolution and feared that a Hungarian national guard would foster subversive ideas; therefore, they wanted no privileges for the Magyars.[87] Lieutenant Colonel Eduard Bartels, pondering solutions even before the *Ausgleich*, perceived the negative effect of Dualism on the other nationalities, mainly the Slavs, who would look for connections to the foreign Slavic powers of Russia, Serbia, and Rumania. He suggested a federation of six independent areas, each with its own Habsburg archduke, government, and army, but all under the rule and at the command of the emperor.[88] However, Franz Joseph, desiring a quick resolution to the constitutional and military situations, remained firm in his conviction to make dualism work. The imperial war minister continued being responsible only to the emperor, but gaining appropriations became harder than before because the military now had to request funds from two parliamentary bodies, the Delegations, representing the legislatures of Austria and Hungary.[89]

Negotiations with Hungary were necessary for passage of the *Wehrgesetz* (military law) of 1868. The new *Wehrgesetz*, the work of over 2 years of discussions on the part of the Austro-Hungarian high command, envisioned large expansion of the Habsburg fighting force to render it comparable with other European powers.[90] According to statistics published in the *ÖMZ*, the Dual Monarchy's peacetime strength in January 1868 amounted to 350,000 men and 791,000 for war, fewer than only the North German Confederation's wartime force of 928,500 and Russia's 1,238,000.[91] After the new military law of 1868, Franz Joseph could call upon 800,000 to over 1,000,000 troops to bear arms during wartime, with an active peacetime strength of 255,000.[92] Soldiers fulfilled an active service term of 3 years in the common army (*k.k.*), 7 years in the reserve, and 2 years in the *Landwehr* or the *Honvéd*, totaling 12 years.[93]

According to Rothenberg, even with this increase, the Habsburg military found itself falling slightly behind the other powers, who had also taken measures to strengthen their forces. The North German Confederation could field over 1,000,000 men, France 1,350,000, and Russia 1,476,000.[94] The numbers given in the *ÖMZ* present a different picture, with the Austro-Hungarian army second only to Russia's 1,279,000 wartime strength for 1870. The Habsburg Empire's 1,058,000 surpassed the North German Confederation's 957,000, France's 772,000, and almost doubled Italy's 573,000, even if the Austro-Hungarian peacetime force did not equal the German and French contingents. By 1874, the *k.k.* army could field 1,135,595 soldiers, compared with Russia's 1,429,700, Germany's 1,314,048, and France's 1,205,000. Thus, while the armies of the other military powers steadily grew in numbers, the Habsburg forces increased by a small percentage, and were superior only to Italy's 647,500. Peacetime statistics showed more clearly the limited growth of the Austro-Hungarian army. From 1870 to 1874, the standing *k.k.* army rose by a mere 1.2% or 3524 men from 298,000 to 301,524, whereas the armed forces of Russia expanded by 5.5% from 726,000 to 765,800, France grew 12.1% from 405,000 to 454,170, and Germany increased 33% from 318,000 to 422,342. Of the major land powers of Europe, only Italy's army decreased, from 183,410 to 159,800 men.[95]

Passage of the military law of 1868 enabled the Habsburg army to compete with the armies of the other European states, at least on paper. The *Wehrgesetz* ensured establishment of a unitary army, with national guards for Austria and Hungary. An imperial war minister responsible to Franz Joseph oversaw military administration. A legal basis existed within which the *k.k.* army could expand because of the introduction of universal conscription throughout the empire. Aside from the issues inherent in the dualistic structure's reliance on the Magyars for budget approval and military support, the 1868 military law laid the foundation for maintaining the Habsburg Empire as a major power. This law met the approval of at least one veteran of 1866: "One had thus made a great achievement, that the highest military boards finally ceased to make almost only administrative adjustments, and recognized the necessity of joining in the progress of modern times in the military and its introduction into the Austrian army."[96] Only 6 years later, the Austro-Hungarian army had failed to keep pace with its rivals. The problem area was implementation of the *Wehrgesetz* and subsequent adjustments.

The high command debated the issue of universal conscription. Kuhn opposed the idea and preferred the old system of calling up a specified number of yearly recruits and allowing those who did not wish to serve to pay a redemption fee instead. The Liberal government of the Austrian half of the empire also preferred this system because its members felt that the more industrialized part of the realm could not endure a long war under universal conscription because of the number of workers called to serve in the army and the drain on financial resources.[97] John, Beck, and Albrecht all saw the necessity of introducing conscription throughout the empire in order to keep up with powers such as Prussia, which had already instituted such a program earlier in the 1860s.[98] As one Austro-Hungarian officer wrote, "It is not to be doubted that by the introduction of universal conscription the stated strength proportions of nearly a million battle-ready fighters will be achieved, if this principle of universal conscription gains actual currency in practical life."[99]

Finally, the Austrian military leaders, including Kuhn, agreed on universal conscription, with no more purchasing of exemptions, as the best means of increasing the army fighting force. Nevertheless, implementation of the new program revealed difficulties inherent within the system. The 1868 military law set the recruit contingent at 95,474, to be determined in subsequent years not by the army but by parliament.

This arrangement signified parliamentary control over the number of men in the army and provoked an ongoing struggle between members of the *Reichsrat* and the Austro-Hungarian high command over whether to raise or lower the recruit contingent, similar to the debates about military budget. Thus, the size of the *k.k.* army depended on the views of the Austrian and Hungarian parliamentary representatives rather than the growing population of the empire or the needs of the military. In addition, not all recruits entered the active army. The draftees drew lots to determine their assignment. Those who drew the lowest numbers joined the active army, whereas those drawing the middle lots served in the *Landwehr* or *Honvéd*. The highest numbers effectively gave the recruits an exemption because they joined the *Ersatzreserve* (supplementary reserve), in which they received no training and entered into military service only during wartime.[100] The reserve received 9574 (10%) of the recruits.[101] Thus, the full 95,474-man recruit contingent did not benefit the standing army in the many ensuing years of peace. Even if the reserves had joined the active forces, they would not have added much to the true military strength of the Austro-Hungarian army because of the paucity of their training. Although parliamentary representatives could take the blame, at least in part, for the small recruit contingent, the army did not use the maximum number of new soldiers to full advantage.

Another problem affecting the recruit contingent arose in the replenishment districts throughout the empire. The commanders in charge of these areas rejected too many recruits as unfit, based on the recruitment instructions that stated the military requirements for accepting new men into the army. The doctors who inspected and measured the recruits followed the prescriptions too stringently or allowed their patients to escape the draft by declaring them unfit for insufficient reasons. In an article published in the *Organ der militärwissenschaftlichen Vereine* (Organ of the Military Science Society), a *k.k.* doctor stated that his purpose was to expose "several deficiencies in the army replenishment directions for the examination of conscripts."[102] The doctor revealed striking statistics showing the serious decline in the number of fit soldiers entering the army, despite the increasing yearly recruit contingent. From 1870 to 1882, the annual number of men eligible for conscription had almost doubled from 496,274 to 830,903. The tally of men declared fit for active service totaled 149,875 (29.3%) in 1870 and only 107,728 (12.9%) in 1882, a drop of nearly a third.[103]

A primary cause of this problem was the tendency of those in charge of selecting recruits to choose only men who displayed every quality desirable in a soldier (powerful physique, good looks, and readiness for training) and rejecting all others as weaklings. The selectors wanted the best recruits for their own branches, such as the technical troops, or cared only about fulfilling the required number of recruits from their sector. Additionally, the commanders of the replenishment regions did not have enough familiarity with their areas because their superiors transferred them too often. During 9 years of working for the army in four different replacement districts, the doctor had seen the transfer of eight recruiting commanders, the same number of recruiting officers, nine *Landwehr* representatives, and eighteen regimental physicians. Under such conditions, no stability or knowledge of the region or its recruits could exist. To combat these defects, the author of the article recommended limiting the frequency of transfers among the recruiting commanders and officers as well as broadening the physical requirements for the designation of fitness. Recruits who did not completely fulfill the standards could still serve in noncombatant positions and allow the more physically fit to take active service roles.[104] Thus, the *k.k.* army would find an internal remedy for the flagging number of recruits without having to beg parliamentary delegates for more funding. The doctor's article reveals the inefficiency within the Habsburg military, where the major problems stemmed not so much from insufficient budgets but rather from inadequate instructions and faulty implementation, in addition to instability caused by excessive transfers with no regard for the good of the army as a whole.

Raising Intellectual Levels: One Year Volunteers and Military Schools

Growth in the number of soldiers alone is not sufficient for success. As one officer pointed out, "A mere numerical addition is certainly still no guarantee for an increase in power; it requires an expanded cadre, produces therefore significantly greater expenditures, demands a large amount of training, clothing, weapons, food, pay, and would be, if not completely fit for war, a burden for the field commander, a weakness for the army, a danger for the state."[105] The leading minds concurred on the necessity of raising not only the number but also the abilities, especially intellectual, of the officer corps, and in particular the junior officers.

In a proposal of 26 December 1866, John communicated to Franz Joseph that the standing army needed an increase both in numbers and in the intellectual level of the officer corps.[106]

The authors of the 1868 *Wehrgesetz* therefore established the *Einjährig-Freiwilligen* (1-year volunteers) to increase the number of officers, especially in the reserve formations, and to raise the general intellectual level of the officer corps. Through this institution, the Austro-Hungarian high command targeted the educated bourgeoisie: "The purpose of the institution of 1-year volunteers in the *k.k.* Austro-Hungarian monarchy," so wrote an officer in 1872, "is to offer the intelligent, young people suited for military duty the opportunity to be able to acquire within 1 year the higher scientific training and an easier intellectual grasp of things, which ought to take the greater part of 3 years."[107] Although this assessment emphasized the benefit for the volunteers, the high command looked upon the bourgeoisie as a source for improvement of the military. Even conservatives like Archduke Albrecht saw the need for 1-year volunteers and reserve officers from the educated middle class because of the perceived beneficial influence of education on the victorious Prussian campaign of 1866. If *k.k.* leaders wished to transform the Habsburg army into an army of the people by universal conscription, they could not reject the intellectual potential of the bourgeois population.[108]

The implementation of this progressive idea of obtaining a group of junior officers from the bourgeoisie proved less helpful than the Austro-Hungarian high command had hoped. By the end of 1870, the number of 1 year volunteers serving in the army was only 1652, with another 3212 on leave of absence with their service deferred.[109] After 1 year of training, the volunteers took a test. If they passed the examination, they received a commission as a reserve officer.[110] However, only roughly half of the 1355 volunteers in 1869 passed the examination, and a mere third of the 1752 applicants of 1870 received reserve commissions.[111]

Over the next 15 years, the numbers did not improve, and only 35% of the 1-year volunteers became reserve officers. By 1878, army statistics listed 5143 officers for the reserve formations, which numbered 524,660 troops, giving a ratio of one officer for every 102 men (1:102).[112] The regular army rolls consisted of 15,594 officers for 806,259 soldiers (ratio of 1:52) in 1878, compared with 20,517 officers (ratio of 1:39) in 1866.[113] Officer statistics for the major European military powers reveal a striking comparison. In 1875, France possessed a ratio of officers to men of 1:16 for the standing army. Germany in 1877 had ratios of 1:22 for peace and 1:41 for war. Russia held a ratio of 1:22 for its peace footing and 1:30 for its war footing.[114] Even including the *Landwehr* and *Honvédség* officers, the Austro-Hungarian army did not have enough non-commissioned officers. Thus, junior officers had to take on duties that sergeants normally handled.[115] This deficiency helps to explain the presence of overqualified officers in positions that lower ranking men normally would have held, especially because there were too many high ranking officers for the available positions befitting higher rank. Once again, as in the case of the recruit contingent, the Habsburg high command proved themselves capable of finding, considering, and debating innovative and even progressive ideas, but did not ensure their success by properly implementing the new measures.

The military schools appeared to be the obvious sphere for instituting reforms that would provide intellectual officers that could rival the Prussians, whom the Austro-Hungarian high command deemed worthy of imitation.[116] Because of the events of 1866 and the fast pace of change in military spheres, many Habsburg army leaders believed success in future wars would depend on intellectual ability.[117] Albrecht and John first aimed at broadening the knowledge of the officer corps by requiring officer aspirants to pass examinations in German and the language of their regiment, mathematics, practical measuring, terrain knowledge and cartography, geography, history, military administration, training and exercise regulations, service regulations, army organization, the tactics of the three main military branches (infantry, cavalry, and artillery), engineering, permanent fortifications, and weaponry. Additionally, these prospective officers from the cadet schools and the regular army had to participate in practical exercises and solve practical military problems.[118] Thus, officers would prove not only their knowledge of all parts of the army and the interconnections of the various branches but also their ability to think under the stress of battlefield conditions.

The increasing prominence of Liberal ideas in the war ministry of Kuhn led to changes in military education. Kuhn promoted reforms to ensure fiscal responsibility and expanded army educational curricula to include more technical and humanistic training. The war minister, with the help of Colonel Eduard Baron Pechmann von Massen, implemented measures to save money by cutting the number of military schools by combining four artillery schools into the Military Technical School and assigning the training of subalterns to troop schools. Kuhn also restricted entrance into higher military institutions until the age of 14.

In an effort to make army education more compatible with public schooling and thus able to provide graduates with skills applicable to civilian life, the war minister and Pechmann required trained officers as teachers for specific courses, more contact for students with society outside the military, and stricter means of measuring worthiness for advancement to higher classes.[119] Thus, the Austro-Hungarian army could save 250,000 florins per year while achieving higher levels of education, a shorter time for training a larger number of subalterns, and an increase in the kind of humanistic and technical training that the Prussians used in their military institutions.[120] Students in the war college had to pass examinations in army organization, tactics, administrative and operative general staff service, military history and strategy, military geography, fortifications, weaponry, terrain, public and international law, economics, business, and the natural sciences, including chemistry and physics. The curriculum also included German literature, ranging from national epics and myths to prose and poetry from the Middle Ages to Leibnitz, Gottsched, Klopstock, Lessing, Kant, Schiller, Goethe, Wieland, Herder, and more recent works of history and philosophy.[121] Such education would not produce officers steeped in backward ideas and conservatism, but progressive thinkers.

These reforms addressed both financial and educational aspects. Combining schools and raising the entrance age saved money, while the introduction of more humanistic and technical training broadened the overall education of Habsburg officers, especially in the *Kriegsschule*. The recurring problem of practical application, however, stymied these measures and brought criticism from Albrecht and others within the Austro-Hungarian army, as discussed later.

Raising Intellectual Levels: Military Journals

Another means used by the high command to raise the intellectual level of the officer corps, especially those who had already graduated from the army's educational institutions, was the newly established Military Science Society and its publication *Organ der militärwissenschaftlichen Vereine*, together with greater emphasis on the role of the *ÖMZ*. In the summer of 1867, several officers in Vienna founded the Military Science Society, "the purpose of which was, in a true patriotic sense, 'to oppose the overgrowing pessimism in the army [from the defeat of 1866] and' to strengthen 'its self-confidence through the cultivation of its moral and scientific element.'"[122] John, the minister of war at that time, promoted the *Verein*, especially as an organization for stimulating the technological training of younger officers: "With the speedy progress in all branches of knowledge, it is necessary for everyone more than in earlier times to think about comprehensive further education."[123] After Kuhn became war minister, he also took charge of the Military Science Society and expanded it to encompass not just the officers in Vienna but the officer corps of the whole army. With his encouragement, the *Verein* began to publish its own journal in 1870, the *Organ der militärwissenschaftlichen Vereine*. This publication grew to include two large volumes of over 1000 pages per year. With an emphasis on military science, the *Organ* published critical articles as well as bibliographical lists of works concerning military topics, including publications from other countries. The articles of this journal focused primarily on analysis of new technology as well as critiques of tactics and strategy from recent publications and conflicts. Thus, the *Organ* provided an opportunity for Habsburg officers to discuss important military questions about modern warfare in a forum promoting truth and frankness. From 600 members in 1870 the Society increased to 3633 by 1900, while fostering the establishment of military science societies in the provincial garrisons.[124]

Overlapping somewhat the work of the *Organ*, the editors of the *ÖMZ* also tried to raise the intellectual level of the Austro-Hungarian officer corps by publishing critical articles from authors both inside and outside the empire in an effort to make the *ÖMZ* the best military journal in Europe. Valentin Streffleur, the editor from 1860 to 1870, numbered the contributors at 214 in 1862, and counted 2439 subscribers by 1869.[125] The journal printed articles about military matters written by captains and lieutenants as well as high-ranking officers who used its pages to spread their views to the officer corps, in many cases anonymously. In addition, the *ÖMZ* published decrees from the emperor and war minister as well as commentaries about changes and transfers in the Austro-Hungarian army. The contributors took great interest in reporting on new technology and the actions of foreign armed forces. Writers devoted long articles to the events of wars both past and contemporary with detailed maps and charts.

In Zitterhofer's index of *ÖMZ* articles, the category of military history has the greatest number of pages with 68. The category, however, includes accounts of modern campaigns that the authors reported as they took place and which belong more to current events than to military history. Tactics occupy the next highest number of pages with 31, then weapons and shooting methods, army and troop histories at 23, army organization 22, and other topics such as troop training and regulations, biography, strategy, military education, and technology with fewer pages.[126] Thus, *ÖMZ* authors covered a broad variety of military topics without stressing any one too greatly. The large number of articles about tactics reveals the importance that theorists gave to the changing battlefield situations of the latter half of the nineteenth century. Although many writers chose to publish analyses of campaigns from earlier Habsburg wars, the topics that aroused the most debate concerned new technology and its effects on strategy and tactics, as well as training and education.

The historian Allmayer-Beck asserted that Archdukes Albrecht and Wilhelm had different goals for the *ÖMZ* from those of Kuhn and the *Organ*. The archdukes saw the secret to the art of war in the classical thoughts of men such as their father Archduke Karl. Kuhn and the Liberals believed their publication should focus on leadership techniques for officers who would have to lead a command in battle, rather than for those who would merely make strategic decisions. Allmayer-Beck maintained that the revival of the *ÖMZ* had no greater success than its first run, because "the transposing of military historical sayings into knowledge founded in reality presupposes an already theoretically schooled officer corps and could be the point just as little after 1866 as before."[127]

This harsh assessment of the value of the *ÖMZ* failed to take into account the views of the editors and contributors, who saw officer training as something more than attempting to apply the maxims of past leaders and theorists to practical situations. Allmayer-Beck did not consider the changes that took place in the *ÖMZ* after 1866 and the efforts of its editors, especially Streffleur, to broaden the knowledge of the officer corps.[128] In addition, the *ÖMZ* printed the writings of the Military Science Society from 1867 until 1870, whereas the *Organ* published articles that did not necessarily correspond to Kuhn's agenda, such as Lieutenant Alois Ritter von Haymerle's defense of the general staff war college.[129] Allmayer-Beck, however, did bring attention to the rivalry between Albrecht and Kuhn and their conflicting ideas by pointing out Kuhn's conviction that the *ÖMZ* did not suffice and another military journal was needed to educate the officers.[130] The redundancy that this rivalry caused, not only in creating the *Organ* but also other periodicals that claimed to belong to "the new era of the army" and "reject the old tradition forever," added to army and officer expenses without bringing about the unity that the Habsburg military needed so much. Streffleur claimed that Austrian intellectuals and artists had only recently begun to show tolerance and cooperation in their pursuit of knowledge. Previously, these men had displayed only envy and censure while tearing down the efforts of others. Members of the military still showed the desire for one-sidedness and self-idolization rather than concerted progress in science.[131] The intensity of this rivalry led one *ÖMZ* writer to lament the propensity of the debaters to lose sight of objectivity as they "tried more often to achieve victory only by personal invective…., when we see things dragged into the street, which in every family are washed in its own house like dirty laundry."[132]

Gauging the impact of the *ÖMZ* and the *Organ* on the Austro-Hungarian officer corps presents difficulties. In 1863, 98 out of 216 general officers subscribed to the *ÖMZ*. Staff officer subscriptions were even lower, with a mere 81 of 464 receiving the journal.[133] By 1869, despite the calls for greater intelligence among the officer corps, only 2439 out of 17,704 officers (13.7%) purchased the *ÖMZ*.[134] In 1867, the *ÖMZ* advertised the introduction of a military library composed of 12 books that would offer a comprehensive knowledge base for officers who could not afford their own collection of all the great martial works. The author of the report lamented the troubles that previous attempts to promote military literature had encountered, especially because of the dearth of participants: "The difficulties with which our own journal itself still has to struggle, despite the ever louder call for the greater diffusion of technical material, gives us the measuring stick of trouble and danger with which other military editorial staffs must also wrestle. There are unfortunately not too many officers among us who earnestly desire to study scientific works, but still fewer who actually buy them."[135]

Financial constraints limited the means of Habsburg officers to purchase subscriptions or books to enhance their intellectual abilities after graduation from one of the military schools. István Deák argued that most officers did not qualify as independently wealthy and that their pay, especially for lieutenants and captains after mandatory expenditures, failed to provide adequate funds for extra expenses such as military journals.[136] Insufficient pay, however, did not account for low subscription rates in all cases. Little interest in intellectual activity can also explain the indifference to martial literature for some officers. Certainly, Arthur Schnitzler's stereotype of the dissolute, arrogant, uncultured, and insipid Lieutenant Gustl did not apply to the Austro-Hungarian officer corps universally.[137] Even if Schnitzler's exaggerated description of Gustl had some basis of truth with regard to certain officers who followed the example of Benedek and had no interest in reading military journals, not all members of the Habsburg officer corps believed that the only important things in life were duels, women, and drinking.

Non-military writers did not register the only complaints about the lack of interest in cerebral pursuits among Habsburg officers. The Liberals, both inside and outside the army, noted the anti-intellectual bent of the officer corps before the Austro-Prussian War, when "the average troop officer did not read much in any case. Reading was considered rather unmanly…"[138] The catastrophe of Königgrätz discredited the anti-intellectual attitude of leaders such as Benedek and Henikstein, who bore responsibility for the disaster. The call to raise the intellectual level of all parts of the armed forces resounded throughout the army. Albrecht and Beck realized the need to train more intelligent officers, especially in the general staff, with better practical application of knowledge through staff rides and realistic maneuvers.[139] Following the close of the 1866 campaign, the *ÖMZ* printed several articles bewailing the inability of Habsburg officers to think during battle and asserting the need for leaders who relied on their practical knowledge of warfare rather than automatons who attempted in vain to achieve victory through brute force and martial spirit.[140] Certainly, the support of the Austro-Hungarian high command for the major military journals after 1866 must have increased the influence of these works. The founding of military science societies in many garrisons throughout the empire afforded officers the opportunity to both give and hear lectures that later appeared in the pages of the journals. The increasing number of articles and authors during the later decades of the nineteenth century also indicates a greater interest in the intellectual side of military pursuits. These journals provide excellent opportunities to see the thoughts and ideas debated by Habsburg officers, while proving that the Dual Monarchy's officer corps did not wallow in backwardness and ultraconservatism as historians such as Gunther Rothenberg and A.J.P. Taylor suggest.

Raising Intellectual Levels: Promotion Regulations

The attempt to reform promotion regulations provides an excellent example of how the Austro-Hungarian high command tried to solve a problem with theory, but failed because of practical application and rivalry. After the defeat of 1866, Albrecht and John realized that the existing promotion regulations contained irregularities and disadvantages. Both men saw that problems had arisen because many officers had requested pensions at the beginning of the war because of age, ill health, or inadequate physical fitness for the strains of a campaign. Therefore, many new and unproven officers gained promotions to replace the old or unfit. During the war, certain units suffered heavy casualties, and thus subalterns with little experience received promotions to fill the gaps in the officer corps. These promotions created a situation in which men who had entered the army in 1866 outranked officers who had served for years. In addition, the need to put the military on a wartime footing required an increase in officers and promotions, which after the war left a large number of officers without commands befitting their rank. The promotion regulations had not proven capable of handling these issues.[141]

On 24 April 1867, the war minister and the army commander instituted reforms to solve the officer promotion problems. In an effort to bring younger and more intelligent men into positions of command, officers who showed outstanding performance in battle could receive promotion. Officer aspirants who had superior test scores in the military academies as well as spotless records would gain promotions more readily. A reserve officer corps would exist for use in time of war. The high command also placed age limits for older officers in active service to eliminate the need to replace a large number of officers who could no longer meet the physical requirements for battle leadership.[142] These reforms offered a beneficial scenario for the army and for officers who displayed intelligence, courage, and skillful command, but they also resulted in an even larger number of pensions and raised the question of how to form and employ a reserve officer corps during a long peace.

This more conservative system never received the chance to prove whether it could solve the problems permanently because Kuhn replaced it quickly with his own more progressive idea of introducing equality throughout the army with testing. The war minister, hoping to advance the most intelligent and talented officers, tried to introduce a meritocracy based on talent. Kuhn eliminated the right of the *Inhaber*, or proprietor of a regiment, to decide promotions. Candidates, even for the ranks of major, lieutenant colonel, and colonel, would prove their abilities by taking competitive examinations. These measures gave the war minister almost complete control over the advancement process, as the emperor usually followed his recommendations.[143] Beck and Albrecht both objected strongly to these innovations because they removed the possibility of extraordinary promotions in peacetime and diminished the importance of the general staff. Kuhn's reforms also caused resentment on the part of older officers, who felt chagrin at seeing themselves subordinate to men younger and less experienced. In addition, Albrecht complained that the testing system contained too much theoretical knowledge rather than practical and necessitated extremely mild grading for anyone to pass.[144]

Kuhn's system, though more suitable for the time of peace in which it operated, resulted in disgruntlement on the part of senior officers and in subjective grading. Theoretically, the liberal war minister's measures appeared feasible on paper. Nevertheless, their practical application failed for two reasons. First, the Habsburg army remained unprepared for the implementation of equality, not necessarily because of antiquated views of the dynastic principle, but because officer candidates came from all over the empire and thus from peoples with extreme differences in education. Second, though the idea of basing promotions on examination appeared to be an objective method, subjectivity unavoidably entered. No system can provide perfection, because once human beings become involved, errors and subjective views affect practical application.

When General der Kavallerie Alexander Baron von Koller of the Constitutional Party replaced Kuhn as war minister in 1874, Beck (head of the imperial military chancellery) and John (who became the new chief of the general staff) introduced a new set of promotion regulations in 1875. These prescriptions greatly limited extraordinary advancement as an honor rather than a right, and based promotions for staff officers on practical knowledge proven during a year of service instead of on competitive examinations.[145] Thus, the general staff gained an elite status as the producer of trained specialists. In this time of technological progress, experts in the various areas of military science held the key to advancement instead of officers who had connections with socially or financially influential people.

Rivalry ruined what good could have come from either Albrecht's or Kuhn's system. The program that finally began at the end of the decade following the Austro-Prussian War introduced a compromise. The Habsburg general staff gained an elite position, similar to the same organ in Prussia, and therefore ended any hopes of all officers, even of the same rank, holding equal status. However, promotions went to officers who displayed superiority in technical knowledge while in practical service, thus demonstrating ability based on merit rather than social influence or financial considerations. Although leadership on the battlefield could come into consideration, the system suited the years of peace that Austria-Hungary experienced until 1878 and then again until 1914.

Rivalry and Reform

Kuhn's reforms regarding the general staff and other positions, such as the general directors of the artillery and special weapons, formed part of his plan "to unite all military power as much as possible in his own hands."[146] By rendering all other Habsburg army commands mere *Hilfsorgane* without any independence, not even the permission to issue instructions to their branches before receiving approval from the war ministry, Kuhn not only recreated the situation of one man wielding too much power, the very situation that Beck wanted to avoid, but also introduced even more bureaucracy into the army.[147] The requirement to obtain the war minister's stamp on all correspondence increased the already vast amount of paperwork within military offices and slowed the workings of the various commands. Testing for advancement in the general staff proved complicated and favored theoretical knowledge rather than practical abilities for battlefield leadership. As Wagner stated, "Hence many false conclusions and irregularities resulted, and even war proven officers often scored worse than others."[148]

Because of these problems, Kuhn's reforms failed to produce the desired results. Instead, they brought about great opposition from both Albrecht and Beck, who did not see liberalization of the army as an improvement. Beck, who normally played the role of peacemaker in the many disputes between Austro-Hungarian military leaders, firmly resisted Kuhn's attempts to abolish the general staff corps. The head of the military chancellery argued that strengthening of the general staff was the key to future army operations by increasing training opportunities, such as maneuvers with large troop formations.[149] The *ÖMZ* editor countered the idea that one man should have total control over the military, particularly in education. Streffleur favored the introduction of a board for discussing suggestions and making decisions affecting the intellectual leadership of military institutions, because of the many areas of study involved in military training.[150] Foreign Minister Andrássy, who according to the war minister possessed a "gypsy nature," considered Kuhn anti-Magyar and thus an opponent. The foreign minister also opposed Kuhn's proposals for war against Russia and revenge on Prussia.[151] Thus, the war minister, like his predecessor, succeeded in antagonizing all the other powerful members of the military and even important government officials.

Kuhn also laid himself open to criticism because of his shortcomings in procurement. Kuhn might have avoided criticism for the slow procurement process if he had not bragged about his accomplishments and lobbied for war against Prussia in 1870. In several messages to the emperor, Kuhn strongly underscored the readiness of the army for war and the advantages of Austro-Hungarian participation with France against Prussia in the Franco-Prussian War. The war minister declared 1870 the best opportunity for Habsburg revenge against Prussia, also offering a chance to weaken Russian aggression in Eastern Europe.[152] The other government officials and military leaders, except ironically Albrecht, rejected Kuhn's proposals. Franz Joseph, even though he permitted partial mobilization for armed mediation, did not fully believe Kuhn's bragging about the military capabilities of Austria-Hungary. The emperor called for a board of inquiry to investigate the army's actual war readiness. The findings of this board revealed grave deficiencies in almost all departments of the *k.k.* military. The infantry still needed 200,000 Werndl rifles and 40 million bullets. The cavalry showed a shortage of 30,000 Werndl carbines, a number that the board considered only a minimum. Although the field artillery had a sufficient number of cannon, the coastal batteries lacked 120 9-cm guns, 100 8-cm guns, and 50 mortars.[153] Fortress artillery required 5000 rifled and 3000 smooth-bore cannon with 500 shots per weapon upon completion of the projected fortification plans throughout the empire. In addition, the infantry showed a deficiency of 30,000 shirts, 28,000 uniform coats, and 14,000 caps. The reserve cavalry needed horses. The telegraph troops had not yet received miles of line, and the railroad divisions revealed a shortage of tools. Apart from the field artillery, only the engineer corps possessed full equipment.[154]

Seeing the unready state of the army, Albrecht did not forfeit this excellent opportunity to lambast his rival publicly. In an anonymous booklet, *Das Jahr 1870 und die Wehrkraft der Monarchie* (The Year 1870 and the Military Power of the Monarchy), the archduke compared the Austro-Hungarian army to the recently victorious Prussians and thus revealed the shortcomings of Kuhn's administration for everyone to see. Albrecht pointed out not only the deficiency in Werndl rifles, which he placed at 340,000–390,000, to arm the reserve forces as well as the line infantry, but also the difficult logistical problems that Habsburg troops would endure if they entered a war with two rifles of different caliber.[155] Although the archduke noted that the parliamentary representatives did not grant enough funds for reserve provisions and that the other ministers opposed the amount requested by the army as unattainable, he lamented the lack of unity within the military as a result of the Dual Monarchy arrangement. Albrecht blamed army administration for negligence and confusion in war preparations, resulting in insufficient provisions and equipment, especially for mobilization. He declared that without agreement and cooperation among leaders, "mutual distrust and ill-will, self-overestimation and despondency, friction and special interests are produced and increase."[156] The archduke targeted Kuhn's attempts to unify the *k.k.* army under his control, as well as his boasts about Austria-Hungary's war readiness and return to great power status.

During the next few years, Albrecht persisted in attacking the war minister's administrative abilities. As inspector general of the army, the archduke had ample opportunities to criticize all aspects of the Habsburg military, including weapons, equipment, training, and tactics. In a military conference in 1873, Albrecht used Kuhn's own liberal ideas against him when he pointed out the burdensome bureaucracy in the *k.k.* army because of the war minister's acquisition of supreme martial power. The archduke recommended the partition of command as an important principle of all constitutional states.[157] Although Albrecht's reports to the emperor never failed to find fault with most of Kuhn's policies, to the point of revealing his personal antipathy for the war minister, the archduke's findings exposed serious problems that Kuhn had not resolved. As Lackey correctly stated, "Kuhn completely rejected the idea that some of the inspector general's observations might have some merit; he saw them only as personal attacks on his character and administration of the armed forces."[158] Thus, the Habsburg military lost any chance of remedying the important issues because of rivalry. The only solution was to find a new war minister; Albrecht, as a member of the royal family, had firm hold over his own position as inspector general of the army.

Kuhn's educational reforms also came under attack. The "Pechmann system" of military education proved unsatisfactory to almost all martial circles, as proclaimed by the military newspapers, especially those with the support of Albrecht. The journal authors contested that the results of the new educational system had not fulfilled the promise of improvement, but had instead worsened the situation. The young sons of officers could not enter military training until the age of 14 and thus created a heavy burden on their families. The general staff's war college fell into neglect. The broadening of subjects and fewer years in the cadet schools rendered the students' education superficial, yet more burdensome. The examiners graded so leniently that a student could better his position by gaining a passing mark in several subjects rather than achieving an excellent grade in one specialty.[159]

The combination of opposition from Albrecht, Beck, and Andrássy doomed Kuhn to eventual replacement.[160] The war minister offered his resignation to Franz Joseph in 1872, though the emperor did not dismiss him until 1874.[161] After only 6 years in office, Kuhn departed and Alexander Baron von Koller took his place. Koller lasted only 2 years in office before retiring because of poor health. In the decade following the Austro-Prussian War, a time of vital importance for reforming the Habsburg military, three men had held its most prominent position. The instability within the war ministry increased the difficulty of introducing measures that would last long enough to solve the main problems.

Conclusion

After 1866, the call for reform spread throughout the *k.k.* military. The entire army leadership recognized the need to resolve critical issues that had resulted in defeat. Many officers proposed solutions. The majority realized that the Habsburg army required new breech-loading rifles and universal conscription to compete with other European powers. Better leadership would result in favorable campaign outcomes. Thus, the new leaders began procuring Werndl rifles and trying to adapt the old Austrian tactics to suit the improved weaponry. Albrecht and John instituted an improved set of promotions regulations. Kuhn tried to transform the military educational establishments with Liberal ideas of scientific testing and advancement by merit. While dealing with a new and much more complex political arrangement because of the *Ausgleich* of 1868, the high command forged a *Wehrgesetz* that could raise Austrian military might to a level that would ensure great power status for the Habsburg Empire.

However, Austro-Hungarian military leaders marred their own attempts at reform by failure in practical application as well as rivalry within the high command. In the decade following the calamity of Königgrätz, three war ministers held office. All the important members of the high command maintained differing positions on the reform program, ranging from keeping the army as a dynastic organ to remodeling the military to resemble civilian institutions. Albrecht, John, Beck, and Kuhn had various ideas that did not always mesh. Each wanted his own part of the military, the war ministry, the *AOK*, the inspectorate, the military chancellery, or the general staff, to control army operations. Except for Beck, each desired absolute power in military affairs. The rivalry that arose, especially the vindictive dislike of Kuhn and Albrecht for each other, crippled attempts to form a united leadership and bring about effective reform. Yet, despite these problems, the Habsburg military did improve in certain areas during the decade after the defeat of 1866.

The ideas and theories that officers raised about improving the status of the troops and rendering them loyal subjects of the emperor sounded excellent. Articles in the military journals proposed learning the languages of the common soldiers for better communication and fulfilling the culturo-historical role of the Habsburg army in making recruits into patriots of the Habsburg Empire. Yet officers did little in practice to effect lasting change. The high command eliminated flogging in 1867 and ordered officers to treat the rank and file with more humanity. Leaders made provisions for better medicinal care and supplies.[162] Nevertheless, critics still blamed the poor conditions of army life for the high mortality rate among Habsburg troops.[163] Various nationalities, especially the Slavic peoples who felt chagrin at the favoritism of dualism for Hungarians and Austrians, saw no reason to give full support to a government that did not treat them fairly.

In tactics, the *k.k.* army showed progress. Attempting to adapt to the new technology of the breech-loading rifle and ever increasing firepower, military leaders advocated the elimination of frontal assaults in closed order. Yet many tacticians still favored the offensive as they strove to find ways to close with the bayonet. Although eschewing cavalry charges against infantry, officers tried to find other roles for mounted troops, such as reconnaissance and security patrols. Nevertheless, some adhered to gallant shock tactics. The desire to learn from the most recent battles resulted in an obsession with Königgrätz and the Franco-Prussian War, campaigns that seemingly proved the decisiveness of the attack against the passivity of defense. However, steps were taken toward more reasonable tactics that could take into account the devastating firepower of the breech-loader and the viability of the defense.

Strategically, almost all Habsburg officers still believed in the effectiveness of permanent fortifications. This view did not take into account the improvements in artillery that rendered fortresses obsolete and at the same time required vast sums of money that parliamentary representatives refused to grant. Although the high command insisted that the stinginess of the delegations hampered procurement of weapons and other necessary reforms, internal corruption and mismanagement of funds held the army back from meaningful progress. Thus, despite concentrated efforts to improve the Austro-Hungarian army, the *k.k.* high command met only partial success before its next military encounter in 1878.

Notes

1. B.P.S., "Unsere Aufgabe," *ÖMZ* 4 (1866), 34.
2. Edmund von Glaise-Horstenau, *Franz Josephs Weggefährte* (Vienna: Amalthea Verlag, 1930), 135.
3. Geoffrey Wawro, "The Austro-Prussian War: Politics, Strategy and War in the Habsburg Monarchy, 1859–1866," (Ph.D. dissertation, Yale University, 1992), 770.
4. Johann C. Allmayer-Beck, "Die Bewaffnete Macht in Staat und Gesellschaft," in *Die Habsburgermonarchie 1848–1918*, Vol. 5 *Die Bewaffnete Macht* (Vienna: Verlag der Österreichischen Akademie der Wissenschaften, 1987), 60.
5. Gunther E. Rothenberg, *The Army of Francis Joseph* (West Lafayette, Indiana: Purdue University Press, 1976), 78–79.
6. Wawro, "The Austro-Prussian War," 804.
7. Rothenberg, *The Army of Francis Joseph*, 72.
8. B.P.S., "Unsere Aufgabe," 34.
9. "Zum Programm des Kriegsministers," *ÖMZ* 4 (1866), 283.
10. Oberst Friedrich von Beck, "Promemoria über Armee-Verhältnisse," August 1867, KA MKSM Sonderreihe, Karton Nr. 66, Studien; Beck, "Theilweise Ursachen des gegenwärtigen schlechten Armee-Geistes und Mittel, welche zur Hebung desselben beitragen dürften," 1867, KA MKSM Sonderreihe, Karton Nr. 66, Studien.
11. FML Erzherzog Albrecht, 14–16/7 Nr. 74 Präsid., Wien am 10. Oktober 1866, KA KM Präsidium, Karton Nr. 243, 1866 CK 14/6–20;

Albrecht, No. 1017 "Allerunterthänigster Vortrag," 21 August 1866, Kriegsarchiv (KA) Militärkanzlei Seiner Majestät (MKSM) Sonderreihe, Karton Nr. 22, 1866; Albrecht, No. 1086 Allerunterthänigster Vortrag, 27 August 1866, Karton Nr. 22, 1866.

12. Albrecht, No. 1086 Allerunterthänigster Vortrag, 27 August 1866, Karton Nr. 22, 1866.
13. Beck, "Promemoria über Armee-Verhältnisse," August 1867, KA MKSM Sonderreihe, Karton Nr. 66, Studien; Glaise-Horstenau, *Franz Josephs Weggefährte*, 141.
14. "Uber die Ursache der Mißerfolge bei der österreichischen Nordarmee im Kriege Preußens gegen Deutschland im Jahre 1866," *ÖMZ* 2 (1866), 361; B.P.S., "Unsere Aufgabe," *ÖMZ* 4 (1866), 142–143; "Der Krieg im Jahre 1866. Im Auszuge nach einem Artikel von Xavier Raymond in der 'Revue des deux mondes'," *ÖMZ* 3 (1866), 101.
15. Allmayer-Beck, "Die Bewaffnete Macht in Staat und Gesellschaft," 57; Rothenberg, *The Army of Francis Joseph*, 83; Walter Wagner, "Die k.(u.)k. Armee - Gliederung und Aufgabenstellung," in *Die Habsburgermonarchie 1848–1918*, Vol. 5 *Die Bewaffnete Macht* (Vienna: Verlag der Österreichischen Akademie der Wissenschaften, 1987), 604.
16. Scott Lackey, *The Rebirth of the Habsburg Army: Friedrich Beck and the Rise of the General Staff* (Westport, CT: Greenwood Press, 1995), 40.
17. *Stenographische Sitzungs-Protokolle der Delegation des Reichsrathes*, 17. Sitzung der 2. Session am 30. August 1869 (Vienna: k.k. Hof—und Staatsdruckerei, 1869), 366–369.
18. Lackey, *The Rebirth of the Habsburg Army*, 40, 45.
19. Carl von Clausewitz, *On War*, edited and translated by Michael Howard and Peter Paret (Princeton, NJ: Princeton University Press, 1976), 87.
20. Oberst Wilhelm Reinländer, *Vorträge über die Taktik* (Vienna: L.W. Seidel & Son, 1870–1871), KA Militärschule, KS Karton Nr. 59, Studienbehelfe: Strategie und Taktik, 1–9.
21. Reinländer, *Vorträge über die Taktik*, 29–32.
22. Reinländer, *Vorträge über die Taktik*, 33–34.
23. Reinländer, *Vorträge über die Taktik*, 49–52.
24. Reinländer, *Vorträge über die Taktik*, 52–62.
25. Wawro, "The Austro-Prussian War," 770.
26. Hauptmann Wendelin Boeheim, "Die Elementar-Taktik der Infanterie in Bezug auf die Grundsätze der Taktik und auf die Praxis," *ÖMZ* 2 (1867), 238.
27. Boeheim, "Die Elementar-Taktik der Infanterie in Bezug auf die Grundsätze der Taktik und auf die Praxis," 238–241.
28. Dr. Alfred Jurnitschek, *Die Wehr-Reform in Österreich-ungarn von 1866 bis 1873* (Vienna: Carl Gerold's Sohn: 1873), XCIV.

29. Oberlieutenant Leopold Auspitz, "Zur Taktik des Hinterladers," *ÖMZ* 4 (1867), 179–195; Oberlieutenant Rudolph Musil, "Die Elemente der Gefechtsführung, durch eine Reihe von Aufgaben erläutert," *Organ der militärwissenschaftlichen Vereine* (*O.*) 2 (1871), 3.
30. Oberst Friedrich von Fischer, "Vorlesungen über Einfachheit u. Sicherheit in der Kriegführung, IV. Vorlesung über den Angriff u. über die Vertheidigung," *ÖMZ* 1 (1870), 126–128.
31. Lackey, *The Rebirth of the Habsburg Army*, 89–90.
32. Hauptmann Ernst Schmedes, "Die Taktik der Preussen beim Ausbruche des Feldzuges 1870 und ihre Änderung im Laufe desselben," *ÖMZ* 4 (1871), 20–23.
33. Oberlieutenant Gustav Ratzenhofer, "Die Taktische Lehren des Krieges 1870–1877," *ÖMZ* 4 (1872), 107–108.
34. B.P.S., "Unsere Aufgabe," 146–148.
35. Lieutenant Carl Landmann, "Die Reiterei im Amerikanische Burgerkrieg 1861–1865," *ÖMZ* 4 (1870), 60–71; F.B.P., "Taktische Studie über Formation und Führung grösserer Cavallerie-Körper und die Thätigkeit ihrer Artillerie," *ÖMZ* 2 (1874), 153–161; Lieutenant Colonel Hotze, "Einige Schlagworte über das Verhalten eines im Vormarsche aufklärenden grösseren Cavallerie-Körpers," *ÖMZ* 3 (1876), 61–70.
36. (Ein alter Soldat), "Die Eintheilung der Cavallerie bei einer Feldarmee," *ÖMZ* 1 (1867), 386–388.
37. Reinländer, *Vorträge über die Taktik*, 62–64.
38. "Die österreichische Armee der Zukunft," *ÖMZ* 1 (1868), 125–129.
39. Albrecht (anonymously), *Das Jahr 1870 und die Wehrkraft der Monarchie* (Vienna: Faesy & Frick, 1870), 21–24.
40. Auspitz, "Zur Taktik des Hinterladers," 183–184.
41. Oberlieutenant Micsin, "Gedanken über die Verwendung der Reiterei im Sinne der modernen Kriegführung mit besonderer Berücksichtigung des Materials, der Organisation u. Ausrüstung der Österreichischen Reiterei," *ÖMZ* 4 (1870), 121–122, 233; Rittmeister Felix Freiherr von Pach zu Berneck, "Über die Vortheile einer bestimmten Gefechtsform grösserer Cavalerie-Körper, sowie über das Feuergefecht und die Methodik der einschlägigen Übungen der Cavalerie," *O.* 10 (1875), 341, 355–357, 361; Major Friedrich Baron Mühlwerth-Gärtner, "Über das Feuergefecht der Cavalerie," *O.* 6 (1873), 386–412.
42. Wawro, "The Austro-Prussian War," 816.
43. Captain Michael Trapsia, "Einige Ursache der Erfolge im Jahre 1870/71," *O.* 10 (1875), 121.
44. István Deák, *Beyond Nationalism: A Social and Political History of the Habsburg Officer Corps, 1848–1918* (New York: Oxford University Press, 1992), 7–8, 127–128.

45. Rothenberg, *The Army of Francis Joseph*, 84.
46. H., "Jomini über den Feldzug 1866 in Böhmen," *ÖMZ* 1 (1867), 150.
47. Fischer, "Vorlesungen über Einfachheit u. Sicherheit in der Kriegführung, IV. Vorlesung über den Angriff u. über die Vertheidigung," *ÖMZ* 1 (1870), 130–132.
48. Dr. Hermann Orges, "Die permanente Befestigung und die Kriegführung der Gegenwart," *O.* 5 (1872), 129–149.
49. Major Bela von Ghyczy, "Über die Zukunft der Festungen," *ÖMZ* 4 (1867), 67–76; Oberlieutenant Moriz Brunner, "Reichsbefestigung und Eisenbahnen," *ÖMZ* 2 (1868), 133–148; "Permanente oder provisorische Festungen? Ein Beitrag zur Lösung dieser Streitfrage," *ÖMZ* 4 (1871), 86–87; "Der gezogene Hinterlade-Mörser und die Fortification," *ÖMZ* 4 (1875), 69–84; "Über Lagerforts u. Verschanzte Lager: Vorschläge zur Erbauung derselben; hiezu erforderliche Geldmittel. Über Reichs-Befestigung," *ÖMZ* 3 (1868), 357–384; "Fortificatorische Studien," *ÖMZ* 3 (1869), 209–230.
50. Albrecht, *Das Jahr 1870 und die Wehrkraft der Monarchie*, 76.
51. Albrecht, No. 25, "Uiber die Vorbereitung eines Kriegsschauplatzes mit besonderer Berücksichtigung der Karpathenländer," July 1871, KA MKSM Sonderreihe, Karton Nr. 64, Studien.
52. Major General Heinrich Freiherr von Scholl, "Denkschriften betr. Befestigungswesen," 1869–1871, KA MKSM Sonderreihe, Karton Nr. 66, Studien; Fol: 1–95 Protokolle No. I bis V, 3–9 April 1868, Reichsbefestigung, KA Generalstab Operationsbüro, Karton Nr. 790, Studien; No. 14, "Vertheidigungs-System der Monarchie 1873," 23. II., Generalstab, KA MKSM Sonderreihe, Karton Nr. 64, Studien.
53. Wagner, "Die k.(u.)k. Armee - Gliederung und Aufgabenstellung," 402.
54. Hauptmann Michael Trapsia, "Welche sind die wichtigsten Erfahrungen aus Dem Kriege des Jahres 1870 zwischen Frankreich und Deutschland?" *O.* 2 (1871), 43–45.
55. Ghyczy, "Über die Zukunft der Festungen," 76.
56. "Die österreichische Armee der Zukunft," *ÖMZ* 1 (1868), 131.
57. Wagner, "Die k.(u.)k. Armee - Gliederung und Aufgabenstellung," 590.
58. *Stenographische Protokolle des Hauses der Abgeordneten des Reichsrathes*, 145. Sitzung der 1. Session am 11. November 1868 (Vienna: k.k. Hof- und Staatsdruckerei, 1868), 4477–4483.
59. *Stenographische Protokolle des Hauses der Abgeordneten des Reichsrathes*, 58. Sitzung der 6. Session am 22. Juni 1871 (Vienna: k.k. Hof- und Staatsdruckerei, 1871), 1228–1230.
60. *Stenographische Protokolle des Hauses der Abgeordneten des Reichsrathes*, 58. Sitzung der 6. Session am 22. Juni 1871, 1227.

61. *Stenographische Protokolle des Hauses der Abgeordneten des Reichsrathes*, 58. Sitzung der 6. Session am 22. Juni 1871, 1250–1251.
62. *Stenographische Protokolle des Hauses der Abgeordneten des Reichsrathes*, 58. Sitzung der 6. Session am 22. Juni 1871, 1241.
63. *Stenographische Sitzungs-Protokolle der Delegation des Reichsrathes*, 9. Sitzung der 2. Session am 17. August 1869 (Vienna: k.k. Hof- und Staatsdruckerei, 1869), 226.
64. *Stenographische Sitzungs-Protokolle der Delegation des Reichsrathes*, 11. Sitzung der 2. Session am 20. August 1869, 283–288.
65. *Stenographische Sitzungs-Protokolle der Delegation des Reichsrathes*, 11. Sitzung der 2. Session am 20. August 1869, 264.
66. *Stenographische Sitzungs-Protokolle der Delegation des Reichsrathes*, 11. Sitzung der 2. Session am 20. August 1869, 268–269.
67. *Stenographische Sitzungs-Protokolle der Delegation des Reichsrathes*, 7. Sitzung der 2. Session am 14. August 1869, 148–149.
68. FML Franz Xavier Freiherr von John, 16–22/1 C.K. No. 5729, Wien am 9. September 1866, KA KM Präsidium, Karton Nr. 243, 1866 CK 14/6–20.
69. Wagner, "Die k.(u.)k. Armee - Gliederung und Aufgabenstellung," 351–352.
70. Beck, "Promemoria über Armee-Verhältnisse," August 1867, KA MKSM Sonderreihe, Karton Nr. 66, Studien.
71. Emperor Franz Joseph, 16–22/1 C.K. No. 5729, Schönbrunn am 15. September 1866, KA KM Präsidium, Karton Nr. 243, 1866 CK 14/6/20.
72. Lackey, *The Rebirth of the Habsburg Army*, 32; Rothenberg, *The Army of Francis Joseph*, 79.
73. Glaise-Horstenau, *Franz Josephs Weggefährte*, 137.
74. Glaise-Horstenau, *Franz Josephs Weggefährte*, 137, 147; Lackey, *The Rebirth of the Habsburg Army*, 32–33; Rothenberg, *The Army of Francis Joseph*, 79.
75. Heinrich von Srbik, *Aus Österreichs Vergangenheit* (Salzburg: O. Müller, 1949), 145; Rothenberg, *The Army of Francis Joseph*, 74; Allmayer-Beck, "Die Bewaffnete Macht in Staat und Gesellschaft," 66–67.
76. Oberst Valentin Ritter von Streffleur, "Österreich am Schlusse des Jahres 1866," *ÖMZ* 1 (1867), 3.
77. Lackey, *The Rebirth of the Habsburg Army*, 34; Rothenberg, *The Army of Francis Joseph*, 79.
78. Oberst Freiherr von Kuhn, "Vorträge über Strategie," *ÖMZ* 2 (1870), 3. Colonel Franz Freiherr Kuhn von Kuhnenfeld gave this lecture to the students of the Habsburg war college for general staff officers.
79. Glaise-Horstenau, *Franz Josephs Weggefährte*, 237.

80. Lackey, *The Rebirth of the Habsburg Army*, 35.
81. Lackey, *The Rebirth of the Habsburg Army*, 36; Wagner, "Die k.(u.)k. Armee - Gliederung und Aufgabenstellung," 374–375; Allmayer-Beck, "Die Bewaffnete Macht in Staat und Gesellschaft," 72.
82. Allmayer-Beck, "Die Bewaffnete Macht in Staat und Gesellschaft," 73.
83. FML Franz Baron Kuhn von Kuhnenfeld, Nachlässe Kuhn, 2 September 1869, Karton Nr. 670, 7.
84. Lackey, *The Rebirth of the Habsburg Army*, 34.
85. Rothenberg, *The Army of Francis Joseph*, 80.
86. For an excellent discussion of various views concerning the *Ausgleich*, see Alan Sked's *The Decline and Fall of the Habsburg Empire, 1815–1918* (London: Longman, 1989), 191–202.
87. Wawro, "The Austro-Prussian War," 800.
88. Eduard Bartels, *Österreich und sein Heer* (Leipzig: Otto Wigand: 1866), 19–20.
89. Rothenberg, *The Army of Francis Joseph*, 75–78.
90. "Ideen über die Mittel zur Heranbildung der für den Bedarf einer Armee in Österreich von der in Neuester Zeit postulirten Stärke - nahezu einer Million Soldaten - nöthigen Anzahl intelligenter Ober- und Unterofficiere," *ÖMZ* 1 (1867), 176. The author considered one million the magic number to ensure great power status both inside and outside the nation. A footnote in the *ÖMZ* says the author of this article also wrote "Praxis und Routine. - Wissenschaft und Kunst. - Betrachtungen über den Kriegsschauplatz in Böhmen von 1866 und die auf demselben stattgehabten Kriegsereignisse dieses Jahres. (Aus den schriften eines Veteranen des österreichischen Heeres)," *ÖMZ* 4 (1866).
91. Hauptmann Ernst Schmedes, "Die Kriegsmacht der europäischen Staaten im Vergleiche mit deren Bevolkerungs- u. Budget-Verhältnisse im Jänner 1868," *ÖMZ* 2 (1868), 54.
92. Lackey, *The Rebirth of the Habsburg Army*, 29; Rothenberg, *The Army of Francis Joseph*, 81.
93. Lackey, *The Rebirth of the Habsburg Army*, 29; Wagner, "Die k.(u.)k. Armee - Gliederung und Aufgabenstellung," 491.
94. Rothenberg, *The Army of Francis Joseph*, 81.
95. Major J. Nosinich, "Machtverhältnisse der Haupt-Staaten Europa's in der alten und neuen Zeit, nebst einem allgemeinen Blicke auf das europäische Gleichgewicht," *ÖMZ* 4 (1875), 24–25.
96. "Ideen über die Mittel zur Heranbildung der für den Bedarf einer Armee in Österreich von der in Neuester Zeit postulirten Stärke - nahezu einer Million Soldaten - nöthigen Anzahl intelligenter Ober- und Unterofficiere," *ÖMZ* 1 (1867), 175.
97. Wagner, "Die k.(u.)k. Armee - Gliederung und Aufgabenstellung," 490.

98. Lackey, *The Rebirth of the Habsburg Army*, 25.
99. "Ideen über die Mittel zur Heranbildung der für den Bedarf einer Armee in Österreich von der in Neuester Zeit postulirten Stärke - nahezu einer Million Soldaten - nöthigen Anzahl intelligenter Ober- und Unterofficiere," *ÖMZ* 1 (1867), 177.
100. Deák, *Beyond Nationalism*, 56; Rothenberg, *The Army of Francis Joseph*, 81.
101. Frederick Martin, Sir John Scott Keltie, Isaac Parker Anderson Renwick, Mortimer Epstein, Sigfrid Henry Steinberg, and John Paxton, *The Statesman's Year-Book: Statistical and Historical Annual of the States of the Civilised World for the Year 1889* (London: Macmillan and Co., 1889), 19.
102. Dr. F. Presl, "Einige Bemerkungen über unsere ungünstigen Heeres-Ergänzungs-Resultate im Hinblicke auf die derzeit giltige Instruction zur ärztlichen Untersuchung der Wehrpflichtigen," *O.* 32 (1886), 197. The Military Science Society began in the summer of 1867.
103. Presl, "Einige Bemerkungen über unsere ungünstigen Heeres-Ergänzungs-Resultate im Hinblicke auf die derzeit giltige Instruction zur ärztlichen Untersuchung der Wehrpflichtigen," 198.
104. Presl, "Einige Bemerkungen über unsere ungünstigen Heeres-Ergänzungs-Resultate im Hinblicke auf die derzeit giltige Instruction zur ärztlichen Untersuchung der Wehrpflichtigen," 199–209.
105. B.P.S., "Unsere Aufgabe," *ÖMZ* 4 (1866), 44.
106. FML Franz Freiherr von John, "Allerunterthänigster Vortrag des Kriegsministers," *Wiener Zeitung*, Nr. 317, 31 December 1866, 1030.
107. Quoted in Allmayer-Beck, "Die Bewaffnete Macht in Staat und Gesellschaft," 77.
108. Allmayer-Beck, "Die Bewaffnete Macht in Staat und Gesellschaft," 76.
109. *Statistisches Jahrbuch für das Jahr 1870* (Vienna: Kaiserlich-Königlich Hof- und Staatsdruckerei, 1872), 528–529.
110. Allmayer-Beck, "Die Bewaffnete Macht in Staat und Gesellschaft," 76.
111. *Militär-statistisches Jahrbuch für das Jahr 1870* (Vienna: Kaiserlich-Königlich Hof- und Staatsdruckerei, 1871), 211.
112. *Statistisches Jahrbuch für das Jahr 1877* (Vienna: Kaiserlich-Königlich Hof- und Staatsdruckerei, 1880), XI, 4–5; Rothenberg, *The Army of Francis Joseph*, 83.
113. *Statistisches Jahrbuch für das Jahr 1877*, XI, 4–5; "Ideen über die Mittel zur Heranbildung der für den Bedarf einer Armee in Österreich von der in Neuester Zeit postulirten Stärke - nahezu einer Million Soldaten - nöthigen Anzahl intelligenter Ober- und Unterofficiere," *ÖMZ* 1 (1867), 177.

114. Frederick Martin, *The Statesman's Year-Book: Statistical and Historical Annual of the States of the Civilised World for the Year 1878* (London: Macmillan and Co., 1878), 70, 102, 380.
115. Rothenberg, *The Army of Francis Joseph*, 83.
116. Wagner, "Die k.(u.)k. Armee - Gliederung und Aufgabenstellung," 494; Bernhard von Poten, *Geschichte des Militär- Erziehungs- und Bildungswesens in Österreich-Ungarn* (Berlin: A. Hoffman & Comp., 1893), 254.
117. A.B., "Über Officiers-Schulen der Truppen," *ÖMZ* 3 (1869), 337.
118. Poten, *Geschichte des Militär- Erziehungs- und Bildungswesens in Österreich-Ungarn*, 260–263; Wagner, "Die k.(u.)k. Armee - Gliederung und Aufgabenstellung," 495; Josef Ritter Rechberger von Rechkron, *Das Bildungswesen im österreichischen Heere vom dreissigjährigen Kriege bis zur Gegenwart* (Vienna: R. V. Waldheim, 1878), 66–67.
119. Poten, *Geschichte des Militär- Erziehungs- und Bildungswesens in Österreich-Ungarn*, 266–268; Rechkron, *Das Bildungswesen im österreichischen Heere vom dreissigjährigen Kriege bis zur Gegenwart*, 30–33; Wagner, "Die k.(u.)k. Armee - Gliederung und Aufgabenstellung," 496.
120. Colonel Eduard Ritter Pechmann von Massen, "Über die Reform der Militär-Bildungsanstalten," *ÖMZ* 2 (1867), 336–346.
121. *Prüfungs-Fragen aus den Studien-Fächern der K.K. Kriegsschule für das Jahr 1877* (Vienna: L.W. Seidl & Sohn, 1877), KA Militärschulen, Karton Nr. 44, Lehrpläne, Stundeneinteilung, Organisation der KS, Denkschrift KS 1852–1877.
122. Zitterhofer, *Streffleurs Militärische Zeitschrift 1808–1908 Eine Geschichte dieser Zeitschrift anlässlich ihres 100jährigen Bestehens* (Vienna: L.W. Seidel & Sohn, 1908), 26.
123. "Mittheilungen aus der Abtheilung für Kriegswissenschaften des k.k. Militär-Casinos in Wien," *ÖMZ* 1 (1868), 203.
124. Zitterhofer, *Streffleurs Militärische Zeitschrift 1808–1908*, 26–31.
125. Zitterhofer, *Streffleurs Militärische Zeitschrift 1808–1908*, 18.
126. Zitterhofer, *Streffleurs Militärische Zeitschrift 1808–1908*, 39–42.
127. Allmayer-Beck, "Die Bewaffnete Macht in Staat und Gesellschaft," 70.
128. Zitterhofer, *Streffleurs Militärische Zeitschrift 1808–1908*, 20–21. Streffleur wrote on a variety of topics spanning from campaign studies, tactics, and topography to railroads, statistics, and marriages in the Russian army.
129. Zitterhofer, *Streffleurs Militärische Zeitschrift 1808–1908*, 27; Alois Ritter von Haymerle, "Über Generalstabsschulen," *O.* 1 (1871), 339–357.
130. Allmayer-Beck, "Die Bewaffnete Macht in Staat und Gesellschaft," 70.
131. Streffleur, "Über die Einsetzung eines Militär-Unterrichtsrathes," *ÖMZ* 1 (1867), 21.
132. "Ein Mahnwort," *ÖMZ* 2 (1870), 225.

133. Rothenberg, *The Army of Francis Joseph*, 62.
134. *Statistisches Jahrbuch für das Jahr 1870*, 528; Zitterhofer, *Streffleurs Militärische Zeitschrift 1808–1908*, 18.
135. .....er, "Literatur. Recension. Österreichische Militär-Bibliothek," *OMZ* 1 (1867), 129.
136. Deák, *Beyond Nationalism*, 120–123.
137. Arthur Schnitzler, *Leutnant Gustl* (Berlin: S. Fischer, 1901).
138. Deák, *Beyond Nationalism*, 110.
139. Feldmarschalleutnant (FML) Erzherzog Albrecht, No. 1017 "Allerunterthänigster Vortrag," 21 August 1866, KA MKSM Sonderreihe, Karton Nr. 22, 1866; Beck, "Theilweise Ursachen des gegenwärtigen schlechten Armee-Geistes und Mittel, welche zur Hebung desselben beitragen dürften," 1867, KA MKSM Sonderreihe, Karton Nr. 66, Studien.
140. Htr., "Degen und Feder," *ÖMZ* 2 (1866), 41–48; "Uber die Ursache der Mißerfolge bei der österreichischen Nordarmee im Kriege Preußens gegen Deutschland im Jahre 1866," *ÖMZ* 2 (1866), 349–352; B.P.S., "Unsere Aufgabe," *ÖMZ* 4 (1866), 38–41; "Praxis und Routine. - Wissenschaft und Kunst. - Betrachtungen über den Kriegsschauplatz in Böhmen von 1866 und die auf demselben stattgehabten Kriegsereignisse dieses Jahres. (Aus den schriften eines Veteranen des österreichischen Heeres)," *ÖMZ* 4 (1866), 181–183; "Ideen über die Mittel zur Heranbildung der für den Bedarf einer Armee in Österreich von der in Neuester Zeit postulirten Stärke - nahezu einer Million Soldaten - nöthigen Anzahl intelligenter Ober- und Unterofficiere," *ÖMZ* 1 (1867), 177–182; "Der österreichische Armee der Zukunft," *ÖMZ* 1 (1868), 127–128.
141. Albrecht and John, "Die Beförderungs-Vorschrift für die k.k. österreichische Landarmee vom 24. April 1867," *ÖMZ* 2 (1867), 137–145.
142. Albrecht and John, "Die Beförderungs-Vorschrift für die k.k. österreichische Landarmee vom 24. April 1867," 146–156.
143. Allmayer-Beck, "Die Bewaffnete Macht in Staat und Gesellschaft," 72–73; Wagner, "Die k.(u.)k. Armee - Gliederung und Aufgabenstellung," 358, 374.
144. Lackey, *The Rebirth of the Habsburg Army*, 50–51.
145. Wagner, "Die k.(u.)k. Armee - Gliederung und Aufgabenstellung," 375.
146. Glaise-Horstenau, *Franz Josephs Weggefährte*, 237.
147. Glaise-Horstenau, *Franz Josephs Weggefährte*, 238.
148. Wagner, "Die k.(u.)k. Armee - Gliederung und Aufgabenstellung," 375.
149. Beck, "Promemoria über Armee-Verhältnisse," August 1867, KA MKSM Sonderreihe, Karton Nr. 66, Studien; Beck, "Theilweise Ursachen des gegenwärtigen schlechten Armee-Geistes und Mittel, welche zur

Hebung desselben beitragen dürften," 1867, KA MKSM Sonderreihe, Karton Nr. 66, Studien; Lackey, *The Rebirth of the Habsburg Army*, 36–37.

150. Streffleur, "Über die Einsetzung eines Militär-Unterrichtsrathes," *ÖMZ* 1 (1867), 19–22; "Über die Errichtung eines Militär Lehrer-Seminars," *ÖMZ* 1 (1867), 239–240.
151. Lackey, *The Rebirth of the Habsburg Army*, 49–50; Srbik, *Aus Österreichs Vergangenheit*, 211.
152. Kuhn, No. 70 "Bitte des Reichs-Kriegs-Ministers FML Frh. v. Kuhn, Gesuch um Enthebung von seinem Posten und seinen politische Gedanken über eine Beteiligung an einem deutsch-französischen Kriege," 20 July 1870, KA MKSM Sonderreihe, Karton Nr. 65, Studien; "Memoire des Kriegsministers Freiherrn v. Kuhn über die Teilnahme der österreichisch-ungarischen Monarchie am Kriege zwischen Deutschland und Frankreich," July 1870, in Glaise-Horstenau, *Franz Josephs Weggefährte*, 457–460.
153. Though coastal batteries do not appear as a necessity for entry into the Franco-Prussian War, the report stated these cannon as a need for any mobilization, such as in the case of a conflict with Italy.
154. 1870 Präs. 16–13/3, 5. Abtheilung des k.k. Reichs-Kriegsministeriums. No. 99/j. "Nachweisung über jene Ausrüstungs-Gegenstände, deren Bestellung anläßig der jüngsten Mobilisirungs-Vorarbeiten angeordnet wurde; ad Reskript Präs. No. 3788 vom 20. Oktober 1870," 14 November 1870, KA KM Präsidium, Karton Nr. 314, 1870 15/33–21/10; 16–13/3, 7. Abtheilung des Reichs-Kriegsministeriums. "Nachweisung in Folge Praesid.-Erlaß No. 3788 vom 20. Oktober 1870, über die wegen der letzten Mobilisirungs-Verhältnisse geschehenen Bestellungen an Heeres-Ausrüstungs-Gegenstände," 25 Oktober 1870, KA KM Präsidium, Karton Nr. 314, 1870 15/33-21/10; Lackey, *The Rebirth of the Habsburg Army*, 39–40.
155. Albrecht, *Das Jahr 1870 und die Wehrkraft der Monarchie*, 71–72.
156. Albrecht, *Das Jahr 1870 und die Wehrkraft der Monarchie*, 39–40, 73.
157. No. 22, "Militär-Conferenz 1873," KA MKSM Sonderreihe, Karton Nr. 64, Studien, 20–23.
158. Lackey, *The Rebirth of the Habsburg Army*, 48–49.
159. Poten, *Geschichte des Militär- Erziehungs- und Bildungswesens in Österreich-Ungarn*, 335–336.
160. Srbik, *Aus Österreichs Vergangenheit*, 216.
161. Lackey, *The Rebirth of the Habsburg Army*, 49–56.
162. Srbik, *Aus Österreichs Vergangenheit*, 185–186.
163. Rothenberg, *The Army of Francis Joseph*, 83.

Bibliography

Unpublished Documents

Kriegsarchiv (KA), Vienna.
Allerhöchster Oberbefehl (AhOB).
Militärkanzlei Seiner Majestät des Kaisers (MKSM) Sonderreihe 1866–1918.
Chef des Generalstabs (GSt) Operationsbüro 1866–1918.
Zentralstellen.
Kriegsministerium (KM) Präsidialbüro (Präsidium) 1866–1918.
Militärerziehungs- und Bildungsanstalten (MEB).
Kriegsschule Wien 1867–1914.

Published Primary Sources

Albrecht, Erzherzog (anonymously). *Das Jahr 1870 und die Wehrkraft der Monarchie* (Vienna: Faesy & Frick, 1870.

Bartels, Eduard. *Österreich und sein Heer*. Leipzig: Otto Wigand, 1866.

John, FML Franz Freiherr von. "Allerunterthänigster Vortrag des Kriegsministers," *Wiener Zeitung*, Nr. 317, 31 December 1866.

Jurnitschek, Dr. Alfred. *Die Wehr-Reform in Österreich-ungarn von 1866 bis 1873*. Vienna: Carl Gerold's Sohn, 1873.

Martin, Frederick. *The Statesman's Year-Book: Statistical and Historical Annual of the States of the Civilised World for the Year 1878*. London: Macmillan and Co., 1878.

Martin, Frederick, Sir John Scott Keltie, Isaac Parker Anderson Renwick, Mortimer Epstein, Sigfrid Henry Steinberg, and John Paxton, *The Statesman's Year-Book: Statistical and Historical Annual of the States of the Civilised World for the Year 1889*. London: Macmillan and Co., 1889.

Militär-statistisches Jahrbuch für das Jahr 1870. Vienna: Kaiserlich-Königlich Hof- und Staatsdruckerei, 1871.

Organ der militärwissenschaftlichen Vereine (*O.*), 1867–1906.

Österreichische Militärische Zeitschrift (*ÖMZ*), 1866–1914.

Poten, Bernhard von. *Geschichte des Militär- Erziehungs- und Bildungswesens in Österreich-Ungarn*. Berlin: A. Hoffman & Comp., 1893.

Rechkron, Josef Ritter Rechberger von. *Das Bildungswesen im österreichischen Heere vom dreissigjährigen Kriege bis zur Gegenwart*. Vienna: R. v. Waldheim, 1878.

Reinländer, Oberst Wilhelm. *Vorträge über die Taktik*. Vienna: L.W. Seidel & Son, 1870–1871.

Schnitzler, Arthur. *Leutnant Gustl*. Berlin: S. Fischer, 1901.

Statistisches Jahrbuch für das Jahr 1870. Vienna: Kaiserlich-Königlich Hof- und Staatsdruckerei, 1872.

Statistisches Jahrbuch für das Jahr 1877. Vienna: Kaiserlich-Königlich Hof- und Staatsdruckerei, 1880.

Stenographische Protokolle des Hauses der Abgeordneten des Reichsrathes. Vienna: k.k. Hof- und Staatsdruckerei, 1863–1871.

Stenographische Sitzungs-Protokolle der Delegation des Reichsrathes. Vienna: k.k. Hof- und Staatsdruckerei, 1869–1911.

Zitterhofer, Oberleutnant [Karl]. *Streffleurs Militärische Zeitschrift 1808–1908: Eine Geschichte dieser Zeitschrift anlässlich ihres 100jährigen Bestehens.* Vienna: L.W. Siedel & Sohn, 1908.

Secondary Sources

Allmayer-Beck, Johann Christoph. "Die Bewaffnete Macht in Staat und Gesellschaft." in *Die Habsburgermonarchie 1848–1918*, Vol. 5 *Die Bewaffnete Macht.* Vienna: Verlag der Österreichischen Akademie der Wissenschaften, 1987.

Clausewitz, Carl von. *On War.* Edited and translated by Michael Howard and Peter Paret. Princeton, New Jersey: Princeton University Press, 1976.

Deák, István. *Beyond Nationalism: A Social and Political History of the Habsburg Officer Corps, 1848–1918.* New York: Oxford University Press, 1992.

Glaise-Horstenau, Edmund von. *Franz Josephs Weggefährte.* Wien: Amalthea Verlag, 1930.

Lackey, Scott. *The Rebirth of the Habsburg Army: Friedrich Beck and the Rise of the General Staff.* Westport, CT: Greenwood Press, 1995.

Rothenberg, Gunther E. *The Army of Francis Joseph.* West Lafayette, IN: Purdue University Press, 1976.

Sked, Alan. *The Decline and Fall of the Habsburg Empire, 1815–1918.* London: Longman, 1989.

Srbik, Heinrich von. *Aus Österreichs Vergangenheit.* Salzburg: O. Müller, 1949.

Wagner, Walter. "Die k.(u.)k. Armee - Gliederung und Aufgabenstellung." in *Die Habsburgermonarchie 1848–1918*, Vol. 5 *Die Bewaffnete Macht.* Vienna: Verlag der Österreichischen Akademie der Wissenschaften, 1987.

Wawro, Geoffrey. "The Austro-Prussian War: Politics, Strategy and War in the Habsburg Monarchy, 1859–1866." Ph.D. dissertation, Yale University, 1992.

CHAPTER 4

Adapting in Bosnia-Hercegovina

Defying the inclemency of extraordinarily unfavorable weather, the hardships of impassible ground and unavoidable privations of every kind, my brave troops have broken the resistance of a misled, fanatical population in glorious battles, have constantly held high the honor of our flags through their exemplary manful discipline and long-standing valor, and successfully solved increasingly difficult tasks in a short time.

The high level of battle discipline, the extraordinary perseverance and marching proficiency, which have been displayed exceptionally by all troops and divisions, have merited undivided acknowledgement; they are the results of the sacrifice and laborious toil of many years, which now may recognize the most beautiful pay in the just recently executed deeds.

I thank the commanders for their circumspect leadership and for their enterprising conduct of operations—I thank the generals, officers, and men of the Second Army - I thank finally all the members of the army, of my navy and of both my *Landwehren*, who were called to contribute to the solution of a difficult task, for their always proven loyalty to duty, for their self-sacrifice, for their perseverance, and for the uniform cooperation of everyone, whereby all results could be achieved, which henceforth will take an honorable place in the history of our fatherland.[1]

With these words, Emperor Franz Joseph praised and congratulated his army for its successful conquest in 1878 of Bosnia-Hercegovina, a small Balkan part of the Ottoman Empire to the south of the Dual Monarchy. The invasion had lasted less than 12 weeks, though the campaign lasted longer than Austria's defeat at the hands of Prussia in

J.A. Dredger, *Tactics and Procurement in the Habsburg Military, 1866–1918*, DOI 10.1007/978-3-319-57678-7_4

the so-called Seven Weeks' War of 1866. Bosnia-Hercegovina presented an excellent scenario for the Austro-Hungarian military to test its new weaponry and tactics as well as the effects of reforms in other areas, such as army organization, military education, and supply network. Although the forces of one small Balkan province of the Ottoman Empire did not qualify as a major European military power, the Bosnian campaign still allowed ample opportunities for judging the battlefield performance of the *k.k.* army. A war against a lesser opponent also presented an easier task than a struggle against Prussia, Russia, France, or even Italy. Victory, though hardly ever in doubt, renewed the confidence of Habsburg troops that had been shaken 12 years earlier. Even parliamentary delegates and public opinion took a more positive view of the Dual Monarchy's armed forces, despite poor spending decisions by the military. Yet, the exaggerated praise of Franz Joseph failed to take into account the problems that the Austro-Hungarian army experienced. Some of these problems also appeared in *k.k.* analyses of the Russo-Turkish War of 1877–1878, especially regarding strategy and tactics.

Lessons from the Russo-Turkish War

The Russo-Turkish war offered an opportunity for Habsburg leaders to learn from the experiences of other armies. Tactically, the Russians "remained true to shock tactics."[2] At Plevna, where the Turks repulsed Russian assaults for four months from 19 July until 12 December 1877, most attacks came from the front and rarely aimed for the flanks of the enemy.[3] Major General L.L. Baron Zeddeler, who led a Russian column against the redoubts of Gorni Dubnik near Plevna and fell wounded by a bullet in the stomach, criticized his superiors for relying on closed order assault formations that aimed for achieving victory with the bayonet rather than using open order and firepower.[4] Despite the heavy losses suffered by Russian attackers while failing to gain their objectives, Austro-Hungarian officers found little of interest in the Russo-Turkish campaigns. One officer even commented, "One cannot draw anything positive from these experiences; at most one can learn how one should not fight."[5] Another officer in his analysis of the war concentrated on the mistakes of the Russians and Turks and especially noted the failure of the Russian generals to adapt their tactics to the needs of the situation. Rather than carefully reconnoitering enemy positions and preparing attacks of sufficient strength, the Russians launched disjointed attacks that did not use the advantages of firepower.[6] Instead of realizing from these campaigns the futility of frontal assaults on entrenched positions and the enormous casualties that would ensue, *k.k.* officers continued to advocate direct attacks, though in swarms rather than columns, as indicated by the next tactical manual from the war college.[7]

Habsburg officers interpreted the lessons of the Russo-Turkish War for cavalry and artillery in the same way as for infantry. Preferring to look at the mistakes of the Russians and Turks rather than trying to apply their experiences to improve Austro-Hungarian methods, *k.k.* analyses of the 1877–1878 Balkan campaigns agreed with Zeddeler's assessments of the inept Russian employment of cavalry and artillery.[8] One Habsburg general staff officer concluded that massed cannon could have a favorable effect on battle and that the Russians had neglected to use their guns effectively.[9] This viewpoint merely confirmed what other *k.k.* officers had argued before the Russo-Turkish War. Similarly, Austro-Hungarian war analysts stated that the numerous Russian mounted troops had little impact on the outcome of the conflict because the Tsar's commanders ordered their cavalry to engage only in scouting missions and guarding the infantry's flanks during battle.[10] A *Honvéd* captain claimed that, mainly because of terrain, positional battles took place instead of *rencontre* (chance) encounters. These battles did not favor mounted units, which sometimes had to fight on foot in entrenched positions. Remarking that infantry could fulfill such tasks better than expensive cavalry could, the *Honvéd* officer ended his article with the exclamation that the next great war should take a completely different course, one suited to mounted warfare. For this reason, according to the writer, Russia increased the number of cavalry in the Tsarist army after the war. As a result, Russian mounted troops outnumbered the Austro-Hungarian and French cavalry forces 3:1 and the German mounted branch 2:1.[11] Russia and Germany had far more mounted troops than the *k.k.* army and France possessed just as many. Thus, the Habsburg high command did not stand alone as a supporter of equipping large numbers of cavalry.

Strategically, despite the slight impact that permanent fortifications had on the war, Habsburg officers continued to adhere to their previous convictions about the usefulness of the cordon system of fortresses. The author of one *ÖMZ* article, citing the Russo-Turkish War and wars from the eighteenth century as proof, even claimed that the cost of improving old fortresses and building new ones did not matter because of their immense influence on war.[12] The 1877–1878 war also proved the advantages of field fortifications. At Plevna, the Turks constructed redoubts and other temporary defenses that thwarted three major Russian assaults, inflicting heavy losses. Some 40,000–50,000 Turkish troops held off Russian forces of 120,000 men and 510 cannon.[13] Only close investment of Plevna by the Russians, resulting in siege rather than pitched battle, and the subsequent shortage of supplies on the side of the Turks ended the engagement with a Russian victory.[14] The effectiveness of field fortifications had already impressed Austro-Hungarian officers before the Russo-Turkish War. Just after the Seven Weeks' War, the author of an *ÖMZ* article criticized the Habsburg leadership for not employing the advantages of entrenchments at Königgrätz.[15] The Franco-Prussian War, the Russo-Turkish War, and the occupation of Bosnia-Hercegovina all strengthened the conviction of *k.k.* officers that field fortifications were essential. These wars, however, did not impress the high command with the uselessness of permanent fortresses, even though the cordon system had very little effect on the outcomes of these conflicts.

Recognizing Railroad Advantages

Austro-Hungarian leaders did think that the Russo-Turkish War proved the usefulness and importance of railroads and engineer forces for mobilizing men, transporting troops on campaign, and bringing supplies. General Staff Captain Carl Regenspursky, who later became the instructor of tactics and strategy for *Landwehr* staff officers, criticized the Russian army for not employing enough technical troops or taking advantage of the Rumanian rail system during mobilization and crossing of the Danube in 1877.[16] The Russo-Turkish conflict confirmed for *k.k.* officers their previous convictions regarding the significance of railroads and the engineering corps. After 1866, First Lieutenant Moriz Brunner, who taught the fortifications course at the Technical Military Academy and had directed the fortification of Przemyśl, advocated tying the imperial cordon system of fortifications together with the railroad lines to enhance communication and transport troops more quickly.[17]

The Franco-Prussian War also provided lessons on the benefits of efficient railroad usage in many aspects of war, such as mobilization; communications; the transport of supplies, munitions, troops, and the sick and wounded; and both offensive and defensive strategic and tactical operations.[18] Despite the recognition of the immense advantages that good utilization of railroads offered, all the European powers except Germany failed to organize their technical troops correctly and provide them with the necessary equipment and training to perform their duties. One *ÖMZ* writer proposed the formation of a railroad division independent from the other technical troops. The rail forces should have sufficient equipment and soldiers specially trained in railroad operations, because civilian administrators and rail workers had proved inadequate in both number and ability during wartime. Finally, the army should operate its own rail line for training purposes.[19]

Members of the Habsburg high command also concurred on the importance of railroads for the *k.k.* army. For years, Beck had advocated expanding the empire's rail network, especially to speed the mobilization process. Kuhn had tried to wrest control over railroad construction away from the civil governments in Vienna and Budapest, particularly to improve lines leading to Galicia, the most probable theater for a war with Russia. The general staff, however, criticized Kuhn's mobilization plans because they did not make adequate use of existing railroads. The general staff report noted the limited rail networks in the northern and eastern parts of the monarchy and the need to build more double-track rail lines for military transportation, deployment, and communications. Archduke Albrecht agreed about the need to construct an extensive rail system to Galicia to connect the cordon system of permanent fortresses and to shuttle troops there in case of a Russian attack.[20] Thus, the Austro-Hungarian high command agreed on the advantages of railroads and wished to make substantial improvements to the empire's rail networks. Habsburg military leaders did not lag behind other European powers in their willingness to adopt new technology and spent great amounts of time and effort planning the best routes and means to attain their goals. In practice, however, these objectives remained difficult to complete and slow to realize, mainly because of financial difficulties. Parliamentary representatives did not always see military necessity as decisive in deciding rail routes, tending to favor routes that fostered business and trade.

The Bosnia-Hercegovina Campaign

The Peace of San Stefano, which ended the Russo-Turkish War, outraged Austria-Hungary. Contrary to secret agreements between Russia and the Dual Monarchy before the war, the Peace of San Stefano entailed an increase in Russia's influence in the Balkans through the establishment of a large Bulgarian state under the patronage of Russia. Although Russia gained immensely by this arrangement, Austria-Hungary did not receive the agreed-upon compensation for taking over Bosnia-Hercegovina. The treaty not only upset the Habsburg state but also other European powers, especially Britain. The powers met at the Congress of Berlin, where they made a new arrangement that split Bulgaria into three sections and allowed Austria-Hungary to occupy Bosnia-Hercegovina indefinitely. With the approval of the other European powers, the Dual Monarchy's army prepared for invasion of the two Turkish provinces.[21]

On 29 July 1878, the XIII Corps of the *k.k.* army with 82,000 troops under the command of *FZM* Joseph Baron Philippović invaded Bosnia from Croatia. On 1 August, the 18th Infantry Division of 9000 men under *FML* Stefan Baron Jovanović entered Hercegovina from Dalmatia.[22] Both military and civilian leaders had expected a simple expedition meeting little resistance. Foreign Minister Julius Count Andrássy expressed his opinion "that it was more a question of a military stroll than a war operation."[23] Only a few members of the army, such as Colonel Friedrich Beck, head of the imperial military chancellery, realized the difficulties inherent in waging a campaign in rugged, undeveloped land with a mostly hostile population.[24] As General Daniel Baron von Salis-Soglio, a veteran of 1866, wrote, "Consequently, from the beginning Austria employed not so many war ready troops as had been actually necessary and were later proven as necessary."[25]

Both the XIII Corps and the 18th Infantry Division met with stiff resistance early in the campaign. Irregular soldiers of the Moslem and Orthodox sections of the population opposed the takeover of their land and did not welcome Catholic invaders, who they felt treated the Slavic peoples within the empire as inferiors. Renegade Turkish regulars with artillery support also fought against the Austro-Hungarian forces.[26] Because of the unexpected number and abilities of the enemy and the inadequate training of *k.k.* troops in countering guerilla tactics, the Habsburg invasion became bogged down, even suffering setbacks in early August.[27] Philippović repeatedly asked for reinforcements, but managed to take his main objective, the Bosnian capital of Sarajevo, on 19 August.[28] Jovanović entered Mostar, the capital of Hercegovina, on 5 August 1878.[29]

The capture of these political centers did not end the campaign. The irregular enemy forces continued to fight throughout the rest of Bosnia and Hercegovina. Realizing the inadequate number of Habsburg forces already engaged, the *k.k.* high command mobilized six more divisions, which raised the total number of Austro-Hungarian troops to 153,000. By the end of this supposedly small campaign, the *k.k.* army had mobilized 250,000 men, one quarter to one third of its wartime strength, although not all fought in battle.[30] The official Habsburg estimate of enemy forces amounted to 79,200 insurgents and 13,800 regulars, making a total of 93,000 men and 75 cannon. Although not all insurgents took part in pitched battles against Austro-Hungarian forces and never appeared on the field simultaneously or under a unified command, especially in Hercegovina, they represented 25% of the Moslem population of Bosnia-Hercegovina and 12% of the total population of both provinces.[31] In all, Habsburg troops fought 61 engagements, ranging from skirmishes to the taking of Sarajevo, and suffered losses of 5020 men and 178 officers dead, wounded, or missing, totaling 5198 casualties.[32]

Difficulties of Counterinsurgency

The occupation of Bosnia-Hercegovina did not qualify as a war against another military power. Rather, the 1878 campaign became more of a counterinsurgency effort in comparison with the recent *k.k.* conflicts of 1848, 1859, 1864, and 1866. From this viewpoint, the great numerical superiority (more than 2.5:1) that Austro-Hungarian forces enjoyed does not appear overwhelming. Instead of interpreting the difficulties that the Habsburg army encountered in Bosnia-Hercegovina as indications of ineptitude in utilizing the vast advantage in numbers and weaponry, military historians should look at the campaign as a small war against an enemy employing mainly guerilla tactics. The US Army aims for at least 3:1 numerical superiority for counterinsurgency operations and a 5:1 ratio for urban assaults, although the Department of Defense's *Handbook on Counter Insurgency* refers to the 10:1 ratio that some military authors set as the minimum requirement for defeating insurgencies.[33] According to these calculations, the *k.k.* operation in Bosnia-Hercegovina had great success, with a strength ratio under the requirements for modern counterinsurgencies. The small number of Habsburg casualties, 2% of all mobilized troops, attests to the overall accomplishment of the Austro-Hungarian army, especially considering the low numbers of dead and wounded rates, 946 and 3980 respectively, and only 272 men missing.[34] The latter number indicates that desertions were not a major problem for *k.k.* forces during this campaign, in contrast to the experiences of 1866.

Conditions in the two provinces rendered normal military operations extremely difficult. Bosnia-Hercegovina possessed little infrastructure. The mountainous terrain with dense forests and few navigable roads made travel laborious and the transport of artillery and supplies onerous. Soldiers had to make heroic exertions to drag cannon "where only the trace of a road existed."[35] Inclement weather added to these arduous circumstances, further hindering transport and communications.[36] Yet, the Habsburg troops covered ground quickly enough to take the political capitals and other strategic locations in less than three weeks from the start of the campaign.

The nature of the *k.k.* army's opponents also provided obstacles that the *k.k.* army had not encountered in most of its recent battles. In the words of one officer, Habsburg troops fought "against a desperately courageous, barbaric enemy, who had beforehand an exact knowledge of the land and clothing suitable for it."[37] According to the official Austro-Hungarian history of the occupation, the local inhabitants possessed a warlike character that had been developed during many years of fighting. Even without the desperation, barbarity, and bellicosity that Habsburg officers attributed to the irregulars, the enemy presented a difficult foe. Usually eschewing the offensive unless holding overwhelming numerical superiority or the advantage of surprise, the irregulars used defensive tactics that skillfully made use of their familiarity with the terrain and the firepower of their rifles. Only about a third carried breech-loaders; the rest used either muzzle-loaders or older guns. Unlike Austro-Hungarian forces, the insurgents did not have to rely on supply trains, but requisitioned provisions from the local population or relied on their leaders, who often held large amounts of land. The simple clothing and equipment of the Bosnians and Hercegovinians helped the irregular forces blend in with the inhabitants and allowed quick movement, which gave them a great advantage over the heavily laden *k.k.* soldiers accustomed to easier terrain and better provisions. The official history summed up the situation: "Difficult terrain, the dearth of resources in most regions, which became theaters of operations, finally the still unbelievably unfavorable weather conditions were the most powerful and faithful allies of the insurgents and compensated by far for any disadvantages that could arise for them from the small number of combatants."[38]

This situation resembled the colonial conflicts of other nations, such as Germany in Southwest Africa from 1904 to 1907. Like the Bosnians and Hercegovinians, the Herero in Southwest Africa held the advantages of familiarity with the terrain and the ability to blend in with local inhabitants. However, the two campaigns had important differences. The Herero at first employed an offensive strategy, attacking German outposts and telegraph lines, whereas the Bosnians and Hercegovinians fought almost exclusively on the defensive. The Herero also possessed better weaponry than those of the Habsburg opponents. In addition, the Austro-Hungarians, as invaders rather than suppressors of a revolt, did not attempt to exterminate their enemies, as the Germans tried to do in Southwest Africa.[39] Unlike the Germans, the Dual Monarchy's army did not advocate absolute destruction of the enemy, but rather the political goal of pacification.

Adapting Tactics: Infantry and Cavalry

To combat the Bosnians and Hercegovinians, Habsburg forces employed an offensive strategy with offensive tactics. This choice of methods corresponded with the overall purpose of the campaign, which required invasion to take possession of the provinces. The success of the operations in Bosnia-Hercegovina confirmed the use of assault in battle. Because the insurgents did not form defensive positions in depth, Austro-Hungarian troops found that flanking movements for attacking the sides and rear of the enemy worked well.[40] The *k.k.* soldiers also made use of their superiority in Werndl breech-loading rifles. The most effective weapon against the irregulars, however, was artillery, especially the recently acquired 80- and 90-mm field guns. Habsburg soldiers discovered the great fear and respect that the insurgents held for cannon, as well as the beneficial effect that one or two artillery shots had in clearing enemy positions.[41] One *k.k.* officer described the effect of the field guns: "In battle there appeared most often the endeavor to shake the enemy with artillery fire and to push him from his most advantageous positions by threats from the flanks and rear."[42] Thus, Austro-Hungarian leaders employed the tactics learned in recent wars: well-placed cannon fire and flanking movements in the spirit of Moltke. As another Habsburg officer wrote of his experiences during the campaign, "Our regulations have proven themselves complete in regard to battle formations, events, and leadership in battle. Strikingly, nothing new has come forward. The events played out in general analogous to those of the spring weapons exercises—the pushes and rushes forward made themselves noticeable."[43] Thus, the Habsburg army still used offensive tactics and emphasized the rush forward to the assault. Yet, the troops also showed flexibility in stressing the importance of artillery and the preference for movement to enable attacks on the flanks and rear of the enemy rather than the front.

The tactical lessons that students in the *k.k.* war college learned reflected these themes, which differed little from the ideas of 1870/1871. Major Anton Gartner's manual, written after the invasion, underscored artillery fire before the attack as an integral part of weakening the firepower of the defender. However, Gartner did not reject the frontal assault with its fulfillment in the bayonet fight.[44] Lieutenant Colonel Alois Hauschka, teacher of tactics for general staff officers, stated emphatically that the Austro-Hungarian exercise regulations did not go to the extreme of avoiding frontal attacks over open ground culminating in the bayonet struggle. Hauschka maintained that neglecting frontal assaults in training exercises stemmed from the overreaction of officers to the events of 1866. Similarly, the lieutenant colonel claimed that the difficult terrain of Bosnia and Hercegovina, not the general uselessness of frontal attacks, dictated the frequent resort to flanking movements. According to Hauschka, the *k.k.* army had returned to the correct way of thinking: "The exercise of the frontal assault is the foundation of correct training of infantry for the battles of a great war."[45] In other words, great powers attacked frontally, despite the lessons of recent conflicts, which showed that modern weapons could halt frontal attacks. Although officers in Bosnia and Hercegovina had adapted to the reality of the battlefield by attacking the flanks and rear of the enemy rather than the front, *Kriegsschule* instructors and writers continued to interpret warfare according to their preconceived notions that favored the offensive.

The cavalry played an insignificant battlefield role in Bosnia-Hercegovina. For the most part, mounted troops executed security and scouting operations while performing important services for communications and supply trains.[46] Only 13,313 horses accompanied the initial invasion force.[47] The Habsburg army sent this small number compared with infantry because of the terrain of the two provinces, where mountains and forests did not prove conducive to cavalry maneuvers. However, the 1881–1882 war college tactical manual still addressed the topic of mounted attacks on infantry, though stressing the importance of artillery or infantry support for the cavalry. Although admitting the difficulties that modern warfare entailed for cavalry charges, Major Gartner insisted that occasions arose when mounted troops could use their speed to assault infantry, such as at the beginning or end of battles when foot soldiers had not settled into their positions or had suffered losses from enemy fire.[48]

Some officers realized that the change in weapons technology reduced the opportunities for shock as an effective form of attack for cavalry. Retired Major Friedrich Baron Mühlwerth-Gärtner, lamenting the paucity of people who understood modern cavalry, asserted the dearth of opportunities for charges. Other than the rare occasions for surprise or assaulting infantry already badly shaken by artillery and rifle fire, mounted attacks constituted "an absurd beginning" and held extremely small chance of success: "All the pluck, the resolute determination to cut the enemy infantry to pieces, are completely useless if the losses of the cavalry during the charge reach a height as on the days of Wörth, Vionville, and Sedan."[49]

At the 1877 *k.k.* cavalry maneuvers near Czegléd, Hungary, Major Karger criticized the overuse of frontal assaults and the few attempts to attack the opponent's flanks.[50] The desire to retain cavalry as a purely offensive weapon with its culmination in shock and saber slashing still permeated the mounted branch of the Austro-Hungarian army and some prominent generals. Major General Johann Baron Waldstätten, who had taught at the war college, published several military works, and commanded the Seventh Infantry Brigade during the occupation of Bosnia, exemplified this view by saying, "Cavalry has not changed its essence for one hundred years, it has no new weapon, no other means than before. The breech-loader and revolver enter very little into the question."[51] The idea of relying on firepower and using a revolver to fire a salvo into the enemy's ranks before the impact of collision had virtually no adherents in the mounted branch of the Habsburg army.[52] Major Emil Dembsher expressed the old feudal view of cavalry when he attempted to refute Karger and Mühlwerth-Gärtner in an 1879 *ÖMZ* article. Claiming that mathematical proofs of the devastating effect of firepower on mounted forces were inconsequential, Dembsher bragged that excellent morale and the offensive spirit could conquer all obstacles. Therefore, the *k.k.* army must engender in its mounted forces cold-bloodedness and scorn for danger in order that the Habsburg cavalry "will remain the descendants of the old knighthood, the noblest of all weapons!"[53] With such ideas within the Austro-Hungarian officer corps, the refusal to reduce the number of mounted troops in the army is no surprise.

Adapting Tactics: Steel-Bronze Artillery

Writers such as *k.k.* Captain Hugo von Molnar agreed that the artillery had gained greater usefulness on the battlefield. The experiences of 1870 proved the benefits of massed cannon formations, as demonstrated at Sedan, where the Prussians achieved victory by hemming in the French with artillery fire along the whole battle line.[54] One lieutenant colonel maintained that even though infantry still decided battles, cannon offered great advantages to military leaders who employed them effectively to support the other branches.[55] The invasion of Bosnia-Hercegovina also supported the increased role of artillery in battle, as insurgents feared the Habsburg cannon shots more than any other part of the *k.k.* army.[56]

Austro-Hungarian artillery had seen substantial improvement just before the invasion of Bosnia-Hercegovina. In 1876 and 1877, the *k.k.* army finally received the new steel-bronze 80-mm and 90-mm field guns that the war ministry had tried to obtain since before the Franco-Prussian War.[57] The chronic problem of financial struggles with parliamentary representatives, who still distrusted the army's procurement decisions, contributed to this delay.[58] Other causes also exacerbated the procurement situation. The fast pace of technological innovation made decisions extremely difficult as new weaponry appeared rapidly. In the 18 years before 1879, the Habsburg army had adopted four different artillery systems in succession.[59] Not only did these quick changes to new cannon cost large sums of money, they also sparked great debate and required extensive testing to assess the new technology.

In 1873, Major General Artur Maximilian Count Bylandt-Rheidt, who would become war minister in 1876, submitted to the imperial military chancellery a report describing the findings of the army's committee for testing new weaponry. With the approval of the committee, Bylandt-Rheidt recommended the procurement of the German Krupp steel breech-loading cannon as the best artillery piece in Europe.[60] Major General von Salis-Soglio, president of the technical and administrative military committee from 1876 to 1880, wrote that the majority of members of the committee in 1875 favored the Krupp steel gun over the steel-bronze version of Major General Franz Baron Uchatius, head of the gun manufacturing division at the *k.k.* army's Vienna arsenal. The steel-bronze barrels weighed far more than the lighter steel of Krupp, like "a corpulent bulldog" compared with "a slender greyhound." Also, the heavier caliber weapons could not withstand the pressure from the burning powder.[61]

Nevertheless, the Habsburg military leaders chose the inferior weapon because of the inability of Austro-Hungarian factories to produce steel barrels and the supposed danger of buying from a foreign firm. In addition, as the Vienna arsenal had already lost the contract for breech-loading rifles to the private manufacturer Josef Werndl, the *k.k.* ordnance experts did not want another lucrative contract to go outside their institution.[62] To start making the steel-bronze barrels, the arsenal needed completely new equipment and by the time production began, the Uchatius guns had already become outmoded. The Krupp cannon shot more efficiently and cost less. As Salis-Soglio later wrote, "Our steel-bronze monster must be considered a stillborn child."[63] Uchatius tried to improve his invention, especially for the higher caliber weapons, which the Habsburg leaders had to order from Krupp. The attempts failed and, consequently, Uchatius committed suicide on 4 June 1881.[64] The episode of choosing steel-bronze over steel reveals the poor decision making of the *k.k.* high command. Austro-Hungarian military leaders chose to reject the advice of the technical committee and instead purchased a far more expensive, but inferior, model rather than buy from a foreign firm. This selection would haunt the *k.k.* army until its demise in the First World War because Habsburg leaders never fully replaced the steel-bronze guns. This example also shows why delegates did not place full trust in the budget requests of the military. Although Liberal representatives preferred the army to buy from local businesses, poor spending choices by the war ministry caused delegates to distrust the army's financial decisions.

After the choice of steel-bronze artillery, Austro-Hungarian officers attempted to proclaim the superiority of Uchatius' invention over Krupp steel by publishing comparisons and tests of the different metals. Steel-bronze somehow always won.[65] According to one *k.k.* officer, "So much the more honorable is the victory which the youthful steel-bronze has carried off over the proven combatant, cast steel.... The halo which mystery mongers and the persisting influence of preconceived opinion have bestowed on cast steel has been annihilated as if by a magic blow."[66] The performance of the Uchatius cannon during the Bosnian campaign even impressed the press.[67] However, the weight of the *k.k.* artillery caused problems in the rugged terrain of Bosnia and Hercegovina, where lighter mountain guns proved more suitable.[68] The Habsburg army continued to test for the best cannon technology, which the Krupp works continued to produce.[69] Despite overwhelming praise for Uchatius' inventions, Austro-Hungarian purchases of German guns and the constant search for improvements in artillery reveal the dissatisfaction with the new products of the Vienna arsenal, although the Habsburg high command would not procure better artillery for many years.

Non-Adapting Strategy: Permanent Fortresses

The occupation of Bosnia-Hercegovina rarely involved the attack or defense of permanent fortifications. Most of the fortresses in the two provinces dated back to feudal times and had fallen into decay. Newer constructions were relatively small and mostly suitable for police forces or protection against robbers. During the war they served to secure communications or as field fortifications rather than as permanent fortresses because they only provided protection against infantry fire.[70] The limited effect of permanent fortifications (*Befestigung*), on the invasion did not dissuade Habsburg officers from their conviction of the usefulness of the cordon system. Austro-Hungarian military journals continued to publish articles favoring permanent fortresses and temporary field fortifications in a permanent style.[71] Even officers who doubted the wisdom of updating old fortresses still believed in the effectiveness of *Befestigung* and showed concern only for the expense of enabling them to withstand modern artillery fire.[72] Clearly, the *k.k.* high command and officer corps failed to realize that the greater maneuverability of modern warfare and the ever-increasing impact of artillery on fortresses had rendered permanent fortifications obsolete. Even while engaged in a guerilla war, fortresses continued to occupy the minds of Austro-Hungarian military thinkers. Thus, instead of abandoning the idea of upgrading old fortresses and building new ones, Habsburg leadership continued to waste money on the cordon system.

Civil-Military Criticism

Although the occupation of Bosnia and Hercegovina proved a success, the press criticized the Habsburg army for its inability to conclude the campaign more quickly. In Vienna, the *Neue Freie Presse*, in answer to the question of why *k.k.* troops had such difficulties defeating "undisciplined hordes" of insurgents, responded that the blame lay not with Philippović but with Andrássy for not providing the army with enough forces.[73] The military papers, not surprisingly, expressed similar sentiments to avert criticism from the Austro-Hungarian army and blame delays on the actions of civilians. Andrássy lashed back by stating that a peaceful occupation should have taken place and accusing Philippović and his subordinates of escalating the danger. According to Andrássy, the commander wanted an exciting adventure full of chances for laurels, not a quiet takeover, which in reality was not feasible. In addition, the foreign minister insisted that Habsburg troops could have seized Sarajevo on 17 August. Instead, Philippović ordered his subordinate *FML* Karl von Tegetthoff to wait for him before entering the city so that the commanding officer could reap the glory of victory.[74] After the invasion, the Liberal newspapers agreed with Andrássy and criticized the army's inadequate handling of the campaign.[75]

Habsburg military leaders, just as after the Austro-Prussian War, publicly blamed civilian officials for army shortcomings in 1878. Officers claimed that the foreign minister had blocked mobilization of sufficient forces at the start of the invasion, despite Philippović's repeated requests for more troops. Military circles issued the usual accusations about parliamentary stinginess in funding the extra expense of occupying Bosnia and Hercegovina.[76] The *Neue Freie Presse* complained that the *k.k.* army had used the 60 million florins that the Delegations had granted the government "for the case when the further development of eastern events should make the development of military strength an unavoidable necessity in regard to maintaining the essential interests of the monarchy." The author of the article did not blame the Habsburg high command for consuming so much money, but rather accused Andrássy of concealing the real reason for the special credit, the seizure of two foreign provinces. Making the situation even worse, the foreign minister in his request for appropriations had not included the cost of civilian administration of Bosnia and Hercegovina after the conclusion of military operations.[77] Although the last accusation had little merit, considering Andrássy's overly optimistic pre-invasion view of easily and inexpensively occupying the two provinces, the article blamed civilians in the Habsburg government rather than the army high command for consuming such a large extraordinary credit so quickly.

Self-Criticism, Recognition, and Learning Lessons

Internally, *k.k.* leaders acknowledged that problems in the military had arisen during the campaign. The high command had projected too small a force for the operation, and even those who saw the numbers as insufficient had acquiesced to the low estimates.[78] *FML* Beck, who headed Franz Joseph's military chancellery and issued the operational orders, had realized the danger of not employing enough force against determined enemies. Nevertheless, Beck had convinced the war ministry and the general staff to reduce the number of troops needed for initial mobilization in order to persuade civilian officials in Vienna and Budapest to approve the occupation. When the invasion forces encountered delays because of heavy resistance by Bosnian irregulars, Beck claimed that the high command had only envisioned a limited mission, not pacification.[79] This argument was not completely truthful because Beck had known that the operation would require more troops than the original number, and provided yet another example of the *k.k.* army's manner of dissembling when dealing with the civilian part of the government in military matters.

Moritz Baron von Auffenberg, war minister from 1911 to 1912, participated in the Bosnian invasion as a general staff officer in the 61st infantry brigade. During and after the campaign, Auffenberg remained unimpressed with the reserve troops and officers, who could not maintain discipline and cohesion on the march. The future minister of war blamed this failure on the insufficient homogeneity between the officers and soldiers, especially because former one-year volunteers did not always speak the language of their men.[80] This assessment differed from that of another staff officer who claimed that the one-year volunteers had performed their duties well, proving the efficacy of instituting the *Einjährig-Freiwilligen* in 1868.[81] Auffenberg admitted that regular troops and reserves fought well enough in battle, although most had no desire or interest in seizing two Turkish provinces for the Habsburg Empire. Austro-Hungarian reserve units merely did their duty against an enemy that had mostly given up. Auffenberg also saw the leadership of several non-commissioned officers as deficient during a river crossing that stalled under enemy fire: "Against an equally matched opponent the undertaking would hardly have succeeded."[82] The future war minister did not regard the Bosnian campaign very favorably, as he did not find there an opportunity for distinction.[83]

The battle leadership of Baron Waldstätten impressed Franz Count Conrad von Hötzendorf, a general staff officer in the Fourth Infantry Division during the invasion of Bosnia and future chief of the general staff.[84] However, Conrad criticized other officers for not leading the troops energetically enough and treating the enemy too leniently.[85] Conrad, a general staff officer, like Auffenberg, who had experienced little direct combat in his first campaign, viewed the war differently from the future war minister. While supervising the stripping of dead bodies to preserve uniforms, Conrad felt that the war revealed "the relentlessness of the struggle for existence."[86] The future chief of the general staff in the Great War saw the seizure of Bosnia and Hercegovina as a very important event, both in underscoring the offensive tactical lessons and aggressive leadership he learned from Waldstätten and in confirming Conrad's social Darwinian ideas that he had acquired before 1878. This aggressive tactical thinking resembled the German military culture of absolute destruction, as described by Isabel Hull (without the emphasis on social Darwinism), rather than the less radical ideas of Albrecht and Beck.[87]

The main problem for the Austro-Hungarian army in Bosnia and Hercegovina, apart from the insufficient number of men at the beginning of the campaign, stemmed from inadequate supply and equipment. Most officers blamed the roughness of the terrain for difficulties in supplying soldiers.[88] Colonel Georg Baron von Holtz, however, claimed that the supply lines failed to function properly because of poor preparation and staff work. The colonel also criticized the tactical arrangements of *k.k.* forces as well as the general staff's intelligence reporting. Because of Habsburg mismanagement, the troops did not possess equipment suitable for mountain warfare.[89] Major Benkiser of the general staff corps agreed that the Hungarian pants and boots worn by some of the soldiers did not meet the demands for fighting in rugged terrain.[90]

For the most part, the *k.k.* high command remained satisfied not only with the overall outcome of the 1878 campaign but also with the performance of individual branches of the army. After an inspection tour in Bosnia during October 1878, Beck reported that the Austro-Hungarian army had successfully broken armed resistance to the occupation, although Habsburg displeasure at the extended campaign resulted in the removal of Philippović from command.[91] Archduke Albrecht headed a commission of inquiry, which expressed overall satisfaction with the military aspects of the invasion.[92] Some army officials criticized Beck for mobilizing so many troops for a small operation against an irregular enemy.[93] Former War Minister Kuhn wrote in his diary that Beck had sent more soldiers to Bosnia and Hercegovina than Radetzky had at his command in Italy in 1848–1849. Kuhn also lamented that Beck, as head of the emperor's military chancellery, had gained control over military leadership within the Habsburg army.[94] Kuhn, however, writing in the secrecy of his personal papers, hardly constituted a prominent member of the high command. His thoughts stemmed as much from resentment for the success of a man who had worked for Kuhn's dismissal as from an unbiased analysis of the Bosnian campaign. Victory, even over a seemingly insignificant foe in the Balkans, proved difficult to belittle.

Success did not mean that the Habsburg army had nothing to learn. When the Austro-Hungarian government attempted to introduce conscription in Bosnia and Hercegovina in 1881, a revolt broke out among the local population. To quell this uprising, the *k.k.* military evacuated small posts instead of trying to defend all positions. The commander in Bosnia, *FZM* Hermann Baron von Dahlen, isolated the area in revolt and called in reinforcements before engaging in battle.[95] Officers avoided distinctive insignia, such as the black trousers, caps, sashes, and swords that differentiated them as leaders and gave the enemy obvious targets. Habsburg soldiers also received better equipment than in 1878, especially boots more suited to the rugged terrain. The troops had learned from their previous experiences to make their own provisions for food rather than rely on supply trains to catch up. The officers shared in the privations of their men and showed great talent for improvisation and humor while trying to alleviate the difficulties of campaigning in challenging conditions.[96] Austro-Hungarian officers, at least in this small operation, had finally started implementing the directives of the *k.k.* manuals, especially in preparing attacks with artillery fire and using terrain advantageously. Leaders as well as the rank and file showed themselves capable once again of adapting to the situation and had learned how to fight better from the recent conflict in Bosnia and Hercegovina.

Yet, certain problems arose just as before. Provisions for troops in the field ran short as the suppression dragged on from November 1881 until May 1882, more than twice as long as the 1878 campaign.[97] The war minister had to issue an order to conserve ammunition in February 1882 because the munitions service had not kept pace with the consumption of supplies. Because of the ensuing revolt, the *k.k.* military had to raise troop commitments to six divisions plus a naval squadron. They also requested an extra eight million florins from the Delegations and spent over 30 million to suppress the uprising.[98] The Habsburg high command responded to the problems and achieved victory over the insurrection, thus showing their ability to adapt and learn from past experience.

Parliamentary Criticism and Favor

Although parliamentary representatives granted the Habsburg high command's requests for extra funding to suppress the revolt, delegates still criticized military spending. During the debate for the 1880 budget, the Moravian delegate Fux, a member of the Delegations' army budget committee, raised the issue of pensions in the Austro-Hungarian army. Although not begrudging a pension to officers who had served their fatherland well and earned their retirement pay, Fux complained of seeing others who had received pensions for ill health gallivanting in "Pensionopolis" (Vienna) and zealously hunting and mountain climbing in other areas. The delegate found it strange how many officers who had passed the intellectual and physical requirements for advancement "suddenly became invalids and quickly obtained a pension." Fux attributed many cases of premature pensions to the *k.k.* practice of allowing influential people to create positions for their protégés by pushing an officer of higher rank to retire. Fux's mention of forming a new commission to test the validity of pension claims met with laughter among the delegates.[99] Obviously, parliamentary representatives did not see the solution to the army's pension problem as yet another board, more proof of the overly bureaucratic Habsburg military. Although the army had made progress during the 1870s, with better promotion and pension regulations, the large number of officers who received pensions because of "nervous breakdown" or "general exhaustion" revealed the increasing leniency of the pension arbitration commission in granting pensions.[100]

Fux also elicited laughter from the delegates when he brought up the common *k.k.* use of overqualified officers for positions that subordinates could easily fill, such as a field marshal commanding a division, a major general leading a brigade, and a colonel heading a *Landwehr* infantry battalion that a captain had commanded earlier and another captain led now. This situation resulted from the superabundance of high ranking officers in the military, together with an insufficient number of non-commissioned officers. The representative pointedly asked, "Why does it not happen also in the realm of civil administration that a governor is replaced by precinct officers or a financial district director by a tax collector?"[101]

Delegate Fux accused the government ministers of self-deception if they believed the Habsburg war ministry's claim of a savings of four million florins in the proposed budget. The parliamentary representative wondered how the army could save so much when its projected reforms would result in a permanent increase in officer wages, a military tax oppressive for the population, better provisions for the rank and file, and the procurement of new fortress cannon. Although Fux supported improving the food supplied to *k.k.* soldiers, the delegate questioned the necessity of fortifying the imperial capital. He also recommended reductions in the "not decisive parade service" and in the number of absentee commanders.[102]

Fux also pointed out that the Austro-Hungarian army had the smallest budget of all the European military states of similar rank. Russian expenses had increased from 219 million florins in 1865 to 365 million in 1879, French outlays had risen by 60% to 270 million, and the Germans spent 213 million or 110% more than in 1865. In the same period, the Habsburg budget had increased by only half a million florins to 115.5 million. The parliamentary delegate believed that the *k.k.* military expenses weighed more heavily on the Austro-Hungarian people than the army budgets of France and Germany did on their populations. The total income of France's population in 1871 amounted to eight billion francs, while Prussia's came to four billion. The income of the Austrian half of the Habsburg Empire was a mere 800 million florins. Despite his criticisms, Fux declared himself ready to vote in favor of the 115 million florin budget that the war minister presented to the Delegations.[103]

Dr. Sturm, speaking on behalf of the Delegations' army budget committee, differed with Fux on the actual sum of the war ministry's proposal. Sturm asserted that the delegates must take into consideration not only the cost of the *Ordinarium* (ordinary budget) but also the *Extraordinarium* (extraordinary budget) as well as the *Landwehr*, the *Honvéd*, and the troops in Bosnia-Hercegovina. All of these sums raised the total to 130 million florins, and thus surpassed the 1865 *k.k.* budget. Sturm, however, was encouraged by the war minister's desire to find ways to save money and hoped that this wish would translate into significant savings in the future.[104] The old problems plaguing promotions and pensions continued to exist, despite the assurances of the war minister *FZM* Artur Maximilian Count Bylandt-Rheidt that Habsburg leaders always took proper measures to avoid errors in awarding advancement and retirement payments.[105] For the most part, the delegates brought up no major objections to the military budget.

None of the delegates spoke of outrageous expenses, although Fux did mention the large sums allocated for fortifications. The Austro-Hungarian high command still favored pouring immense amounts of money into permanent fortresses. The Habsburg military did not stand alone in its convictions about the importance of fortifications. According to Captain Hugo von Molnár of the general staff, France spent over 35 million florins on upgrading the fortresses along the German border, and Germany 100 million for the expansion of 23 fortified sites throughout its empire. Even the Italian government granted 18 million florins for improving fortresses, especially along the Austro-Hungarian border. By contrast, Habsburg parliamentary delegates balked at giving 200,000 florins to continue fortifying the supposedly crucial fortress of Przemyśl in Galicia.[106] However, after 1878, delegates had fewer objections to military spending.

Fruits of Victory: Public and Parliamentary Approval

One reason for this change in the attitude of the parliamentary representatives stemmed from the success of Austro-Hungarian armed forces in Bosnia and Hercegovina. According to Andrássy's biographer, Eduard von Wertheimer, the residents of the Habsburg Empire had formed their opinion of the *k.k.* military primarily from the defeats of 1859 and 1866 and, since then, from parliamentary debates. The victorious occupation of the two Turkish provinces in 1878 presented the army as the triumphant arm of the government, more effective than diplomats. Because Austro-Hungarian troops had fulfilled the mandate of the Congress of Berlin to take Bosnia and Hercegovina, public opinion both within the Habsburg Empire and abroad now saw the *k.k.* army as proof of the great power status of the Habsburg Empire.[107] The press also helped promote this victorious image of the military through their reporting of the progress of *k.k.* forces during August, September, and October 1878. The *Wiener Sonn- und Montags-Zeitung* even boasted that the campaign had eliminated national differences between the various peoples of the empire: "Germans, Slavs, Hungarians, and Italians fulfilled their duty in equal fashion and fought with equal enthusiasm for the honor and good of their common fatherland."[108] Without the exaggerated style of the press, Major Benkiser wrote truthfully that most parliamentary representatives in both halves of the empire honored the army in their speeches, while public opinion toward the military took "a completely different position than was the case just a few years before."[109] Foreign newspapers also noted the support of the Austro-Hungarian people for the army in Bosnia. The French newspaper *Le Figaro* reported that even the Hungarian population rejoiced at the fall of Sarajevo.[110] The British press published a British statesman's view of Austria-Hungary as a strong power and one of the best administered in Europe.[111]

Delegation debate over the expenses of the Habsburg navy in 1880 illustrates the change in attitude of the parliamentary representatives. Hardly any discussion took place, even though the war ministry asked for funds to build new ships, an unusual request during the 1870s and 1880s. The presenter of the report from the Delegations' budget commission, Dr. Ruß, succinctly stated that the first installment for a new battleship, the *Tegethoff*, appeared now in the *Extraordinarium* rather than the *Ordinarium* and that the first two installments for two new gunboats appeared in the *Ordinarium*. The deduction that the commission recommended for the two gunboats came from a desire for better business accounting methods, not because the two new boats were considered unnecessary. When the president of the Delegations opened the floor for general debate concerning the naval budget, no discussion took place. The special debate consisted merely in delegate approval for the various parts of the *Ordinarium* request, amounting to 7,674,552 florins, and for the *Extraordinarium*, an additional 900,350 florins. Even the first installment of 600,000 florins for building the new battleship did not raise any objections.[112]

Naval expenses comprised a small part of the total budget of 197,961,512 florins for the *k.k.* military, a mere 4.4% and roughly half of the expense needed to maintain troops in Bosnia and Hercegovina.[113] Outlays for the maritime branch of the Habsburg armed forces did not consume excessive amounts of funding. However, of all the great military powers of Europe, Austria-Hungary had the least cause to build a fleet of battleships. Britain and France had already held overseas possessions for many years. Germany, Russia, and Italy had also begun to acquire colonies in the latter half of the nineteenth century. Franz Joseph, however, did not engage wholeheartedly in the imperialist drive to gain lands in Asia and Africa. Therefore, the *k.k.* navy saw its main purpose as protection of the Habsburg part of the Adriatic coast and its few ports. Although Admiral Wilhelm von Tegetthoff had defeated Italy at the battle of Lissa in 1866, Austria-Hungary still felt that the Italian navy constituted the greatest threat. During the political isolation of the Habsburg Empire before signing the Dual Alliance with Germany in 1879 and the Triple Alliance that included Italy along with Germany and Austria-Hungary in 1881, the *k.k.* military believed in upgrading its naval strength. This view did not coincide with the reality of the Habsburg situation, which did not require great naval power to defend the empire's Adriatic coast. The funds spent on the navy could have gone to other more vital needs, such as the procurement of Krupp cannon. Nevertheless, delegates granted the florins that the war minister requested for the navy.

The more favorable attitude of parliamentary representatives also stemmed from the economizing measures of the war minister, *FZM* Bylandt-Rheidt, in whom Dr. Sturm expressed confidence during the 1880 budget debate.[114] Bylandt-Rheidt, a veteran of 1848–1849 in Hungary and a general staff officer in Italy in 1859, had presided over the Artillery Committee in 1864 and the Technical and Administrative Military Committee in 1869 before becoming war minister in June 1876.[115] Bylandt-Rheidt, a proponent of more constitutional government, held the position of war minister until 1888, longer than any other Austro-Hungarian war minister, thus giving stability to the *k.k.* military during his tenure.

Conclusion

The occupation of Bosnia and Hercegovina in 1878 gave the Habsburg army a chance to test the new reforms and weaponry that the high command had implemented over the previous 12 years. Even though the irregular opponents encountered by Austro-Hungarian forces in the two Turkish provinces did not compare with the armies of the military powers of Europe, *k.k.* troops had ample opportunities to prove the benefits of the reforms since the catastrophe of 1866. The breech-loading Werndl rifles gave the Habsburg infantry a distinct advantage over the insurgents. The 80-mm and 90-mm field guns as well as the new mountain mortars instilled fear in the enemy and provided devastating firepower for destroying prepared positions. Although having little influence in battle, the cavalry proved valuable by performing security and reconnaissance services and supporting difficult communications in undeveloped lands. The emphasis on more open tactics with flank attacks, rather than closed frontal assaults, found success on the Bosnian and Hercegovinian battlefields. Officers and men fought well together, with the officers sharing in the hardships of the rank and file and no nationalistic problems arising. In general, the *k.k.* army had adapted to rough conditions and performed well in 1878, and again in 1881–1882 when insurgents rose in revolt in the two provinces.

Problems, however, still existed. The supply system had broken down. The campaigns had lasted longer than expected and required a large number of additional troops. Tactical manuals continued to advocate frontal attacks culminating in the bayonet fight. A significant number of cavalry officers still believed in the primacy of shock tactics and *élan* in the use of the mounted branch. The Habsburg high command insisted on maintaining and upgrading the cordon system of permanent fortresses. Rivalry persisted among military leaders, though Bylandt-Rheidt had succeeded in bringing more stability to the war ministry.

The Russo-Turkish War of 1877–1878 gave another opportunity to observe the changes in modern warfare. This conflict revealed the increasing importance of massed artillery on the battlefield as well as the inanity of frontal assaults on fortified positions. Cavalry contributed more than ever before, not by participating in battle but by performing vital reconnaissance and security roles. Temporary fortifications proved extremely effective, especially at Plevna. The mobilization process showed the need for greater use of technical troops and railroads for quick and effective deployment of forces. Habsburg officers tended to interpret the lessons of the Russo-Turkish War in ways that reinforced their previous ideas, whether right or wrong, instead of rethinking the methods of war.

Chronic financial difficulties continued to exist. The *k.k.* high command had still not solved excessive pensioning and the influence of patronage on promotions. The Habsburg army also spent vast amounts on permanent fortifications. Parliamentary representatives questioned spending money on parades and absentee commanders. Yet, the delegates devoted less time to debating military budgets than before and mentioned fewer examples of army wastefulness. Victory not only covered the army's deficiencies but also improved the way that delegates and the public viewed the army.

Major Benkiser made a very significant point at the end of his article on the occupation of Bosnia and Hercegovina: "The principal benefit of the last campaign consists of the raising of the self-confidence of the army."[116] Even with the introduction of the new *Wehrgesetz* in 1868 and the procurement of better weaponry for all branches of the armed forces, the *k.k.* military needed an opportunity to prove its worth on the battlefield. Invasion of the two Turkish provinces at the behest of the other European powers at the Congress of Berlin delivered the desired result: military success for the Habsburg troops. With the renewed confidence of the press and civilian government, the Austro-Hungarian army could enter the next phase of its development as the high command endeavored to compete with the rest of Europe in the ever-increasing pace of technological innovation during the last two decades of the nineteenth century.

Notes

1. Franz Josef, "Armee-Befehl vom 19.10.1878," *Österreichische Militärische Zeitschrift (ÖMZ)* 3 & 4 (1878): 1–2.
2. General Baron Zeddeler, "Das Gefecht der russischen Infanterie im letzten Kriege," *ÖMZ* 3–4 (1878): 221.
3. Thilo von Trotha, "Tactical Studies on the Battles around Plevna," translated by First Lieutenant Carl Reichmann U.S. Army (Kansas City, MO: Hudson-Kimberley Publishing Co., 1896), 210–211. Von Trotha held the rank of captain in the German army.
4. Zeddeler, "Das Gefecht der russischen Infanterie im letzten Kriege," 222–223. Zeddeler had warned the Russian high command earlier about the dangers of attacking troops equipped with breech-loading rifles, but to no avail. See Bruce W. Menning, *Bayonets Before Bullets: The Imperial Russian Army, 1861–1914* (Bloomington & Indianapolis: Indiana University Press, 1992), 71.
5. Lieutenant Colonel Victor Ritter von Neuwirth, "Das Gefecht der russischen Infanterie im Feldzuge 1877–78, im Vergleiche mit unseren tactischen Vorschriften," *ÖMZ* 1–2 (1879): 294.
6. Hauptmann Emil Medycki, "Die tactischen Lehren, welche aus dem russisch-türkischen Kriege 1877–78 resultiren," *Organ der militärwissenschaftlichen Vereine (O.)* 22 (1881): 17–18, 29.
7. K.u.k. KS Taktik I. Jahrgang 1881/2 Vortrage des Major Anton Gartner, KA Militärschule, KS Karton Nr. 59, Studienbehelfe: Strategie und Taktik; Lieutenant Colonel Alois Hauschka, "Zur Entwicklung der Kampfweise der österreichischen Infanterie seit 1867," *ÖMZ* 3–4 (1879): 170–172.

8. Zeddeler, "Das Gefecht der russischen Infanterie im letzten Kriege," 223–224.
9. Neuwirth, "Das Gefecht der russischen Infanterie im Feldzuge 1877–78, im Vergleiche mit unseren tactischen Vorschriften," 289–291; Medycki, "Die tactischen Lehren, welche aus dem russisch-türkischen Kriege 1877–78 resultiren," 20–21.
10. Neuwirth, "Das Gefecht der russischen Infanterie im Feldzuge 1877–78, im Vergleiche mit unseren tactischen Vorschriften," 287.
11. Captain Alexander Pervulesco, "Einiges über der Verwendung der russischen Cavallerie," *ÖMZ* 1–2 (1880): 189–201.
12. Captain Alexander Pervulesco, "Über Befestigungen," *ÖMZ* 3–4 (1878): 116–124.
13. Lieutenant Colonel Carl Geissner, "Über flüchtige Befestigungen mit Rücksicht auf die jüngsten Kriegs-Erfahrungen und Übungen mit dem Infanterie-Spaten," *O.* 20 (1880): 313.
14. Menning, *Bayonets Before Bullets: The Imperial Russian Army, 1861–1914*, 60–74.
15. "Die flüchtigen Befestigungen auf dem Schlachtfelde bei Königgrätz," *ÖMZ* 3 (1866): 327–328, 333–334.
16. Captain Carl Regenspursky, "Vorträge über den russisch-türkischen Krieg im Jahre 1877," *O.* 16 (1878): 20–21.
17. First Lieutenant Moriz Brunner, "Reichsbefestigung und Eisenbahnen," *ÖMZ* 2 (1868): 133–134, 147–148.
18. A., "Die Eisenbahnen im deutsch-französischen Kriege 1870," *ÖMZ* 1 (1871): 191; Colonel Winterhalder, "Eisenbahnen als Kriegsmittel. Mit Rückblicken auf ihre Leistungen im Kriege 1870–71," *ÖMZ* 1 (1876).
19. "Die russische Bahnbenützung im Jahre 1877. Eine Aufforderung zur Reorganisation der Feld-Eisenbahn-Truppen," *ÖMZ* 4 (1877): 23–28.
20. Scott Lackey, *The Rebirth of the Habsburg Army: Friedrich Beck and the Rise of the General Staff* (Westport, CT: Greenwood Press, 1995), 43–44, 61, 113.
21. Barbara Jelavich, *The Habsburg Empire in European Affairs, 1814–1918* (Chicago: Rand McNally & Co., 1969), 119–122; C.A. Macartney, *The Habsburg Empire, 1790–1918* (London: Weidenfeld and Nicolson, 1968), 592.
22. *Die Occupation Bosniens und der Hercegovina durch k.k. Truppen im Jahre 1878* (Vienna: k.k. Generalstab and L.W. Seidel & Sohn, 1879), 114, 276–277.
23. FZM Daniel Freiherr von Salis-Soglio, *Mein Leben und was ich davon erzählen will, kann und darf*, vol. II (Stuttgart and Leipzig: Deutsche Verlags-Anstalt, 1908), 76.
24. Lackey, *The Rebirth of the Habsburg Army*, 77.

25. Salis-Soglio, *Mein Leben und was ich davon erzählen will, kann und darf*, vol. II, 76.
26. Gunther E. Rothenberg, *The Army of Francis Joseph* (West Lafayette, IN: Purdue University Press, 1976), 101–102.
27. *Die Occupation Bosniens und der Hercegovina durch k.k. Truppen im Jahre 1878*, 126–146, 242–257.
28. *Die Occupation Bosniens und der Hercegovina durch k.k. Truppen im Jahre 1878*, 420–451; Lackey, *The Rebirth of the Habsburg Army*, 78–79.
29. *Die Occupation Bosniens und der Hercegovina durch k.k. Truppen im Jahre 1878*, 288–296.
30. Lackey, *The Rebirth of the Habsburg Army*, 79; Rothenberg, *The Army of Francis Joseph*,, 102.
31. *Die Occupation Bosniens und der Hercegovina durch k.k. Truppen im Jahre 1878*, 884–885.
32. *Die Occupation Bosniens und der Hercegovina durch k.k. Truppen im Jahre 1878*, Beilage 12, II–X.
33. Major Joshua Thiel, "COIN Manpower Ratios: Debunking the 10 to 1 Ratio and Surges," *Small Wars Journal* (Jan. 15, 2011): 1.
34. *Die Occupation Bosniens und der Hercegovina durch k.k. Truppen im Jahre 1878*, Beilage 12, X.
35. Major von Benkiser, "Rückblick auf die Operationen zur Besetzung Bosniens und der Hercegovina im Jahre 1878," *O.* 18 (1879), 418–419.
36. *Die Occupation Bosniens und der Hercegovina durch k.k. Truppen im Jahre 1878*, 888.
37. Benkiser, "Rückblick auf die Operationen zur Besetzung Bosniens und der Hercegovina im Jahre 1878," 418.
38. *Die Occupation Bosniens und der Hercegovina durch k.k. Truppen im Jahre 1878*, 885–888.
39. Hull, *Absolute Destruction: Military Culture and the Practices of War in Imperial Germany*, 7–43.
40. Captain Norbert Spaleny, "Eindrücke and Wahrnehmungen während der Occupations-Campagne in Bosnien vom Standpuncte des Troupiers," *O.* 19 (1879): 169.
41. Spaleny, "Eindrücke and Wahrnehmungen während der Occupations-Campagne in Bosnien vom Standpuncte des Troupiers," 170; *Die Occupation Bosniens und der Hercegovina durch k.k. Truppen im Jahre 1878*, 888.
42. Benkiser, "Rückblick auf die Operationen zur Besetzung Bosniens und der Hercegovina im Jahre 1878," *O.* 18 (1879), 418.
43. Spaleny, "Eindrücke and Wahrnehmungen während der Occupations-Campagne in Bosnien vom Standpuncte des Troupiers," 173.

44. K.u.k. KS Taktik I. Jahrgang 1881/2 Vortrage des Major Anton Gartner, KA Militärschule, KS Karton Nr. 59, Studienbehelfe: Strategie und Taktik, 78–79.
45. Hauschka, "Zur Entwicklung der Kampfweise der österreichischen Infanterie seit 1867," 170–172.
46. Benkiser, "Rückblick auf die Operationen zur Besetzung Bosniens und der Hercegovina im Jahre 1878419; Spaleny, "Eindrücke and Wahrnehmungen während der Occupations-Campagne in Bosnien vom Standpuncte des Troupiers," 172.
47. *Die Occupation Bosniens und der Hercegovina durch k.k. Truppen im Jahre 1878*, 98, Beilage 7.
48. K.u.k. KS Taktik I. Jahrgang 1881/2 Vortrage des Major Anton Gartner, KA Militärschule, KS Karton Nr. 59, Studienbehelfe: Strategie und Taktik, 170.
49. Major Friedrich Freiherrn Mühlwerth-Gärtner, "Der Reiterangriff auf Infanterie," *O.* 17 (1878): 29–30. Large bodies of French cavalry suffered heavy losses in futile attacks on Prussian infantry in 1870.
50. Major Karger, "Czegléd. Studie über die im September 1877 dort stattgehabten Cavallerie-Manöver," *ÖMZ* 3–4 (1878): 51.
51. Major Emil Dembsher, "Cavallerie-Attaken," *ÖMZ* 1–2 (1879): 245.
52. Pervulesco, "Einiges über der Verwendung der russischen Cavallerie," 197.
53. Dembsher, "Cavallerie-Attaken," 258–260.
54. Captain Hugo von Molnar, "Die Verwendung der deutschen Artillerie in der Schlacht bei Sedan," *O.* 20 (1880).
55. Lieutenant Colonel Hotze, "Reglement-Studie XXXV. Das Exercir-Reglement der k.k. Artillerie. Für Infanterie- und Cavallerie-Officiere," *ÖMZ* 1–2 (1879): 148.
56. Benkiser, "Rückblick auf die Operationen zur Besetzung Bosniens und der Hercegovina im Jahre 1878," 418; Spaleny, "Eindrücke and Wahrnehmungen während der Occupations-Campagne in Bosnien vom Standpuncte des Troupiers," 170; *Die Occupation Bosniens und der Hercegovina durch k.k. Truppen im Jahre 1878*, 888.
57. Walter Wagner, "Die k.(u.)k. Armee - Gliederung und Aufgabenstellung," in *Die Habsburgermonarchie 1848–1918*, Vol. 5 *Die Bewaffnete Macht* (Vienna: Verlag der Österreichischen Akademie der Wissenschaften, 1987), 450.
58. Lackey, *The Rebirth of the Habsburg Army*, 45.
59. Lieutenant Colonel Michael Trapsia, "Beitrag zur Verwendung der Streitkräfte. (Der Kampf der Infanterie.)" *O.* 18 (1879): 217–218.
60. GM Artur Maximilian Graf Bylandt-Rheidt, No. 5 Memoire uber den Stand der Bewaffnungsfrage, 22. XI. 1873, KA MKSM Sonderreihe, Karton Nr. 64, Studien.

61. Salis-Soglio, *Mein Leben und was ich davon erzählen will, kann und darf*, vol. II, 69–70.
62. Rothenberg, *The Army of Francis Joseph*, 84.
63. Salis-Soglio, *Mein Leben und was ich davon erzählen will, kann und darf*, vol. II, 70.
64. Salis-Soglio, *Mein Leben und was ich davon erzählen will, kann und darf*, vol. II,70; Rothenberg, *The Army of Francis Joseph*, 844.
65. "Die Ring-Hohlgeschosse des Generals von Uchatius," *ÖMZ* 4 (1875): 119–126; Hauptmann Ottomar Volkmer, "Über Stahl-Bronce," *O.* 10 (1875): 246–247; Volkmer, "Vergleichende Gegenüberstellung des neuen österreichischen und deutschen Feld-Artillerie-Materiales," *ÖMZ* 1 (1877): 160.
66. "Die Uchatius-Kanonen," *ÖMZ* 3 (1875): 107.
67. "Die Feuerprobe unserer Wehrverfassung," *Wiener Sonn- und Montags-Zeitung*, 21. October 1878, Nr. 83, 2.
68. Benkiser, "Rückblick auf die Operationen zur Besetzung Bosniens und der Hercegovina im Jahre 1878," 419.
69. v.B., "Die neuesten Versuche mit der Krupp'schen Panzerkanone," *ÖMZ* 4 (1877): 112–114.
70. *Die Occupation Bosniens und der Hercegovina durch k.k. Truppen im Jahre 1878*, 52–53.
71. "Verschanzungen und Festungen," *O.* 19 (1879): 157–159.
72. Graf Geldern-Egmond, "Über die neuesten Versuche mit Eisenpanzern und deren Anwendung auf die Lösung der Befestigungsfrage," *O.* 16 (1878): 355–371.
73. "Die Occupation," *Neue Freie Presse*, 20. August 1878, Nr. 5021, 2.
74. Eduard von Wertheimer, *Graf Julius Andrássy, sein Leben und seine Zeit*, vol. III (Stuttgart: Deutsche Verlags-Anstalt, 1913), 152–155.
75. *Tagespost*, 15. January 1879, Graz.
76. Ludwig Ritter von Przibram, *Erinnerungen eines alten Österreichers* (Stuttgart-Leipzig: Deutsche Verlags-Anstalt, 1912), vol. II, 78–79.
77. "Wien, 19. August," *Neue Freie Presse*, 20. August 1878, No. 5021, 1.
78. Rothenberg, *The Army of Francis Joseph*, 102.
79. Lackey, *The Rebirth of the Habsburg Army*, 77–79.
80. Moritz Freiherr von Auffenberg-Komarów, *Aus Österreichs Höhe und Niedergang - eine Lebensschilderung* (Munich: Drei Masken Verlag, 1921), 44–45.
81. Benkiser, "Rückblick auf die Operationen zur Besetzung Bosniens und der Hercegovina im Jahre 1878," 419.
82. Auffenberg, *Aus Österreichs Höhe und Niedergang - eine Lebensschilderung*, 46.
83. Auffenberg, *Aus Österreichs Höhe und Niedergang - eine Lebensschilderung*, 50.

84. Lawrence Sondhaus, *Franz Conrad von Hötzendorf: Architect of the Apocalypse* (Boston: Humanities Press, 2000), 20.
85. Franz Graf Conrad von Hötzendorf, *Mein Anfang: Kriegserinnerungen aus der Jugendzeit 1878–1882* (Berlin: Verlag für Kulturpolitik, 1925), 31–35.
86. Sondhaus, *Franz Conrad von Hötzendorf*, 20.
87. Hull, *Absolute Destruction*, 1–4.
88. Benkiser, "Rückblick auf die Operationen zur Besetzung Bosniens und der Hercegovina im Jahre 1878," 419; Spaleny, "Eindrücke and Wahrnehmungen während der Occupations-Campagne in Bosnien vom Standpuncte des Troupiers," 172.
89. Georg Freiherr von Holtz, *Von Brod bis Sarajevo* (Vienna, Leipzig: Stern, 1907), 184–191.
90. Benkiser, "Rückblick auf die Operationen zur Besetzung Bosniens und der Hercegovina im Jahre 1878," 419.
91. Lackey, *The Rebirth of the Habsburg Army*, 80. Philippović officially requested permission to return to his previous position as commanding general in Prague.
92. Rothenberg, *The Army of Francis Joseph*, 246; see note 77.
93. Lackey, *The Rebirth of the Habsburg Army*, 82.
94. FML Franz Baron Kuhn von Kuhnenfeld, Nachlässe Kuhn, Karton Nr. 670, 14–15, 34.
95. Rothenberg, *The Army of Francis Joseph*, 103.
96. Josef Maria Aloysius Graf von Stürgkh, *Politische und militärische Erinnerungen* (Leipzig: Paul List Verlag, 1922), 35, 48–49.
97. Charles Jelavich, "The Revolt in Bosnia-Hercegovina, 1881–2," *The Slavonic and East European Review* 31, No. 77 (June 1953): 434.
98. "Wien, 27. Januar", "Inland," *Neue Freie Presse*, 28. Januar 1882, Nr. 6258, 1–3; Charles Jelavich, "The Revolt in Bosnia-Hercegovina, 1881–2," 424; Rothenberg, *The Army of Francis Joseph*, 104.
99. *Stenographische Sitzungs-Protokolle der Delegation des Reichsrathes*, 4. Sitzung der 12. Session am 6. Februar 1880 (Vienna: k.k. Hof- und Staatsdruckerei, 1880), 75.
100. István Deák, *Beyond Nationalism: A Social and Political History of the Habsburg Officer Corps, 1848–1918* (New York: Oxford University Press, 1992), 151–152.
101. *Stenographische Sitzungs-Protokolle der Delegation des Reichsrathes*, 4. Sitzung der 12. Session am 6. Februar 1880, 74.
102. *Stenographische Sitzungs-Protokolle der Delegation des Reichsrathes*, 4. Sitzung der 12. Session am 6. Februar 1880, 74–76.

103. *Stenographische Sitzungs-Protokolle der Delegation des Reichsrathes*, 4. Sitzung der 12. Session am 6. Februar 1880, 73.
104. *Stenographische Sitzungs-Protokolle der Delegation des Reichsrathes*, 4. Sitzung der 12. Session am 6. Februar 1880, 71–72, 79–80.
105. *Stenographische Sitzungs-Protokolle der Delegation des Reichsrathes*, 4. Sitzung der 12. Session am 6. Februar 1880, 78.
106. Hauptmann Hugo von Molnár, "Über Heeres-Budgets. Eine militärstatistische Studie," *O.* 14 (1877): 130–131.
107. Eduard von Wertheimer, *Graf Julius Andrássy, sein Leben und seine Zeit*, vol. III (Stuttgart: Deutsche Verlags-Anstalt, 1913), 156–157.
108. "Die Feuerprobe unserer Wehrverfassung," *Wiener Sonn- und Montags-Zeitung*, 21. October 1878, Nr. 83, 2.
109. Benkiser, "Rückblick auf die Operationen zur Besetzung Bosniens und der Hercegovina im Jahre 1878," 419–420.
110. "La Presse Étrangère au Jour le Jour," *Le Figaro*, 25 August 1878, 2.
111. "Arrival of the English Mail," *The Argus*, 12 September 1878, 6.
112. *Stenographische Sitzungs-Protokolle der Delegation des Reichsrathes*, 4. Sitzung der 12. Session am 6. Februar 1880, 84–86.
113. *Budget Übersicht, 1868–1911*, KA Generalstab Operationsbüro, Karton Nr. 806, Budget-Entwurfe.
114. *Stenographische Sitzungs-Protokolle der Delegation des Reichsrathes*, 4. Sitzung der 12. Session am 6. Februar 1880, 72.
115. *Österreichisches Biographisches Lexikon 1815–1950* Vol. 1 (Vienna: Verlag der Österreichischen Akademie der Wissenschaften, 1957), 132.
116. Benkiser, "Rückblick auf die Operationen zur Besetzung Bosniens und der Hercegovina im Jahre 1878," 419.

Bibliography

Unpublished Documents

Kriegsarchiv (KA), Vienna.
Allerhöchster Oberbefehl (AhOB).
Militärkanzlei Seiner Majestät des Kaisers (MKSM) Sonderreihe 1866–1918.
Chef des Generalstabs (GSt) Operationsbüro 1866–1918.
Zentralstellen.
Kriegsministerium (KM) Präsidialbüro (Präsidium) 1866–1918.
Militärerziehungs- und Bildungsanstalten (MEB).
Kriegsschule Wien 1867–1914.

Published Primary Sources

Auffenberg-Komarów, Moritz Freiherr von. *Aus Österreichs Höhe und Niedergang - eine Lebensschilderung*. Munich: Drei Masken Verlag, 1921.

Conrad von Hötzendorf, Franz Graf *Mein Anfang: Kriegserinnerungen aus der Jugendzeit 1878–1882*. Berlin: Verlag für Kulturpolitik, 1925.

Die Occupation Bosniens und der Hercegovina durch k.k. Truppen im Jahre 1878. Vienna: k.k. Generalstab and L.W. Seidel & Sohn, 1879.

Holtz, Georg Freiherr von. *Von Brod bis Sarajevo*. Vienna, Leipzig: Stern, 1907.

Le Figaro, 1878.

Neue Freie Presse, 1878.

Organ der militärwissenschaftlichen Vereine (O.), 1867–1906.

Österreichische Militärische Zeitschrift (ÖMZ), 1866–1914.

Przibram, Ludwig Ritter von. *Erinnerungen eines alten Österreichers*. Stuttgart-Leipzig: Deutsche Verlags-Anstalt, 1912.

Salis-Soglio, FZM Daniel Freiherr von. *Mein Leben und was ich davon erzählen will, kann und darf.* Stuttgart and Leipzig: Deutsche Verlags-Anstalt, 1908.

Stenographische Sitzungs-Protokolle der Delegation des Reichsrathes. Vienna: k.k. Hof- und Staatsdruckerei, 1869–1911.

Stürgkh, Josef Maria Aloysius Graf von. *Politische und militärische Erinnerungen*. Leipzig: Paul List Verlag, 1922.

Tagespost, 1879.

The Argus, 1878.

Trotha, Thilo von. "Tactical Studies on the Battles around Plevna," translated by First Lieutenant Carl Reichmann U.S. Army. Kansas City, MO: Hudson-Kimberley Publishing Co., 1896.

Wertheimer, Eduard von. *Graf Julius Andrássy, sein Leben und seine Zeit.* Stuttgart: Deutsche Verlags-Anstalt, 1913.

Wiener Sonn- und Montags-Zeitung, 1878.

Secondary Sources

Deák, István. *Beyond Nationalism: A Social and Political History of the Habsburg Officer Corps, 1848–1918*. New York: Oxford University Press, 1992.

Hull, Isabel V. *Absolute Destruction: Military Culture and the Practices of War in Imperial Germany*. Ithaca: Cornell University Press, 2005.

Jelavich, Barbara. *The Habsburg Empire in European Affairs, 1814–1918*. Chicago: Rand McNally & Co., 1969.

Jelavich, Charles. "The Revolt in Bosnia-Hercegovina, 1881–1882." *The Slavonic and East European Review* 31, No. 77 (June 1953): 420–436.

Lackey, Scott. *The Rebirth of the Habsburg Army: Friedrich Beck and the Rise of the General Staff.* Westport, CT: Greenwood Press, 1995.

Macartney, C.A. *The Habsburg Empire 1790–1918*. London: Weidenfeld and Nicolson, 1969.

Menning, Bruce W. *Bayonets before Bullets: The Imperial Russian Army, 1861–1914*. Bloomington & Indianapolis: Indiana University Press, 1992.

Österreichisches Biographisches Lexikon 1815–1950 Vol. 1. Vienna: Verlag der Österreichischen Akademie der Wissenschaften, 1957.

Rothenberg, Gunther E. *The Army of Francis Joseph*. West Lafayette, Indiana: Purdue University Press, 1976.

Sondhaus, Lawrence. *Franz Conrad von Hötzendorf: Architect of the Apocalypse*. Boston: Humanities Press, 2000.

Thiel, Major Joshua. "COIN Manpower Ratios: Debunking the 10 to 1 Ratio and Surges." *Small Wars Journal* (Jan. 15, 2011), http://smallwarsjournal.com/jrnl/art/coin-manpower-ratios-debunking-the-10-to-1-ratio-and-surges (accessed 10 January 2012).

Wagner, Walter. "Die k.(u.)k. Armee—Gliederung und Aufgabenstellung." in *Die Habsburgermonarchie 1848–1918*, Vol. 5 *Die Bewaffnete Macht*. Vienna: Verlag der Österreichischen Akademie der Wissenschaften, 1987.

CHAPTER 5

From Progress to Reversion

Captain Reska, a retired Habsburg cavalry captain, drawing from the writings of the German Hegelian philosopher Conrad Hermann on the philosophy of history, stated, "As once force had to be overcome by sense of honor in order to bring the moral element to supremacy, so in future handicraft will be surpassed by science in order to bring the intellectual into prominence.—This is the next stage in the progress of history, that certainly appears threatened by a still closer reaction, which at least in our army will be prevented only by a universal effort."[1]

Reska aptly assessed the most important aspects of the age that all European armies had entered by the 1880s. The era of fast-paced technological innovation created a quandary for military high commands. In the presence of multiple versions of new weapons, in particular the repeating rifle and ever-improving artillery, leaders had to make the right decisions for procurement and also choose quickly enough to stay ahead or at least keep pace with the other powers. At the same time, as technology presented more and more inventions for the use of armies, too early a choice would result in an obsolete weapons system. High-ranking officers had the responsibility of choosing correctly among all the alternatives, thereby asserting the supremacy of the intellect through science over mere handicraft. For the Habsburg high command, less funding than the other European powers created even more difficulty. Imprudent spending decisions only exacerbated this situation as the Austro-Hungarian army wasted large sums on needless permanent fortifications and naval expenditures.

J.A. Dredger, *Tactics and Procurement in the Habsburg Military, 1866–1918*, DOI 10.1007/978-3-319-57678-7_5

Military establishments had to make difficult decisions in a rapidly advancing technological environment, and leaders had to fend off the backward-looking members of the army, especially older officers and those in the cavalry, where advocates of shock and *élan* still had great influence. Such reactionary attitudes remained embedded in the Austro-Hungarian mounted forces as well as in other branches and prompted Reska's remark that concerted opposition to retrogression was necessary, a reference to Franz Joseph's personal motto *Viribus Unitis*. Under the general peace of the last two decades of the nineteenth century, the *k.k.* high command had to persevere in its attempts to adapt to the requirements of modern warfare. After the 1878 campaign in Bosnia and Hercegovina and the revolt there in 1881–1882, Austro-Hungarian leaders had to update tactics, procure new weaponry, decide the role of each branch, prepare defenses for the empire, improve the railroad and communications network, and raise the standards of military education, all without the benefit of testing reforms in actual combat or observing the wars of other powers. Moreover, the high command faced the ever-present obstacle of convincing the Delegations to fund the expensive demands of the armed forces. Following the victory of 1878, however, the *k.k.* military appeared capable of successfully overcoming these challenges.

Despite the difficulties of this era, the Austro-Hungarian high command improved the weaponry of the infantry and adapted the role of cavalry to the modern battlefield. The war ministry remained stable and relations with the Delegations continued favorably. The first half of the 1890s, however, proved a disastrously harmful turning point for *k.k.* development as the offensive *à outrance* returned to the tactical sphere with the rise of Conrad von Hötzendorf and the death of Archduke Albrecht. Together with these events, the increasing problem of numerical inferiority in comparison with the other European powers as well as mismanagement of funds foretold future ruin for the Austro-Hungarian military.

Repeater Rifles and Tactics

One of the most important tasks for Habsburg military leaders was procuring a repeating rifle with magazines to compete with other European powers. The Prussian field marshal Helmuth von Moltke, victorious in 1866 against Austria and in 1870 against France, stated before the German parliament that the magazine rifle epitomized the competitive strivings of all great powers to retain their status of major military might and, thus, the procurement of repeaters became unavoidable.[2] A military chancellery memorandum of October 1886 detailed the history of the repeater, with the advantages and disadvantages of the various models based on the extensive testing that the *k.k.* army had carried out with the new weapons. The memorandum's main emphasis lay in stressing the necessity of acquiring magazine rifles for Austro-Hungarian troops, not only for the main army but also for the reserves. The Werndl breech-loaders, already 12–14 years old, had reached the end of their usefulness. Now Habsburg forces needed the technological superiority of the repeater to render the army battle-ready.[3]

The Austro-Hungarian high command and the officer corps almost universally supported the acquisition of repeating rifles and thus displayed a continuing interest in new technology. War Minister *FZM* Artur Maximilian Count Bylandt-Rheidt underscored the importance of the new weapon to the budget committee of the Hungarian Delegation thus: "Do you have the courage to set our army with its present rifle against an enemy with the repeating weapon? I don't!"[4] Years before, at the request of the *k.k.* leadership, officers had engaged in experiments to find the best model of magazine rifle. One officer optimistically concluded that the procurement of the repeater for the Habsburg infantry would raise the Austro-Hungarian army to the highest rank of all European states, most of which had already begun exploring the capabilities of magazine rifles. The French navy had even started to issue repeaters to its sailors in 1879.[5]

Although Franz Joseph approved the procurement of the Mannlicher repeating rifle for the Habsburg military in 1886, the new weapon did not reach soldiers until 1889.[6] This rifle, the invention of the Austrian arms designer Ferdinand Baron von Mannlicher, used a straight-pull bolt action and a five-round *en bloc* clip. Although prone to collect mud and dirt that clogged the bolt action, the Mannlicher repeater shot accurately and dependably because it contained fewer components than most other rifle designs. Thus, the new rifle represented a significant upgrade over the single-shot Werndl.[7] Austro-Hungarian army leaders realized the necessity of introducing the magazine rifle to keep pace with other European nations and thus maintain the Habsburg Empire's status as a major military power. According to one of the favorite sayings of contributors to the *ÖMZ* and the *Organ der militärwissenschaftlichen*

Vereine, "Standing still is a step backwards."[8] This saying aptly fit the *k.k.* view on the necessity of acquiring the Mannlicher magazine rifle.

Questions arose, however, regarding how the repeating rifle would affect tactics. Austro-Hungarian officers agreed that the new weapon would change how armies fought, though there differences of opinion arose on how much change would take place. One officer argued that the principles of fire tactics ought to remain unchanged, but the depth of troop formations might have to alter.[9] Another officer incredibly advocated thicker square formations in the face of repeating weapons.[10] Lieutenant Colonel Gustav Ratzenhofer of the general staff corps, the leading interpreter of the 1874 *k.k.* regulations, author of several tactical manuals, and one of the only officers to assert his doubts publicly about the wisdom of arming Habsburg troops with repeaters, warned about the dangers of wasting ammunition at an extraordinary rate with magazine rifles. Basing his judgment on the target practice of Austro-Hungarian soldiers, who shot only three bullets per minute rather than the six or seven a trained marksman would, Ratzenhofer reiterated his belief that *k.k.* infantryman received poor training. Unlike peacetime target practice, when there is no pressure to shoot quickly, the battlefield presents a completely different situation. During a firefight, the nervous and poorly trained soldier will shoot as quickly as he can and waste all his ammunition. The magazine rifle would only exacerbate this problem. Therefore, regardless of the obvious advantages of the repeater, the Habsburg army would have to instill fire discipline in the troops before the men could make efficient use of the new weaponry.[11]

Despite the exponential increase in firepower given by the repeating rifle, the Austro-Hungarian high command failed to adapt *k.k.* battle tactics correctly to account for this dramatic rise in destructive force. In 1870, a division could fire 40,000 rounds per minute with breech-loaders. By 1890, the same division could shoot 200,000 rounds per minute with magazine rifles.[12] *FML* Zeno Count Welser von Welsersheimb, a former adjutant of Archduke Albrecht in 1866 and land defense minister from 1880 to 1905, pointed out that the new 1889 infantry regulations failed to emphasize the art of shooting. Welser stressed the importance of gaining fire superiority with accurate shooting rather than relying on the number of bullets fired. Explaining that a soldier could shoot an average of 100 bullets in 10 min, the land defense minister calculated that each man would consume all his ammunition within half an hour and thus become inoperative for battle. Well-aimed shots would produce more hits and bring about victory through more efficient and effective firepower.[13]

Nevertheless, tactical manuals from the Habsburg war college continued to advocate frontal assaults culminating in bayonet charges, and train future general staff officers to adhere to these ideas.[14] Although *k.k.* infantry regulations emphasized the great difficulties of frontal assault, the instructions impressed upon officers the need to bring firepower forward for decisive results. In field exercises, troop leaders continued to drive toward the enemy and instill an offensive mindset in the soldiers. The contradictory stance of stressing the importance of firepower while constantly pressing forward ensured that an attacking spirit remained in the Austro-Hungarian army.[15] Despite this spirit, the Habsburg military had made progress since 1866 in adapting tactics to the increased fire of breech-loading and repeating rifles. With more emphasis on firepower, Albrecht and Ratzenhofer opposed the offensive *à outrance* of the past and allowed the defensive to enter tactical debates. This improvement began to end with the rise of Franz Count Conrad von Hötzendorf to prominence within the *k.k.* military.

Conrad's Offensive Tactics and the 1889 Infantry Regulations

Conrad, future chief of the general staff and architect of Austria-Hungary's war plans in 1914, taught at the *Kriegsschule* as a tactics instructor from 1888 to 1892. Hötzendorf's early career recommended him for the position. First in his class at the war college, Conrad demonstrated an excellent grasp of the principles of education for staff officers. During the 12 years between his graduation and appointment as instructor of tactics, Hötzendorf had gained some combat experience and received medals in Bosnia. He had also established a reputation as a tactical innovator, stemming from articles written for the *Organ*, in which Conrad argued for the benefits of earthworks and open order tactics in addition to more practical mapping.[16] During his tenure as chief of staff for the 11th Infantry Division at Lemberg, Conrad von Hötzendorf achieved prominence for his stance against excessive use of the parade ground and establishment of the first modern training ground in Austria-Hungary. This accomplishment as well as the articles influenced high-ranking members of the Habsburg army to consider Conrad an innovative and dynamic thinker who would help the Dual Monarchy's military continue its progress toward modernization. Thus, Beck, who served as chief of the general staff from 1882 until 1906, appointed Conrad to the most influential post in the *Kriegsschule*.[17]

While teaching tactics, Conrad emphasized the importance of the offensive and morale as necessary for achieving decisive results. Tactical and strategic tasks and exercises in the years that he taught focused almost completely on attack and very little on defense, except for rear-guard actions on the march.[18] Conrad's teaching notes, which he published as a commentary on the new *k.k. Exerzirreglements* of 1889, called for more exercises with the bayonet (a part of infantry training that had declined since 1866).[19] Constantly focusing on the role of morale and psychology in battle, Conrad instilled in his students a love of the offensive at all costs, while denigrating the benefits of defense and field fortifications, a change from his earlier writings.[20]

The introduction of smokeless powder for rifles eliminated any chance of running under the cover of smoke, as Colonel Reinländer had proposed for attacking breech-loaders in 1871.[21] The combination of repeating rifles and smokeless powder made frontal attacks over open ground suicidal. Yet the new infantry regulations of 1889, written to incorporate the Mannlicher repeater into *k.k.* tactics, took on a more offensive spirit than the previous regulations of 1874. Although acknowledging the superiority of firepower, the regulations maintained the possibility of platoons or swarms of soldiers using ground cover to attack an enemy being bombarded by artillery and thus thwart the advantages of the defense. The bayonet charge would form the final stage of the assault. The authors of the regulations realized that 30% casualties would be likely during such offensive maneuvers.[22] The Austro-Hungarian infantry instructions prophesied the battles of the First World War 25 years before they took place, although the casualty estimates proved optimistically low.

The 1889 infantry regulations made official a growing desire among the Habsburg officer corps to return to past tactics of shock and *élan*, which some officers had never given up. During the 1880s, some *k.k.* military writers expressed reservations about the success of bayonet attacks, especially with untrained reserves.[23] Preference for the offensive and the decisive role of morale, however, had never left the war theory of the Austro-Hungarian army. As one *ÖMZ* author said, "For a moment the danger appeared to lie near that one—just as in past centuries—will seek salvation in the rigid defensive, but finally the conviction that positive results are to be found only in the offensive maintained the field."[24] Trying to solve the problem of how to attack enemies possessing increasingly greater firepower, while proving unwilling to consider the defensive as a viable option, Habsburg officers looked to earlier methods of successful assaults.

This view belonged especially to younger officers who had not experienced the effect of the breech-loader in battle. One *Landwehr* major advocated a return to mass linear tactics, claiming, with poor timing, that the age of guerilla warfare had passed.[25] Relying on examples from the seventeenth and eighteenth centuries, as well as more recent campaigns such as a successful Boer attack on British troops in Africa on 27 February 1881, another *k.k.* officer argued that there was no case in which attacking troops had been annihilated by firepower: "The attack with shining weapons, the storm, the old reliable thrust tactics, the shock on foot, is unstoppable, unconquerable, just like the shock of cavalry, if fresh troops not unnerved by long *Schnellfeuer* lead." Even the repeating rifle could not withstand the assault of troops defying death and wielding the nimble bayonet.[26] Clearly, even after the 1874 infantry regulations emphasized firepower, the offensive spirit remained strong within the *k.k.* officer corps. Archduke Albrecht, inspector general of the Habsburg army, dismissed as absurd the idea that no closed order advances in deep formations took place any more, despite the lessons of recent wars, especially the Austro-Prussian War, the Franco-Prussian War, and the Russo-Turkish War, with their appalling losses and unsuccessful assaults.[27] Habsburg officers misinterpreted these lessons because, even though frontal assaults failed for the most part during these campaigns, the victor in each war (France in 1859, Prussia in 1866 and 1870, Russia in 1877–1878, and Austria-Hungary in 1878) had employed offensive strategy and tactics.

After publication of the 1889 infantry regulations and introduction of the Mannlicher magazine rifle, the offensive spirit gained even more intensity. As tactics teacher at the Habsburg war college, Conrad had significant influence over the 100 general staff officers from the 1888–1890 and 1890–1892 classes, who would implement the new regulations in maneuvers and instruct soldiers how to use the new weaponry. By the end of the First World War, 60 of the 70 students from Conrad's classes who remained in the army had reached the rank of colonel, with 51 achieving major general or higher. Thus, throughout the last quarter century of the Austro-Hungarian Empire, Conrad's protégés had an increasing influence on *k.k.* strategy and tactics.[28] This influence meant inculcation of the offensive spirit *à outrance* that stemmed from Conrad's mixture of Clausewitzian thought and social Darwinism in military matters: "The goal of war is the lasting conquest of the enemy's will."[29] These words resembled Clausewitz's saying, "War is thus an act of force to compel our enemy to do our will."[30] Conrad, however, interpreted the need to dominate the opponent's will as a call for the offensive: "The attack works not only by paralyzing the enemy, but also by inspiring one's own troops; it lends them a higher zeal, enables thereby their own power, demands the moral annihilation of the enemy, and works against their own moral depression, - it works therefore doubly on the goal, as what is described as 'moral superiority.'"[31]

Other officers also expressed ideas that corresponded with Conrad's words. Instead of seeing the advantages that the increase in firepower from repeating rifles gave the defensive, contributors to the *ÖMZ* and the *Organ* continued to advocate the attack as the stronger form of war, primarily because the repeater did not grant more morale to the defender.[32] Likewise, smokeless powder did not render the defensive more powerful.[33] One author asserted that all great commanders from antiquity to the present possessed the offensive spirit, which maintained the power of the initiative and imposed the will of the attacker on the defender: "It is better to be the hammer than the anvil."[34] One officer, who admitted the rarity of successful frontal assaults in modern warfare, even contended that the offense still provided a better option than the defense because military history revealed that the great aggressive leaders gained decisive victories. The advantage belonged to the attacker who had a positive goal and acted to fulfill a plan rather than the defender who remained passively waiting to react to the move of the offensive side.[35] One writer under the pseudonym *Éclair* argued that troops who possess excellent morale would always conquer an enemy with superior weaponry but lower morale. *Éclair*, as well as other officers, loved to repeat the famous words of Suvarov, an eighteenth century Russian general, "The bullet is a fool, the bayonet a hero."[36] Like Conrad, these officers stressed the importance of the attack to enhance morale and impose one's will on the enemy.

In addition, *k.k.* military writers put great trust in the lesson gleaned from studying past campaigns, that the aggressor always won crushing battles. Instructors, including Conrad, remained especially obsessed with the masterpieces of Moltke, the Bohemian campaign of 1866 and the Prussian victories in 1870. The *Kriegsschule* tactical manuals contained examples almost exclusively from these campaigns.[37] Thus, Moltke's ideas of the superiority of the offensive and envelopment maneuvers became embedded in Austro-Hungarian officers more than ever before. Although most officers agreed with the 1889 infantry regulations on the necessity of achieving fire superiority, the push forward, or *Drang nach vorwärts*, still took priority. Attack formed the best method of battle; the enveloping attack was the best method of attack as long as firing did not hinder the *Drang nach vorwärts*.[38] This line of thought made sense for the *k.k.* high command because the Habsburg army would probably fight any future wars allied with Germany in Moltke's style of warfare, even though the offensive did not fit the abilities of the smaller Austro-Hungarian military.

Military Education: Intellectual Training and Tactics

Bylandt-Rheidt, war minister from 1876 to 1888, continued education in Austro-Hungarian military institutions in the manner that his predecessors, *FML* Franz Baron Kuhn von Kuhnenfeld and General der Kavallerie Alexander Baron von Koller, had established for civil schools. Perceiving the benefits for both military institutions and students, Bylandt-Rheidt regulated the curriculum of each *k.k.* officer school to correspond as closely as possible with public educational institutions.[39] Thus, students entering army academies from civil schools could make smooth transitions to military institutions, just as officers who had graduated from army schools could adjust easily to public educational facilities. Some Habsburg officers, including Ratzenhofer, even envisioned military training as part of the public school curriculum. This innovation would make sense for any state using universal conscription and would enhance the army's fighting ability. The military could then employ soldiers who had already received some training before entering the army and save both time and money in forming the new recruits into battle-ready warriors.[40]

Realizing the problems of Kuhn's system of testing, which relied too much on theory, Bylandt-Rheidt stressed the importance of both theoretical and practical knowledge. The war minister wanted military graduates, especially among the general staff, to be proficient in all branches of the art of war. Therefore, military schools emphasized familiarity with the most recent innovations in warfare as well as target practice and staff rides. Two years of service in one of the army branches solidified the theoretical knowledge gained in educational institutions.[41] Practical training also formed a recurrent theme in *ÖMZ* articles on education. While still maintaining the merits of theory, officers emphasized the need for practical application in the form of war games and field exercises, especially for tactics.[42]

During the 1880s and after, staff rides became a prominent part of military training for both staff officers and general officers. Archduke Albrecht and, especially, *FML* Friedrich von Beck-Rzikowsky proved instrumental in establishing these practical exercises. As chief of the general staff (1881–1906), Beck had great influence over the staff rides and tried to make all field exercises as realistic as possible. Beck and Albrecht also expanded these training practices to include all branches of the army, including reserves in the *Landwehr* and *Honvéd*, in both offensive and defensive roles. The Habsburg military held the first exercises ever to take place in Europe involving more than one corps on each side in 1893 at Güns in Hungary.[43] Because of these measures, the *k.k.* army showed great progress in realistic training for the modern battlefield.

Within the *k.k.* academic institutions, tactics had the greatest emphasis. In the infantry cadet schools, students of the third year studied tactics for three hours each week and fourth year students for four hours. No other subject received as much attention, especially in the third and fourth years, although cadets of the fourth year spent four and a half hours per week on fortifications and fortress warfare. They also studied terrain and the German language for more total hours but spread out over more years. The general staff war college stressed tactics even more obviously. In this institution, students spent four and a half hours per week on the tactical course until 1885 when the number of hours was increased to six, twice as much time as students spent studying strategy, three times more than the terrain course, and four times more than the courses in weaponry, army organization, engineering and fortification, and military penal law.[44] This emphasis on tactical training explains the influence that the instructor of tactics had on prospective staff officers. Conrad, who began teaching tactics at the *Kriegsschule* 3 years after the expansion of the tactics course, took advantage of the additional time to instill his ideas in the classes of 1888–1892. Along with Conrad's charismatic teaching style, the extra hours spent absorbing his views reinforced the conviction of the future high-ranking officers of the Habsburg army of World War I that it was necessary to retain the initiative and the offensive at all costs.

Even with the great emphasis on practical training and tactics, some officers criticized the educational system of the *k.k.* army. Major-General Alois Baron von Haymerle, the author of various political works and a biography of *FML* Josef Count Radetzky, revealed that despite reforms the Austro-Hungarian educational institutions suffered from frequent turnover of instructors and incompetent teachers who had too much freedom in methodology. Haymerle also complained that cadet schools placed too great an emphasis on mathematics and not enough on tactics.[45] Another officer revealed how instructors, especially incompetent substitutes, wasted up to one quarter of instruction time, both in the classroom and during field exercises, with inadequate preparation and frequent breaks.[46] Once again, the Habsburg army had difficulty in practical application. The reforms had merit, yet the high command did not ensure competence and stability in the teaching body.

Creating a united military capable of offensive actions formed a significant part of Austro-Hungarian training. As one *k.k.* first lieutenant wrote, the psychological side of education took greater prominence in modern times because "weapons techniques and the raising of great masses of warriors can find a limit, but the psychological, inner worth of an army cannot."[47] According to Habsburg officers, not only could an Austro-Hungarian military united in love of fatherland and monarch carry out successful offensive operations, but also compensate for inferior numbers. Therefore, *k.k.* officers increasingly advised their comrades to take on the role of teachers for the rank and file coming from so many ethnic backgrounds within the empire. Only officers could perform the vital social task of educating the population in love of monarch and fatherland, performance of duty, courage in the presence of death, and repression of selfish nationalistic feelings.[48] Because officers as true patriots had no nationality or politics, the corps was the perfect group for transmitting the military spirit to recruits and, thus, the rest of society.[49] To achieve this goal, the new military school instructions issued in the 1890s stressed intellectual training and practical knowledge to enhance morale, so that officers would learn to think and, in turn, teach soldiers to think.[50] Conrad's charismatic style of instruction, which encouraged discussion and input from the student body, suited this impetus well and increased his popularity.

Tactical and Numerical Disconnection

The offensive tactics of Conrad and the 1889 infantry regulations failed to coincide with the numerical inferiority of the *k.k.* army compared with the major European militaries. Calculations of the peacetime and war strengths of the European powers in 1891 put Habsburg forces at a numerical disadvantage because years of smaller recruit contingents had widened the gap between Austria-Hungary's forces and most of the other military powers. The *k.k.* army's standing army amounted to 300,499 men, or 350,708 including the *Landwehr* and the *Honvéd*. Germany had a peacetime footing of 511,657, France 591,188, and Russia 602,186, or 818,033 with the reserve troops. Only Italy with 276,013 men had a smaller land army than Austria-Hungary. The war footing numbers gave an even starker picture of the declining Habsburg military strength. The *k.k.* army could put 1,010,310 soldiers in the field, or a total of 1,862,249 including all reserves, *Landwehr*, *Honvéd*, and the third line of troops, the *Landsturm*, which contained all able-bodied men between the ages of 18 and 42, though with extremely little training. In contrast, Germany could mobilize 2,416,300 men not counting reserves; France 1,395,000, or 3,040,000 including reserves and territorial armies; and Russia 1,187,951, or 2,420,746 with the second reserve line but without the third. Even Italy's wartime army amounted to 679,517 men and 2,844,339 reserves and militia.[51] Of all the major continental European military powers, Austria-Hungary possessed the smallest wartime army and the second-smallest peacetime footing. These numbers did not indicate the offensive option as the best Habsburg choice for strategy and tactics, especially considering the very real possibility of a multifront war with some combination of Russia, Italy, and the Balkan states. Yet, as one *k.k.* captain wrote to prove the eternal predominance of the offensive, "One shortened the bayonet, and formed the rifle into the present precision weapon – and Austria's combat strategy remains the attack!"[52] Offensive strategy and tactics filled the *k.k.* officer corps with pride and feelings of the worthiness of Austria-Hungary as a first-rate military power.

The Realistic View

Some voices of reason did exist among *k.k.* officers. Adolf Horsetzky von Hornthal, a lieutenant-colonel in the general staff and teacher of strategy at the war college from 1884 to 1888, offered a different perspective on frontal attacks. As a veteran of Königgrätz in 1866 and the Bosnian campaign in 1878, Horsetzky had more battle experience than Conrad and many of the younger officers advocating the offensive. The lieutenant-colonel noted that frontal assaults hardly ever proved successful, even in Napoleon's time, and far less so in modern warfare.[53] Horsetzky's experience and reputation as a noted military writer in Austria-Hungary lent credibility to his thoughts. However, when Conrad became tactical instructor at the *Kriegsschule* in 1888, the same year Horsetzky ended his time at the war college, the general staff students latched onto the younger man's charismatic way of teaching and became devoted not only to Conrad's ideas but also to his person. According to his former students, Conrad encouraged open debate and discussion in the classroom in order to arrive at solutions to tactical problems. In this way, he became not only an instructor but also the friend of his students while guiding them to accept his theories.[54]

Another officer asserted the greater difficulty of the attack because of the distinct advantage in firepower that every improvement in rifle technology grants the defensive. Troops who use the repeating rifle well should repulse every assault, even offensives of far superior manpower, while inflicting heavy casualties before the attackers reach a point 100 paces in front of the defensive line. Thus, the defenders should never have to retreat.[55] The land defense minister, Welser von Welsersheimb, contended that the attempt to gain fire superiority while attacking was illusory and a fatal mistake against a well-chosen defensive position. Swarm lines could be effective, not in deep formations but in small groups that could take advantage of the initiative and surprise the enemy.[56]

Lieutenant-Colonel Nikolaus Ritter von Wuich's weapons study guide for first year war college students in 1890–1891 explained how the bayonet played a lesser role on the modern battlefield because of the increased firepower of breech-loading and repeating rifles. Statistics revealed that wounds from bayonets or sabers during the 1866 Bohemian campaign totaled a mere 3% of all Austrian casualties, whereas only 1% of Prussian losses at the battle of Pravelotte in 1870 came from *blanken Waffen*. In addition, Wuich showed the negative impact that the bayonet had on accurate shooting. A bayonet affixed to a rifle added to its weight and partially blocked the aim of the shooter, resulting in lower accuracy. Habsburg troops also engaged in much less target practice with a fixed bayonet because it fatigued the men faster. Because of these drawbacks, infantry regulations prescribed fixing the bayonet onto the rifle only just before the final assault.[57] Nevertheless, the same students who heard these views from Wuich listened to the ideas of Conrad and preferred the tactical instructor's liking for shock and the bayonet attack.

Another voice that should have had great influence on the Habsburg officer corps was that of Archduke Albrecht. The inspector general wrote in 1888 about the dangers that a long peace presented for the military. The longer an army fights no wars, the more the officers forget the lessons of previous campaigns. New leaders gain little experience and learn "the precepts of theoretical doctrinaires, incompetent armchair pedagogues of smooth training grounds." The archduke saw the same situation occurring with the *k.k.* military as took place before 1866. Too much formalism in battle methods had become rooted in the Austro-Hungarian army as well as a great desire to follow the latest trend that seemed to lead unswervingly to victory. Neglecting the impact of firepower on advancing troops and the demoralizing effect of suffering heavy losses in a matter of minutes, theorists called for frontal assaults in specific formations without flexibility. Albrecht noted that the era of Napoleonic tactics had passed and that firepower had given superiority to the defensive. No specific formation can render one side unconquerable in battle but instead leads to passivity and loss of initiative. Every battle presents different obstacles. All officers, from the highest ranks down to corporals, must display independence of thought, quickly grasp the situation, and prove their ability to act on their own to achieve favorable results through proper use of terrain and flank attacks.[58] Even the words of the most experienced and successful commander in the Habsburg army, the victor of Custozza in 1866, could not dissuade the majority of *k.k.* officers, including Conrad and his followers, from the mistake of looking to the offensive, and especially shock tactics, as the only means of victory. Without the charisma of Conrad or close contact with the rising generation of staff officers in the war college, the aged Albrecht did not have the same opportunity to influence young military students as the popular tactical instructor did.

Cavalry Tactics: Shock Versus Reconnaissance

The tactical employment of cavalry also involved the use of shock tactics. Most Austro-Hungarian officers took a more realistic approach regarding this branch of the army because of the realities of the modern battlefield.

Mounted troops presented much larger targets for the increasingly accurate and far-shooting rifles of the late nineteenth century, while the rapidity of breech-loader and repeater fire negated the main advantage of cavalry, speed of movement. Therefore, according to an experienced soldier such as Lieutenant-Colonel Viktor Baron von Neuwirth, a veteran of the Italian campaigns in 1859 and 1866, mounted forces should devote their energy to reconnaissance and securing the flanks of infantry against enemy cavalry charges rather than attempt to participate in pitched battles.[59] As another officer stated, "The times of great cavalry attacks in battle are over; this is a principle of recent war leadership."[60] The lessons of the Franco-Prussian War supported this view of the ineffectiveness of cavalry against infantry. The murderous fire of breech-loaders sobered the enthusiasm of military leaders for mounted charges. The introduction of magazine rifles raised even more doubts about the use of cavalry, "and maintained a cautious *noli me tangere* as advisable, perhaps up to the lessons of the next campaign."[61] Thus, the Habsburg cavalry continued to adapt to the realities of modern warfare by reducing the role of mounted troops in combat.

Yet, there was a note of doubt. The insinuation that the next war might change the battlefield back to favoring cavalry contained hopes of reviving the glorious days of horsemen swooping down on infantry and laying waste with sword and pike. Even the officer who asserted the end of the days of great cavalry attacks believed exceptions to this principle existed.[62] Most of the officers who believed in preserving the honor of the cavalry by insisting on the battle worthiness of the mounted branch belonged to the cavalry. Major Emil Dembsher, in a series of articles for the *ÖMZ*, claimed that proponents of the breech-loader exaggerated the weapon's effect. Mounted charges could still ensure success as long as the horsemen took advantage of conditions to surprise opposing infantry. Thus, cavalry should not become mere mounted infantry, a role that constituted an exception in the cavalry regulations.[63] Officers persisted in affirming the possibility of successful assaults on infantry, but with the proviso of surprise. The regulations supported these assertions, suggesting that attacks take place in swarms or even lines.[64] One officer even proposed a return to deep formations to use shock to full advantage. This same officer maintained that, as infantry could no longer assault enemies armed with repeating rifles, cavalry should take the offensive because mounted troops could employ surprise and terrain better than infantry could and charge before the enemy could fire.[65]

Fantasies such as mounted forces charging so fast that infantry cannot fire even one salvo indicated the desperation of cavalry officers to retain the glory of past Austrian horse units in the days of Prince Eugene of Savoy and Empress Maria Theresa. The desire to preserve the honor and glory of the Habsburg cavalry drove officers to seek the offensive as a means to instill this sense of past greatness in the troops. Major Heinrich Baron von Pitreich of the general staff, who would later become commandant of the war college and then minister of war in 1902, wrote of cavalry going, "not shaken, forward! and, if necessary, headlong into battle!" Using the well known "Better to be the hammer than the anvil" slogan, Pitreich asserted in 1881 that mounted warriors still valued greatness and expected nothing more than undertakings full of honor.[66] Ten years later, a colonel used almost the exact same words as Pitreich while stating his conviction that fortune favors the bold. Even if the results of charging headlong into battle turn out unfavorably, cavalry "remain the weapon of glory" as "modern horsemen, despite the improved fire weapons, wish to remain true to the example of their glory crowned ancestors."[67]

The new roles of reconnaissance and communications did not suit dreams of honor and renown for the mounted branch. *FML* Leonidas Baron von Popp, a general staff officer; former instructor of strategy at the central cavalry school; veteran of 1859, 1866, and 1878; and head of the imperial military chancellery from 1881 to 1889, proposed eliminating the engineer companies (*Pioniere*) attached to cavalry units so that mounted forces could perform more important tasks without the encumbrance of technical troops. Popp even suggested that by removing the *Pioniere* the army could add another cavalry regiment and save the paltry sum of 4875 florins.[68] To fund the extra cavalry regiment, instead of saving money or procuring more and better artillery, the Austro-Hungarian military requested 433,858 more florins in the ordinary budget submission and an additional 195,000 florins for the extraordinary budget for 1891. This request for more cavalry stemmed from the desire to keep pace with the other European powers, which all had more mounted troops.[69] Ideas about enlarging the number of *k.k.* cavalry also resulted from dreams of great feats and disdain for subsidiary duties such as reconnaissance and communications. Major Dembsher expressed the cavalry officer's view and explained that the successful charges against infantry during field exercises demonstrated how mounted forces could fulfill greater tasks than mere "postal service."[70]

Hopes of restoring past grandeur also sparked debates about the best weaponry for cavalry. After 1866, the Austrian high command issued carbines to the mounted troops, though the Uhlan regiments, traditionally lance regiments, received only 32 carbines per squadron. The attempt to equip men with both weapons failed because of the extra weight and the burden of learning to wield both a lance and a carbine. In 1880, the number of carbines per Uhlan squadron rose to 48.[71] This situation caused Lieutenant Colonel Markus von Czerlien, an intelligent Uhlan officer, to quote from *Modern Cavalry* by the Canadian officer George Taylor Denison, an award-winning expert on cavalry: "Cavalry in most armies is equipped almost exactly as it was at the time when Alexander the Great led them against the Persians."[72] Only in 1884 did every man in Uhlan regiments discard the lance and take up the short rifle.[73] This decision to end the use of lances put the Austro-Hungarian military far in advance of the other major European powers, which still employed the outdated weapon for cavalry.

These changes in favor of firepower for cavalry brought about a wave of objections from mounted officers who feared that the introduction of firearms would harm the dash and spirit of the equestrian branch.[74] Major Dembsher complained that forcing cavalry to fight on foot and rely on firepower, a situation that in his opinion happened too often during maneuvers, would cause the men to renounce success with *blanken Waffen* and resort too easily to the defensive.[75] Even a voice from the infantry, who acknowledged the overall importance of firepower, claimed that cavalry could profit little from rifles. Though mounted troops should know how to fire effectively, speed, saber, and lance comprised the main weapons of horse warriors.[76] In 1889, a call to bring back the lance issued from the pages of the *ÖMZ*. A return to the pike would restore the flagging morale of the *k.k.* cavalry and enable the first wave of horsemen to crash into the enemy with greater impact. The Viennese arsenal had even stored away the old lances, which all Uhlans hoped would return to their hands in the near future.[77]

Habsburg cavalry officers did not stand alone in their preference for the lance and saber. Among the various European military powers during this time of technological change and modification, as Lieutenant Colonel Czerlien attested, "a veritable chaos of principles had come into employment." The French cavalry no longer used lances but the Germans issued no revolvers to their mounted troops. French, German, and Russian Cuirassiers rarely used carbines, although the Russian

Cossacks went into battle with pike, carbine, and revolver. German Uhlans and Italian *Lancieri* carried a lance and carbine. Most nations distributed lances to Uhlans, Cuirassiers, and Hussars. Only France equipped its cavalry with both revolver and carbine, whereas Turkey was the only nation to issue a magazine rifle to mounted forces.[78] Thus, Austria-Hungary showed no more backwardness than most other states. Other than France, the Habsburg Empire proved the most capable of adapting cavalry weapons and tactics to the requirements of the modern battlefield and its dominating firepower.

Certain *k.k.* officers called for the Habsburg high command to instill belief in the prospect of successful charges by imitating their German allies, whose cavalry performed numerous massed attacks on infantry during training exercises.[79] Although Habsburg officers, such as Conrad, admired the Prussian victories of 1866 and 1870 and devoted great energy in trying to incorporate the ideas of Moltke into the *k.k.* army, Austro-Hungarian exercises revealed that the heavy losses of recent mounted assaults had affected Habsburg military thinking. In 1881, one lieutenant colonel complained that *k.k.* peace exercises contained too little realism. Military leaders contrived situations that allowed big battles and daring deeds at the expense of training cavalry for the more important task of reconnaissance.[80] By 1889, however, complaints arose from the opposing camp that Habsburg cavalry no longer learned how to attack infantry and hardly ever practiced charges during exercises.[81] One officer, who had declared the need for more cavalry training for attacking infantry in 1884, had reversed his position by 1893. Instead of exercises in shock tactics, the officer promoted reconnaissance training, both strategic and tactical, as the primary task of mounted troops unable to assault infantry armed with repeaters.[82]

During the decade following the Bosnian campaign of 1878 and the Russo-Turkish War of 1877–1878, the Austro-Hungarian cavalry made progress in adapting to the modern battlefield. The Habsburg high command emphasized reconnaissance and security operations rather than charges and shock tactics during maneuvers and exercises. Most of the *ÖMZ* and *Organ* contributors who wrote articles about the cavalry during the 1890s affirmed reconnaissance as the primary task of cavalry and the great difficulty of charging infantry under modern battlefield conditions.[83] As one author said, "All theoretical affectations with assault forms and assault lines against infantry physically or psychologically unbroken or awaiting the attack are and remain idle paper wishes."[84]

Because of this stress on duties outside pitched battle, the *k.k.* mounted troops exchanged their lances and sabers for revolvers and carbines. Even though some cavalry officers disputed the wisdom of such changes, Austro-Hungarian leaders implemented reforms that revealed Habsburg progress beyond most of the other major European military powers.

Artillery: Tactics and Numbers

For the third military branch, Habsburg leaders agreed on the importance of field guns and the use of artillery in battle. Therefore, less debate regarding cannon took place in the *k.k.* military journals. Austro-Hungarian officers concurred about employing artillery in masses to produce the greatest amount of firepower and thus gain superiority over the enemy at decisive points.[85] Although artillery still formed a supporting weapon for infantry, officers considered field guns essential for attaining effective levels of firepower and achieving ultimate victory.[86] The army required field guns both for offensive and defensive purposes. Even though artillery itself could not charge and thus appeared defensive, infantry required cannons to weaken the enemy before a successful assault could take place.[87] At the same time, artillery had to provide an invincible wall for shattering enemy attacks.[88] As one *k.k.* captain expressed the role of field guns on the battlefield, "In the attack-battle breaking a path for the masses of infantry in a destructive way, in the defense the iron rock, on which even the most violently rushing waves of the enemy assault smash powerlessly."[89] Cannoneers also needed high morale for effective battlefield performance. Gunners had to display composure and cold-bloodedness, especially in the face of charging infantry and cavalry, to fulfill the tasks of modern artillery.[90]

Compared with rifles, cannon had not developed as quickly and dramatically from 1877 to 1892, according to First Lieutenant Anton Christl of the *Kriegsschule*. Whereas European armies had changed infantry equipment at least twice during these years, artillery had remained the same except for an expansion in number and an increasing recognition of the importance of field guns in battle.[91] Although Christl spoke mainly for Austria-Hungary, this situation did not present difficulties as long as all armies possessed similar cannon. If even one state, however, made significant improvements to field artillery, then the other military powers would have to imitate the innovations or find even better technology.[92] During the 1880s, Habsburg officers remained convinced of the excellence of the Uchatius steel-bronze cannon and maintained that the *k.k.* field guns met all the requirements of the modern battlefield better than the weapons of other states. A *Landwehr* officer, concurring with a Prussian artillery major, claimed that the field guns of the Viennese arsenal rivaled the Krupp artillery of Prussia as the best in Europe, while Italian cannon ranked a close third.[93] Nevertheless, by the 1890s, Habsburg officers realized that the *k.k.* artillery needed to take advantage of technological innovations and procure better field guns. Because infantry rifles had increased in firing speed, accuracy, and range, cannon needed to fire faster and farther to compensate for these improvements in handguns.[94] One officer, citing the example of the Russian field artillery's inability to destroy the Turkish fortifications at Plevna in 1877, advocated mortars with their higher trajectory for obliterating improved fieldworks and raising the effectiveness of *k.k.* artillery.[95] Once again, Habsburg officers realized the importance of new technology and engaged in debates on how to employ innovations to improve battlefield performance.

The main problem for the Habsburg high command was the *k.k.* army's numerical inferiority in field guns. In an 1882 memorandum regarding advisable changes in the organization of the field artillery, *FML* Archduke Wilhelm, the general artillery inspector and younger brother of Albrecht, stated the need to increase the number of field pieces to between 1540 and 1620. Although this augmentation would significantly improve the Austro-Hungarian artillery branch, the additional guns would not raise the *k.k.* army to the level of the other major European military powers.[96] By 1891, Habsburg leaders had still not remedied the deficiency in cannon. Austro-Hungarian officers realized the financial sacrifice required to procure more field guns.[97] One officer proposed more and better training to attain fire superiority on the battlefield without spending money on purchasing more guns or improved material.[98] This solution could only partially compensate for the far greater numbers and superior material that other armies possessed. Even though the *k.k.* leadership realized the importance of the artillery branch in modern warfare, the official statistics from 1891 revealed the small number of soldiers assigned to field guns. Of the 1,015,792 men in the Habsburg army, only 80,343 (8%) served in the field artillery compared with 639,154 (62.9%) in the infantry and 91,278 (9%) in the cavalry. Adding the fortifications artillery (20,929 or 2%) and technical artillery (2814 or 0.3%) brought the artillery forces to 104,086 (10.2%) of the total strength of the *k.k.* military.[99] The other major European armies dedicated a higher percentage of men to artillery than the Habsburg army: France 14%, Italy 14%, Germany 12.5%, and Russia 11%.[100] The Austro-Hungarian military needed more funding or, better yet, more responsible and purposeful spending of the funds available from the Delegation grants.

In 1891, the Habsburg high command requested 4,607,600 florins to upgrade the artillery branch. This budget submission included 2,100,000 florins to improve or replace the M.1861 muzzle-loading guns that the Austro-Hungarian army stationed in many fortresses. The *k.k.* artillery still employed 30-year-old cannons in 1891 and proposed to replace these outdated weapons with M.1875s and other steel-bronze Uchatius guns.[101] Clearly, the Habsburg artillery suffered from not only antique weaponry but also the inferior quality of the cannon from the Vienna arsenal. The plan to continue to arm permanent fortifications with these guns merely compounded the errors because these weapons would come into action only if potential enemies chose to attack the fortresses defended by these cannon. Surely, it would have been much better for Habsburg leaders to use the 2,100,000 florins to upgrade the *k.k.* field artillery by procuring superior Krupp guns and thereby bridge the gap between the Austro-Hungarian military and other leading European powers. The Habsburg high command, however, viewed the Uchatius cannon as adequate artillery, based on tests such as those cited by the *Landwehr* officer in his article.[102] The *k.k.* leaders also believed in the necessity of the cordon system of permanent fortresses to defend Austro-Hungarian borders from invasion in the case of a multifront war.

Permanent Waste: The Cordon System

As in previous decades, the Habsburg high command could have saved large sums of money in the area of permanent fortifications. The cordon system continued to consume vast numbers of florins that the *k.k.* army could have used for procuring more and better artillery. Yet, Austro-Hungarian officers insisted on the need to upgrade and expand old fortresses and build new ones. One engineer captain explained the rationale for this view in a lecture at the Military Science Society at the Galician fortress of Przemyśl in 1882. Weighing the advantages and disadvantages of permanent fortifications, the captain concluded that Austria-Hungary needed the cordon system because future wars would most probably involve multiple fronts. In order for the *k.k.* army to fight in more than one theater, military leaders would have to use fortresses to strengthen the various parts of the divided Habsburg army. The captain argued that permanent fortifications could also influence a whole province, such as Galicia where Przemyśl stood, and provided the only means to secure an open area like Galicia while ensuring a safe connection with the rest of the empire. Despite the high cost of fortresses, their immobility, and the need to employ field-worthy troops for garrisons, permanent fortifications remained the best method of supporting the *k.k.* military both offensively and defensively.[103]

Students at the *Kriegsschule* also subscribed to these ideas. Captain Heinrich von Vefsel praised the merits of fortifications in his manual on *Befestigung* for 1887–1888. For Vefsel, the purpose of fortifications was to enable a small amount of power for the greatest possible resistance. This definition applied primarily to the defensive but also indirectly to the offensive.[104] Such ideas corresponded perfectly with the Austro-Hungarian military's view of its weak geographical position with regard to future wars. Facing potential enemies on three sides, with Russia to the northeast, Italy to the southwest, and the volatile Balkans to the south, *k.k.* military leaders saw the cordon system of permanent fortifications as the best means to defend against multiple threats simultaneously.[105] This consideration appeared logical, especially because of the small number of troops that Austria-Hungary could field compared with the other European powers. Therefore, little debate concerning the advantages and disadvantages of permanent fortresses took place in the *k.k.* military journals during the 1880s and 1890s.

Instead of debating the merits of the cordon system, Habsburg officers argued about the worth of fieldworks. Many writers advocated the use of temporary works. Captain Vefsel's *Befestigung* manual applied to both permanent and temporary fortifications.[106] Another officer viewed Austria-Hungary as the foremost pioneer in employing fieldworks because the Habsburg high command issued spades to all the infantry on 25 February 1870, before the outbreak of the Franco-Prussian War. The *k.k.* army continued to emphasize the importance of building temporary fortifications by only equipping engineer troops with tools and not with rifles.[107] One *k.k.* officer revealed the effect of fieldworks in battle by comparing the casualties of French and German forces at Gravelotte. French troops who fought in trenches and behind earthen walls suffered only 3.5% losses, whereas French units that erected no defenses lost 15% of their men.

The Turkish works at Plevna in 1877 only confirmed the immense benefits of building temporary fortifications on the battlefield.[108]

As one officer wrote in an article entitled, "Temporary fortifications in the service of the offensive," the main objection to temporary fortifications stemmed from the belief that fieldworks implied an overly defensive approach to war.[109] Lieutenant Colonel Wenzel Porth, who had turned to military writing after suffering a serious wound during the Austro-Prussian War and had published numerous articles, warned against trusting immobile positions because this overly defensive mindset gave up the advantages of the offensive and let the enemy dictate the battle conditions.[110] Another officer called temporary fortifications "harmful palliatives" and attempted to prove fieldworks less effective in war than permanent fortresses.[111] According to officers who followed these ideas, temporary fortifications harmed the *Drang nach vorwärts* that the infantry regulations emphasized "from the last man to the highest leader."[112] Thus, whether of the opinion that fieldworks did not provide enough defensive advantages or that temporary fortifications proved too defensive, *k.k.* officers insisted on the need to build or upgrade permanent fortresses, especially in the vulnerable province of Galicia.[113] Lieutenant Colonel Ernst Baron von Leithner acknowledged that improvements in smokeless powder and artillery maneuverability, along with better observation through use of electric lights and balloons, rendered permanent fortresses indefensible. However, even he suggested better methods of defense as an alternative to abandoning fortifications. Leithner, who would later become inspector general of the engineer corps, advocated stronger armor to protect fortress walls and a more complex system of fortifications, similar to those of the famous seventeenth century French engineer Vauban.[114]

The Habsburg military did not stand alone as a proponent of permanent fortifications. Other European states, including Germany, France, and Russia, also began building complicated fortress systems with expensive metal plating. In 1894, the French army held fortification maneuvers in which infantry storm assaults and artillery barrages tested the quality of the new methods of construction.[115] The main problem for the Austro-Hungarian high command was the large size and vulnerability of the Habsburg Empire. Forming defensible frontiers against possible opponents drove the *k.k.* leadership to spend vast sums on the cordon system of permanent fortresses to alleviate the difficulties of multifront conflicts, instead of using the funds to procure more artillery.

This objective applied specifically to the province of Galicia, the most likely theater of any future war with Russia. The geographical conditions of Galicia presented a difficult task for military operations, especially for defense. An 1889 general staff report described the impracticability of maintaining forces and establishing bases in Galicia's numerous swamps and heavy forests. The challenging conditions rendered the gathering of resources and finding adequate quarters for troops problematic. The author of the report concluded, "In its totality the Russian-Galician theater of war gives no attractive picture." Only hard work and exertion would provide a solution.[116] The northern and eastern frontiers provided no defensible positions nor did the three rivers, the Dniester, the Moldova, and the Ceremuş, that crossed the province. With little road and rail access through the Carpathian Mountains bordering Hungary, the Habsburg army faced a more difficult predicament than Russia in waging a campaign in Galicia.[117]

Nevertheless, the *k.k.* high command considered no option other than defending the province with permanent fortifications, especially Przemyśl. *FML* Anton Baron von Schönfeld, chief of the general staff from 1876 to 1881, stressed the need to complete and extend the fortresses of Przemyśl and Krakau. Temporary fortifications were merely a help and even an opiate for theorists who believed in the superiority of fieldworks.[118] Officers writing in the military journals agreed with Schönfeld's assessment of permanent fortifications as the only means of securing Galicia against Russian invasion.[119] The chief of the general staff, *FML* Beck invariably recommended further upgrades and completion of the Galician fortresses in his annual memorandum for the emperor.[120]

Upgrading the defenses of Przemyśl and Krakau cost the *k.k.* army vast amounts of money. In 1891 alone, the Habsburg high command asked for 2 million florins from the Delegations for improvement of the Galician fortresses. In this request, the military recognized the significant progress of artillery technology and acknowledged the inadequacy of previous methods of rendering the fortifications strong enough to resist modern guns. Therefore, engineers would have to build new works as well as transform temporary sections of the fortresses into permanent constructions with metal armor.[121] Recognition of technological advances in artillery indicated that the permanence of these upgrades would not last forever. Austro-Hungarian military leaders had already spent over 10 million florins on these fortifications.[122] With more innovations in the future, the fortresses would soon require costly improvements yet again.

The Habsburg army could have spent the millions of florins used to upgrade permanent fortifications on improving the military in other ways. Instead of requesting 2,320,000 florins for fortresses in 1891, not including improvements at Krakau, and indicating the need for another 1,200,000 for the completion of permanent works in the Tirol along the Italian border and at Cattaro, one of Austria-Hungary's main ports on the Adriatic, the *k.k.* high command could have used the funding for necessary procurements, such as more repeaters or smokeless powder. In the same year, the army submitted a request for 4 million florins for magazine rifles and 3 million for smokeless powder.[123] Military leaders could have used the 2,320,000 florins for fortresses and the 628,858 florins for the unnecessary new cavalry regiment (totaling 2,948,858 florins) to cover the costs of the 1891 installment for repeating rifles or smokeless powder. The high command could also have used the money to procure weapons and equipment for 14 new batteries of field artillery.[124]

Parliamentary Favor

Delegates from the parliaments of the two parts of the Dual Monarchy hardly ever granted the full amounts that the Habsburg high command requested. The reductions stemmed from a desire not to burden inhabitants of the various parts of the empire rather than disapprobation of the army's spending decisions.[125] The heated exchanges of the 1860s and early 1870s between war ministers and parliamentary representatives did not take place during the terms of Bylandt-Rheidt and his successor *FZM* Ferdinand Baron von Bauer, who served as minister of war from 1888 to 1893. Bylandt-Rheidt especially impressed the delegates with his efforts to curtail expenditure, while Bauer's responses during the debates displayed good will and understanding about the various concerns of the representatives.[126] By gaining the trust of the majority of the representatives, Bylandt-Rheidt and Bauer proved capable of obtaining adequate funding and most delegates appeared willing to work with the needs of the war ministry. These good relations coincide with British historian Alan Sked's argument that even nationalists within Austro-Hungary did not desire dissolution of the resilient Habsburg Empire.[127]

The main issues that delegates had with the Austro-Hungarian military concerned better conditions for the rank and file as well as increased army purchases from imperial businesses instead of foreign firms.[128] Although parliamentary representatives preferred to grant the *k.k.* army's budget requests in smaller installments than the Habsburg high command desired, delegates had few criticisms of the requests themselves. Neither permanent fortifications nor battleships raised difficulties other than disagreements about the installment amounts. Some delegates even shared the concerns of certain officers, such as the possibility of wasting ammunition with repeating rifles, and proposed similar suggestions about the possibility of public schools providing some military training before students entered the army.[129]

With regard to the fleet, delegates approved the navy's increased reliance on Austro-Hungarian industry for procurement. The Delegations did not object to granting 11,834,122 florins for naval expenses, including 1,372,000 florins out of 5,940,000 that the navy requested for new battleships and Danube submarines. The representatives argued in the same way as the military that the Habsburg Empire needed more warships to compete with the navies of other European powers. Great Britain possessed 58 fully modern battleships, France 26, Russia and Germany 17 each, Italy 12, and Spain 8. Austria-Hungary had only three, the same number as Greece, hardly a major maritime power. The ships that the *k.k.* navy had built in the 1860s and 1870s no longer met the requirements of modern sea battles. Thus, the Habsburg fleet required new battleships to continue the great success that the representatives proudly remembered.[130] Although Austria-Hungary did not qualify as a seafaring power, both military men and parliamentary delegates shared the belief that the Habsburg Empire must increase the *k.k.* fleet dramatically to maintain its great power status. This consideration, as well as the benefits that naval orders for ships gave to imperial businesses and industries, convinced representatives to grant millions of florins over a number of years for battleships and submarines that would become obsolete very quickly, if not by the time of completion.

The success of the *k.k.* army during the 1878 campaign in Bosnia-Hercegovina persisted in the minds of the delegates, along with the efforts of Bylandt-Rheidt to save money wherever possible in military spending. With favorable relations between the Delegations and the war ministry, Habsburg officers had little to complain about funding. Although the representatives usually chose to grant army requests in installments rather than in full, the delegates rarely disapproved of the reasons for which the war ministers made the requests. The causes of the *k.k.* army's financial problems stemmed more from the Habsburg high command's choices in spending, such as inordinately expensive permanent fortresses and battleships, rather than parliamentary stinginess.

Stability in the High Command

Parliamentary favor resulted from a more stable war ministry, where *FZM* Bylandt-Rheidt maintained control until 1888 when ill health forced him to retire. During his 12-year tenure, Bylandt-Rheidt gave stability to an essential part of the *k.k.* high command, a position that had been held by three men in the previous 10-years. With more solidity and less squabbling within the military administration, Bylandt-Rheidt proved capable of greatly improving the Habsburg army and gaining the trust of parliamentary representatives. The war minister succeeded in convincing the Delegations to fund introduction of the Mannlicher repeating rifle. Under his direction, military education continued to progress in both war and civil fields. The Army Shooting School took on a greater role as a permanent establishment, with an inspector and resident instructors who formed an advising committee for training and procurement.[131] Under Bylandt-Rheidt, the *k.k.* military continued to show interest in adapting to new technology. Just as the Habsburg Empire improved economically and politically during the latter half of the nineteenth century, as historians David Good, Barbara Jelavich, and Alan Sked argue, the Austro-Hungarian army also made progress.[132]

Railroads formed an important area for the war minister, who fought against decentralization of the state railways.[133] Beck, now chief of the general staff, fully supported Bylandt-Rheidt in this struggle against private interests taking over the railroads, because the army could use rail lines under state control much more easily during war time. The general staff chief had long noted the inadequacy of Austro-Hungarian railroads and thus worked diligently with the war minister to remedy this situation, especially regarding the lines connecting Galicia to the rest of the empire. Beck annually informed Franz Joseph of the status of the imperial railways in his detailed memoranda and made recommendations for future improvements.[134] During the 1880s, rolling stock for the Galician railroads increased by 50%, and by 1891 96 trains could depart daily for the northeastern province, almost three times more than in 1881.[135] Bylandt-Rheidt and Beck also influenced the creation of a general directorate for state railroads in 1882, which would combine with the *k.k.* army's rail directorate for military transport that the war minister had formed in 1878.[136] The main reason for dramatic development of the railroads to Galicia at this time was the desire to prove the ability of the Habsburg military in any future war with Russia. Because Germany could mobilize enough troops to launch an offensive against the Russians, Austro-Hungarian war planners wished to show how the *k.k.* army could successfully cooperate with its ally. If Germany defeated Russia alone, Austria-Hungary would face the humiliation of having failed an ally, along with the question of Habsburg worthiness as a great power. As Beck wrote to Franz Joseph in 1883, the *k.k.* army needed victories too.[137]

Bylandt-Rheidt also simplified organization of the Austro-Hungarian military by making more boards and organs directly answerable to the war ministry. The minister of war thus succeeded in establishing the war ministry's independence from Archduke Albrecht, the inspector general of the army. Instead of occupying a subordinate position to the inspectorate, Bylandt-Rheidt promoted the war ministry as responsible only to the emperor. The war minister even proposed that Albrecht's report reach Franz Joseph through the ministry of war rather than directly. As a result, these reforms engendered the resentment of the archduke. The emperor approved Bylandt-Rheidt's proposals. Although Albrecht remained displeased with this arrangement, he acquiesced.[138] Even though tension existed between Albrecht and Bylandt-Rheidt, the bitter antagonism of the Kuhn era remained outside the *k.k.* high command and hindered neither reform nor adaptation to the needs of modern warfare. Clearly, the Habsburg army had made definite progress.

The next war minister, *FZM* Ferdinand Baron von Bauer, a graduate of the engineering academy, worked to improve the technical abilities of the Habsburg military, especially the artillery and *Pioniere*. Under Bauer's term, the infantry obtained the Mannlicher repeating rifles and smokeless powder that Bylandt-Rheidt had received permission to procure. After his sudden death from sickness in 1893, *FZM* Rudolph Baron von Merkl held the war ministry for less than 2 months before General der Kavallerie Edmund Baron von Krieghammer took the position from 1893 to 1902.[139] Relations between the various components of the high command remained relatively amicable during the tenures of Bauer and Merkl and made possible the continued progress of the *k.k.* military. Krieghammer, however, brought much more tension to the Habsburg army than the previous three war ministers.

Albrecht: Voice of Tactical Reason

Krieghammer did not have many quarrels with Albrecht as the archduke died on 18 February 1895. Historians such as Gunther Rothenberg and Walter Wagner have blamed Albrecht for holding back the Austro-Hungarian army from adapting to the requirements of modern warfare.[140] This criticism unjustly blames the archduke for the failings of the Habsburg military. Certainly, Albrecht held antiquated views on strategy, as his support of the cordon system of permanent fortresses proved.[141] The archduke's insistence on fortifying Przemyśl not only cost the Imperial and Royal (*kaiserlich und königlich*; *k.u.k.*) army millions of florins that could have been used to procure better artillery, but also proved fatal for thousands of soldiers in the First World War. The formation of more cavalry was also an important part of the archduke's military thinking.[142] Yet, the rest of the Habsburg high command shared Albrecht's ideas on *Befestigung* and the need for more cavalry. Therefore, the archduke cannot take all the blame, or even the majority, for decisions made by those who agreed with him.

Albrecht did take part in the rivalry within the high command. As a member of the house of Habsburg and a proponent of the dynastic principle, the archduke always argued that the army formed the strongest bulwark of the monarchy against ethnic divisions as well as socialist and liberal ideas.[143] This idea proved true as the Austro-Hungarian army held together thousands of soldiers from various ethnic backgrounds until the very end of the Habsburg Empire, even after the government had started to collapse.[144] Albrecht's viewpoint solidified his own position in the military because of his imperial status and high rank. Thus, when differences arose between the various members of the high command over power, especially with the war ministers Kuhn and Bylandt-Rheidt, Albrecht strove to retain the control he had held previously at the time of the *Armeeoberkommando*. Gradually, however, he relented and accepted a lesser role in the army.[145] Although the archduke took part in bitter disputes, in particular with Kuhn, the blame should not fall entirely on Albrecht for the rivalries. Disputes with the war ministers mainly centered on army organization and control. Although opposing certain suggestions, the archduke argued for maintaining stability in the military and opposed change for the sake of change.[146]

The archduke did not try to thwart the technological advancement of the Austro-Hungarian army but rather proposed the procurement of better weaponry, especially infantry rifles.[147] Albrecht also desired better equipment for the troops in the form of lighter packs, tougher shoes, and warmer clothing in case of a war with Russia that might require a winter campaign.[148] Later *k.u.k.* military leaders, including Conrad, sadly did not share the archduke's concern for the rank and file, as revealed by the troops' sufferings because of inadequate clothing during the 1915 Carpathian winter campaign.[149]

To remedy Habsburg numerical inferiority compared with other European military powers, a problem that Albrecht clearly recognized, the archduke called for soldiers to stay in wartime formations during peace instead of dividing into separate units spread throughout the empire. In this way, mobilization could proceed more quickly without the confusion of forming new units. In addition, commanders should reside with their troops, rather than remaining absentee and only joining their commands at the outbreak of war.[150] These practical considerations exemplified the archduke's approach to war. For Albrecht, practicality reigned, especially in the realm of tactics. Proving his ability to learn and adapt to the changes in warfare, the archduke realized that success on the modern battlefield consisted of achieving firepower supremacy. Therefore, Albrecht insisted that no frontal assaults over uncovered ground take place against breech-loaders or repeating rifles. Instead, the practical use of terrain and artillery should direct every officer's analysis of the battle situation and determine the action, whether offensive or defensive, that the troops should take. If the offensive promised the most success, flank attacks should provide the best chances. Formalism embodied in adhering to only one method, such as the offensive *à outrance*, should never rule the commander on the battlefield.[151] When a return to more offensive tactics arrived in the form of the 1889 infantry regulations and the writings of Conrad, the Habsburg army lost its most influential voice against the offensive at all costs with the death of Albrecht in 1895.

Conclusion

The early 1890s proved a decisive turning point for the Austro-Hungarian army. The high command issued new Mannlicher repeaters and smokeless powder to the troops and issued new infantry regulations. These manuals instructed officers to strive for the offensive and revived the bayonet assault, which had fallen out of favor in the previous two decades. At the same time, the appointment of Conrad as teacher of tactics at the *Kriegsschule* gave great impetus to offensive ideas for the classes of 1889–1890 and 1890–1891. These general staff students formed the majority of high ranking officers during the First World War and inculcated the Habsburg army on all levels with these tactical ideas. The most prominent voice against a reversion to previous tactics of shock and *élan* was lost with the death of Albrecht. Although the *k.k.* military made progress in employing mounted troops for security and reconnaissance duties, many cavalry officers welcomed the return to shock tactics in the infantry and hoped for the same revival in the mounted branch.

Artillery use remained stable, emphasizing massed formations to support both offensive and defensive combat. The main problem for the artillery, however, was numerical inferiority in comparison with other European powers. As the Austro-Hungarian army lagged farther and farther behind Germany, France, and Russia in numbers of men and weapons, the Habsburg high command continued to make questionable spending decisions. Instead of taking advantage of parliamentary favor to procure more and better cannon, the *k.k.* army insisted on wasting millions of florins on the inferior steel-bronze Uchatius cannon and on permanent fortifications, especially the fortresses of Galicia, decisions that would prove detrimental to the Austro-Hungarian army in World War I.

In education, Habsburg leaders stressed the importance of practical application of theory in exercises, maneuvers, and staff rides. Intellectual ability among the officer corps continued to be a major objective of *k.k.* training. Practical application, however, remained a constant problem for the Austro-Hungarian high command because officers still favored the offensive on the training grounds. Growing emphasis on tactics in the *Kriegsschule* opened the way for Conrad's view of the tactical offensive to spread throughout the army.

During the 1880s, the Austro-Hungarian high command remained stable under the leadership of Bylandt-Rheidt and Bauer as war ministers, along with Beck as chief of the general staff. The bitter friction and rivalry of the Kuhn years no longer embroiled *k.k.* military leaders. Although Albrecht had differed with the war ministers over organization of the high command and control of the army as a whole, the archduke relented on many of his ideas and took a lesser role. Beck continued his work as peacemaker between the other leaders. Not until the appointment of Krieghammer to the war ministry did major friction return once again to the high command. The combination of rivalry at the top of the Habsburg army's structure with a revival of offensive shock tactics and continual mismanagement of funds forecast future disaster for the Austro-Hungarian military.

Notes

1. Rittmeister des Ruhestandes Reska, "Die neue Aera," *Organ der militärwissenschaftlichen Vereine* (*O.*) 15 (1877): 101.
2. Lieutenant-Colonel Gustav Ratzenhofer, "Die Taktik des Repetirgewehres," *Österreichische Militärische Zeitschrift* (*ÖMZ*) 1 (1887): 230.
3. No. 6 Memoire über die Nothwendigkeit der Beschaffung von Repetirgewehren, Oktober 1886, Kriegsarchiv (KA) Militärkanzlei Seiner Majestät (MKSM) Sonderreihe, Karton Nr. 64, Studien, 29–30.
4. Ratzenhofer, "Die Taktik des Repetirgewehres," 230.
5. Oberlieutenant Franz Tscherin, "Über Repetir-Gewehre," *O.* 20 (1880): 183–188.
6. Major-Auditor Dr. Emil Dangelmaier, "Unser Kaiser als militärischer Gesetzgeber," *ÖMZ* 4 (1898): 246.
7. "Miscellen. Das Repetir-Gewehr von Mannlicher," *O.* 15 (1877): 343–344; John Walter, *The Rifle Story* (London: Greenhill Books, 2006), 190.
8. "Modificirter Gewehr-Aufsatz, Modell 1873/77," *ÖMZ* 1 (1881): 94.
9. Hauptmann Freiherrn La Motte, "Über die Anwendung der Anschlagsrichtungen mit den Infanterie- und Jäger Gewehren M. 1873/77 und M. 1867/77," *O.* 32 (1886): 86–87.
10. Major Kasimir Zaiaczkowski Ritter de Zareba, "Die taktische Gliederung im Kampfe mit Rücksicht auf die Feuerkraft des Repetir-gewehres und die Inversion," *ÖMZ* 1 (1889): 258.
11. Ratzenhofer, "Die Taktik des Repetirgewehres," 220–228.
12. Geoffrey Wawro, *Warfare and Society in Europe, 1792–1914* (New York: Routledge, 2000), 138.
13. FML Zeno Graf Welser von Welsersheimb, 8: Taktische Studie, Jänner 1890, KA MKSM Sonderreihe, Karton Nr. 67, Studien.
14. Ritter von Czibulka, Taktik II. Jahrgang 1883/1884, KA Militärschule, Kriegsschule, Karton Nr. 59, Studienbehelfe: Strategie und Taktik; Oberstlieutenant Alfred von Englisch-Popparisch, K.u.k. KS Taktik I. Jahrgang 1889/1890, II. Theil, KA Militärschule, KS, Karton Nr. 59, Studienbehelfe: Strategie und Taktik.
15. Oberst Maximilian Freiherr von Pitreich, *Lemberg 1914* (Wien: Adolf Holzhausens Nachfolger, 1929), 127.

16. Conrad von Hötzendorf, "Einiges über den süd-hercegovinischen Karst in militärischer Hinsicht," *O.* 24 (1882): addendum; Conrad, "Ueber militär-geographische Behelfe," *O.* 26 (1883): 411–423.
17. Lawrence Sondhaus, *Franz Conrad von Hötzendorf: Architect of the Apocalypse* (Boston: Humanities Press, 2000), 37–38.
18. K.u.k. KS Lehrstoff und Übungen, Wien 1891 (Studienjahre 1889/90 und 1890/1), Grundsätze der Strategie, KA Militärschulen, Karton Nr. 44, Lehrpläne, Stundeneinteilung, Organisation der KS, Denkschrift KS 1852–1877.
19. Franz Conrad von Hötzendorf, *Zum Studium der Taktik. I. Theil: Einleitung und Infanterie* (Vienna: L.W. Seidel & Sohn, 1891), 111–112.
20. Sondhaus, *Franz Conrad von Hötzendorf: Architect of the Apocalypse*, 44–45.
21. Colonel Wilhelm Reinländer, *Vorträge über die Taktik* (Vienna: L.W. Seidel & Son, 1870–71), KA Militärschule, KS Karton Nr. 59, Studienbehelfe: Strategie und Taktik, 1–9.
22. Sondhaus, *Franz Conrad von Hötzendorf: Architect of the Apocalypse*, 41–42.
23. "Der Anlauf mit dem Bajonnet," *ÖMZ* 1 (1882): 262–270.
24. F. Ebh., "Einige Betrachtungen über den Infanterie-Angriff mit Hinblick auf die Bestimmungen des Reglements," *ÖMZ* 3 (1883): 229.
25. Major Baron Boecklin, "Das Infanterie-Feuer im Gefechte. Eine tactische Studie," *O.* 22 (1882): 444.
26. Hauptmann Ferdinand Kudelka, "Feuer und Bajonett," *O.* 25 (1882): 322–323.
27. Erzherzog Albrecht, 2: Bemerkungen zum Bericht über die Manöver des 8. und 9. Korps im August 1885, Arco, 6. XII. 1885, KS MKSM Sonderreihe, Karton Nr. 67, Studien.
28. Sondhaus, *Franz Conrad von Hötzendorf*, 40.
29. Conrad, *Zum Studium der Taktik*, 4.
30. Carl von Clausewitz, *On War*, edited and translated by Michael Howard and Peter Paret (Princeton, NJ: Princeton University Press, 1976), 75.
31. Conrad, *Zum Studium der Taktik*, 14.
32. E.K., "Der moderne Infanterie-Angriff," *ÖMZ* 1 (1893): 182.
33. Hauptmann Gaj, "Betrachtungen über den Einfluss des rauchschwachen Pulvers auf Taktik, Ausbildung und Erziehung von Oberst Wentzel Porth, Commandant des Inf.-Regiments Nr. 101," *ÖMZ* 2 (1892): 68–69.
34. "Initiative und Offensive," *O.* 38 (1889): 166–187.
35. Major von Czogler, "Einflüsse der modernen Kleincalibergewehre und des rauchschwachen Pulvers im Gefechte," *ÖMZ* 3 (1891): 48–49.

36. *Éclair*, "Bajonnett und moralische Erziehung," *ÖMZ* 1 (1893): 37, 42.
37. Ritter von Czibulka, Taktik II. Jahrgang 1883/4, KA Militärschule, Kriegsschule, Karton Nr. 59, Studienbehelfe: Strategie und Taktik; Oberstlieutenant Alfred von Englisch-Popparisch, K.u.k. KS Taktik I. Jahrgang 1889/90, II. Theil, KA Militärschule, KS, Karton Nr. 59, Studienbehelfe: Strategie und Taktik.
38. Hauptmann Ferdinand Fidler von Isarborn, "Studie über den Infanterie-Angriff," *ÖMZ* 2 (1892): 230.
39. Bernhard von Poten, *Geschichte des Militär- Erziehungs- und Bildungswesens in Österreich-Ungarn* (Berlin: A. Hoffman & Comp., 1893), 337.
40. "Über militärische Erziehung der Volksjugend," *ÖMZ* 1 (1881): 220; Major E.M., "Vortrag über die theoretische und praktische Ausbildung des Unterofficiers und Soldaten der Infanterie," *ÖMZ* 3 (1883): 215; General-Major Alois Ritter von Haymerle, "Unsere Infanterie-Cadetenschulen," *ÖMZ* 1 (1884): 245–246; S., "Eine Studie über unser Militär-Erziehungs- und Bildungswesen," *ÖMZ* 4 (1890): 180.
41. Poten, *Geschichte des Militär- Erziehungs- und Bildungswesens in Österreich-Ungarn*, 370, 391, 412–413.
42. Major E.M., "Vortrag über die theoretische und praktische Ausbildung des Unterofficiers und Soldaten der Infanterie," 218; Haymerle, "Unsere Infanterie-Cadetenschulen," 241–242; Oberst -w-, "Aphorismen über Schulung und Ausbildung der Truppen," *ÖMZ* 2 (1884): 89; S., "Eine Studie über unser Militär-Erziehungs- und Bildungswesen," 185; E.v.C., "Zur theoretischen Fortbildung der Officiere und Cadetten," *O.* 50 (1895): 171–179.
43. Scott Lackey, *The Rebirth of the Habsburg Army: Friedrich Beck and the Rise of the General Staff* (Westport, CT: Greenwood Press, 1995), 91–94.
44. Poten, *Geschichte des Militär- Erziehungs- und Bildungswesens in Österreich-Ungarn*, 413–415, 428–432.
45. Haymerle, "Unsere Infanterie-Cadetenschulen," 241–250.
46. Major E.M., "Vortrag über die theoretische und praktische Ausbildung des Unterofficiers und Soldaten der Infanterie," 216–218.
47. Oberlieutenant Ludwig Uhle, "Über das Anerziehen des Muthes," *O.* 21 (1880): 96.
48. Oberlieutenant Friedrich Lax, "Die sociale Aufgabe des Officiers," *ÖMZ* 2 (1893): 235–236, 245–246; Hauptmann Stefan von Buchwald, "Zur Psychologie des Soldatenstandes," *ÖMZ* 4 (1895): 148; L.S., "Der Officier als Lehrer der Mannschaft," *ÖMZ* 4 (1895): 277–281.
49. O.v.St., "Soldatengeist und Soldatenpflicht," *ÖMZ* 1 (1893): 134–136.

50. Lax, "Die sociale Aufgabe des Officiers," 86; Oberstlieutenant Franz Rieger, "Über den Wert und die Pflege der moralischen Kraft," *ÖMZ* 4 (1895): 34–45; E.v.C., "Zur theoretischen Fortbildung der Officiere und Cadetten," 148.
51. "Die Stärken aller Armeen Europas," *ÖMZ* 1 (1893): 76–77.
52. Isarborn, "Studie über den Infanterie-Angriff," 215.
53. Oberstlieutenant Adolf Horsetzky von Hornthal, "Ueber Napoleonische und moderne Offensiv-Operationen," *O.* 32 (1886): 151.
54. August Urbański von Ostrymiecz, *Conrad von Hötzendorf* (Graz-Leipzig-Vienna: Ulrich Mosers Verlag, 1938), 66; Sondhaus, *Franz Conrad von Hötzendorf*, 39–40.
55. Oberst Alexander Ulmansky, "Über die Änderungen in der Taktik der Infanterie, welche die Einführung des Repetirgewehres bedingt," *O.* 38 (1889): 24–26.
56. FML Zeno Graf Welser von Welsersheimb, 8: Taktische Studie, Jänner 1890, KA MKSM Sonderreihe, Karton Nr. 67, Studien.
57. Oberstlieutenant Nikolaus Ritter von Wuich, k.u.k. KS Waffenwesen I. Jahrgang 1890/1, KA Militärschule, KS, Karton Nr. 66, Studienbehelfe: Waffenwesen, 1–2.
58. Erzherzog Albrecht, "Aphorismen über Infanterie-Ausbildung," Wien, December 1888, KA MKFF, Karton Nr. 21, Studien.
59. Oberstlieutenant Viktor Ritter von Neuwirth, "Über den Aufklärungsdienst der Cavallerie und dessen Verwerthung bei der Befehlgebung der höheren Commanden im Felde," *ÖMZ* 1 (1881): 219.
60. L., "Zur Cavallerie-Verwendung im Gefecht," *ÖMZ* 1 (1885): 243.
61. "Über die Ausbildung der Cavallerie für den Kampf mit der Infanterie," *ÖMZ* 1 (1889): 209.
62. L., "Zur Cavallerie-Verwendung im Gefecht," 243.
63. Major Emil Dembsher, "Über Verwendung und Ausbildung der Reiterie im Feuergefecht zu Fuss," *ÖMZ* 2 (1881): 1, 18–19; Dembsher, "Hat die Cavallerie aufgehört eine Waffe zu sein?" *ÖMZ* 2 (1881): 281–282; Dembsher, "Kleine Beiträge fur die Ausbildung und das Dienstleben im Heere. 12. Cavallerie gegen Infanterie," *ÖMZ* 3 (1881): 248.
64. "Angriffs-Formation der Cavallerie auf Infanterie," *ÖMZ* 1 (1889): 197–199.
65. Oberst Gaudernak, "Die Cavallerie und das jetzige Infanteriegewehr," *O.* 43 (1891): 3–4, 15–17.
66. Major Heinrich Freiherr von Pitreich, "Cavallerie im Dienste der Strategie," *ÖMZ* 1 (1881): 90.
67. Gaudernak, "Die Cavallerie und das jetzige Infanteriegewehr," 20.
68. FML Leonidas Freiherr von Popp, No. 48 Memoire über die Aufstellung eines 42. Kavallerie-Regiments und über die Ausrüstung der Kavallerie

mit Feld-Telegraphen-Material, 1888, KA MKSM Sonderreihe, Karton Nr. 65, Studien.

69. Summar über das Gesammt-Erfordernis des stehenden Heeres für das Jahr 1891. Sub-Beilage III zu Beilage A2, KA Generalstab Operationsbüro, Karton Nr. 806, Budget-Entwurfe, 4–5; Beilage B2, 17.
70. Dembsher, "Kleine Beiträge für die Ausbildung und das Dienstleben im Heere. 12. Cavallerie gegen Infanterie," 248.
71. "Abschaffung der Pike bei den k.k. Uhlanen," *ÖMZ* 1 (1889): 214.
72. Oberstlieutenant Markus von Czerlien, "Ueber Einheits-Cavalerie und einige die Ausbildung und Verwendung der Reiterei berührende Fragen," *O.* 22 (1881): 309.
73. "Abschaffung der Pike bei den k.k. Uhlanen," *ÖMZ* 1 (1889): 214.
74. Czerlien, "Ueber Einheits-Cavalerie und einige die Ausbildung und Verwendung der Reiterei berührende Fragen," 317.
75. Dembsher, "Über Verwendung und Ausbildung der Reiterei im Feuergefecht zu Fuss," 1.
76. Hauptmann Ludwig Freiherr von Gottesheim, "Die Cavallerie in den Kriegen der Neuzeit," *ÖMZ* 3 (1882): 183, 193–195.
77. "Abschaffung der Pike bei den k.k. Uhlanen," 223–224.
78. Czerlien, "Ueber Einheits-Cavalerie und einige die Ausbildung und Verwendung der Reiterei berührende Fragen," 274.
79. M.v.B., "Ein Beitrag zu dem Thema 'Der Reiter-Angriff auf Infanterie'," *ÖMZ* 1 (1884): 171.
80. Oberstlieutenant Felix Freiherr von Pach, "Der Friedensübungen der Cavalerie," *O.* 22 (1881): 640.
81. M.v.B., "Ein Beitrag zu dem Thema 'Der Reiter-Angriff auf Infanterie'," 171; "Über die Ausbildung der Cavallerie für den Kampf mit der Infanterie," 209.
82. M.v.B., "Ein Beitrag zu dem Thema 'Der Reiter-Angriff auf Infanterie'," 171; M.v.B., "Einiges über Aufklärungs- und Gefechtsübungen grösserer Cavalleriekörper," *ÖMZ* 4 (1893): 127–128.
83. Gaj, "Betrachtungen über den Einfluss des rauchschwachen Pulvers auf Taktik, Ausbildung und Erziehung von Oberst Wentzel Porth, Commandant des Inf.-Regiments Nr. 101," 67–68; M.v.B., "Einiges über Aufklärungs- und Gefechtsübungen grösserer Cavalleriekörper," 127–128; Oberstlieutenant Ferdinand Schneider, "Cavallerie vor! Eine kriegsgeschichtliche Studie," *O.* 46 (1893): 293–294; "Manöver-Reflexionen," *ÖMZ* 1 (1894): 39–41.
84. o, "Die Friedens-Arbeit der österr.-ung. Cavallerie. Von Marcus von Czerlien, k.u.k. Generalmajor," *ÖMZ* 1 (1895): 291.
85. Major Otto Maresch, "Über die Führung der Artillerie im Manöver und Gefechte," *O.* 26 (1883): 382–398; Major Karl Edler von Reznicek,

"Ein Beitrag zur Ausbildung der Technik des Infanterie-Gefechtes," *O.* 38 (1889): 218; Oberst Hugo von Molnár, "Einiges über Verwendung der Feld-Artillerie," *O.* 46 (1893): 1–3; Hauptmann Bodo Roebbelen, "Über Bildung und Leitung grösserer Artilleriekörper im Gefechte," *O.* 46 (1893): 367; Oberstlieutenant Ludwig Baron Gottesheim, "Die Artillerie in den Kriegen der Neuzeit," *ÖMZ* 3 (1895): 258–259.

86. Gottesheim, "Die Artillerie in den Kriegen der Neuzeit," 258.
87. Gottesheim, "Die Artillerie in den Kriegen der Neuzeit," 258; Gaj, "Betrachtungen über den Einfluss des rauchschwachen Pulvers auf Taktik, Ausbildung und Erziehung von Oberst Wentzel Porth, Commandant des Inf.-Regiments Nr. 101," 68.
88. Molnár, "Einiges über Verwendung der Feld-Artillerie," 16; Gottesheim, "Der Artillerie in den Kriegen der Neuzeit," 259–260.
89. Roebbelen, "Über Bildung und Leitung grösserer Artilleriekörper im Gefechte," 368.
90. Reznicek, "Ein Beitrag zur Ausbildung der Technik des Infanterie-Gefechtes," 218; Gottesheim, "Der Artillerie in den Kriegen der Neuzeit," 262.
91. Oberlieutenant Anton Christl, "Über das Schießen der Feld-Artillerie," *ÖMZ* 2 (1892): 231–232.
92. Hauptmann Justus Jahn von Jahnau, "Die Schnellfeuer-Kanonen und der Zukunftsfortschritt der Feld-Artillerie," *O.* 38 (1889): 207.
93. Hauptmann Alexander Pervulesco, "Vergleichende Schilderung der Bewaffnung der Feld-Artillerien in den fünf grossen Militär-Staaten Europa's, insbesondere mit Rucksicht auf die Beweglichkeit und Feuerwirkung derselben," *ÖMZ* 2 (1881): 43–44.
94. Jahnau, "Die Schnellfeuer-Kanonen und der Zukunftsfortschritt der Feld-Artillerie," 207; Christl, "Über das Schießen der Feld-Artillerie," 232; Oberstlieutenant Nikolaus Ritter von Wuich, "Das Zukunfts-Feldgeschütz," *O.* 46 (1893): 143–151.
95. J.v.M., "Die Feldmörser," *O.* 38 (1889): 324–339.
96. Erzherzog Wilhelm, FML, General-Artillerie-Inspector, No. 50 Denkschrift über vorzunehmende Änderungen in der Organisation der Feld-Artillerie, Jan. 1882, KA MKSM Sonderreihe, Karton Nr. 65, Studien.
97. Jahnau, "Die Schnellfeuer-Kanonen und der Zukunftsfortschritt der Feld-Artillerie," 207; Oberlieutenant Anton Christl, "Das Schiessen von Brisanzgeschossen aus Feldgeschützen," *ÖMZ* 2 (1891): 124.
98. Roebbelen, "Über Bildung und Leitung grösserer Artilleriekörper im Gefechte," 367–368.
99. "Militärische Statistik des österreichisch-ungarischen Heeres für das Jahr 1891," *ÖMZ* 4 (1892): 229.

100. J. Scott Keltie, ed., *The Statesman's Yearbook: Statistical and Historical Annual of the States of the World for the Year 1891* (London: Macmillan and Co., 1891), 479, 538, 693, 868–869.
101. Summar über das Gesammt-Erfordernis des stehendes Heeres für das Jahr 1891. Beilage B2. KA Generalstab Operationsbüro, Karton Nr. 806, Budget-Entwurfe, 2–4.
102. Pervulesco, "Vergleichende Schilderung der Bewaffnung der Feld-Artillerien in den fünf grossen Militär-Staaten Europa's, insbesondere mit Rucksicht auf die Beweglichkeit und Feuerwirkung derselben," 43–44.
103. Hauptmann Franz Schlögelhofer, "Ueber permanente Befestigung," *O.* 26 (1883): 29–54.
104. Hauptmann des Geniestabes Heinrich Ritter von Vefsel, k.k. KS Befestigungskunst 1887/8, KA Militärschule, KS Karton Nr. 61, Studienbehelfe: Befestigung und Festungskriege, 1–2.
105. Schlögelhofer, "Ueber permanente Befestigung," 30, 35–37.
106. Vefsel, k.k. KS Befestigungskunst 1887/8, KA Militärschule, KS Karton Nr. 61, Studienbehelfe: Befestigung und Festungskriege.
107. Mgg., "Über das Verhalten der Infanterie beim Angriffe und der Vertheidigung flüchtiger und Feldbefestigungen," *ÖMZ* 2 (1884): 104–105.
108. Hauptmann Franz Rieger, "Die flüchtige Befestigung im Dienste der Offensive," *O.* 29 (1884): 282.
109. Rieger, "Die flüchtige Befestigung im Dienste der Offensive," 274.
110. Oberstlieutenant Wenzel Porth, "Das Vertrauen auf starke Positionen," *ÖMZ* 1 (1887): 300.
111. Schlögelhofer, "Ueber permanente Befestigung," 31–34.
112. Oberlieutenant Alois Hein, "Über „flüchtige Befestigung"; deren Verwendung im modernen Kampfe; Friedensausbildung," *ÖMZ* 4 (1892): 157.
113. Major Alfred Miksch, "Der Realismus im Festungskriege," *O.* 50 (1895): 237; Toilow, "Studie über Länderbefestigung," *ÖMZ* 1 (1895): 195.
114. Oberstlieutenant Ernst Freiherr von Leithner, "Der heutige Stand der Befestigungsfrage," *O.* 50 (1895): 19–20.
115. Leithner, "Der heutige Stand der Befestigungsfrage," 23–26.
116. Generalstabs-Oberst Wasiliew, Militärische Würdigung des Grenzgebietes Russland-Galizien zwischen Weichsel und Bug, 1889, KA Generalstab Operationsbüro, Karton Nr. 800, Diverse Studien 1882–1914.
117. Graydon A. Tunstall, *Blood on the Snow: The Carpathian Winter War of 1915* (Lawrence: University Press of Kansas, 2010), 3.

118. Chef des Generalstab FML Anton Freiherr von Schönfeld, No. 54 Memoire über die Nothwendigkeit des Ausbaues von Przemyśl und Krakau, KA MKSM Sonderreihe, Karton Nr. 65, Studien.
119. Schlögelhofer, "Ueber permanente Befestigung," 31; Toilow, "Studie über Länderbefestigung," 195.
120. FML Friedrich Graf Beck-Rzikowsky, "Denkschrift für 1893," "Denkschrift für 1894," "Denkschrift für 1895," KA Generalstab Operationsbüro, Karton Nr. 740, Denkschriften des Chef des Generalstabes 1893–1900.
121. Summar über das Gesammt-Erfordernis des stehendes Heeres für das Jahr 1891. Beilage B2. KA Generalstab Operationsbüro, Karton Nr. 806, Budget-Entwurfe, 12.
122. Walter Wagner, "Die k.(u.)k. Armee - Gliederung und Aufgabenstellung," in *Die Habsburgermonarchie 1848–1918*, Vol. 5 *Die Bewaffnete Macht* (Vienna: Verlag der Österreichischen Akademie der Wissenschaften, 1987), 405.
123. Summar über das Gesammt-Erfordernis des stehendes Heeres für das Jahr 1891. Beilage B2. KA Generalstab Operationsbüro, Karton Nr. 806, Budget-Entwurfe, 1, 4, 11–13, 17; Sub-Beilage III zu Beilage A2, 4.
124. Summar über das Gesammt-Erfordernis des stehendes Heeres für das Jahr 1898. Sub-Beilage zur Beilage B. KA Generalstab Operationsbüro, Karton Nr. 806, Budget-Entwurfe, 15.
125. *Stenographische Sitzungs-Protokolle der Delegation des Reichsrathes*, 3. Sitzung der 27. Session am 2. December 1891 (Vienna: k.k. Hof- und Staatsdruckerei, 1891), 48.
126. *Stenographische Sitzungs-Protokolle der Delegation des Reichsrathes*, 4. Sitzung der 12. Session am 6. Februar 1880 (Vienna: k.k. Hof- und Staatsdruckerei, 1880), 79–80; 3. Sitzung der 27. Session am 2. December 1891, 51–54.
127. Alan Sked, *The Decline and Fall of the Habsburg Empire, 1815–1918* (London: Longman, 1989), 299–300.
128. *Stenographische Sitzungs-Protokolle der Delegation des Reichsrathes*, 3. Sitzung der 27. Session am 2. December 1891, 47–48, 51, 123, 133, 137–138.
129. *Stenographische Sitzungs-Protokolle der Delegation des Reichsrathes*, 3. Sitzung der 27. Session am 2. December 1891, 49–50.
130. *Stenographische Sitzungs-Protokolle der Delegation des Reichsrathes*, 3. Sitzung der 27. Session am 2. December 1891, 137–144.
131. Walter Wagner, *Geschichte des K. K. Kriegsministeriums, II. Band 1866–1888* (Wien-Köln-Graz: Hermann Böhlaus: 1971), 251–252.
132. Sked, *The Decline and Fall of the Habsburg Empire, 1815–1918*; Barbara Jelavich, *The Habsburg Empire in European Affairs, 1814–1918*

(Chicago: Rand McNally & Co., 1969); David Good, *The Economic Rise of the Habsburg Empire, 1750–1914* (Berkeley: University of California Press, 1984).

133. *Österreichisches Biographisches Lexikon 1815–1950* Vol. 1 (Vienna: Verlag der Österreichischen Akademie der Wissenschaften, 1957), 132.
134. Beck, "Denkschrift für 1893," "Denkschrift für 1894," "Denkschrift für 1895," KA Generalstab Operationsbüro, Karton Nr. 740, Denkschriften des Chef des Generalstabes 1893–1900.
135. Lackey, *The Rebirth of the Habsburg Army*, 114–115.
136. Lackey, *The Rebirth of the Habsburg Army*, 115; Wagner, *Geschichte des K. K. Kriegsministeriums, II. Band 1866–1888*, 174.
137. Lackey, *The Rebirth of the Habsburg Army*, 115.
138. Wagner, *Geschichte des K. K. Kriegsministeriums, II. Band 1866–1888*, 228–235; Wagner, "Die k.(u.)k. Armee - Gliederung und Aufgabenstellung," –365.
139. *Österreichisches Biographisches Lexikon 1815–1950* Vol. 1, 55, Vol. 6, 231, Vol. 4, 271–272.
140. Gunther E. Rothenberg, *The Army of Francis Joseph* (West Lafayette, IN: Purdue University Press, 1976), 101, 112, 122; Wagner, *Geschichte des K. K. Kriegsministeriums, II. Band 1866–1888*, 10.
141. Albrecht, No. 25, "Uiber die Vorbereitung eines Kriegsschauplatzes mit besonderer Berücksichtigung der Karpathenländer," July 1871, KA MKSM Sonderreihe, Karton Nr. 64, Studien.
142. Albrecht (anonymously), *Das Jahr 1870 und die Wehrkraft der Monarchie* (Vienna: Faesy & Frick, 1870), 21–24. The Habsburg army adopted the title k.u.k. (*kaiserlich und königlich*) instead of k.k. (*kaiser-lich-königlich*) in 1889 as a concession to Hungary for the passage of the 1889 army law. Hungarian politicians viewed this addition of the 'u' as recognition of the equal status of Hungary with Austria according to the *Ausgleich* of 1867.
143. Albrecht, No. 27, "Hauptbedingungen für den Bestand und das Gedeihen der Armee," August 1873, KA MKSM Sonderreihe, Karton Nr. 64, Studien.
144. Rothenberg, *The Army of Francis Joseph*, 216.
145. Wagner, *Geschichte des K. K. Kriegsministeriums, II. Band 1866–1888*, 228–235.
146. Albrecht, No. 27, "Hauptbedingungen für den Bestand und das Gedeihen der Armee," August 1873, KA MKSM Sonderreihe, Karton Nr. 64, Studien.
147. Albrecht, No. 1086 Allerunterthänigster Vortrag, 27 August 1866, Karton Nr. 22, 1866.

148. Albrecht, No. 49 "Memorandum (Organisations-Studie betr. Mobilisierung)," Ende Jan. 1888, KA MKSM Sonderreihe, Karton Nr. 65, Studien.
149. Tunstall, *Blood on the Snow*, 3.
150. Albrecht, No. 49 "Memorandum (Organisations-Studie betr. Mobilisierung)," Ende Jan. 1888, KA MKSM Sonderreihe, Karton Nr. 65, Studien; Albrecht, No. 28 "Promemoria über die Zutheilung und Verwendung von Generalen des Ruhestandes," Feb. 1887, KA MKSM Sonderreihe, Karton Nr. 64, Studien; Albrecht, No. 38 "Studie über die Vermehrung der Wehrkraft der Monarchie," Ende Dez. 1886, KA MKSM Sonderreihe, Karton Nr. 65, Studien.
151. Erzherzog Albrecht, "Aphorismen über Infanterie-Ausbildung," Wien, December 1888, KA MKFF, Karton Nr. 21, Studien.

Bibliography

Unpublished Documents

Kriegsarchiv (KA), Vienna.
Allerhöchster Oberbefehl (AhOB).
Militärkanzlei Seiner Majestät des Kaisers (MKSM) Sonderreihe 1866–1918.
Militärkanzlei des Generalinspektors der gesamten bewaffneten Macht Erzherzog Franz Ferdinand (MKFF) 1898–1914.
Chef des Generalstabs (GSt) Operationsbüro 1866–1918.
Zentralstellen.
Kriegsministerium (KM) Präsidialbüro (Präsidium) 1866–1918.
Militärerziehungs- und Bildungsanstalten (MEB).
Kriegsschule Wien 1867–1914.

Published Primary Sources

Albrecht (anonymously). *Das Jahr 1870 und die Wehrkraft der Monarchie.* Vienna: Faesy & Frick, 1870.
Conrad von Hötzendorf, Franz. *Zum Studium der Taktik.* Vienna: L.W. Seidel & Sohn, 1891.
Keltie, J. Scott, ed. *The Statesman's Yearbook: Statistical and Historical Annual of the States of the World for the Year 1891.* London: Macmillan and Co., 1891.
Organ der militärwissenschaftlichen Vereine (O.), 1867–1906.
Österreichische Militärische Zeitschrift (ÖMZ), 1866–1914.
Ostrymiecz, August Urbański von. *Conrad von Hötzendorf.* Graz-Leipzig-Vienna: Ulrich Mosers Verlag, 1938.
Pitreich, Oberst Maximilian Freiherr von. *Lemberg 1914.* Wien: Adolf Holzhausens Nachfolger, 1929.

Poten, Bernhard von. *Geschichte des Militär- Erziehungs- und Bildungswesens in Österreich-Ungarn*. Berlin: A. Hoffman & Comp., 1893.

Reinländer, Oberst Wilhelm. *Vorträge über die Taktik*. Vienna: L.W. Seidel & Son, 1870–71.

Stenographische Sitzungs-Protokolle der Delegation des Reichsrathes. Vienna: k.k. Hof- und Staatsdruckerei, 1869–1911.

Secondary Sources

Clausewitz, Carl von. *On War*. Edited and translated by Michael Howard and Peter Paret. Princeton, New Jersey: Princeton University Press, 1976.

Good, David. *The Economic Rise of the Habsburg Empire, 1750–1914*. Berkeley: University of California Press, 1984.

Jelavich, Barbara. *The Habsburg Empire in European Affairs, 1814–1918*. Chicago: Rand McNally & Co., 1969.

Lackey, Scott. *The Rebirth of the Habsburg Army: Friedrich Beck and the Rise of the General Staff*. Westport, CT: Greenwood Press, 1995.

Österreichisches Biographisches Lexikon 1815–1950 Vol. 1. Vienna: Verlag der Österreichischen Akademie der Wissenschaften, 1957.

Rothenberg, Gunther E. *The Army of Francis Joseph*. West Lafayette, IN: Purdue University Press, 1976.

Sked, Alan. *The Decline and Fall of the Habsburg Empire, 1815–1918*. London: Longman, 1989.

Sondhaus, Lawrence. *Franz Conrad von Hötzendorf: Architect of the Apocalypse*. Boston: Humanities Press, 2000.

Tunstall, Graydon A. *Blood on the Snow: The Carpathian Winter War of 1915*. Lawrence: University Press of Kansas, 2010.

Wagner, Walter. "Die k.(u.)k. Armee - Gliederung und Aufgabenstellung." in *Die Habsburgermonarchie 1848–1918*, Vol. 5 *Die Bewaffnete Macht*. Vienna: Verlag der Österreichischen Akademie der Wissenschaften, 1987.

Wagner, Walter. *Geschichte des K. K. Kriegsministeriums, II. Band 1866–1888*. Wien-Köln-Graz: Hermann Böhlaus: 1971.

Walter, John. *The Rifle Story*. London: Greenhill Books, 2006.

Wawro, Geoffrey. *Warfare and Society in Europe, 1792–1914*. New York: Routledge, 2000.

CHAPTER 6

Financial Shock: Conradian Tactics and Wasteful Spending

"Woe to the weak!"[1] was how the *Neue Freie Presse* of Vienna described the international situation at the end of the nineteenth century. Europe had formed two groups aligned against each other: the *Dreibund* (Triple Alliance) of Austria-Hungary, Germany, and Italy, and the *Zweibund* (Dual Alliance) of France and Russia. With a peace footing of 359,878 men and a war footing of 1,826,940 in 1901, the Habsburg Empire, with its low yearly conscription numbers, definitely had fewer soldiers than the other major continental powers. In peacetime, Germany had 580,023 soldiers, France 589,444, and Russia 1,100,000. Only Italy possessed smaller numbers with 263,684 troops. In war, the inferiority of Austria-Hungary stood out more starkly as Germany could put over 3,000,000 men in the field, France 2,500,000, and Russia 4,600,000. Even Italy could field 3,308,650, though more than 2,000,000 of these qualified as territorial militia.[2] The numerical superiority of the Russo-French alliance with its 7,100,000 troops compared with under 5,000,000 men of Germany and Austria-Hungary brought this weakness into even greater contrast. Because Germany and Austria-Hungary could not rely upon the assistance of Italy, the untrustworthy member of the alliance and former foe of the Habsburg Empire, the *Dreibund* remained at a disadvantage to the *Zweibund*.

Austria-Hungary needed to take significant measures to compensate for the numerical disadvantages of its military position. With the constant burden of inferiority weighing upon the Habsburg army, the *k.u.k.* high command continued to develop the imperial forces in ways

J.A. Dredger, *Tactics and Procurement in the Habsburg Military, 1866–1918*, DOI 10.1007/978-3-319-57678-7_6

that would compensate for the lack in numbers while maintaining Austria-Hungary's great power status. However, Habsburg officers perpetuated the same mistakes that had plagued the *k.u.k.* military previously. Tactics took on an even more offensive course, with emphasis on the will and spirit to overcome superior numbers. The high command poured increasingly large sums into permanent fortifications and battleships while neglecting the procurement of better artillery. During the two decades before the First World War, the last chance for the Austro-Hungarian army to remedy the failures of earlier years, *k.u.k.* military leaders repeatedly failed to learn the lessons of modern warfare, which favored the defensive, and implement the necessary requirements for an army in the weak position of the Habsburg Empire.

Solution for Numerical Inferiority: Morale

Near the close of the nineteenth century, several authors commented that the end of the million-man army drew near. The German staff officer, Major Wilhelm Leopold Colmar Freiherr von der Goltz, prophesied the rise of a new Alexander the Great, who would use a small force of well-trained and well-equipped men to defeat the numberless hordes of the enemy.[3] Similarly, a *k.u.k.* captain pointed out the numerous occasions throughout history when troops, smaller in number but better armed and trained, defeated more numerous opponents. In his opinion, this success meant that immense armies were unnecessary.[4] Even more emphatically, retired *FML* Adolf Baron von Sacken in several articles of the *ÖMZ* argued for elimination of the unwieldy and expensive armed forces that would flood the battlefields of Europe with millions of destructive men and weapons. Massive militaries with universal conscription and the support of the whole populace would bring about wars of annihilation and battles of despair, which the states would lead *à outrance* until "the last reserves, the last levy of the defeated have been utterly destroyed." Then the victors, amid countless cripples and sick, will remap Europe while slicing up the conquered lands, and thereby leave the losers full of thoughts of revenge.[5]

Such a ghastly war filled Austro-Hungarian military leaders with trepidation, especially as the outcome did not look propitious for the weaker Habsburg army. The peace conferences of the 1890s held no guarantees of everlasting peace and the European states continued to enlarge their military might.[6] Therefore, the idea of returning to a professional army of volunteers rather than a massive force of conscripts understandably appealed to *k.u.k.* officers. A study of the means to develop the war power of the Habsburg military summed up the difficulty: "Universal conscription exists among us only in theory, but not in reality, because the claims for exception by the available able-bodied people liable for conscription are completely heterogeneous."[7] Although certain reasons for exception merited consideration, too many received exemptions. Those men who qualified for conscription were divided into three classes: 3-year recruits for the standing army, 2-year recruits for the *Landwehr*, and the rest for the *Landsturm*, which never received any training. The army remained far too small to fight a successful war against another great power and would have to employ the *Landwehr* in the front lines from the beginning of any war instead of as reserve forces.[8] Incapable of raising the number of Austro-Hungarian troops dramatically, Habsburg theorists looked for other solutions to the predicament of inferior numbers. The option of falling from the ranks of the great military powers or failing to fulfill the duties of the alliance with Germany never entered into consideration.[9]

Therefore, *k.u.k.* officers studied history for precedents showing how smaller forces had conquered larger adversaries. One officer attributed victory not so much to overwhelming numerical advantage but rather to superior leadership, equipment, and weaponry as well as luck.[10] Other officers emphasized the necessity of the "inner worth" of the army. Sacken wrote, "Not in numerical strength but in the inner ability and solidity, in the mobility and impulsive power is the true worth of the army to be sought and in this direction must its development also be sought." After all, Prussia had defeated France in 1870–1871 without the benefits of universal conscription.[11]

Conradian Tactics: The Superior Morale of the Offensive

This view meshed perfectly with the tactical doctrine of Franz Conrad von Hötzendorf, the influential tactical instructor at the *Kriegsschule* from 1888 to 1892, foremost interpreter of the *k.u.k.* infantry regulations, and chief of the general staff from 1906 to 1911 and again from 1912 to 1917. Conrad believed in achieving moral superiority over the enemy as the means to victory. Only the offensive could give this advantage to soldiers, while demoralizing opponents who depended on the will of the attacker by taking defensive positions.[12] Belief in the power of the offensive spirit coincided with Conrad's Social Darwinism, which set the stronger over the weaker no matter who possessed numerical superiority.[13] The stronger always attacked. This view also suited Conrad's desire to raise the sunken prestige of Austria-Hungary and restore the Habsburg Empire to great power status. As chief of the general staff, Conrad constantly tried to convince the emperor, war ministers, foreign ministers, and anyone else he could find that Austria-Hungary must engage in preventive wars to raise the prestige of the Habsburg monarchy.[14]

Conrad's *Zum Studium der Taktik* provides the essential points of his tactical thought. Hötzendorf compiled this 815-page work as a publication of his teaching notes at the war college. Throughout the introduction, Conrad discussed victory and defeat, the principle of superiority, initiative, activity and passivity, and attack and defense. He stressed the need to seize the initiative, achieve activity and the attack, and force the enemy to remain passive in defense and merely react to the moves of the attacker. All depended on maintaining superior morale in order to inflict one's will upon the opponent: "The goal of war is the permanent conquest of the enemy's will."[15]

In this spirit, Conrad devoted 105 pages (13% of the whole book) to the attack and only 45 pages (5.5%) to defense. Although the author discussed artillery for 115 pages, the section on infantry encompassed 168 pages. Hötzendorf focused on infantry as the decisive offensive weapon in the most important section of the work. This 155-page section entitled "*Vom Gefecht*" described the actions that infantry should take during battle to achieve offensive victory by an assault culminating in a bayonet attack.[16] The combination of superior morale and infantry offensive epitomized the tactical thought of Conrad, which he strove to instill in the Habsburg officer corps, especially the general staff officers.

Conradian Influence: The *Kriegsschule* and the Officer Corps

When Conrad became chief of the general staff in 1906, he stipulated changes in the curriculum and teaching methods of the *Kriegsschule*. Placing more emphasis on tactics and the character of the general staff officer, Conrad stressed the ability of officers relying on superior morale to organize and lead troops, even in frontal assaults, and therefore to gain experience in offensive exercises.[17] Several years later, he put greater weight on the psychological training of staff officers than on the calculation of numbers in the Clausewitzian spirit of the philosophy of war. Conrad recommended his own study, *Zum Studium der Taktik*, with its idealization of the offensive, rather than the Prussian theorist's discussion of defense and attack.[18]

The curriculum of the *k.u.k.* war college revealed the influence of the former instructor of tactics. Even before Conrad became chief of the general staff, tactical courses focused on the offensive far more than the defensive. Lists of study themes for tactics from 1902 to 1906 persisted in asking for assessments of the armies fighting offensive battles rather than the defenders. These lists especially concentrated on the Austro-Prussian War of 1866 and the Franco-Prussian War of 1870–1871, with primary emphasis on the attacking side. For the 1902–1903 list, 22 of 33 study questions referred to 1866 or 1870–1871; in the 1903–1904 list, 28 of 36 focused on 1866 and 1870–1871; and for the 1905–1906 list, 21 of 32. Most of the other themes also stressed the importance of the attack in studying offensive battles from the Russo-Turkish War of 1877–1878 and the Russo-Japanese War of 1904–1905. The same predominance of Prussian offensive victories in 1866 and 1870–1871 appeared in the study theme lists for strategy and military history.[19] The Habsburg army's obsession with the theories of Moltke and offensive warfare had not diminished, but rather increased over the three or four decades since the Austro-Prussian and Franco-Prussian conflicts. The Prussian commander Moltke, as the conqueror of both the Austrian army in 1866 and the French army (supposedly the best military in Europe) in 1870, held the primary place of honor in the eyes of most Habsburg officers. Conrad's immense knowledge of the 1870–1871 war and the ideas of his "hero" Moltke influenced the exaggerated role of the Prussian field marshal's battles in the education of future *k.u.k.* general staff officers.[20]

After Conrad became chief of the general staff, the emphasis on offensive tactics, especially the victories of Moltke, and the need for superior *élan* took even greater precedence in the *Kriegsschule*. Lesson plans revealed how Conrad had incorporated his ideas of the primacy of the offensive and superior morale into the curriculum of the war college. In the second year of tactical instruction, students toured the battlefields of Bohemia and Moravia. The third year military history course focused on the 1866 Bohemian campaign and the Franco-Prussian War as examples of modern offensive war. The Bohemian and Moravian battles, however, were an essential part of every year of study, not just the second and third.[21] In all classes and study rides, the instructors emphasized the need to seize and hold the initiative and the offensive, as well as the importance of will and spirit for superior morale.[22] Thus, the Habsburg military saw the secret to success on the battlefield as emulating the offensive victories of maneuver that the Prussians achieved in 1866 and 1870.

Other documents showed the same emphasis on the offensive. An analysis of the Battle of Spichern in 1870 concluded that the Germans did not press the attack vigorously enough and thus could not dislodge the weaker French adversary.[23] On a different occasion during the Franco-Prussian War, according to a *k.u.k.* study guide, a German unit successfully charged across an open field and broke through two numerically superior French lines with bayonets, because of will power and confidence in their own superior abilities.[24] The author of another Austro-Hungarian tactical study remarked that an attack across open ground in the face of modern infantry fire could still succeed. The German failure at St. Privat in 1870 had resulted from poor leadership and insufficient numbers, not the terrain or devastating firepower of the French rifles.[25] Conrad pointed out the battle of Mars-la-Tour in 1870 as the best engagement for detailed study and testing.[26]

Habsburg tactical instructors tried to apply Moltke's ideas to future campaigns. The writer of a *k.u.k.* study of Austro-Hungarian advance into Galicia against the Russians compared the Habsburg movements with Moltke's invasion of France in 1870. The main danger was the possibility of the three projected armies becoming too greatly separated during the advance. To counter this problem, the study author recommended that *k.u.k.* forces live off the land to move faster and overrun the enemy before the Russians could realize the Austro-Hungarian weaknesses.[27] This study proved accurate in depicting the difficulty for Habsburg troops to maintain contact with each other and not allow large gaps to occur while advancing in the face of numerically far superior forces.[28] The offensive ideas of Moltke did not alleviate the problems for the *k.u.k.* army in 1914 and the recommendations to live off the land for faster movement and overrun the enemy before Habsburg weaknesses became obvious portrayed an impossible hope. Glossing over the problems with hopeful yet unrealizable solutions, rather than rectifying the faulty strategy with a defensive operational scheme, only confirmed the fixation of Austro-Hungarian theorists for the offensive. No prominent *k.u.k.* strategists or tacticians even considered the defense as a viable option, because they believed that great military powers gained victory only by attack, not by defenses that merely reacted to the will of the opponent.

The extreme emphasis on tactics in the *Kriegsschule* led Major General Alfred Krauss, commandant of the war college from 1910 until 1914, to lament that instructors taught tactics as the most important topic, completely detached from all others, and therefore only led exercises for independent units in battle situations rather than maneuvers involving all aspects of war. Thus, instead of working together with the operational general staff service and taking into consideration the great significance of provisions and supplies for soldiers in the field, tacticians treated their work in isolation. Krauss, however, like most other Austro-Hungarian military writers, used examples from the Austro-Prussian and Franco-Prussian wars to illustrate his point.[29] The fixation on Moltke's campaigns had even infected men like Krauss, who found fault with the exaggerated importance of tactics in Habsburg military education.

The obsession with the Prussian victories of 1866 and 1870 spread throughout the Habsburg officer corps during the two decades before the First World War even more than in previous years. After Conrad began publishing his tactical works, hardly any writers expressed opinions contrary to the ideas of Conrad or failed to mention the ideas and victories of Moltke. This agreement became pronounced, especially during the last half of the 1890s. Article writers emphasized the importance of seizing the initiative and maintaining high morale as well as the constant *Drang nach vorwärts* (push forward), while repeatedly referencing Conrad's *Zum Studium der Taktik* and the infantry regulations of 1889.[30] In the words of one author, "The good soldier will constantly decide for the attack where feasible in small and great conditions. Let us always remain mindful that posterity rarely weaves a wreath of glory for the successful defender."[31] Once again, Austro-Hungarian theorists strongly advocated the offensive as the only means to victory and military prestige.

Few voices of reason in line with the thoughts of Archduke Albrecht surfaced at this time. Most of these writers, unwilling to put their own names on criticisms of the prevalent ideas in the Habsburg army, published their articles in the military journals anonymously. Questioning the wisdom of incessantly striving for the offensive, these officers showed the advantages that repeating rifles and smokeless powder offered for the defensive, while asserting that certain situations called for defensive fighting.[32] One writer, taking the name Simplex in a demand for simplicity in tactical theory, called for a golden mean between attack and defense and accused *k.u.k.* tacticians of returning to the Middle Ages by instructing infantry to use rifles like lances because of the bayonet.[33] Another officer agreed that bayonets offered no advantage, not even psychological, but instead hindered shooting, wasted time because they needed to be fixed to the gun, and helped little in hand to hand combat because men instinctively used the rifle butt to club the enemy.[34] A third author complained that, during field exercises, judges invariably ruled the attacking forces victorious over the defenders no matter how the troops performed, because the offensive side always possessed more soldiers.[35] Even among these dissenting officers, most did not propose a defensive strategy and tactics for the Austro-Hungarian army but instead assessed the offensive as the more desirable form of battle while emphasizing the importance of gaining the initiative for high morale.[36] No one dared to offer an effective solution for the increasing numerical gap between the *k.u.k.* military and the other European powers by proposing a strategical and tactical defensive, with the goal of taking the offensive only after the exhaustion of futile enemy attacks.

The maneuvers of the Habsburg army during the decade preceding the First World War exhibited the preference for the offensive.[37] *FML* Karl Maria von Lang, a well-known military writer in Austria-Hungary, commented on the emphasis on assault during the large army exercises of 1907, 1908, and 1909.[38] Regarding the relationship of attack and defense, Lang wrote, "The attacker remains constantly in the advantage and superior to the defender."[39] Likewise, Lang stated the need for every soldier to maintain the fundamental conviction that "safety and victory lie only in the attack."[40] A general staff colonel commented that troop exercises contained more and more frontal attacks without artillery support in the last years before the Great War.[41] Judges declared that the side that brought more units most quickly to certain "decisive points" had won the exercise, regardless of the interaction of infantry and artillery. Even though all officers knew that both branches must work together to achieve victory, in practice this close support never took place.[42] War Minister Auffenberg also noted the insistence on constant *Drang nach vorwärts* to increase *élan* during maneuvers, with little consideration for artillery or losses.[43] This stress on the offensive continued up to the First World War, even to the point of ordering massed cavalry to charge entrenched infantry at the maneuvers of 1913.[44] The obvious purpose of the great Habsburg field exercises was to inculcate every member of the Austro-Hungarian army with the offensive *à outrance* as preparation for the next war. This methodology revealed a failure to grasp and implement the lessons of the most recent wars.

Failure to Learn: Lessons of the Boer War

During the first years of the twentieth century, *k.u.k.* officers rethought the tactical instructions of the 1889 infantry regulations because of the surprising events of the Boer War. This conflict between the Boers, or Dutch settlers in South Africa, and the British from 1899 to 1902 gave stark proof of the advantages that modern weaponry gave to the defender. With repeating rifles, machineguns, smokeless powder, and excellent defensive positions, the Boers succeeded in inflicting heavy casualties while stopping British assaults. Thus, the British had to change tactics. Instead of the combination of fire and movement culminating in a bayonet charge, British leaders sent half a million men into the field, employing flying columns of British mounted infantry along with attacks on Boer farms and the incarceration of Boers in concentration camps. With such drastic measures the British gained victory, but not with frontal assaults.[45]

The surprising tactical success of the Boer defense sobered the optimistic offensive view of some Habsburg officers. Because of the strong impression given by the Boer fire discipline, field fortifications, and economic use of ammunition, Austro-Hungarian military writers tempered the overly offensive viewpoint of the 1889 infantry regulations. *FML* Gustav Ratzenhofer, the lead interpreter of *k.u.k.* infantry regulations before the rise of Conrad, stated that the Boer War reinforced the lessons of 1866 and 1870: frontal assaults against modern rifles only worked in peacetime maneuvers, not on the battlefield. British troops, like the Austrians in the Austro-Prussian War, made the capital mistake of relying too heavily on mere courage to gain victory.[46] Other officers stressed the importance of firepower, especially precise shooting rather than mass fire.[47] Storm tactics could only prove effective if fire had already broken the resistance of the enemy.[48]

Even the new infantry regulations of 1903, the product of a commission led by Archduke Franz Ferdinand, heir to the Habsburg throne, and including Conrad, emphasized the need for the attacker to establish fire superiority before storming defensive positions. Yet these same regulations instructed officers to lead their troops as close as possible to the enemy before opening fire and then to use denser swarm lines to achieve as much firepower as possible.[49] In effect, the new *k.u.k.* infantry regulations, which the Habsburg high command had designed to take into consideration the lessons of the Boer War, merely restated the fire and movement tactics of the British with a greater emphasis on gaining fire superiority before the bayonet charge. Austro-Hungarian tacticians failed to learn the real lessons of British defeat and Boer victory and chose to maintain the offensive spirit rather than turn to the defensive first and then look for opportunities to counterattack, according to the ideas of Clausewitz. After all, the offensive side had won the war in the end.

The main *k.u.k.* tactical theorist, Conrad von Hötzendorf, misinterpreted the events of the Boer War. In his book *Infanterische Fragen und die Erscheinungen des Boerenkrieges*, Conrad claimed that poor British morale and insufficient *élan* had caused disaster for the offensive forces. The increased firepower of magazine rifles and machine guns had not brought victory to the defensive-minded Boers. Other successful attackers in previous wars, such as the Prussians in 1870, had won despite heavier casualties than the British suffered. Hötzendorf concluded that the British had not carried out the assaults correctly. Besides, European soldiers would never aim as well as the Boers, who learned how to shoot at an early age. Therefore, the offensive still maintained superiority over the defensive and would prove effective in future wars.[50]

Most Habsburg officers followed Conrad's analysis of the Boer War in their own articles. While expressing admiration for the impressive defense of the Boers, *k.u.k.* military writers blamed the British for poor reconnaissance and attack preparation. Their solutions to the problem of successful attack echoed Conrad and the infantry regulations of 1903. Calling for more initiative and higher morale, officers advocated gaining fire superiority over the enemy by advancing as close as possible with as many rifles as possible before shooting, and then charging with the bayonet. Though proposing more target practice because accurate fire raises morale, these authors still concluded that modern weaponry required a greater sense of *Drang nach vorwärts*.[51] The bayonet remained an essential part of Austro-Hungarian tactics, despite the insignificant role *blanken Waffen* played in the Boer War because the British attackers hardly ever reached the defenses and the Boers possessed no bayonets.[52]

Some *k.u.k.* officers recognized the excellent morale of the Boers as the source of success. This realization meant that the defenders possessed a greater psychological advantage as well as fire superiority over the British attackers, who became demoralized because they could not even see the Boers behind their field fortifications.[53] Nevertheless, in an effort to prove the merits of the *k.u.k.* insistence on offensive operations, Habsburg military authors censured the Boers for defending in a purely passive manner with no plan for counterattacking.[54] The British won the war in the end as the attacker.[55] Thus, despite recognition of the superiority of fire and the advantages that modern weaponry gave to the defender, the majority of Austro-Hungarian officers agreed with Conrad and the 1903 infantry regulations that the offensive offered the only means for victory.

Failure to Learn: Lessons of the Russo-Japanese War

The Russo-Japanese War of 1904–1905 confirmed the *k.u.k.* preference for the offensive and trust in the superiority of high morale. At Port Arthur, the Japanese attacked the excellent Russian defensive positions no less than six times between August and November 1904 with no effect, while suffering heavy casualties. Not only had the Russians fortified the town with extensive mutually supportive forts and trenches, but they used the new technology of recoilless quick-firing artillery, howitzers, and explosive shells. The combination of firepower from rifles and cannon with entrenched defense in depth thwarted Japanese attempts to break the Russian lines and rendered the battlefield a precursor to the warfare of the First World War.[56] To achieve victory, the Japanese had to resort to methodical siege tactics, which brought about the capitulation of Port Arthur because the Russians ran out of ammunition and provisions.[57]

The other major land battle of the Russo-Japanese War involved a flanking movement in the spirit of Moltke by the Japanese at Mukden. This attempt, however, did not result in a brilliant victory of maneuver, but rather 3 weeks of incessant shelling and failed assaults. Although the Russians retreated from Japanese bombardment, the Japanese could hardly claim victory because the casualties of both sides roughly equaled each other. Nor could the Japanese press the advantage because of their heavy losses, and thus allowed the Russians to escape. The war ended because of the Japanese naval victory of Tsushima and the ensuing domestic turmoil in Russia, not because of the superiority of the offensive.[58]

The Japanese, the attacking combatant, had won the war and the Russians, fighting on the defensive, had lost. For Habsburg military theorists, the answer to Japanese success and Russian failure had to lie in the offensive strategy and tactics of the victorious side. Therefore, *k.u.k.* officers tried to explain the superiority of Japanese tactics. Instead of blaming the failure of Japanese frontal assaults on the futility of attacking opponents in heavily fortified positions and holding destructive weaponry, the Austro-Hungarians praised the incessant *Drang nach vorwärts* of the attacks. Because offensive fire had proved incapable of dislodging the Russians from their fortifications, the Japanese had resorted to bayonet charges. Even though these assaults rarely had any positive effect, Habsburg theorists equated the offensive shock tactics with the overall success of the Japanese military during the war.[59]

The good morale and offensive spirit of Japanese warfare impressed *k.u.k.* officers most. The Japanese soldiers displayed, in the eyes of Austro-Hungarian military thinkers, the highest level of the offensive *à outrance*. Not only did the Japanese attack at all costs, but they had also won the war. Thus, Habsburg officers believed that the tactics of Conrad and the *k.u.k.* infantry regulations had been confirmed and pushed for the offensive even more as the only means for victory.[60] The success of Japan in a war against a numerically superior enemy inspired Austro-Hungarian theorists to think that the Habsburg army could use the same methods and win future conflicts. Therefore, *k.u.k.* officers continued to stress the offensive and the development of morale as the answer to the problems of inferior numbers and weaponry during the years before World War I.[61] Statistics reporting a lower percentage of casualties for attacking troops during the Russo-Japanese War than in previous conflicts appeared to support the view that the offensive provided the greatest chance for success.[62] German historian Günther Kronenbitter stated correctly that Austro-Hungarian officers firmly believed that the outcome of the Russo-Japanese War proved the superiority of the attack filled with *élan*, even over more numerous defenders.[63] Instead of learning the real lessons of the war in Manchuria, Dual Monarchy officers, especially in the general staff, used the Russo-Japanese experiences to confirm their pre-existing preference for the offensive, which stemmed from the adoration of Moltke's victories in 1870–1871.[64]

In articles analyzing the causes of victory, many Habsburg officers used the phrase *Wille zum Siege*, or "will to victory," to define the winning psychological attitude of the Japanese soldiers, and thus of every conquering army.[65] Austro-Hungarian military authors began using this phrase in 1906, the same year that the second edition of the German philosopher Friedrich Nietzsche's *Der Wille zur Macht* came into publication. The concept of the "will to power" in a military sense meant the desire to overpower the enemy by means of superior morale. This idea coincided perfectly with the views of Conrad in *Zum Studium der Taktik* and other *k.u.k.* writers who stressed the paramount importance of morale and impressing one's own will on the enemy.[66] The 1909 sketch for the new infantry regulations used the phrase *Wille zu siegen* as one of the all-important means of spurring the troops on to self-sacrifice, perseverance, and a spirit of enterprise.[67] As one *k.u.k.* major said, "The attacker's senses and striving culminate in the strong will: forward to the enemy, cost what it will."[68]

The views held by the Habsburg army were also expressed by other Viennese authors, such as the psychologist Alfred Adler, who incorporated Nietzsche's ideas into his theory of individual psychology, and the English-born and pro-German Houston Stewart Chamberlain, who wrote a series of war essays entitled *Der Wille zum Sieg und andere Aufsätze* during the First World War.[69] The excessive emphasis on the power of the will for victory corresponded with the increasing importance of the individual in the years before World War I. Austro-Hungarian military writers expressed the need to develop the thinking ability and personality of each officer and the discipline and intelligence of every soldier.[70] Colonel Rudolf Rudel stated this idea best: "The intellectual and psychological power of the individual is in today's nerve-shattering battle, despite all the progress of technology, the best and most successful weapon."[71] By stressing the importance of the psychological strength of each officer and soldier in training, the Habsburg army employed philosophical ideas prevalent during the first decade of the twentieth century to drive soldiers on to offensive victory.

The other European military powers also saw the Japanese victory as the result of an attacking spirit and the passivity of the Russian defense. This view confirmed the preference for the offensive, which permeated the infantry regulations of modern armies.[72] The *k.u.k.* infantry regulations were most similar to the 1906 German regulations.[73] This likeness stemmed not only from the alliance between the two states, but also from the fixation of Austro-Hungarian theorists such as Conrad on Moltke's offensive ideas and the Prussian victories of 1866 and 1870–1871.

The Japanese infantry instructions exuded the offensive spirit, emphasizing "lust for the attack," the "iron will" of commanders and troops, and the decisiveness of the bayonet for victory.[74] The new Japanese 1909 exercise regulations for infantry, written to incorporate the lessons of the Russo-Japanese War, expressed the offensive spirit even more than previous editions.[75] Stressing the need to seize the initiative and maintain superior morale, the Japanese regulations, as translated by the Evidence Bureau of the *k.u.k.* general staff, stated, "The attack is in general the only way to victory, the commander chooses another means only when pressed by necessity."[76] The Japanese regulations impressed Habsburg officers as the instructions of a victorious yet smaller military power against the largest European military, an army that Austria-Hungary would very probably face in a future war. Although the extreme offensive spirit of the Japanese regulations greatly inspired *k.u.k.* thinkers, many Habsburg theorists found the source of this spirit, and thus the most important factor in Japanese success, to be the love of fatherland and monarch that Japanese soldiers and the whole population possessed.[77] The excellent morale and enthusiasm of the Japanese people and army appealed to Austro-Hungarian officers, who still considered that the role of the *k.u.k.* military as educator of the various peoples of the empire in patriotism was paramount.[78] Thus, everything about the Japanese victory over Russia inspired Habsburg theorists: a smaller army defeating a larger one, offensive spirit, and patriotic support of the population.

New Infantry Regulations: Conradian Offensive

When Conrad determined to write a new set of infantry regulations for the *k.u.k.* army, the ideas of the Japanese military had a strong influence.[79] The 1909 draft of the new infantry tactical regulations displayed devotion to attack as the only means of success, the culmination of assaults in bayonet storms, and the prominence of morale in inflicting one's will on the enemy and seizing the initiative. The regulations significantly underscored these points: "An infantry filled with lust for attack, physically and psychologically persevering, well-trained and well-led will fight successfully against a numerically superior enemy." Regarding morale, the regulations spoke emphatically: "The strength of morale forms in war the most powerful driving force of all performance, it stimulates the use of the means of battle and is often of greater significance for success than the relationship of numbers and the skill of leadership."[80]

The instructions also emphasized the need for frontal attacks: "The attack alone with the all-inspiring and never tiring thought 'forward toward the enemy' brings decisive results." Although the regulations emphasized fire superiority as the means to victory, the storm with bayonet charge remained the final step for breaking the resistance of the defender. The infantry assault "remains irresistible in the most difficult situations, if an effective, powerful fire prepares the way." Artillery must prepare the attack and make the assault easier for the infantry. The ground troops, however, must never become dependent on the artillery or wait for artillery fire to attack. The frontal infantry assault culminating in the bayonet charge "forms an essential and unavoidable part of the whole infantry attack and becomes the rule for the greatest part of the battle front." Thus, although acknowledging the importance of firepower, the new regulations emphasized Conrad's ideas of morale, the will for victory, and the offensive as the necessary means of achieving victory.

A board of 33 of the highest ranking generals and colonels in the *k.u.k.* army, including Archduke Franz Ferdinand and Archdukes Friedrich and Eugen, reviewed the draft of the new infantry regulations and offered critiques, but did not discuss the overemphasis on the offensive. The majority (19) approved the new instructions as essential progress, although Archduke Eugen and several other generals recognized the difficulties in the requirement for more initiative and independent action from subordinates, and called for intensive training of non-commissioned officers.[81]

Ten reviewers took a middle position on the proposed infantry regulations. These men expressed concern that the call for more individual training in battle discipline, and thus less formalism and drill, did not correspond to the special situation of the Austro-Hungarian military. Because of the multi-ethnic composition of the Habsburg army and the low level of intellectual training that many recruits received before entrance into the armed forces, these ten reviewers felt that *k.u.k.* officers and soldiers might not prove capable of implementing the instructions, although the new regulations promised progress and adaptation to the modern battlefield.[82]

The four reviewers who rejected the new infantry regulations included Franz Ferdinand and *FZM* Oskar Potiorek, who would command the *k.u.k.* army against Serbia in World War I. These high-ranking men criticized the new instructions for replacing training and drill on the exercise field and in parades with education that focused too heavily on the individual soldier. Fearful of losing the Habsburg tradition of discipline and cohesion among troops, Franz Ferdinand, Potiorek, and two other generals could not approve regulations that emphasized the initiative and independence of lower ranking officers. However, these four men had little criticism of the tactical sections, focusing on details rather than the main ideas.[83] Thus, none of the 33 reviewers found fault with the draft's devotion to attack as the only means of success, the culmination of assaults in bayonet storms, and the importance of morale in inflicting one's will on the enemy and seizing the initiative. These men, most of whom would hold important commands during the First World War, all agreed with the offensive *à outrance* of Conrad's tactical ideas. Infatuation with the attack had consumed the most influential members of the Habsburg officer corps as well as the general staff, who had absorbed Conrad's views at the war college and would assist in drawing up battle plans for the next war.

Failure to Learn: Lessons of the Balkan Wars

The Balkan Wars of 1912–1913 provided the last opportunity for Habsburg officers to assess the state of modern warfare. A *Kriegsschule* report on the lessons of these conflicts expressed the same ideas that Austro-Hungarian military theorists had previously held. Although acknowledging the great effect of firepower, especially from artillery, and the difficulty of attacking under heavy shrapnel and rifle fire, the author of the report asserted the possibility of successful assaults. The attackers must spring forward with lightning quickness and charge through the places empty of enemy shots. The bayonet, though rarely useful during the day, gave good results at night. Because of the doubtfulness of achieving fire superiority, psychological superiority offered the means to victory. Lance and saber instilled fear in the enemy, proving the indispensability of *blanken Waffen*. Likewise, assaults with music and unfurled flags boosted morale immensely and brought success. The report concluded, "One may smile in peace about such things as flags and music, but whoever took part in this war could say as the first lesson which he took home that the value of morale is higher than the value of shooting, higher than the value of numbers, higher even than the value of tactics and practicality."[84] With these ideas, *k.u.k.* officers tried to compensate for the inferior numbers and weaponry of the Habsburg army. Such an approach, however, could only lead to disaster in a war against a numerically far superior and better equipped opponent such as Russia or a more experienced enemy such as Serbia.

Cavalry Tactics: Theory and Practice

Austro-Hungarian officers took a more realistic view of cavalry. Instead of adhering to the offensive *à outrance*, mounted troops focused increasingly on reconnaissance and security duties. With the advent of repeating rifles, smokeless powder, and more effective artillery fire, *k.u.k.* military writers realized that cavalry could no longer assault opposing infantry and artillery with shock tactics as in previous centuries.[85] Although these authors insisted on the importance of morale and cavalry spirit, and the possibility, though rare, of attacking infantry and artillery if enemy weakness and the chance of surprise existed, the paucity of articles in the Habsburg military journals showed the sparse debate on the use of mounted forces.[86] Even Conrad declared that cavalry had little hope of success in attacking infantry, unless the foot troops were already demoralized or the cavalry used surprise.[87]

The experiences of recent wars, especially the Russo-Japanese War, revealed no new lessons about cavalry. Austro-Hungarian officers noted the poor performance of mounted troops on both sides in 1904–1905. The mountainous terrain and, according to one *k.u.k.* officer, the absence of a mounted tradition and cavalry spirit in Japanese soldiers, limited the Japanese cavalry to the role of mounted infantry.[88] With few recent examples of successful mounted warfare, Habsburg military writers returned to the experiences of 40 years earlier in the American Civil War and the Franco-Prussian War.[89] Germany too continued to promote the possible success of mounted shock with *blanken Waffen* against infantry during maneuvers. Most, however, realized that the time of cavalry charges against infantry and artillery had passed.[90] Austro-Hungarian officers advocated equipping cavalry with machine guns and rifles to achieve firepower superiority and training cavalry to fight as mounted infantry. The *k.u.k.* military authors also favored employing modern technology, such as telegraphs and other communication devices in addition to bicycles and automobiles, to help the cavalry with reconnaissance.[91] By the advent of the First World War, only the cavalry of the Dual Monarchy, unlike other European mounted troops, no longer carried lances.[92] Thus, the Habsburg army proved once again an interest in new techniques and a willingness to try the latest technological innovations.

This theoretical interest did not gain as much practical application as some officers had hoped. A 1911 general staff study guide ignored the more recent wars and gave examples only from 1866 and 1870 for security and reconnaissance services. The Austro-Hungarian high command failed to implement the new ideas stemming from the experiences of the Boer War and the Russo-Japanese War and did not equip the *k.u.k.* cavalry with sufficient firepower, especially machine guns. As a result, the Habsburg mounted branch entered the First World War with the same attacking mindset as the infantry, despite the new regulations and the theoretical writings of many officers.[93]

Artillery: Insufficient Numbers and Quality

Technology certainly played a major role in the artillery, which had become more effective on the battlefield as a result of the advent of smokeless powder and increasingly greater range, faster rate of fire, and higher precision of arms as well as the availability of recoilless cannon, heavy howitzers, and high-explosive shells.[94] In 1905, one military writer asserted that the effect of artillery had become 24 to 35 times greater than in the Franco-Prussian War, and that one modern field gun could fire in 1 min as much as 500 rifles.[95] Artillery officers realized the greater significance that artillery would have in future wars.[96]

Statistics from the Russo-Japanese War created doubt among some infantry officers on the impact of field guns in the next conflict. One officer published a chart indicating the declining effect of artillery on the battlefield. In 1870–1871, French troops had suffered 25% dead and wounded from cannon fire, 70% from rifles, and 5% from *blanke Waffe*. In 1904–1905, Japanese losses from artillery amounted to only 13.09%, whereas rifles had inflicted 83.15% of casualties and *blanke Waffe* 3.76%.[97] Captain Ignaz Rodić agreed, although publishing his own figures for the Russo-Japanese War: less than 8% losses from artillery, over 90% from rifle fire, and less than 1% from *blanke Waffe*. To emphasize the decreasing influence of field guns, Rodić also provided statistics to show that the Russians and Japanese used far more artillery in 1904–1905 than the French and Germans in 1870–1871. The number of rounds in the latter war surpassed the former by at least three to four times, though with much less effect.[98]

This assertion elicited a strong response, not only from *k.u.k.* artillery officers but also from a German general.[99] These writers issued rebuttals against Rodić's view, stating that mere numbers did not provide adequate proof of success or failure in war. Tactical results determined the effectiveness of field guns, which had caused great loss of morale during the Russo-Japanese War while thwarting attacks and destroying defenses. This demoralizing impact of artillery resulted in both offensive and defensive troops becoming passive and incapable of achieving their objectives.[100] Rapid-firing field guns had annihilated whole columns of infantry within minutes.[101] Artillery officers attributed the smaller hit percentage of Russian and Japanese field guns to the differences in size and roughness of terrain in France and Korea, as well as the greater use of cover and open order tactics in 1904–1905.[102] In addition, most officers concurred that the Russians and Japanese had failed to employ artillery for maximum effect.[103]

The Balkan Wars of 1912–1913 gave a foretaste of World War I combat and confirmed Habsburg officers' belief in the increasing impact of field guns during battle. The *Kriegsschule* report on the lessons of the Balkan Wars devoted six out of ten pages to artillery, concluding that field guns had more material and psychological effect than ever before.[104] In the same manner, the author of an *ÖMZ* article on these wars claimed greater damage in both numbers and morale for artillery against infantry. This writer even asserted that field guns had proven vital for frontal assaults and, therefore, for victory and that artillery had more material and psychological impact than infantry fire.[105]

Despite all the indications from the Russo-Japanese War and the Balkan Wars, Conrad, chief of the general staff and the most important man in the Habsburg military, continued to focus on infantry as capable of gaining victory through assaults without artillery support. Even though Conrad devoted a large section of his tactical study to artillery and the role of field guns in achieving firepower superiority, the 1911 infantry regulations, largely a product of Conrad's ideas, insisted on the independence of foot troops: "The infantry is the main arm. Able to fight at long range or at close quarters, in defense or in attack, the infantry can use its weapons with success against any enemy, in every type of terrain, by day as well as by night. It decides battles: even without support from other arms and against a numerically superior enemy it is capable of attaining the laurels of victory, if only it has trust in itself and has the will to fight."[106] Conrad and the rest of the *k.u.k.* high command feared that too much reliance on artillery would harm the will to attack.[107] Under the influence of this erroneous belief, the Habsburg army suffered catastrophic losses in the early campaigns of the Great War.

The greatest problem for the *k.u.k.* artillery remained the same as in previous decades, numerical inferiority. Austria-Hungary lagged far behind the other main military powers of continental Europe. According to an 1899 *ÖMZ* article, the Habsburg army possessed 43 field pieces per division. Germany had 78, France 63, Russia 56, and even Italy surpassed the *k.u.k.* artillery with 48 guns.[108] By 1911, the ratio had worsened, with Austria-Hungary having only 6 cannon per division for every 8 in Russia, 9 in Serbia, and 12 in Germany.[109]

Not only did the Austro-Hungarian artillery suffer from inferior numbers but also from deficient quality. In the last decade of the nineteenth century and first decade of the twentieth, the Habsburg army still used the steel-bronze Uchatius cannon from 1875. This weapon weighed more yet shot rounds half the weight of Germany's Krupp 1893 model, with a maximum range shorter by about 1000 meters.[110] The French M.97 could fire 18 rounds per minute with 300 pieces of shrapnel per round (5400 pieces altogether), equivalent to the fire from 386 rifles. The German M.96 shot 10 rounds per minute with 300 shrapnel pieces (3000 total), equal to 214 rifles. The *k.u.k.* M.75 could shoot only 6 times per minute with 173–250 pieces of shrapnel (1038–1500 total), as much as 74–107 rifles. At maximum output, the Habsburg weapon barely shot more than the Russian and Italian field guns, which shot roughly 1400 pieces of shrapnel per minute, corresponding to 100 rifles. The artillery officer who published these statistics estimated that, in overall performance and quality, the German cannon surpassed the *k.u.k.* pieces by 120%, and the Russian weapons outperformed the Uchatius by 100%. The Italian guns exceeded the Austro-Hungarian cannon by 25%, and the most modern field guns displayed 300–400% greater ability.[111]

A universal call for new and more field guns arose from the Habsburg artillery officer corps. Reluctantly admitting that the Uchatius pieces no longer met the requirements of modern warfare, officers analyzed various weapons (especially howitzers) and how they could be used with greatest benefit on future battlefields.[112] The *k.u.k.* high command set up a commission in 1896 to upgrade the M.75 and construct new artillery weapons. Representatives from the technical military committees, the Vienna arsenal, and the Blumauer powder factory met under the presidency of the inspector general of the artillery.[113] With the presence of members of the arsenal and the Blumauer factory, the commission did not even consider foreign suppliers such as Krupp. To gain favor with Austro-Hungarian politicians and public opinion, necessary to obtain sufficient funding for expensive cannon, the Habsburg military looked to businesses within the empire for the manufacture of new artillery.[114] Only halting progress was made because of political unrest within the empire, which brought parliament to a halt from 1897 to 1902. Therefore, the *k.u.k.* army could not renew the 10-year military agreement between the two parts of the Dual Monarchy, scheduled for 1899, nor could there be any progress with artillery until the unrest had subsided.[115]

Although the commission quickly approved upgrades to the M.75, which became the M.96, the procurement of new weaponry did not come until much later.[116] In 1908, the *k.u.k.* artillery had still not completed the last stage of procuring new guns, and only in 1909, 13 years after the commission began, did all regiments finally receive and train with the new M.5.[117] With these new cannon, the Habsburg artillery now equaled the Germans and French with 144 guns per corps and surpassed the Russians with 120 and the Italians with 108.[118] Although these numbers showed great progress for the Austro-Hungarian army, statistics for the total amount of artillery and guns per division just before the First World War (42 for Austria-Hungary, 48 for Russian, and 54 for Germany) revealed the vast inferiority of the Habsburg military.[119] By 1913, Germany had raised the number of cannon per corps to 160 and France to 184. For every 1000 men, Germany had 6.5 guns, Great Britain 6.3, France 5, Italy 4, Austria-Hungary 3.8–4.0, and Russia 3.75. Even Rumania had more cannon per 1000 soldiers than the Habsburg army did.[120] Furthermore, the *k.u.k.* artillery did not supply each field piece with as much ammunition as the other powers and thus negated any advantages that came from equal or superior numbers of guns per corps.[121]

Habsburg artillery officers therefore attempted to compensate for inferior numbers in other ways. Many *k.u.k.* writers called for more training, as well as the ever-present demand for higher morale and the will for victory for every individual soldier.[122] The new artillery regulations that came with the issue of the new weapons also stressed the need for more practical training.[123] Tactically, officers advocated that artillery support infantry to gain fire superiority and that the highest task of field guns was to enable assaults.[124] Despite recognition of the need for cooperation between infantry and artillery in the regulations, practical application on the exercise field failed to instill this idea in the troops.[125] For the Habsburg military, the *Drang nach vorwärts* applied just as much to artillery as to infantry. These ideas fit perfectly with the tactical views of Conrad, the *k.u.k.* infantry regulations of 1911, and the regulations of every other European power.[126]

The idea of compensating for inferior numbers by more training, resulting in greater precision shooting, could have worked for a different army. The 2-year military service of Austria-Hungary did not give enough time to train recruits to reach a level surpassing all the other militaries of Europe. As one anonymous author wrote in the *ÖMZ*, "The previous conduct of our neighbors for war gives us no right to this arrogant assumption."[127] In addition, the Habsburg army did not provide enough ammunition and time for artillery shooting practice.[128] Each battery in the *k.u.k.* army fired only 208 shots per year in comparison with 464 in Germany, 390 in France, 366 in Italy, and 480 in Russia.[129] The decision to pursue offensive tactics at all costs, even to the point of "exposing oneself recklessly," could never compensate for numerical inferiority in the face of well-trained opponents.[130] The Austro-Hungarian high command desperately wanted to keep pace with the rest of Europe, and thus refused to admit inferiority.[131] Once again, the combination of *Drang nach vorwärts* with the desire to maintain the appearance of a great power did not coincide with the weak military reality of the Habsburg Empire.

As always, finances remained decisive for the *k.u.k.* military in procurement decisions. New artillery cost enormous sums of money. In 1902, the Habsburg army received 38 million Kronen as a one-time extraordinary credit for new artillery weaponry and 15 million in 1904. In 1905, the war minister asked for and received an additional 50 million Kronen as another extraordinary credit, and requested 119 million more for the future.[132] The Austro-Hungarian army continued to receive extraordinary grants for artillery: 20 million Kronen in 1906, 30 million in 1907, 15 million in 1908 and again in 1909, 8 million in 1910, and 4 million in 1911, totaling 195 million Kronen over the 10 years since 1902.[133]

Even with these large sums, the *k.u.k.* high command considered another series of large extraordinary credits necessary for the further development of the artillery branch. With finalization of a new military law for the Dual Monarchy in 1912, the first since 1889, and the ensuing rise in recruitment allotment, Habsburg military leaders requested an extraordinary credit of 250 million Kronen at a rate of 41 million per year over the next 6 years. Of the 250 million, the chief of the general staff *General der Infanterie* (*GdI*) Blasius Schemua projected 170–185 million for cannon, howitzers, and mortars, whereas the war minister *FML* Baron Moritz Auffenberg von Komarów forecast 198 million for more divisions and more ammunition per cannon.[134]

The rapid pace of technological innovation precipitated the need for such vast amounts of money for new guns. The backward state of the *k.u.k.* artillery also necessitated an upgrade. Even though the Habsburg artillery had received new weapons in 1909, just 3 years earlier, some antique guns were still in use. The 51-year-old M.61s defended permanent fortifications and 13-year-old M.99s and two other models served in the mountain artillery.[135] Even the relatively new M.5s had overly heavy Uchatius steel-bronze barrels with short range.[136] In addition, by the time all troops received the new weapons 6 years later, the M.5s would be outdated 13-year-old artillery and the army would need more modern guns. The other more recent models would suffer similar fates. Understandably, the *k.u.k.* high command tried to render such a large expense palatable to the finance ministers and parliamentary delegates by stretching the funding over 6 years. This plan, however, contained the significant flaw of prolonging procurement. Not only did the Austro-Hungarian army ensure that some weapons would face obsolescence almost before their date of issue, but also that most troops would never receive artillery that met the requirements of modern warfare before the outbreak of World War I.

Financial Imprudence: Permanent Fortifications

The Habsburg high command's insistence on spending money in the wrong areas only aggravated the problem of procuring new artillery quickly. As in previous decades, maintaining permanent fortresses comprised a major part of the *k.u.k.* budget. From 1894 to 1899, the Austro-Hungarian army spent 31,975,000 Kronen (18,550,000 on fortresses themselves and 13,425,000 on arming fortifications).

During the next 6 years another 20,860,000 (6,860,000 for fortresses and 14,000,000 for arming) went to *Befestigung*. At the end of 1904, the war ministry wanted an additional 49,500,000, but requested only 16,500,000. The Galician fortresses of Krakau and Przemyśl absorbed more than half of these sums.[137] The high command deemed these amounts insufficient because of the need to upgrade old fortifications to withstand modern siege artillery. In 1908, Conrad estimated that 450 million Kronen were necessary to render the borders of the Habsburg Empire defensible.[138] In 1911, the war ministry calculated another 36,300,000 for permanent fortresses.[139] Of the 250 million extraordinary credit request of 1912, the war minister bookmarked 27 million for permanent fortresses and the chief of the general staff projected 55 million.[140] More *Befestigung* also required more fortress artillery.[141] Instead of placing these guns in permanent fortifications that might or might not see action in the next war, the Habsburg high command could have deployed more artillery in the army and thus helped to compensate for the deficiency in field weaponry.

According to the calculations of twentieth century Austrian historian Walter Wagner, the Austro-Hungarian army spent 178 million Kronen on *Befestigung* from 1868 to 1912. This figure does not include the millions that the *k.u.k.* high command requested but the delegates cut back. Although, as Wagner points out, this number was little over 1% of all military expenditure, a comparison with figures for weaponry procurement presents a different point of view. From 1868 to 1876, arming the Habsburg army with Werndl breech-loading rifles had cost 69,180,000; adapting the Werndls for better ammunition and procuring an ammunition reserve by 1886 cost another 16,290,000. The Austro-Hungarian military spent 144,550,000 on Mannlicher repeating rifles by 1905, bringing the total to 229,970,000. Similarly, from 1899 to 1912, the *k.u.k.* high command spent 31,250,000 on the M.75 Uchatius steel-bronze cannon, 34,780,000 for the acquisition of smokeless powder, and 193,810,000 for new weaponry, totaling 259,840,000 for artillery.[142] Between 1910 and 1912, 147,560,000 Kronen was spent on artillery costs and 112,280,000 up to 1910. Thus, the *k.u.k.* army spent more on permanent fortresses up to 1910 than on modern artillery. Even so, Conrad complained about the extremely small budget devoted to fortresses, especially in comparison with Italy.[143] Minister of War Auffenberg also bemoaned the insufficient spending on permanent fortifications, which resulted in too much reliance on aged fortresses such as

Przemyśl.[144] Clearly, *Befestigung* ranked high among the military priorities of the Habsburg Empire and rivalled the acquisition of new rifles and cannon, despite the obvious lesson from 1866 that an army with inferior weapons cannot win a war, regardless of how many permanent fortresses exist.

The Austro-Hungarian officer corps continued to support the cordon system of permanent fortifications throughout the empire as a means of defending the borders during a multifront war and thus compensate for inferior numbers of soldiers. Although some military writers observed that the French fortresses had failed to thwart Prussian forces in 1870–1871, hardly anyone called for the abandonment of costly fortification upgrades. Instead of logically concluding that the immense power of modern artillery and the ability of armies to bypass permanent fortifications had rendered fortresses obsolete, *k.u.k.* officers merely stated the need to change the style of *Befestigung* and make walls and redoubts stronger.[145] Only the engineer general inspector *FML* Baron Ernst von Leithner opposed pouring more money into the permanent fortifications of Galicia. Leithner based this judgment on the open nature of the land, which fortresses could not control, rather than the inability of antiquated permanent fortifications to resist modern artillery.[146]

Habsburg military authors also stressed the increasing importance of field fortifications. Conrad realized that the more expensive permanent fortresses became, the greater significance provisory fortifications would hold.[147] The strength of the Boer and Russian defensive positions in the Boer War and the Russo-Japanese War supported this idea. Although Austro-Hungarian officers showed the ability to learn lessons from the most recent conflicts, *ÖMZ* articles centered on the advantages of field fortifications for the offensive and how to attack fortified positions.[148] The spade, rather than hindering the offensive spirit, increased morale and prepared the victory that the rifle won.[149] It seemed that even the engineers had absorbed the *Drang nach vorwärts* concept of Conradian tactics as well as the Nietzschean supremacy of the *Wille zur Siege*. As one author wrote, "We have seen that victory does not belong to the one who contents himself with pure repelling in strong positions, but to the one who pursues a positive goal through the offensive with the strong will to victory."[150]

During the decade before the First World War, the *k.u.k.* military spent a large sum on coastal fortifications. The army high command deemed this expenditure necessary because of the greatly expanded

Habsburg navy. The fleet needed fortified ports for protection in dock.[151] Even Conrad, the foremost proponent of offensive warfare, supported the idea of upgrading coastal fortresses because of his successful amphibious assault on the important port of Pola during maneuvers.[152] The first proposal for coastal fortifications amounted to 112,500,000 Kronen and rose to the outrageous sum of 300–350 million. Realizing that the Delegations would never grant such an enormous amount, the war minister and the chief of the general staff reduced the request to fit the minimal program of 155 million Kronen for all fortifications.[153]

Financial Imprudence: The Navy

The navy demanded an immense amount of funding. Between 1873 and 1912, the Austro-Hungarian military consumed 818,370,000 on ship building, 606,910,000 of that between 1905 and 1912.[154] The former amount represented more than the Habsburg army spent on rifles, smokeless powder, artillery, and permanent fortifications combined between the Austro-Prussian War and World War I. The naval budget had almost tripled from 56,080,000 Kronen in 1904 to 170,200,000 in 1912.[155] Yet, the chief of the navy, Vice-admiral Count Rudolf Montecuccoli degli Erri, protested against rejection of his budget proposal during the ministerial meeting on 8–9 July 1912.[156] Despite this temporary setback, the navy continued to receive vast credits. Conrad expressed his surprise and complained to the emperor in 1913 and 1914 that the navy had been granted 426 million Kronen, which was more than the 400 million Conrad wanted for the ground forces that would decide the future of the monarchy.[157]

The enormous expenditure on the *k.u.k.* fleet appeared justifiable to the Austro-Hungarian high command for several reasons. Even though three 20,000-ton battleships had cost 100 million Kronen each, or more than the Habsburg army had spent on rifles or artillery during the previous 40 years, the naval section of the war ministry rationalized such an outlay. The primary cause for naval spending resulted from the Austro-Hungarian fear of falling too far behind the other European states. World powers ruled the sea. Germany and Russia had built strong fleets to take part in the rampant imperialism of the decades before the First World War. The Habsburg Empire needed to do the same to prove itself a world power.[158] Even Italy, Austria-Hungary's main rival for control of the Adriatic Sea, where the only Habsburg ports were sited, had embarked on a major push for naval funding. The Italian navy received a grant of 566,600,000 lire for use from 1912 to 1918.[159] Montecuccoli, the last of the *k.u.k.* admirals who had fought at the victorious battle of Lissa in 1866, strongly believed that the Austro-Hungarian navy must match Italy's fleet in order to compete for domination in the Adriatic and Mediterranean seas.[160] The rest of the Habsburg high command, including Conrad and Franz Ferdinand, also desired a powerful fleet to raise the Dual Monarchy's position among the other great European powers.[161]

The *k.u.k.* military wanted to protect the imperial coast and also project Habsburg power throughout the world in order to reach a prominent position as a world power. Only a strong navy with attack capabilities could achieve this goal, which coincided perfectly with the offensive mindset of Austro-Hungarian military doctrine. All the other powers had already gained overseas acquisitions. The Habsburg Empire could not remain behind. The geographical position and meager coastline of imperial lands made no difference. In addition, a big fleet would stimulate industry and business. The *k.u.k.* navy cost Austro-Hungarian citizens a mere 3.5 Kronen per head in comparison to 4 Kronen in Japan, 6.8 in Italy, 8.5 in Germany, 10.6 in France, and 23.6 in Great Britain. The people of the Habsburg Empire could afford an increase in naval expenditures, according to one Dual Monarchy officer. The only requirement for success was the will of the people.[162]

Parliamentary Favor

The will of the people, according to newspapers in both Vienna and Budapest, did not accord with the will of the military, even if parliament voted to grant large sums for the *k.u.k.* army and navy.[163] In 1904, the year of debates on the first major increase in naval expenditures, many delegates who opposed these grants, and even some of those who approved funding for the military, also voiced the concerns of the people about the increasing tax burden for military expenditures.[164] These same concerns entered the 1911 debates over the extraordinary budget request for 1912.[165] However, for some of the populace, the desire for a strong navy grew. The Austrian Navy League, founded in 1904 on the model of the popular German Navy League, had 25 local chapters in large cities with a total of 4389 members by 1910 and 44,617 by 1914.[166] This organization enjoyed the sponsorship of Franz

Ferdinand, heir to the Habsburg throne, as well as other prominent politicians and industrialists who wanted a larger navy to stimulate business and industry.[167] In addition, the Austrian Navy League canvassed for Dreadnoughts, primarily to create a powerful naval strike force for the Habsburg Empire.[168] The League's monthly paper, *Die Flagge*, expressed the organization's viewpoint: "History teaches us that no nation can maintain its great power status in the long run without naval prestige, without sea power!"[169] This naval enthusiasm and desire for great power status through a large navy infected parliamentary representatives and a growing number of the populace.[170]

The main issue for delegates in both 1904 and 1911 was army and naval support for business and industry.[171] Representatives from the western half of the Dual Monarchy accused the Habsburg military, especially the navy, of giving too many contracts to Hungarian firms.[172] Delegates from Hungary supported the budget requests of the navy in particular because, even though the cost of producing ships within the Habsburg Empire surpassed foreign manufacture by 10%, the *k.u.k.* marine commandants always tried to purchase within the empire and had promised contracts for Hungarian industry.[173]

Some delegates also criticized the army for issues that did not involve economics. Slavic representatives raised the usual complaints during the debates of 1904 and 1911 about favoritism for German and Hungarian speakers in the army and described the language difficulties for soldiers of different ethnic backgrounds who could not communicate with their officers.[174] Other delegates brought up the need for better treatment of recruits, pension reform, and elimination of superfluous officials.[175] Most of these demands came from delegates who approved the military budget requests and desired the *k.u.k.* high command to continue improvements in these areas in return for parliamentary favor toward army and navy funding. Although problems of pensioning and too much bureaucracy still existed in the Habsburg military, politicians did not find these issues of overwhelming importance in comparison with economic concerns.

Only a small number of representatives, including the Social Democrat Dr. Wilhelm Ellenbogen, objected to granting military requests for strategic or tactical reasons. Asserting the impossibility of rivaling any of the major naval powers that Austria-Hungary might face in a future war, such as Great Britain, France, or even Italy, these delegates declared that spending 400 million Kronen for four Dreadnoughts would not render the Habsburg fleet the equal of any of these nations.

The *k.u.k.* navy would require four times the funding to give Austro-Hungarian ships enough offensive power to attack in the way the naval command desired. In addition, sea battles, whether losses or victories, would never affect a war decisively for a land power such as the Habsburg Empire. Instead of building four Dreadnoughts, which would become obsolete by the time of launching, the *k.u.k.* navy should stay within the boundaries of financial responsibility by investing in smaller vessels, such as submarines, torpedo boats, and mine ships, to defend the small coastline and few ports of Dalmatia. Protecting Austria-Hungary's small merchant marine did not warrant the immense expense of producing modern battleships.[176]

The parliamentary delegates who supported the army and navy budget requests disagreed emphatically with these wise assessments. Echoing the ideas of the *k.u.k.* military, these representatives repeatedly argued that the Habsburg Empire must maintain or restore its great power status. Only large credits would enable the army and navy to keep pace with the other powers, who continued to spend exorbitant amounts on arming, and to remain a dependable ally capable of helping Germany and waging campaigns without assistance. If Austria-Hungary chose to lag behind Germany, France, Russia, Italy, and Great Britain, and thus become a second-rate power, Habsburg business and political interests would suffer greatly. Overseas business required a strong fleet for support. Therefore, the army needed enough funding to carry out offensive operations and the navy needed sufficient credits to build Dreadnoughts to attack enemy ships. Parliamentary speakers even brought up the lessons of the Russo-Japanese war and the importance of spirit and morale to compensate for inferiority in numbers and weaponry. Additionally, delegates appealed to their colleagues to vote for the military credits so that Austro-Hungarian soldiers (relatives and constituents of the representatives) would not go to war with outdated weapons against vastly superior rifles and artillery.[177] By voting for the military credits, the majority of parliamentary representatives approved the *k.u.k.* desire to retain great power status.

Major support for army and navy budget requests also stemmed from the economic benefits that delegates realized for both their voters and themselves. Whether representing industrial firms or making profits from private investments, these politicians both in 1904 and in 1911 trusted the war ministers *FZM* Heinrich Baron von Pitreich (minister of war 1902–1906) and *GdI* Franz Baron Schönaich (minister of war 1906–1911) as well as the naval commanders-in-chief Admiral Hermann von Spaun and Admiral Rudolf Count Montecuccoli to give army and navy contracts to Austro-Hungarian businesses.[178] Similar to the years of good relations between the army and the Delegations during the tenure of *FZM* Arthur Maximilian Count Bylandt-Rheidt in the 1880s, the representatives voiced confidence in the *k.u.k.* high command on several occasions, especially compared with the antagonism that war minister *General der Kavallerie* Edmund Baron von Krieghammer had inspired.[179] As one delegate said, "If there is a question of military matters, the opinion of the experts stands far higher to me than the opinion of Dr. Ellenbogen."[180]

These same military experts claimed that Austria-Hungary should spend hundreds of millions on a fleet that could never have a major influence in a future war rather than using the funding to procure modern artillery more quickly. Replacing outdated field guns would have rendered the *k.u.k.* army more battle-ready than four Dreadnoughts that hardly left port during World War I. These experts also underscored the need to make all parts of the Habsburg military into offensive forces, despite obvious inferiority in numbers and weaponry in both the army and navy. Although parliamentary delegates must share part of the blame for approving funding for unnecessary ships and permanent fortresses, the largest fault lies with the Austro-Hungarian high command for judging the fleet and *Befestigung* worthy of such prominence in military spending. Thus, the claim made by apologists for the Austro-Hungarian army such as Hugo Kerchnawe and Oskar Regele, as well as historians such as C. A. Macartney, that parliamentary stinginess caused Habsburg military defeat does not explain the reality of the situation.[181] The Dual Monarchy's high command received sufficient funding from the Delegations. The procurement choices that military leaders made, however, displayed poor judgment in how they spent parliamentary grants.

Financial Imprudence: Tank Rejection

A good example of poor judgment in budget expenditures is the *Motorgeschütz* of First Lieutenant Gunther Burstyn, an engineer in the *k.u.k.* railroad regiment. Burstyn had designed an armored car that had proven battle-worthy during the 1906 maneuvers, especially because of its ability to flank the enemy quickly.[182] Seeing the success of his motorized vehicle, Burstyn invented a tank with the capability of swiftly traversing any terrain and obstacles. This vehicle would possess armor for resisting infantry fire and shrapnel and a light *Schnellfeuer* cannon to knock out opposing artillery and machine guns.[183] Although only in model form and without battlefield testing, this tank created the possibility of greatly enhancing the movement and firepower of the Austro-Hungarian army, especially in offensive actions.

Burstyn submitted his tank model to the war ministry, but without success. The inventor did not have a self-propelled version and thus could not demonstrate the full abilities of his armored vehicle. Three months later, the war ministry passed the model on to department after department until the invention received a negative appraisal from the Technical-Administrative Military Committee. Viewing Burstyn's tank model as nothing more than another armored car, Lieutenant Colonel Robert Wolf, an artillerist in charge of the automobile section with no training as an engineer, judged the invention useless for transporting cannon or any other purpose. Therefore, the *k.u.k.* army did not grant funds to develop and test a working model.[184]

In rejecting Burstyn's invention, the Technical-Administrative Military Committee lost an excellent opportunity to upgrade both the firepower and movement capabilities of the Habsburg army. Wolf failed to recognize the usefulness of the tank in battle and made the same mistake as the German army. The Artillery Commission in Berlin also judged Burstyn's model impracticable and not a new weapon.[185] None of the other European powers had developed tanks or foreseen the great battlefield advantages of all-terrain vehicles equipped with cannon. The failure of the *k.u.k.* military to test Burstyn's tank and put it into production stemmed not from technological backwardness or conservatism but rather from misjudgment and poor financial decision making. By 1912, the Austro-Hungarian high command had determined to spend extraordinary credits from the Delegations on much needed artillery, but also on Dreadnoughts and permanent fortresses. Instead of wasting millions on extremely expensive but useless battleships and quickly obsolete fortifications, the *k.u.k.* army would have taken a far greater step toward restoring the great power status of the Habsburg Empire by investing in Burstyn's tank.

The High Command: Stability and Views of Technology

During the decade before World War I, the Habsburg high command regained the trust of parliamentary representatives antagonized by Krieghammer during his term as war minister from 1893 to 1902. As a cavalry troop officer, Krieghammer brought little organizational and statesmanlike experience to the war ministry. Instead of carrying on the good relations that had existed in the tenures of Bylandt-Rheidt and his successor *FZM* Ferdinand Baron Bauer, Krieghammer antagonized not only the Austrian and Hungarian parliaments but also the chief of the general staff *FML* Friedrich von Beck-Rzikowsky and the naval commander-in-chief Spaun. As the friction became insupportable and Krieghammer proved incapable of coming to an agreement with the Hungarian parliament on a new army bill, Emperor Franz Joseph finally removed Krieghammer from office.[186] The next war ministers, Pitreich, Schönaich, *GdI* Moritz Baron Auffenberg von Komarów (war minister 1911–1912), and *FZM* Alexander Baron von Krobatin (war minister 1911–1917), restored parliamentary confidence in the war ministry.[187] This restored confidence helps to explain the favor that the Delegations showed the Habsburg army during budget debates.

During the decade before the First World War, Franz Ferdinand, heir to the throne and a man of extremely strong opinions, had great influence on the *k.u.k.* army. The *Thronfolger* (successor) took some of the responsibilities of Archduke Albrecht in 1895 as a roving inspector of all aspects of the military. Franz Ferdinand also formed his own 16-member military chancellery that rivalled the chancellery of the emperor but received better intelligence from a complex and wide network of sources.[188] The imperial heir played a large role in the appointments and dismissals of members of the high command. Franz Ferdinand influenced the removals of Beck as chief of the general staff, Pitreich and Schönaich as war ministers, and *GdI* Blasius Schemua as general staff chief, as well as the appointments of Schönaich, Schemua, and Auffenberg.[189] The primary reason for the heir's involvement in dismissals and appointments stemmed from his wish for men of action to lead Austria-Hungary as a great military power in international relations. This desire led the *Thronfolger* to welcome Aloys Count Lexa von Ährenthal to the foreign ministry and favor Pitreich, Conrad, and Auffenberg rather than Beck and Schemua.[190] The need to act like a great power dominated the thinking of the *k.u.k.* high command, including the heir to the throne.[191]

Conrad in particular appeared to Franz Ferdinand as a man of fire and energy, the right choice for the most important position in the army, chief of the general staff. Conrad's performance during the 1905 maneuvers in the Tyrol, where he served as Franz Ferdinand's chief of staff and won as both attacker and defender, particularly impressed the heir to the throne. Thus, Conrad became the obvious choice to replace the aging and less active Beck.[192] Both the imperial heir and the new general staff chief shared the ideas of forming a united state and army as well as opposing any concessions to Hungary, although Conrad's view of the other half of the Dual Monarchy did not approach Franz Ferdinand's unmitigated hatred. However, Franz Ferdinand and Conrad did not agree on all topics. As an ardent Catholic and devoted husband, the *Thronfolger* despised the general staff chief's religious indifference and attachment to Gina von Reininghaus, the wife of another man. In addition, Franz Ferdinand disliked Conrad's constant warmongering and desire for preventive war. They also differed in their views on the role of the army. Conrad saw the army as an aggressive force to support a strong foreign policy, whereas Franz Ferdinand viewed it as an internal peace-keeping force rather than a means of external aggression. The imperial heir emphasized military appearance, especially in the form of impressive parades, drills, and exercises with cavalry charges rather than realistic maneuvers. Despite these differences, Ferdinand still regarded Conrad as the right man to raise the Austro-Hungarian military from its stagnant status.[193]

With regard to technology, the *Thronfolger* presented a paradox. Franz Ferdinand enthusiastically supported the navy and the budding Austro-Hungarian military aviation branch. He also willingly used automobiles during maneuvers, remarking that the future belonged to the motorized vehicle.[194] Nevertheless, Franz Ferdinand believed in the superiority of devotion to the fatherland, obedience, and confidence as the means to victory. In addition, during maneuvers the imperial heir revealed his penchant for the offensive, ignoring the lessons about firepower from the Boer War and the Russo-Japanese War and ordering a cavalry charge against entrenched infantry in 1913.[195] As Auffenberg commented after the Great War, certain members of the high command held "an aversion for technical perfections," regarding "the most modern means of war more or less as sport," while seeing "the cavalryman brandishing the sword as still the ideal warrior and combatant."[196]

This neglect of technology did not infect the whole *k.u.k.* military, nor even the whole house of Habsburg. Archduke Leopold Salvator, as general artillery inspector, called for an extensive and intensive increase in the number and quality of artillery using the latest technology.[197] Archduke Wilhelm had called for more modern artillery 30 years earlier.[198] Archduke Albrecht had promoted the procurement of breech-loading and repeating rifles. Even Emperor Franz Joseph did not deserve the reputation for skepticism regarding technology that historians have given him. Stories of Franz Joseph's aversion for modern technology, such as telephones, elevators, and motor cars, provide entertaining anecdotes.[199] However, these episodes exaggerate the notion of the emperor's backwardness. Franz Joseph, especially later in his reign, trusted his military advisors and did not oppose the procurement of new weaponry. During the corps maneuvers of 1906, the emperor expressed his displeasure and disdain for Burstyn's armored vehicles, which frightened his horse. Yet, Franz Joseph also praised the performance of the automobile troops and recognized the usefulness of motor cars on the battlefield.[200]

In general, the Austro-Hungarian high command and officer corps showed great interest in modern technology. The plethora of articles in the *k.u.k.* military journals, establishment of technical schools for the army, recognition of the military possibilities of aviation, and various studies on new weapons all prove that aversion to technology did not constitute a problem for the Habsburg army.[201] Imprudent decisions on how to spend the limited funds of the Austro-Hungarian military led to defeat during the early campaigns of the First World War.

Conclusion

Combination of the infatuation with the offensive *à outrance* and inept financial choices doomed the *k.u.k.* military to defeat in the First World War. With the appointment of Conrad as chief of the general staff and the rise of his former war college students to high-ranking positions, no more voices against the constant *Drang nach vorwärts* arose in the army. *Kriegsschule* courses drilled ideas of attack into general staff students, who would develop battle plans and lead troops in World War I. Learning the wrong lessons from the Russo-Japanese War, *k.u.k.* theorists saw the example of Japan, a smaller power, defeating the much larger army of Russia as a model of how to conquer a probable future opponent. Austro-Hungarian officers viewed patriotism, *élan*, and the offensive spirit of the Japanese soldiers as the secrets to success. Habsburg military thinkers hoped to compensate for inferior numbers and weaponry with offensive strategy and tactics combined with high morale.

Austria-Hungary spent less on military purposes than the other European powers but the *k.u.k.* inferiority in men and weapons was not just a result of a shortage of funding. The main problem for the Habsburg army came from incompetent spending decisions. The high command considered pouring money into the fleet more important than procuring rifles and artillery because of the desire to obtain overseas acquisitions and protect commerce, like the other European powers. Similarly, permanent fortresses ranked high among *k.u.k.* priorities, higher than developing a tank for mobile warfare. Such choices, in addition to the desire to attack at all costs, created a situation in which Habsburg forces entered war at a grave disadvantage. Both love of the offensive and poor choices in spending arose from the desire to maintain great power status for the Dual Monarchy. Nevertheless, these decisions resulted in exactly the opposite: the loss not only of great power status but also of the monarchy.

Notes

1. A.S., "Zur Geschichte des Krieges. Ein Ausblick in die Zukunft," *Österreichische Militärische Zeitschrift* (*ÖMZ*) 1 (1897): 148. The author of this article is most likely the retired FML Adolf Freiherrn von Sacken, a former teacher of tactics at the *Kriegsschule*, director of the military history bureau in the war archives of Vienna, and author of numerous military-political works.
2. Frederick Martin, Sir John Scott Keltie, Isaac Parker Anderson Renwick, Mortimer Epstein, Sigfrid Henry Steinberg, and John Paxton, *The Statesman's Year-Book: Statistical and Historical Annual of the States of the Civilised World for the Year 1902* (London: Macmillan and Co., 1902), 396, 572–573, 647, 806, 1002.
3. Wilhelm Leopold Colmar Freiherr von der Goltz, *Das Volk in Waffen. Ein Buch über Heerwesen und Kriegführung unserer Zeit* (Berlin: R. v. Decker's Verlag: 1883), 4–5.
4. Hauptmann Otto Berndt, *Die Zahl im Kriege. Statistische Daten aus der neueren Kriegsgeschichte in graphischer Darstellung* (Wien: G. Freytag & Berndt, 1897), 133–134, 142–144. The Habsburg army adopted the title k.u.k. (*kaiserlich und königlich*) instead of k.k. (*kaiserlich-königlich*) in 1889 as a concession to Hungary for the passage of the 1889 army law. Hungarian politicians viewed this addition of the 'u' as recognition of the equal status of Hungary with Austria according to the *Ausgleich* of 1867.

5. A.S., “Zur Geschichte des Krieges. Ein Ausblick in die Zukunft,” *ÖMZ* 1 (1897): 107–151; A.S., “Der Zukunftskrieg und die Staatswehr. Eine militärisch-politische Studie,” *ÖMZ* 3 (1897): 1–32; A.S., “Das Ende der Millionenheere. Ein Mahnruf zur Jahreswende,” *ÖMZ* 4 (1897): 193–205.
6. Oberstlieutenant Auditor Dr. Emil Dangelmaier, “Die Friedens-Conferenz,” *ÖMZ* 1 (1899): 243–246.
7. “Studie über den Ausbau unserer Wehrmacht auf Grund des neuen Wehrgesetzes,” Wien. Aus der kaiserlich-königlichen Hof- und Staatsdruckerei, 1894, KA MKSM Sonderreihe, Karton Nr. 70, Ausbau der Wehrmacht 1896, 3.
8. “Studie über den Ausbau unserer Wehrmacht auf Grund des neuen Wehrgesetzes,” Wien. Aus der kaiserlich-königlichen Hof- und Staatsdruckerei, 1894, KA MKSM Sonderreihe, Karton Nr. 70, Ausbau der Wehrmacht 1896, 3–4.
9. A.S., “Zur Geschichte des Krieges. Ein Ausblick in die Zukunft,” 107.
10. Berndt, *Die Zahl im Kriege. Statistische Daten aus der neueren Kriegsgeschichte in graphischer Darstellung*, 130.
11. A.S., “Zur Geschichte des Krieges. Ein Ausblick in die Zukunft,” 150; A.S., “Das Ende der Millionenheere. Ein Mahnruf zur Jahreswende,” 196–197, 205.
12. Franz Conrad von Hötzendorf, *Zum Studium der Taktik. I. Theil: Einleitung und Infanterie* (Vienna: L.W. Seidel & Sohn, 1891), 14, 25–26.
13. Dieter Hackl, “Der Offensivgeist des Conrad von Hötzendorf,” (Mag. Phil. Diplomarbeit, Universität Wien, 2009), 107.
14. K. und k. Chef des Generalstabes. Geh. Nr. 141, n.d., KA Generalstab Operationsbüro, Karton Nr. 738, Conrad: Persönliche Studien, Studien über Festungskrieg, Korrespondenz mit Ährenthal, Korrespondenz mit Berchtold und Potiorek; Korrespondenz in Angelegenheiten Ährenthal: Geheimes Promemoria 15 August 1909, KA Generalstab Operationsbüro, Karton Nr. 738, Conrad: Persönliche Studien, Studien über Festungskrieg, Korrespondez mit Ährenthal, Korrespondez mit Berchtold und Potiorek; Gerhard Ritter, *Staatskunst und Kriegshandwerk*, (München: R. Oldenbourg, 1954–1968), 2 Bd., 284–286; Edmund Glaise-Horstenau, Josef Brauner, Eduard Czegka, Jaromir Diakow, Friedrich Franek, Walther Heydendorff, Rudolf Kiszling, Franz Mühlhofer, Ernst Wisshaupt und Georg Zobi, *Österreich-Ungarns letzter Krieg 1914–1918* (*ÖULK*) (Wien: Verlag der Militärwissenschaftlichen Mitteilungen, 1930–1938) 1: 41.
15. Conrad, *Zum Studium der Taktik*, 4–28.
16. Conrad, *Zum Studium der Taktik*, 31–347, 359–473, 547–701.

17. Conrad, "Gesichtspunkte für die Reorganisation der Kriegsschule," 1907, KA Militärschulen, Karton Nr. 44, Lehrpläne, Stundeneinteilung, Organisation der KS, Denkschrift KS 1852–1877, 8.
18. Conrad, "Direktiven für die Leitung der Kriegsschule," Wien am 6./X. 1910, KA Militärschulen, Karton Nr. 43, Kriegsschulakten 1886/1914, Mobilisierungsplan, Befehle für die Lehrer (aus dem Nachlaß Theodor Körner).
19. K.u.k. KS Verzeichnis der Studienthemen im Jahre 1902/3; K.u.k. KS Verzeichnis der Studienthemen im Jahre 1903/4; K.u.k. KS Verzeichnis der Studienthemen im Jahre 1904/5; K.u.k. KS Verzeichnis der Studienthemen im Jahre 1905/6, KA Militärschulen, Karton Nr. 44, Lehrpläne, Stundeneinteilung, Organisation der KS, Denkschrift KS 1852–1877.
20. Lawrence Sondhaus, *Franz Conrad von Hötzendorf: Architect of the Apocalypse* (Boston: Humanities Press, Inc., 2000), 39.
21. K.u.k. Kriegsschule 1910. Lehrplan für die k.u.k. Kriegsschule und Anhaltspunkte für die Feststellung der Studienerfolge. Befehle für die Lehrer (aus dem Nachlaß Theodor Körner). KA Militärschulen, Karton Nr. 43, Kriegsschulakten 1886/1914, Mobilisierungsplan, Befehle für die Lehrer (aus dem Nachlaß Theodor Körner), 10, 17–18.
22. K.u.k. Kriegsschule 1910. Lehrplan für die k.u.k. Kriegsschule und Anhaltspunkte für die Feststellung der Studienerfolge. Befehle für die Lehrer (aus dem Nachlaß Theodor Körner). KA Militärschulen, Karton Nr. 43, Kriegsschulakten 1886/1914, Mobilisierungsplan, Befehle für die Lehrer (aus dem Nachlaß Theodor Körner), 16; Conrad, "Gesichtspunkte für die Reorganisation der Kriegsschule," 1907, KA Militärschulen, Karton Nr. 44, Lehrpläne, Stundeneinteilung, Organisation der KS, Denkschrift KS 1852–1877, 12–15; Nr. 14 res. de 883, 16 Beilagen zum Studienplan, 2 Taktik, KA Militärschulen, Karton Nr. 43, Kriegsschulakten 1886/1914, Mobilisierungsplan, Befehle für die Lehrer (aus dem Nachlaß Theodor Körner).
23. K.u.k. KS I. Jahrgang 19.../... Taktik. Verteidigung des Kaninchen Berges in der Schlacht von Spichern am 6. August 1870, KA Militärschule, KS Karton Nr. 69, Studienbehelfe: 1912/1914.
24. "Das Detachement Bolstenstern am 26. u. 27. Dezember 1870," KA Militärschulen, KS Karton Nr. 67, Studienbehelfe: 1912/1914.
25. K.u.k. Kriegsschule I. Jahrgang 19... Taktik. Angriff der 1. Gardeinfanteriebrigade auf St. Privat am 16. August 1870. Bemerkungen. KA Militärschulen, KS Karton Nr. 68, Studienbehelfe: 1912/1914.
26. K.u.k. Chef des Generalstabes. Korpsbefehl Nr. 24. Wien, am 24. Oktober 1910. KA Militärschulen, Karton Nr. 43, Kriegsschulakten

1886/1914, Mobilisierungsplan, Befehle für die Lehrer (aus dem Nachlaß Theodor Körner).

27. K. und k. Kriegsschule. Res. No. 706. Wien, am 10. Dezember 1913. KA Militärschulen, Karton Nr. 43, Kriegsschulakten 1886/1914, Mobilisierungsplan, Befehle für die Lehrer (aus dem Nachlaß Theodor Körner), 1–2, 9, 12.
28. Graydon A. Tunstall, *Blood on the Snow: The Carpathian Winter War of 1915* (Lawrence: University Press of Kansas, 2010), 15–16.
29. Generalmajor Alfred Krauss, k.u.k. Kriegsschule. Res. Nr. 91. Uebungsreise 1911. Abschrift der Zuschrift an Hauptmann d. Glst. von Langer. Wien, am 22. Februar 1911, KA Militärschulen, Karton Nr. 43, Kriegsschulakten 1886/1914, Mobilisierungsplan, Befehle für die Lehrer (aus dem Nachlaß Theodor Körner).
30. Oberst z.D. Maschke, "Die Infanterietaktik der Gegenwart, Eine Studie," *ÖMZ* 3 (1896): 97–169; Oberstlieutenant des Generalstabs-Corps Johann Schirmbeck, "Zum Dienst-Reglement für das k. und k. Heer. II. Theil, 3. Auflage, 1896," *Organ der militärwissenschaftlichen Vereine* (*O.*) 53 (1896): 241–284; Oberstlieutenant Strobl, "Über Taktik-Aufgaben auf kriegsgeschichtlicher Grundlage," *ÖMZ* 1 (1897): 208–234; Oberstlieutenant des Generalstabs-Corps Wilhelm Buschek, "Der taktische Verband im Gefechte," *ÖMZ* 2 (1897): 157–177; Hauptmann Albert Margutti, "Die Entscheidungsuchende Vertheidigung," *O.* 54 (1897): 190–206; *Hónved* Hauptmann Dionys Horvath de Nagyvarad, "Der Wert der Anerziehung der Initiative," *O.* 54 (1897): 319–344; Oberst Ebhardt, "Hauptmomente der Entwicklung der Taktik im österreichischen Heer von der Zeit Kaiser Maximilian I. bis Gegenwart," *ÖMZ* 3 (1898): 1–30; Oberlieutenant Orestes Ritter von Bischoff, "Die Erziehung des Soldaten zu besonders anstrengenden und gefahrvollen Unternehmungen," *ÖMZ* 1 (1899): 75–95.
31. E.v.K., "Taktiksche Meinungen und Mahnungen," *ÖMZ* 2 (1896): 108–133.
32. Margutti, "Die Entscheidungsuchende Vertheidigung," 190–206; H. von W., "Die Infanterie im Schlachtenfeuer der Zukunft," *ÖMZ* 3 (1898): 193–226; S., "Beiträge zum Studium des Infanterie-Angriffes in der Bataille rangée," *ÖMZ* 4 (1899): 105–137.
33. Simplex, "Die verbannte Einfachheit," *ÖMZ* 4 (1896): 1–20.
34. S., "Beiträge zum Studium des Infanterie-Angriffes in der Bataille rangée," 135–136.
35. lr., "Ein Wort zur Frage des Infanterie-Angriffes," *ÖMZ* 4 (1896): 193–195; lr., "Ein Wort zu § 20 der Instruction für die Waffenübungen des k.u.k. Heeres," *ÖMZ* 1 (1897): 42–45.

36. lr., "Ein Wort zur Frage des Infanterie-Angriffes," 193–195; Margutti, "Die Entscheidungsuchende Vertheidigung," 190–196; H. von W., "Die Infanterie im Schlachtenfeuer der Zukunft," 193–202; S., "Beiträge zum Studium des Infanterie-Angriffes in der Bataille rangée," 105–106.
37. Moritz Freiherr von Auffenberg-Komarów, *Aus Österreichs Höhe und Niedergang: Eine Lebensschilderung* (München: Drei Masken Verlag, 1921), 173.
38. FML Karl von Lang (GdI), "Betrachtungen über die Armeemanöver 1908 in Westungarn mit Rücksicht auf applikatorische Besprechungen hierüber," *ÖMZ* 2 (1909): 1829–1854; Lang, "Betrachtungen über die Manöver des 3 und 14 Korps im Kärnten vom 2 bis 7 September 1907," *ÖMZ* 1 (1910): 699–730; Lang, "Betrachtungen über die großen Herbstmanöver in Mähren vom 8 bis 11 Sept. 1909," *ÖMZ* 2 (1910): 1193–1234.
39. Lang, "Betrachtungen über die Armeemanöver 1908 in Westungarn mit Rücksicht auf applikatorische Besprechungen hierüber," 1853.
40. Lang, "Betrachtungen über die Manöver des 3 und 14 Korps im Kärnten vom 2 bis 7 September 1907," 730.
41. Oberst Maximilian Freiherr von Pitreich, *Lemberg 1914* (Wien: Adolf Holzhausens Nachfolger, 1929), 129–130.
42. General der Infanterie Alfred Krauß, *Die Ursachen unserer Niederlage: Erinnerungen und Urteile aus dem Weltkrieg* (München: J.F. Lehmanns Verlag, 1921), 96.
43. Moritz Auffenberg-Komarów, *Aus Österreich-Ungarns Teilnahme am Weltkriege* (Wien: Ullstein & Co., 1920), 52–53.
44. Rudolf Kiszling, *Erzherzog Franz Ferdinand von Österreich-Este: Leben, Pläne und Wirken am Schicksalsweg der Donaumonarchie* (Graz: Hermann Böhlaus Nachf., 1953), 263–264.
45. Geoffrey Wawro, *Warfare and Society in Europe, 1792–1914* (New York: Routledge, 2000): 139–144.
46. FML Gustav Ratzenhofer, "Rückblick auf den Krieg in Südafrika," *ÖMZ* 1 (1901): 97–103.
47. Hauptmann Rudolf Meißner, "Moderne Infanterie," *O.* 64 (1902): 163–214; Hauptmann Wilhelm von Reinöhl, "Die Entwicklung der Feuertaktik der Infanterie," *O.* 68 (1904): 1–33.
48. z, "Taktische Folgerungen aus dem Burenkriege nach Boguslawski," *ÖMZ* 1 (1903): 227–240; z, "Infanterische Fragen und die Erscheinungen des Boerenkrieges von F.C.v.H.," *ÖMZ* 1 (1904): 12–29.
49. Generalmajor Otto Meixner, "Das Exerzierreglement für die k.u.k. Fußtruppen vom Jahre 1903," *O.* 70 (1905): 93–110.

50. Franz Conrad von Hötzendorf, *Infanterische Fragen und die Erscheinungen des Boerenkrieges* (Wien: Seidel & Sohn, 1903), 6, 14, 58.
51. Oberst von Kirchgaesser, "Erfahrungen und Lehren aus dem südafrikanischen Krieg," *ÖMZ* 1 (1900): 230–237; Kirchgaesser, "Kritische Betrachtungen über die Ereignisse auf dem südafrikanischen Kriegs-Theater," *ÖMZ* 3 (1900): 99–112; Generalstabs-Officier, "Zusammengewürfelte Gedanken über unsere Reglements. Der Kampf um die infanteristische Feuerüberlegenheit," *ÖMZ* 1 (1901): 22–31; "Der Kampf um die infanteristische Feuerüberlegenheit," *ÖMZ* 1 (1901): 264–269; Generalstabs-Officier, "Zusammengewürfelte Gedanken über unsere Reglements. Nochmals: 'Der Kampf um die infanteristische Feuerüberlegenheit.' - Die Formation der zum Feuergefechte bestimmten Compagnien. - Der eigentliche Angriff under der Bajonnetkampf," *ÖMZ* 2 (1901): 74–87; "Die neuen Infanterie-Reglements in Frankreich und in Österreich-Ungarn," *ÖMZ* 4 (1901): 283–316; Hauptmann Freiherrn Henriques de Ben, "Vergleich des Entwurfes zum Exercier-Reglement für die k.und k. Fußtruppen mit dem bisher in Kraft gestandenen Reglement," *O.* 64 (1902): 310–343; Oberlieutenant J.L., "Über den Angriff im alten und neuen Reglement," *O.* 64 (1902): 344–355; L.F.v.G., "Schlagworte über die Taktik der Zukunft," *ÖMZ* 2 (1903): 831–840; Hauptmann des Generalstabskorps Franz Schnetzer, "Die modernen Angriffsströmungen und unser Exerzierreglement," *ÖMZ* 2 (1903): 899–927, 1003–1029; Smekal, "Einiges über den Infanterieangriff," *O.* 69 (1904): 257–299.
52. Kirchgaesser, "Kritische Betrachtungen über die Ereignisse auf dem südafrikanischen Krieg," 235; Generalstabs-Officier, "Zusammengewürfelte Gedanken über unsere Reglements. Nochmals: 'Der Kampf um die infanteristische Feuerüberlegenheit.' - Die Formation der zum Feuergefechte bestimmten Compagnien. - Der eigentliche Angriff under der Bajonnetkampf," 85–87; Henriques de Ben, "Vergleich des Entwurfes zum Exercier-Reglement für die k.und k. Fußtruppen mit dem bisher in Kraft gestandenen Reglement," 318–319; Schnetzer, "Die modernen Angriffsströmungen und unser Exerzierreglement," 1024–1025; Smekal, "Einiges über den Infanterieangriff," 265, 299; Meixner, "Das Exerzierreglement für die k.u.k. Fußtruppen vom Jahre 1903," 98–99.
53. Kirchgaesser, "Erfahrungen und Lehren aus dem südafrikanischen Krieg," 236; L.F.v.G., "Schlagworte über die Taktik der Zukunft," 839–840; Reinöhl, "Die Entwicklung der Feuertaktik der Infanterie," 26–27; T.R.v.Z., "Über Angriffstaktik nach den Erfahrungen des südafrikanischen Krieges," *O.* 68 (1904): 133–135.

54. Kirchgaesser, “Erfahrungen und Lehren aus dem südafrikanischen Krieg,” 230–231; Smekal, “Einiges über den Infanterieangriff,” 259; Oberst Wenzel von Porth, “Kriegslehren,” *O.* 70 (1905): 212–213.
55. z, “Infanterische Fragen und die Erscheinungen des Boerenkrieges von F.C.v.H.,” 24.
56. Wawro, *Warfare and Society in Europe, 1792–1914*, 152–155.
57. Major des Geniestabes Alexander Kuchinka, “Vorträge. Der Kampf um Port Arthur,” *ÖMZ* 2 (1905): 892; Major des Generalstabscorps Maximilian Ritter von Hoen, “Der russisch-japanische Krieg,” *O.* 70 (1905): 168–169.
58. Wawro, *Warfare and Society in Europe, 1792–1914*, 156–159.
59. Hoen, “Vorträge. Der russisch-japanische Krieg,” *ÖMZ* 1 (1905): 679; Hoen, “Der russisch-japanische Krieg,” 158–159, 169; Oberstleutnant Albin Regele, “Port Arthur,” *O.* 71 (1905): 81–82; “Der russisch-japanische Krieg: Urteile und Beobachtungen von Mitkampfern,” *ÖMZ* 1 (1906): 120–121; Oberleutnant Erwin Franz, “Vorträge. Episoden und Eindrücke aus dem mandschurischen Feldzuge auf japanischer Seite,” *ÖMZ* 1 (1906): 449–452; Hauptmann des Generalstabskorps Karl Kratochwil des Szt. Keresztheg<y, “Vorträge. Der russisch-japanische Krieg: Betrachtungen und Folgerungen,” 1101–1102; Major Adalbert von Dani, “Der russisch-japanische Krieg: Urteile und Beobachtungen von Mitkämpfern. Die Infanterie der I. japanischen Armee im Feldzug gegen Rußland,” *ÖMZ* 2 (1906): 1773; Dani, “Der russisch-japanische Krieg: Urteile und Beobachtungen von Mitkämpfern. Die Infanterie der I. japanischen Armee im Feldzug gegen Rußland,” *ÖMZ* 1 (1907): 107–119; Hauptmann Silvio von Spieß, “Bemerkungen zur infanteristischen Aufklärung und Angriffstechnik,” *ÖMZ* 1 (1908): 24–31; Lang, “Das Infanteriegefecht,” *ÖMZ* 1 (1908): 417–419, 595; Generalmajor Otto Meixner, “Truppenausbildung und Truppenführung,” *ÖMZ* 1 (1908): 807–808; Oberst Rudolf Rudel, “Das neue Exerzierreglement für die k.u.k. Fußtruppen,” *ÖMZ* 1 (1912): 415.
60. Hoen, “Der russisch-japanische Krieg,” 168–170; Hauptmann Josef Putzker, “Lose Gedanken über das moderne Gefecht,” *O.* 71 (1905): 243–248; “Der russisch-japanische Krieg: Urteile und Beobachtungen von Mitkämpfern,” 120–121; Franz, “Vorträge. Episoden und Eindrücke aus dem mandschurischen Feldzuge auf japanischer Seite,” 452; Kratochwil, “Vorträge. Der russisch-japanische Krieg: Betrachtungen und Folgerungen,” 1101; Dani 1907, 107; C.H., “Über das innere Wesen der japanischen und neuzeitlichen Offensive. Eine kriegspsychologische Studie,” *ÖMZ* 2 (1907): 1426–1428; Spieß, “Bemerkungen zur infanteristischen Aufklärung und Angriffstechnik,” 45–50; Lang, “Das Infanteriegefecht,” 417–419; Hauptmann Lehar,

"Kriegsmoral; deren Vorbereitung im Frieden. Auf Grund des Studiums des russisch-japanischen Feldzuges," *ÖMZ* 2 (1910): 1729–1733.

61. Putzker, "Lose Gedanken über das moderne Gefecht," 243–248; Lang, "Uber die taktische Ausbildung der Infanterie," *O.* 72 (1906): 219–244; "Der Infanterieangriff über offenes Terrain," *ÖMZ* 1 (1907): 393–403; Lang, "Das Infanteriegefecht," 792; FML von Woinovich, "Die Schlacht von Maximilian Csicserics v. Bacsány, k.u.k. Oberst," *ÖMZ* 2 (1908): 1326–1327; "Mitteilungen der Armeeschießschule. Heroische Zug eines Unteroffiziers," *ÖMZ* 2 (1908): 1215–1216; "Mitteilungen der Armeeschießschule. Schüttere und dichte Schwarmlinie im Feuerkampfe," *ÖMZ* 2 (1908): 1841; "Mitteilungen der Armeeschießschule. Über das Sprungweise Vorgehen," *ÖMZ* 1 (1909): 843; Major Wilde, "Die Technik des Infanterieangriffes auf Grund reglementarischer Bestimmungen," *ÖMZ* 2 (1910): 1509–1524; "Neuerungen im Heereswesen im Laufe des Jahres 1910," *ÖMZ* 1 (1911): 822; Rudel, "Das neue Exerzierreglement für die k.u.k. Fußtruppen," 403, 422–425; Hauptmann Albert von Ungard, "Betrachtungen über das Problem der Feuerüberlegenheit," *ÖMZ* 1 (1913): 689–697; Nn., "Neue Reglements. Eine kritische Studie," *ÖMZ* 1 (1913): 981–983; Ein Truppenkommandant, "Über die moralische Vorbereitung zum Kriege," *ÖMZ* 1 (1914): 577–608.
62. Lang, "Das Infanteriegefecht," 795–796.
63. Günther Kronenbitter, *"Krieg im Frieden." Die Führung der k.u.k. Armee und die Großmacht politik Österreich-Ungarns 1906–1914* (Munich: Oldenbourg, 2003), 84.
64. Auffenberg, *Aus Österreich-Ungarns Teilnahme am Weltkriege*, 51–52.
65. "Der russisch-japanische Krieg: Urteile und Beobachtungen von Mikämpfern," 121; Franz, "Vorträge. Episoden und Eindrücke aus dem mandschurischen Feldzuge auf japanischer Seite," 452; Kratochwil, "Vorträge. Der russisch-japanische Krieg: Betrachtungen und Folgerungen," 1101; Spieß, "Bemerkungen zur infanteristischen Aufklärung und Angriffstechnik," 50; Lehar, "Kriegsmoral; deren Vorbereitung im Frieden. Auf Grund des Studiums des russisch-japanischen Feldzuges," 1733; Ungard, "Betrachtungen über das Problem der Feuerüberlegenheit," 697; Ein Truppenkommandant, "Über die moralische Vorbereitung zum Kriege," 608.
66. Conrad, *Zum Studium der Taktik*, 4, 14; Woinovich, "Die Schlacht von Maximilian Csicserics v. Bacsány, k.u.k. Oberst," 1326–1327; "Mitteilungen der Armeeschießschule. Schüttere und dichte Schwarmlinie im Feuerkampfe," 1841; Wilde, "Die Technik des Infanterieangriffes auf Grund reglementarischer Bestimmungen," 1521; Ungard, "Betrachtungen über das Problem der Feuerüberlegenheit," 690–691.

67. Entwurf. Taktisches Reglement für die k.u.k. Fustruppen. II. Heft. Gefecht. (Wien: k.k. Hof- und Staatsdruckerei, 1909), KA Generalstab Operationsbüro, Karton Nr. 743, Exercierreglement und Entwurfe 1907–1911, 1–4, 12–13, 15.
68. Wilde, "Die Technik des Infanterieangriffes auf Grund reglementarischer Bestimmungen," 1521.
69. Viktor E. Frankl, *Man's Search for Meaning* (Boston: Beacon Press, 1959), 104; Houston Stewart Chamberlain, *Der Wille zum Sieg und andere Aufsätze* (München: Hugo Bruckmann, 1918).
70. "Der Infanterieangriff über offenes Terrain," 407; Wilde, "Die Technik des Infanterieangriffes auf Grund reglementarischer Bestimmungen," 1512–1513; Rudel, "Das neue Exerzierreglement für die k.u.k. Fußtruppen," 425; Ungard, "Betrachtungen über das Problem der Feuerüberlegenheit," 690–691.
71. Rudel, "Das neue Exerzierreglement für die k.u.k. Fußtruppen," 425.
72. Meixner, "Das Exerzierreglement für die k.u.k. Fußtruppen vom Jahre 1903," 98; Wilde, "Die Technik des Infanterieangriffes auf Grund reglementarischer Bestimmungen," 1509–1510.
73. Lang, "Das Infanteriegefecht," 429–432.
74. Evidenz-Bureau des k.u.k. Generalstabes. Japan 1907. Infanterie Exercierreglement 2. Teil. Das Gefecht. Exercierreglement Fol: 593–622. KA Generalstab Operationsbüro, Karton Nr. 743, Exercierreglement und Entwurfe 1907–1911. The Evidenz-Bureau collected documents and statistics of foreign armies and drew up reports on these topics for the chief of the general staff.
75. Generalstabhauptmann Theodor von Lerch, "Das neue japanische Infanteriereglement," *ÖMZ* 1 (1908): 260–278.
76. "K.u.k. KS I. Jahrgang 1912/13 Taktik. Studie über die sukzessive Entwicklung des Angriffsverfahrens der japanischen Infanterie und die wichtigsten Bestimmungen über das Gefecht im japanischen exerzierreglement für die Infanterie vom Jahre 1907/:Entwurf:/u. 1909," KA Militärschulen, KS Karton Nr. 67, Studienbehelfe: 1912/1914, 15.
77. "K.u.k. KS I. Jahrgang 1912/13 Taktik. Studie über die sukzessive Entwicklung des Angriffsverfahrens der japanischen Infanterie und die wichtigsten Bestimmungen über das Gefecht im japanischen exerzierreglement für die Infanterie vom Jahre 1907/:Entwurf:/u. 1909," KA Militärschulen, KS Karton Nr. 67, Studienbehelfe: 1912/1914, 15; Franz, "Vorträge. Episoden und Eindrücke aus dem mandschurischen Feldzuge auf japanischer Seite," 452; Kratochwil, "Vorträge. Der russisch-japanische Krieg: Betrachtungen und Folgerungen," 1103; Lehar, "Kriegsmoral; deren Vorbereitung im Frieden. Auf Grund des Studiums des russisch-japanischen Feldzuges," 1733.

78. Oberstleutnant Oskar von Shießler, "Die Ausbildung unserer Jungmannschaft," *ÖMZ* 1 (1909): 787.
79. Abt. 5. Nro. 3882 von 1909. Referat über den Stand des neuen Exerzierreglements für die Fußtruppen—Ende Oktober 1909. Mit 11 Beilage. KA Fischer 6282/O-KA/94 Fol: 343–429, KA Generalstab Operationsbüro, Karton Nr. 743 Exercierreglement und Entwurfe 1907–1911, 1–2; zu Res. Glstb. Nr. 122 von 1911, KA Fol: 1–74: KA Generalstab Operationsbüro, Karton Nr. 743, Exercierreglement und Entwurfe 1907–1911.
80. Entwurf. Taktisches Reglement für die k.u.k. Fusstruppen. II. Heft. Gefecht. (Wien: k.k. Hof- und Staatsdruckerei, 1909), KA Generalstab Operationsbüro, Karton Nr. 743, Exercierreglement und Entwurfe 1907–1911, 1–4, 12–13, 15.
81. Abt. 5. Nro. 3882 von 1909. Referat über den Stand des neuen Exerzierreglements für die Fußtruppen—Ende Oktober 1909. Mit 11 Beilage. KA Fischer 6282/O-KA/94 Fol: 343–429, KA Generalstab Operationsbüro, Karton Nr. 743 Exercierreglement und Entwurfe 1907–1911, 6–7; Beilage 12 zum Erlaß Abt. 5. Nr. 3882 von 1909. General der Infanterie Liborius Frank, KA Fischer 6282/O-KA/94 Fol: 343–429, KA Generalstab Operationsbüro, Karton Nr. 743 Exercierreglement und Entwurfe 1907–1911; Beilage 13 zum Erlaß Abt. 5. Nr. 3882 von 1909. F.M.Lt. Boroević, KA Fischer 6282/O-KA/94 Fol: 343–429, KA Generalstab Operationsbüro, Karton Nr. 743 Exercierreglement und Entwurfe 1907–1911; Beilage 14 zum Erlaß Abt. 5. Nro. 3882 von 1909. Generalmajor Stephan Sarkotić, KA Fischer 6282/O-KA/94 Fol: 343–429, KA Generalstab Operationsbüro, Karton Nr. 743 Exercierreglement und Entwurfe 1907–1911.
82. Abt. 5. Nro. 3882 von 1909. Referat über den Stand des neuen Exerzierreglements für die Fußtruppen - Ende Oktober 1909. Mit 11 Beilage. KA Fischer 6282/O-KA/94 Fol: 343–429, KA Generalstab Operationsbüro, Karton Nr. 743 Exercierreglement und Entwurfe 1907–1911, 6; Beilage 9 zum Erlaß Abt. 5. Nr. 3882 von 1909. General der Infanterie Artur Ritter von Pino, KA Fischer 6282/O-KA/94 Fol: 343–429, KA Generalstab Operationsbüro, Karton Nr. 743 Exercierreglement und Entwurfe 1907–1911; Beilage 10 zum Erlaß Abt. 5. Nro. 3882 von 1909. FML Blasius Schemua, KA Fischer 6282/O-KA/94 Fol: 343–429, KA Generalstab Operationsbüro, Karton Nr. 743 Exercierreglement und Entwurfe 1907–1911; Beilage 11 zum Erlaß Abt. 5. Nr. 3882 von 1909. Oberst Ferdinand Ritter von Marterer, KA Fischer 6282/O-KA/94 Fol: 343–429, KA Generalstab

Operationsbüro, Karton Nr. 743 Exercierreglement und Entwurfe 1907–1911.

83. Abt. 5. Nro. 3882 von 1909. Referat über den Stand des neuen Exerzierreglements für die Fußtruppen - Ende Oktober 1909. Mit 11 Beilage. KA Fischer 6282/O-KA/94 Fol: 343–429, KA Generalstab Operationsbüro, Karton Nr. 743 Exercierreglement und Entwurfe 1907–1911, 5–6; Beilage 7 zum Erlaß Abt. Nr. 3882 von 1909. Generaltruppeninspektor General der Infanterie Ferdinand Fiedler, KA Fischer 6282/O-KA/94 Fol: 343–429, KA Generalstab Operationsbüro, Karton Nr. 743 Exercierreglement und Entwurfe 1907–1911; Beilage 8 zum Erlaß Abt. 5. Nr. 3882 von 1909. General der Infanterie Oskar Potiorek, KA Fischer 6282/O-KA/94 Fol: 343–429, KA Generalstab Operationsbüro, Karton Nr. 743 Exercierreglement und Entwurfe 1907–1911; General der Kavallerie und Admiral Erzherzog Franz Ferdinand. Res. No. Me/2. Entwurf des neuen Exerzierreglements, Wien, am 15. Dezember 1910. KA Fol: 1–74: KA Generalstab Operationsbüro, Karton Nr. 743, Exercierreglement und Entwurfe 1907–1911; General der Kavallerie Erzherzog Franz Ferdinand Res. No. M/177. Taktisches Reglement für die Fußtruppen. 4. September 1909. Bemerkungen zum Entwurfe des taktischen Reglements für die k.u.k. Fusstruppen. KA Fol: 1–74: KA Generalstab Operationsbüro, Karton Nr. 743, Exercierreglement und Entwurfe 1907–1911.

84. K.u.k. KS Res. Nr. 594 Beiliegend wird eine Sammlung von Erfahrungen und Beobachtungen, die während des Balkankrieges von Mitkämpfern und Augenzeugen gemacht wurden, zur Verwertung ausgegeben. Wien, am 10. November 1913, KA Militärschulen, Karton Nr. 43 Kriegsschulakten 1886/1914, Mobilisierungsplan, Befehle für die Lehrer (aus dem Nachlass Theodor Körner), 1–10.

85. Major Wilhelm Buschek, "Aufklärung und Verschleierung," *ÖMZ* 2 (1896): 218; Hauptmann H. Sallagar, "Über Verwendung der Cavallerie im Aufklärungsdienste," *ÖMZ* 1 (1899): 8; Hauptmann Ludwig Berger, "Infanterie gegen Reiterei," *ÖMZ* 4 (1899): 82; Ein Honvéd-Officier, "Infanterie gegen Reiterei," *ÖMZ* 2 (1900): 139–168; Pk., "Berittene Infanterie," *ÖMZ* 4 (1901): 50; Ein General, "Treffenformation grösserer Kavalleriekörper," *ÖMZ* 1 (1906): 886; General der Kavallerie Gaudernak, "Der Kavalleriekampf," *ÖMZ* 1 (1907): 185; Gstbsmajor Franz Graf Zedtwitz, "Dienst und Verwendung der Divisionskavallerie," *ÖMZ* 1 (1911): 655; Generalmajor Ernst von Horsetzky, "Zur Frage der Divisionskavallerie," *ÖMZ* 1 (1913): 33–34; Obstl. Franz Graf Zedtwitz, "Über Kavallerieverwendung bei Übunge aller Waffen," *ÖMZ* 1 (1914): 609–620.

86. Buschek, "Aufklärung und Verschleierung," 212; Feldmarschall-Lieutenant von Molnár, "Ein Wort zur Frage der Divisions-Cavallerie," *ÖMZ* 1 (1899): 1–7; Bdt., "Gedanken über unsere Waffe', der österreichisch-ungarischen Kavallerie gewidmet," *ÖMZ* 1 (1906): 593; Ein General, "Treffenformation grösserer Kavalleriekörper," 886; "Über Angriffsformen grösserer Kavalleriekörper," *ÖMZ* 1 (1907): 905.
87. Conrad, *Zum Studium der Taktik*, 351.
88. Hoen, "Vorträge. Der russisch-japanische Krieg," 679; Franz, "Vorträge. Episoden und Eindrücke aus dem mandschurischen Feldzuge auf japanischer Seite," 450–451; Kratochwil, "Vorträge. Der russisch-japanische Krieg: Betrachtungen und Folgerungen," 1102; Dani, "Der russisch-japanische Krieg: Urteile und Beobachtungen von Mitkämpfern. Die Kavallerie der I. japanischen Armee im Feldzug gegen Rußland," *ÖMZ* 1 (1907): 624–627; Hauptmann Ignaz Rodić, "Chancen von Reitermassen in Flanke und Rücken des Feindes," *ÖMZ* 2 (1908): 1275–1277.
89. Oberstlieutenant A. Strobl, "Cavalleristische Kriegsspiele auf kriegsgeschichtlicher Grundlage," *ÖMZ* 2 (1897): 201–203; Ein General, "Treffenformation grösserer Kavalleriekörper," 878; "Über Angriffsformen grösserer Kavalleriekörper," 891; Rodić, "Chancen von Reitermassen in Flanke und Rücken des Feindes," 1275–1277.
90. Rodić, "Über Feldartilleriewirkung. Eine Replik," *ÖMZ* 2 (1912): 1687.
91. Hauptmann August Urbanski, "Militärische Ausnützung des Fahrrades," *ÖMZ* 4 (1899): 217–266; Pk., "Berittene Infanterie," 47; Hauptmann Höfer, "Vorträge. Radfahrer und berittene Infanterie," *ÖMZ* 1 (1905): 676; "Eine neue Schießinstruktion für die Kavallerie," *ÖMZ* 2 (1905): 1385–1398; Höfer, "Radfahrer und berittene Infanterie," *O.* 70 (1905): 21–42; Bdt., "Gedanken über unsere Waffe', der österreichisch-ungarischen Kavallerie gewidmet," 594; "Verwendung und Leistungsfähigkeit der Maschinengewehre bei den grösseren Manövern in Böhmen 1905," *ÖMZ* 1 (1906): 704–713; Oberstleutnant Berndt, "Über Maschinengewehre und Feuergefecht der Kavallerie," *ÖMZ* 2 (1906): 1737–1761; Rodić, "Chancen von Reitermassen in Flanke und Rücken des Feindes," 1286–1288; "Mitteilungen der Armeeschießschule. Bekämpfung feindlicher, Schutz der eigenen Maschinen-gewehre im Reiterkampfe," *ÖMZ* 1 (1910): 949–957; Hauptmann Kosmutza, "Die neuen Technischen Unterrichte für die Infanterie und Kavallerie," *ÖMZ* 1 (1911): 657–674; Oblt. des Kriegsministeriums Eduard Brunner, "Unsere Radfahrerkompagnien," *ÖMZ* 2 (1912): 1663–1669.
92. Auffenberg, *Aus Österreich-Ungarns Teilnahme am Weltkriege*, 41.

93. Heinrich Mast, "Die Aufklärungstätigkeit der österr.-ung. Kavallerie bei Kriegsbeginn 1914," *ÖMZ* Sonderheft I (1965): 9–10.
94. Fl., "Einfluß moderner Artilleriewirkung auf den Aufklärungs- und Sicherungsdienst," *ÖMZ* 1 (1914): 621–635.
95. Major Franz Ruprecht, "Über moderne Artillerieverwendung," *ÖMZ* 1 (1905): 27, 178–179.
96. Hauptmann Alois Kalteis, "Die Kräfte-Verhältnisse und die Schießausbildung der Feld-Artillerien der continentalen Großmachte," *ÖMZ* 1 (1901): 4; Hf., "Zur Feldartilleriefrage," *ÖMZ* 2 (1905): 875–877; Casey, "Die schmalspurigen Feldhaubitzen bei den Manövern in Südtirol," *ÖMZ* 1 (1906): 193–194; Oberst Ernst von Horsetzky, "Eindrücke vom Artillerieinformationskurse in Hajmáskér 1908," *ÖMZ* 1 (1909): 245–247; Oberleutnant Johann Hanika, "Ist die Artilleriefrage gelöst?" *ÖMZ* 2 (1910): 533, 549; Fl., "Einfluß moderner Artilleriewirkung auf den Aufklärungs- und Sicherungsdienst," 621–635; Hauptmann Ludwig R. v. Eimannsberger, "Unsere Artillerietaktik," *ÖMZ* 2 (1914): 1021–1034; Oberst M. Gärtner, "Über Verwendung der Feldartillerie im Balkankriege 1912/13," *ÖMZ* 2 (1914): 1035–1061, 1185–1212.
97. Dani, "Der russisch-japanische Krieg: Urteile und Beobachtungen von Mitkämpfern. Die Artillerie der I. japanischen Armee im Feldzug gegen Rußland," *ÖMZ* 1 (1907): 642.
98. Rodić, "Welchen Einfluß dürfte die Feldartillerie auf den Gefechtsverlauf in einem kommenden Kriege üben?" *ÖMZ* 2 (1910): 1530–1532.
99. Rodić, "Über Feldartilleriewirkung. Eine Replik," 1685–1702, 1865–1876.
100. Oberleutnant Anton Schiebl, "Der artilleristische Standpunkt," *ÖMZ* 1 (1911): 1269–1272.
101. Casey, "Die schmalspurigen Feldhaubitzen bei den Manövern in Südtirol," 193–194.
102. Hauptmann Theodor Baeck, "Über Feldartilleriewirkung. Ein Beitrag zu ihrer Einschätzung auf Grund der Ergebnisse des russisch-japanischen Krieges," *ÖMZ* 1 (1911): 832–844.
103. Baeck, "Über Feldartilleriewirkung. Ein Beitrag zu ihrer Einschätzung auf Grund der Ergebnisse des russisch-japanischen Krieges," 840–841; Franz, "Vorträge. Episoden und Eindrücke aus dem mandschurischen Feldzuge auf japanischer Seite," 450; Hoen, "Vorträge. Der russisch-japanische Krieg," 680; Hoen, "Der russisch-japanische Krieg," 162–163.
104. K.u.k. KS Res. Nr. 594 Beiliegend wird eine Sammlung von Erfahrungen und Beobachtungen, die während des Balkankrieges von Mitkämpfern und Augenzeugen gemacht wurden, zur Verwertung ausgegeben. Wien, am 10. November 1913, KA Militärschulen, Karton Nr.

43 Kriegsschulakten 1886/1914, Mobilisierungsplan, Befehle für die Lehrer (aus dem Nachlass Theodor Körner), 1–10.

105. Gärtner, "Über Verwendung der Feldartillerie im Balkankriege 1912/13," 1035, 1038, 1061, 1209.
106. *Exerzierreglement für die k.u.k. Fußtruppen* (Wien: k.k. Hof- und Staatsdruckerei, 1911), 1.
107. Erich Gabriel, "Die wichtigsten Waffen der österreichisch-ungarischen Armee 1918," *ÖMZ* 6 (1968): 436.
108. Kalteis, "Die Kräfte-Verhältnisse und die Schießausbildung der Feld-Artillerien der continentalen Großmachte," 8.
109. Auffenberg, *Aus Österreich-Ungarns Teilnahme am Weltkriege*, 42.
110. Oberstlieutenant Johann Witsch, "Das zukünftige Feldgeschütz und die Schnellfeuer-Kanonen," *O.* 52 (1896): 374.
111. Ruprecht, "Über moderne Artillerieverwendung," 28–29.
112. Witsch, "Das zukünftige Feldgeschütz und die Schnellfeuer-Kanonen," 395; "Die mobile Belagerungs-Artillerie der europäischen Militärstaaten," *ÖMZ* 4 (1897): 176–184; S., "Die Organisation der Feld-Artillerie," *ÖMZ* 1 (1902): 189–191; A.N.O., "Anfangsgeschwindigkeit. Ein Beitrag zur Feldgeschützfrage," *ÖMZ* 1 (1902): 223; Major Adolf Weigner, "Vom Feldgeschütz," *ÖMZ* 1 (1903): 58–74; -i-, "Die Feldgeschützfrage," *ÖMZ* 1 (1904): 131–141; Ruprecht, "Über moderne Artillerieverwendung," 26–44, 178–194; Hf., 871–883; "Zur Reorganisation der Feldartillerie," *O.* 72 (1906): 33–49; Artillerieingenieur Kühn, "Leichte Feldhaubitzer," *ÖMZ* 1 (1907): 78–99, 280–290; Hauptmann Adler, "Uber die Zugehörigkeit der Belagerungshaubitzdivisionen," *ÖMZ* 2 (1907): 1023–1032; Hauptmann des Generalstabskorps Paul Winterstein, "Über Führung und Ausbildung der Feldartillerie," *ÖMZ* 1 (1908): 228; A.B.C., "Mehr Haubitzen!" *ÖMZ* 2 (1908): 1931–1935; Hanika, "Ist die Artilleriefrage gelöst?" 531–554, 731–748; Hauptmann Moriz Mansch, "Betrachtungen über Einstellung schwerer Geschütze in der Feldartillerie," *ÖMZ* 2 (1910): 1235–1250; Oberstleutnant Ludwig Sündermann, "Über Artillerieverwendung," *ÖMZ* 1 (1912): 33–35.
113. -i-, "Die Feldgeschützfrage," 131.
114. "Zur Reorganisation der Feldartillerie," 33.
115. Gunther E. Rothenberg, *The Army of Francis Joseph* (West Lafayette, IN: Purdue University Press, 1976), 129–136.
116. -i-, "Die Feldgeschützfrage," 131–132.
117. "Neuerungen im eigenen Heerwesen. Die Reorganisation der Feld- und Gebirgsartillerie," *ÖMZ* 1 (1908): 1083; "Neuerungen im Heerwesen im Sommerhalbjahr 1909," *ÖMZ* 2 (1909): 1815.

118. Oberstleutnant Alois Vollgruber, "Die Geschützzahl und die taktische Artilleriereserve," *ÖMZ* 2 (1913): 1847.
119. Rothenberg, *The Army of Francis Joseph*, 174.
120. Evidenzbureau des Generalstabes. A. Nr. 98 Res. Übersicht der bei den Divisionen (Korps) fremder Armeen organisationsgemäsen Dotierung mit Artillerie. 30 Sept. 1913, KA Generalstab Operationsbüro, Karton Nr. 739, Vorträge und Referate 1910–1914.
121. Vollgruber, "Die Geschützzahl und die taktische Artilleriereserve," 1858.
122. S., "Artillerie im Infanteriefeuer," *ÖMZ* 4 (1900): 97–146; Kalteis, "Die Kräfte-Verhältnisse und die Schießausbildung der Feld-Artillerien der continentalen Großmachte," 5, 19; Ruprecht, "Über moderne Artillerieverwendung," 194; Hauptmann Wilhelm Knobloch, "Schweres Mörserfeuer," *ÖMZ* 2 (1908): 1415; Horsetzky, "Eindrücke vom Artillerieinformationskurse in Hajmáskér 1908," 245–252; Kommando der Schießschulabteilung der Feldartillerie, "Erwiderung auf 'Eindrücke vom Artillerieinformationskurse in Hajmáskér 1908'," *ÖMZ* 1 (1909): 771; Leutnant Viktor Cajanek, "Erfahrungen des russisch-japanischen Krieges für die Verwendung der Feldartillerie im Feldkriege," *ÖMZ* 2 (1910): 1059–1071; Hauptmann Max Kralupper, "Die Ausbildung unserer Festungsartillerie für den Angriffskrieg," *ÖMZ* 1 (1913): 465; Eimannsberger, "Unsere Artillerietaktik," 1033–1034.
123. "Neuerungen im Heerwesen im Sommerhalbjahr 1909," 1816–1817.
124. Knobloch, "Die Artillerie im Kampfe gestern und heute," *O.* 68 (1904): 308–309; Dani, "Der russisch-japanische Krieg: Urteile und Beobachtungen von Mitkämpfern. Die Artillerie der I. japanischen Armee im Feldzug gegen Rußland," 636–637; Winterstein, "Über Führung und Ausbildung der Feldartillerie," 226; A.B.C., "Mehr Haubitzen!" 1935; Cajanek, "Erfahrungen des russisch-japanischen Krieges für die Verwendung der Feldartillerie im Feldkriege," 1061–1061; Mansch, "Betrachtungen über Einstellung schwerer Geschütze in der Feldartillerie," 1245; Sündermann, "Über Artillerieverwendung," 33; Oberstleutnant Karl Hroch, "Disponierung der Artillerie im Gefecht," *ÖMZ* 1 (1912): 594–597; Oberleutnant Geza Lajtos von Szentmaria, "Unterstützung des Infanterieangriffes durch Artillerie, bei besonderer Berücksichtigung der Tätigkeit der Artillerie," *ÖMZ* 1 (1912): 599–617; Casey, "Zur Disposition der Artillerie im Gefechte," *ÖMZ* 1 (1913): 115; Major Lottspeich, "Zur Disposition der Artillerie im Gefechte," *ÖMZ* 2 (1913): 1677; Eimannsberger, "Unsere Artillerietaktik," 1023–1029; Gärtner, "Über Verwendung der Feldartillerie im Balkankriege 1912/13," 1061.
125. Auffenberg, *Aus Österreich-Ungarns Teilnahme am Weltkriege*, 54–55.

126. Vollgruber, "Die Geschützzahl und die taktische Artilleriereserve," 1848.
127. S., "Die Organisation der Feld-Artillerie," 222.
128. S., "Artillerie im Infanteriefeuer," 145; Winterstein, "Über Führung und Ausbildung der Feldartillerie," 228; Cajanek, "Erfahrungen des russisch-japanischen Krieges für die Verwendung der Feldartillerie im Feldkriege," 1071; Kralupper, "Die Ausbildung unserer Festungsartillerie für den Angriffskrieg," 465.
129. Kalteis, "Die Kräfte-Verhältnisse und die Schießausbildung der Feld-Artillerien der continentalen Großmachte," 18.
130. Eimannsberger, "Unsere Artillerietaktik," 1034.
131. Eimannsberger, "Unsere Artillerietaktik," 1021.
132. Summar über das Gesammterfordernis des Heeres für das Jahr 1905. Beilage D. Vorlage des gemeinsamen Kriegsministeriums, A. Heer, an die Delegation des hohen Reichsrates, betreffend das Ansuchen um die Bewilligung des Teilbetrages von 50,000.000 K als einmaliges ausserordentliches Erfordernis zur Fortsetzung der Beschaffung des neuen Feldartilleriematerials. KA Generalstab Operationsbüro, Karton Nr. 807, Budget-Entwurfe. In 1892 Austria-Hungary adopted the gold standard and set the value of the Krone, the new currency, as 2 Kronen for 1 florin.
133. Summar über das Gesamt-Erfordernis des stehenden Heeres für das Jahr 1912. Beilage F. Vorlage des Kriegsministeriums, A. Heer, an die Delegation des hohen Reichsrates, betreffend das Ansuchen um die Bewilligung des Teilbetrages von 4,000.000 K als einmaliges ausserordentliches Erfordernis zur Fortsetzung der Beschaffung des neuen Feldartilleriematerials. KA Generalstab Operationsbüro, Karton Nr. 806, Budget-Enwurfe.
134. Zusammensetzung des ausserordentlichen Kredites von 250 Mill. Kr. KA Generalstab Operationsbüro, Karton Nr. 808, Budget, Besondere Kredite; Spezialkredit 1912 Vorlage des Kriegsministeriums, Erfordernis für die Beschaffung von Kriegsmaterial und zur Durchführung fortifikatorischer Maßnahmen. 250 Millionen Kredit. KA Generalstab Operationsbüro, Karton Nr. 808, Budget, Besondere Kredite.
135. Spezialkredit 1912 Vorlage des Kriegsministeriums, Erfordernis für die Beschaffung von Kriegsmaterial und zur Durchführung fortifikatorischer Maßnahmen. KA Generalstab Operationsbüro, Karton Nr. 808, Budget, Besondere Kredite.
136. Rothenberg, *The Army of Francis Joseph*, 174.
137. Walter Wagner, "Die k. (u.)k. Armee - Gliederung und Aufgabenstellung," in *Die Habsburgermonarchie 1848–1918*, Vol. 5 *Die Bewaffnete Macht* (Vienna: Verlag der Österreichischen Akademie der Wissenschaften, 1987), 408–409.

138. Denkschrift 1908: 8. Abtheilung Zu int. res. No. 106/mob. von 1908, Beitrag zur Denkschrift für das Jahr 1908. KA Generalstab Operationsbüro, Karton Nr. 742, Denkschriften des Chef des Generalstabes 1906–1914.
139. 1911 Budget: VII PermanenteBefestigungen. KA Generalstab Operationsbüro, Karton Nr. 808, Budget, Besondere Kredite.
140. Spezialkredit 1912 Vorlage des Kriegsministeriums, Erfordernis für die Beschaffung von Kriegsmaterial und zur Durchführung fortifikatorischer Maßnahmen. 250 Millionen Kredit. KA Generalstab Operationsbüro, Karton Nr. 808, Budget, Besondere Kredite.
141. "Neuerungen im Heerwesen," *ÖMZ* 2 (1912): 1148–1149.
142. Wagner, "Die k. (u.)k. Armee - Gliederung und Aufgabenstellung," 589.
143. FML Franz Graf Conrad von Hötzendorf, *Aus Meiner Dienstzeit 1906–1918* (Wien: Rikola Verlag, 1921), 1: 424.
144. Auffenberg, *Aus Österreich-Ungarns Teilnahme am Weltkriege*, 44–45.
145. F., "Gedanken über Festungen, Festungskrieg und die Feuertaktik in demselben," *ÖMZ* 4 (1896): 196–209; Major Karl Kuk, "Die Vertheidigungsfronten einer Festung," *O.* 54 (1897): 101–134; Oberst M. Magdalenitsch, "Die Staatenvertheidigung und die Fortification am Endes des XIX Jahrhunderts," *ÖMZ* 1 (1899): 97–152; Oberlieutenant Max von Schönowsky, "Der Grenzschutz," *ÖMZ* 2 (1901): 59–73; "Die Grundzüge des zukünftigen Landesbefestigungssystem in Deutschland," *ÖMZ* 4 (1901): 80–85; Hauptmann August Zell, "Folgerungen aus den Kriegen in Südafrika und Ostasien für den Angriff auf Befestigungen," *ÖMZ* 2 (1907): 1565–1590; Oberleutnant Johann Hanika, "Neuerungen in der permanenten Fortifikation. Ein Vorschlag," *ÖMZ* 1 (1908): 229–260; Major Graf Lavaulx, "Die Wirtschaftsfrage in der Befestigung," *ÖMZ* 2 (1910): 1549–1568.
146. Franz Forstner, *Przemyśl: Österreich-Ungarns bedeutendste Festung* (Wien: Österreichischer Bundesverlag, 1987), 57–58.
147. K.u.k. Chef des Generalstabes. Allerunteränigster Vortrag. KA Generalstab Operationsbüro, Karton Nr. 742, Denkschriften des Chef des Generalstabes 1906–1914.
148. Pionnier-Hauptmann Rudolf Seissl, "Über Befestigung der Schlacht- und Gefechtsfelder," *ÖMZ* 4 (1897): 127–146; Kuk, "Die Vertheidigungsfronten einer Festung," 101–134; "Die Grundzüge des zukünftigen Landesbefestigungssytem in Deutschland," 80–85; Oberst Ernst Freiherr von Leithner, "Ein Plevna von einst und jetzt," *O.* 65 (1902): 329–346; R.S., "Einfluß der modernen Feuerwaffen auf die flüchtigen Befestigungsanlagen der Infanterie," *ÖMZ* 2 (1906): 1576–1582; Hauptmann Hans Schwalb, "Moderne Schlachtfeldbefestigung im Lichte russisch-japanische Kriegserfahrungen," *O.* 72 (1906):

277–318; Zell, "Folgerungen aus den Kriegen in Südafrika und Ostasien für den Angriff auf Befestigungen," 1565–1590; "Anhaltspunkte für die Durchführung von Feldbefestigungen bei der Infanterie," *ÖMZ* 1 (1908): 995–1016; Lavaulx, "Die Wirtschaftsfrage in der Befestigung," 1549–1568; Hauptmann Freiherr von Majneri-Kampen, "Widerstandsdauer einer Sperre," *ÖMZ* 2 (1912): 1181–1186; Hauptmann Ludwig Berger, "Beitrag zur Taktik des Festungskrieges," *ÖMZ* 2 (1913): 1321–1343.

149. Leithner, "Ein Plevna von einst und jetzt," 346; "Anhaltspunkte für die Durchführung von Feldbefestigungen bei der Infanterie," 1012–1013.
150. Schwalb, "Moderne Schlachtfeldbefestigung im Lichte russisch-japanische Kriegserfahrungen," 318.
151. Berger, "Küstenbefestigung," *ÖMZ* 1 (1912): 427–454.
152. Sondhaus, *Franz Conrad von Hötzendorf: Architect of the Apocalypse*, 65.
153. Wagner, "Die k.(u.)k. Armee - Gliederung und Aufgabenstellung," 411–414.
154. Wagner, "Die k.(u.)k. Armee - Gliederung und Aufgabenstellung," 589.
155. Wagner, "Die k.(u.)k. Armee - Gliederung und Aufgabenstellung," 591.
156. Besondere Kredite 250 Mill. Ministerkonferenzen Juli 1912. K.u.k. Chef des Generalstabes. Bericht über den Verlauf des gemeinsamen Ministerrates am 8 und 9 Juli 1912. KA Generalstab Operationsbüro, Karton Nr. 808, Budget, Besondere Kredite.
157. K.u.k. Chef des Generalstabes. Rapport bei Sr. Majestät, Schönbrunn 15 Oktober 1913, KA Generalstab Operationsbüro, Karton Nr. 739, Vorträge und Referate 1910–1914; Rapport bei Sr. Majestät am 4/6 1914, KA Generalstab Operationsbüro, Karton Nr. 739, Vorträge und Referate 1910–1914.
158. LSchK.v.B., "Kriegsschifftypen und ihre Anwendung auf unsere Verhältnisse," *ÖMZ* 1 (1909): 607–624.
159. Besondere Kredite 250 Mill. Ministerkonferenzen Juli 1912. K.u.k. Militärattaché in Rom. Abschrift. Nr. 22/3 Neuer 60 Millionen Kredit für das Heer und 21 ½ Millionen für die Kriegsmarine. 1. Juni 1912. KA Generalstab Operationsbüro, Karton Nr. 808, Budget, Besondere Kredite.
160. Lothar Höbelt, "Die Marine" in *Die Habsburgermonarchie 1848–1918*, Vol. 5 *Die Bewaffnete Macht* (Vienna: Verlag der Österreichischen Akademie der Wissenschaften, 1987), 716–718.
161. Kronenbitter, *"Krieg im Frieden."* 183–184.
162. Linienschiffsleutnant Alfred Dietrich Edlen von Sachsenfels, "Die Bedeutung einer Flotte," *ÖMZ* 2 (1914): 1063–1079.
163. "Die Delegationen," *Pester Lloyd*, 5. Februar 1911, Nr. 31, 6; "Wien, 4. Februar," *Neue Freie Presse*, 5. Februar 1911, Nr. 16688, 1.

164. *Stenographische Sitzungs-Protokolle der Delegation des Reichsrates*, 3. Sitzung der 40. Session am 30. Mai 1904 (Vienna: k.k. Hof- und Staatsdruckerei, 1904), 90, 4. Sitzung der 40. Session am 31. Mai 1904, 278, 298–302, 5. Sitzung der 40. Session am 1. Juni 1904, 380.
165. *Stenographische Sitzungs-Protokolle der Delegation des Reichsrates*, 10. Sitzung der 45. Session am 1. März 1911 (Vienna: k.k. Hof- und Staatsdruckerei, 1911), 459, 486, 504, 507–508, 510, 516, 12. Sitzung der 45. Session am 2. März 1911, 906, 13. Sitzung der 45. Session am 3. März 1911, 946.
166. Lawrence Sondhaus, *The Naval Policy of Austria-Hungary, 1867–1918: Navalism, Industrial Development, and the Politics of Dualism* (West Lafayette, IN: Purdue University Press, 1994), 194; Milan N. Vego, *Austro-Hungarian Naval Policy 1904–1914* (Portland, OR: Frank Cass, 1996), 56.
167. 28 25.09.1904. Verein zur Förderung der österreichischien Schiffahrt an Erzh. F.F. betr. Vereins-gründung, KA MKFF, Karton Nr. 208, Nichtprotokollierte Stücke 1898–1914.
168. Vego, *Austro-Hungarian Naval Policy 1904–1914*, 56.
169. Sondhaus, *The Naval Policy of Austria-Hungary, 1867–1918: Navalism, Industrial Development, and the Politics of Dualism*, 178.
170. Kronenbitter, *"Krieg im Frieden."* 183.
171. *Stenographische Sitzungs-Protokolle der Delegation des Reichsrates*, 3. Sitzung der 40. Session am 30. Mai 1904, 92–93, 94–98, 100–104, 109, 4. Sitzung der 40. Session am 31. Mai 1904, 286, 296, 5. Sitzung der 40. Session am 1. Juni 1904, 375–379; *Stenographische Sitzungs-Protokolle der Delegation des Reichsrates*, 10. Sitzung der 45. Session am 1. März 1911, 471–474, 478–484, 490, 493–496, 499–501, 505, 513, 11. Sitzung der 45. Session am 2. März 1911, 627, 650–652, 12. Sitzung der 45. Session am 2. März 1911, 902–903, 908–909, 911–912, 917–918, 13. Sitzung der 45. Session am 3. März 1911, 941, 945, 956–960, 15. (Schluß-) Sitzung der 45. Session am 4. März 1911, 1105–1110, 1115, 1120.
172. *Stenographische Sitzungs-Protokolle der Delegation des Reichsrates*, 5. Sitzung der 40. Session am 1. Juni 1904, 373–375, 382; *Stenographische Sitzungs-Protokolle der Delegation des Reichsrates*, 10. Sitzung der 45. Session am 1. März 1911, 467, 488–489, 492, 496–498, 506, 512, 12. Sitzung der 45. Session am 2. März 1911, 910, 13. Sitzung der 45. Session am 3. März 1911, 941, 960.
173. "Die Delegationen," *Pester Lloyd*, 5. Februar 1911, Nr. 31, 6; "Die Delegationen," *Pester Lloyd*, 14. Februar 1911, Nr. 38, 4; *Stenographische Sitzungs-Protokolle der Delegation des Reichsrates*, 5. Sitzung der 40. Session am 1. Juni 1904, 388; *Stenographische*

Sitzungs-Protokolle der Delegation des Reichsrates, 12. Sitzung der 45. Session am 2. März 1911, 918.

174. *Stenographische Sitzungs-Protokolle der Delegation des Reichsrates*, 3. Sitzung der 40. Session am 30. Mai 1904, 87, 118, 5. Sitzung der 40. Session am 1. Juni 1904, 375–377; *Stenographische Sitzungs-Protokolle der Delegation des Reichsrates*, 10. Sitzung der 45. Session am 1. März 1911, 477, 492, 11. Sitzung der 45. Session am 2. März 1911, 631, 640, 13. Sitzung der 45. Session am 3. März 1911, 947–950, 15. (Schluß-) Sitzung der 45. Session am 4. März 1911, 1104–1105.
175. *Stenographische Sitzungs-Protokolle der Delegation des Reichsrates*, 3. Sitzung der 40. Session am 30. Mai 1904, 94–95; *Stenographische Sitzungs-Protokolle der Delegation des Reichsrates*, 10. Sitzung der 45. Session am 1. März 1911, 507–508, 511, 517, 11. Sitzung der 45. Session am 2. März 1911, 636–638, 642, 12. Sitzung der 45. Session am 2. März 1911, 903, 907, 13. Sitzung der 45. Session am 3. März 1911, 945, 954–955, 957–958, 15. (Schluß-) Sitzung der 45. Session am 2. März 1911, 1104–1105, 1114, 1119–1121, 1124, 1141.
176. *Stenographische Sitzungs-Protokolle der Delegation des Reichsrates*, 10. Sitzung der 45. Session am 1. März 1911, 459–469, 474–476, 485–487, 489, 504–505, 508, 516, 12. Sitzung der 45. Session am 2. März 1911, 912.
177. *Stenographische Sitzungs-Protokolle der Delegation des Reichsrates*, 3. Sitzung der 40. Session am 30. Mai 1904, 86, 102, 118, 4. Sitzung der 40. Session am 31. Mai 1904, 277–285, 296, 304, 306, 320–322, 5. Sitzung der 40. Session am 1. Juni 1904, 372–373, 375–377, 379, 386; *Stenographische Sitzungs-Protokolle der Delegation des Reichsrates*, 10. Sitzung der 45. Session am 1. März 1911, 456–457, 478–481, 499–504, 901–902, 906–909, 911–912, 917, 920, 11. Sitzung der 45. Session am 2. März 1911, 625–626, 646–647, 652, 12. Sitzung der 45. Session am 2. März 1911, 901–902, 906–909, 911–912, 917, 920, 13. Sitzung der 45. Session am 3. März 1911, 945, 956, 15. (Schluß-) Sitzung der 45. Session am 4. März 1911, 1103, 1115–1118, 1122, 1128, 1130, 1133–1136.
178. *Stenographische Sitzungs-Protokolle der Delegation des Reichsrates*, 4. Sitzung der 40. Session am 31. Mai 1904, 286, 5. Sitzung der 40. Session am 1. Juni 1904, 375–377, 388; *Stenographische Sitzungs-Protokolle der Delegation des Reichsrates*, 10. Sitzung der 45. Session am 1. März 1911, 465, 471–474, 479, 493, 499, 513, 11. Sitzung der 45. Session am 2. März 1911, 627, 12. Sitzung der 45. Session am 2. März 1911, 902, 912, 924,13. Sitzung der 45. Session am 3. März 1911, 941, 15. (Schluß-) Sitzung der 45. Session am 4. März 1911, 1136.

179. *Stenographische Sitzungs-Protokolle der Delegation des Reichsrates*, 10. Sitzung der 45. Session am 1. März 1911, 493, 13. Sitzung der 45. Session am 3. März 1911, 948, 15. (Schluß-) Sitzung der 45. Session am 4. März 1911, 1131, 1136.
180. *Stenographische Sitzungs-Protokolle der Delegation des Reichsrates*, 15. (Schluß-) Sitzung der 45. Session am 4. März 1911, 1115.
181. Hugo Kerchnawe, *Die Vorgeschichte von 1866 und 19??* (Vienna: C.W. Stern Verlag, 1909), 5; Oskar Regele, *Feldzeugmeister Benedek und der Weg nach Königgrätz* (Vienna: Verlag Herold, 1960), 2–6; C.A. Macartney, *The Habsburg Empire 1790–1918* (London: Weidenfeld and Nicolson, 1969), 791.
182. R.L. DiNardo and Austin Bay, "The First Modern Tank: Gunther Burstyn and His Motorgeschütz," *Military Affairs* Vol. 50, No. 1 (Jan. 1986): 13.
183. Oberleutnant Gunther Burstyn, "Das Motorgeschütz," *ÖMZ* 1 (1912): 305.
184. Daniela and Ewald Angetter, *Gunther Burstyn (1879–1945): Sein 'Panzer' - eine bahnbrechende Erfindung zur falschen Zeit am falschen Ort* (Wien: Verlag der Österreichischen Akademie der Wissenschaften, 2008), 46–49; Walther Albrecht, *Gunther Burstyn (1879–1945) und die Entwicklung der Panzerwaffe* (Osnabrück: Biblio Verlag, 1973), 82–84.
185. Angetter, *Gunther Burstyn (1879–1945): Sein 'Panzer' - eine bahnbrechende Erfindung zur falschen Zeit am falschen Ort*, 50; W. Albrecht, *Gunther Burstyn (1879–1945) und die Entwicklung der Panzerwaffe*, 85–86.
186. *Österreichisches Biographisches Lexikon 1815–1950* Bd. 4 (Wien: Verlag der Österreichischen Akademie der Wissenschaften, 1957), 272; "Der Rücktritt des Kriegsministers Baron Krieghammer," *Neue Freie Presse*, 19. December 1902, Nr. 13763, 1–2; "Wien, 20. December," *Neue Freie Presse*, 21. December 1902, Nr. 13765, 1–2; "Baron Krieghammer †," *Pester Lloyd*, 21. August 1906, Nr. 190, 1; Edmund von Glaise-Horstenau, *Franz Josephs Weggefährte* (Vienna: Amalthea Verlag, 1930), 364–365.
187. *Stenographische Sitzungs-Protokolle der Delegation des Reichsrates*, 13. Sitzung der 45. Session am 3. März 1911, 948, 15. (Schluß-) Sitzung der 45. Session am 4. März 1911, 1131, 1136.
188. Rothenberg, *The Army of Francis Joseph*, 141.
189. Rothenberg, *The Army of Francis Joseph*, 137, 147, 161, 164, 167–168; Nr. 4/Vstd. betr. Reichskriegsminister Schönaich, Rücktritt, 1 Reservatexhibiten des Vorstandes der Militärkanzlei 1911, KA MKFF, Karton Nr. 207, Reservatakte.

190. Rothenberg, *The Army of Francis Joseph*, 140; Geoffrey Wawro, *A Mad Catastrophe: The Outbreak of World War I and the Collapse of the Habsburg Empire* (New York: Basic Books, 2014), 48.
191. "Austria-Hungary. The Military Question." *The Advertiser*, Monday 2 January 1911, 9. *The Advertiser* was published in Adelaide, Australia.
192. Rothenberg, *The Army of Francis Joseph*, 142; Sondhaus, *Franz Conrad von Hötzendorf: Architect of the Apocalypse*, 77.
193. Rothenberg, *The Army of Francis Joseph*, 144–145; Sondhaus, *Franz Conrad von Hötzendorf: Architect of the Apocalypse*, 78–79; Wawro, *A Mad Catastrophe*, 48–49, 79.
194. W. Albrecht, *Gunther Burstyn (1879–1945) und die Entwicklung der Panzerwaffe*, 14–15.
195. 9 Antrag Sr. k.u.k. Hoheit über freizügige Anlage der Kaisermanöver 1901, KA MKFF, Karton Nr. 201, Studien; 16 Moritz Ritter von Auffenberg, GdI. Studie: Stellung und Aufgaben eines nächsten Kriegsministers, Nov. 1910 (mit einem Referat der Militärkanzlei), KA MKFF, Karton Nr. 201, Studien (reference is in Referat, 4); Kiszling, *Erzherzog Franz Ferdinand von Österreich-Este*, 63–64, 263–264; Kronenbitter, *"Krieg im Frieden."* 91–92.
196. Auffenberg, *Aus Österreich-Ungarns Teilnahme am Weltkriege*, 43.
197. 7 K.u.k. Generalartillerieinspektor. Res. Nr. 308. Sanierung der Offiziersverhältnisse der Zahl u. Qualitat. Erz. Leopold Salvator, FZM to FF, n.d. KA MKFF, Karton Nr. 201, Studien.
198. Erzherzog Wilhelm, FML, General-Artillerie-Inspector, No. 50 Denkschrift über vorzunehmende Änderungen in der Organisation der Feld-Artillerie, Jan. 1882, KA MKSM Sonderreihe, Karton Nr. 65, Studien.
199. Rothenberg, *The Army of Francis Joseph*, 127.
200. "Die Manöver des 1. und 2. Korps in Schlesien vom 31. August bis 4. September 1906," *ÖMZ* 2 (1906): 1723; W. Albrecht, *Gunther Burstyn (1879–1945) und die Entwicklung der Panzerwaffe*, 14–15.
201. *ÖMZ* and *O.*, passim; *Inventar des Kriegsarchiv Wien*, I. Band (Wien: Ferdinand Berger, 1953), 174; Referat über den Versuch mit dem Caterpillar am 31. März 1914 bei Malacka, Hptm. Josef Schitler, KA Generalstab Operationsbüro, Karton Nr. 800, Diverse Studien 1882–1914; Studie über das erste Einschießen mit Granaten, Jänner 1896, Oberst Jdiczukh, KA Generalstab Operationsbüro, Karton Nr. 799, Diverse Studien 1882–; Studie über Fesselballon, Oberst Schleyer, KA Generalstab Operationsbüro, Karton Nr. 799, Diverse Studien 1882–; Über Fragen des Telgr. Büro, 1907, Schleyer, KA Generalstab Operationsbüro, Karton Nr. 799, Diverse Studien 1882–.

Bibliography

Unpublished Documents

Kriegsarchiv (KA), Vienna.
Allerhöchster Oberbefehl (AhOB).
Militärkanzlei Seiner Majestät des Kaisers (MKSM) Sonderreihe 1866–1918.
Militärkanzlei des Generalinspektors der gesamten bewaffneten Macht Erzherzog Franz Ferdinand (MKFF) 1898–1914.
Chef des Generalstabs (GSt) Operationsbüro 1866–1918.
Zentralstellen.
Kriegsministerium (KM) Präsidialbüro (Präsidium) 1866–1918.
Militärerziehungs- und Bildungsanstalten (MEB).
Kriegsschule Wien 1867–1914.

Published Primary Sources

Auffenberg-Komarów, Moritz. *Aus Österreich-Ungarns Teilnahme am Weltkriege*. Wien: Ullstein & Co., 1920.

Auffenberg-Komarów, Moritz Freiherr von. *Aus Österreichs Höhe und Niedergang - eine Lebensschilderung*. Munich: Drei Masken Verlag, 1921.

Berndt, Hauptmann Otto. *Die Zahl im Kriege. Statistische Daten aus der neueren Kriegsgeschichte in graphischer Darstellung*. Wien: G. Freytag & Berndt, 1897.

Chamberlain, Houston Stewart. *Der Wille zum Sieg und andere Aufsätze*. München: Hugo Bruckmann, 1918.

Conrad von Hötzendorf, FML Franz Graf. *Aus Meiner Dienstzeit 1906–1918*. Wien: Rikola Verlag, 1921.

Conrad von Hötzendorf, Franz. *Infanterische Fragen und die Erscheinungen des Boerenkrieges*. Wien: Seidel & Sohn, 1903.

Conrad von Hötzendorf, Franz. *Zum Studium der Taktik*. Vienna: L.W. Seidel & Sohn, 1891.

Exerzierreglement für die k.u.k. Fußtruppen. Wien: k.k. Hof- und Staatsdruckerei, 1911.

Glaise-Horstenau, Edmund, Josef Brauner, Eduard Czegka, Jaromir Diakow, Friedrich Franek, Walther Heydendorff, Rudolf Kiszling, Franz Mühlhofer, Ernst Wisshaupt und Georg Zobi, *Österreich-Ungarns letzter Krieg 1914–1918 (ÖULK)*. Wien: Verlag der Militärwissenschaftlichen Mitteilungen, 1930–1938.

Goltz, Wilhelm Leopold Colmar Freiherr von der. *Das Volk in Waffen. Ein Buch über Heerwesen und Kriegführung unserer Zeit*. Berlin: R. v. Decker's Verlag: 1883.

Kerchnawe, Hugo. *Die Vorgeschichte von 1866 und 19??* Wien: C.W. Stern Verlag, 1909.

Krauß, General der Infanterie Alfred. *Die Ursachen unserer Niederlage: Erinnerungen und Urteile aus dem Weltkrieg.* München: J.F. Lehmanns Verlag, 1921.

Martin, Frederick, Sir John Scott Keltie, Isaac Parker Anderson Renwick, Mortimer Epstein, Sigfrid Henry Steinberg, and John Paxton, *The Statesman's Year-Book: Statistical and Historical Annual of the States of the Civilised World for the Year 1902.* London: Macmillan and Co., 1902.

Neue Freie Presse, 1902, 1911.

Organ der militärwissenschaftlichen Vereine (O.), 1867–1906.

Österreichische Militärische Zeitschrift (ÖMZ), 1866–1914.

Pester Lloyd, 1906, 1911.

Pitreich, Oberst Maximilian Freiherr von. *Lemberg 1914.* Wien: Adolf Holzhausens Nachfolger, 1929.

Stenographische Sitzungs-Protokolle der Delegation des Reichsrathes. Vienna: k.k. Hof- und Staatsdruckerei, 1869–1911.

The Advertiser, 1911.

Secondary Sources

Albrecht, Walther. *Gunther Burstyn (1879–1945) und die Entwicklung der Panzerwaffe.* Osnabrück: Biblio Verlag, 1973.

Angetter, Daniela and Ewald. *Gunther Burstyn (1879–1945): Sein 'Panzer' - eine bahnbrechende Erfindung zur falschen Zeit am falschen Ort.* Wien: Verlag der Österreichischen Akademie der Wissenschaften, 2008.

DiNardo, R.L., and Austin Bay, "The First Modern Tank: Gunther Burstyn and His Motorgeschütz." *Military Affairs* Vol. 50, No. 1 (Jan. 1986): 12–15.

Forstner, Franz. *Przemyśl: Österreich-Ungarns bedeutendste Festung.* Wien: Österreichischer Bundesverlag, 1987.

Frankl, Viktor E. *Man's Search for Meaning.* Boston: Beacon Press, 1959.

Glaise-Horstenau, Edmund von. *Franz Josephs Weggefährte.* Wien: Amalthea Verlag, 1930.

Hackl, Dieter. "Der Offensivgeist des Conrad von Hötzendorf." Mag. Phil. Diplomarbeit, Universität Wien, 2009.

Höbelt, Lothar. "Die Marine." in *Die Habsburgermonarchie 1848–1918*, Vol. 5 *Die Bewaffnete Macht.* Vienna: Verlag der Österreichischen Akademie der Wissenschaften, 1987.

Inventar des Kriegsarchiv Wien, I. Band. Wien: Ferdinand Berger, 1953.

Kiszling, Rudolf. *Erzherzog Franz Ferdinand von Österreich-Este: Leben, Pläne und Wirken am Schicksalsweg der Donaumonarchie.* Graz: Hermann Böhlaus Nachf., 1953.

Kronenbitter, Günther. *"Krieg im Frieden." Die Führung der k.u.k. Armee und die Großmachtpolitik Österreich-Ungarns 1906–1914*. Munich: Oldenbourg, 2003.

Macartney, C.A. *The Habsburg Empire 1790–1918*. London: Weidenfeld and Nicolson, 1969.

Österreichisches Biographisches Lexikon 1815–1950 Vol. 1. Vienna: Verlag der Österreichischen Akademie der Wissenschaften, 1957.

Regele, Oskar. *Feldzeugmeister Benedek und der Weg nach Königgrätz*. Wien: Verlag Herold, 1960.

Ritter, Gerhard. *Staatskunst und Kriegshandwerk*, München: R. Oldenbourg, 1954–1968.

Rothenberg, Gunther E. *The Army of Francis Joseph*. West Lafayette, IN: Purdue University Press, 1976.

Sondhaus, Lawrence. *Franz Conrad von Hötzendorf: Architect of the Apocalypse*. Boston: Humanities Press, 2000.

Sondhaus, Lawrence. *The Naval Policy of Austria-Hungary, 1867–1918: Navalism, Industrial Development, and the Politics of Dualism*. West Lafayette, IN: Purdue University Press, 1994.

Tunstall, Graydon A. *Blood on the Snow: The Carpathian Winter War of 1915*. Lawrence: University Press of Kansas, 2010.

Vego, Milan N. *Austro-Hungarian Naval Policy 1904–1914*. Portland, OR: Frank Cass, 1996.

Wagner, Walter. "Die k.(u.)k. Armee - Gliederung und Aufgabenstellung." in *Die Habsburgermonarchie 1848–1918*, Vol. 5 *Die Bewaffnete Macht*. Vienna: Verlag der Österreichischen Akademie der Wissenschaften, 1987.

Wawro, Geoffrey. *A Mad Catastrophe: The Outbreak of World War I and the Collapse of the Habsburg Empire*. New York: Basic Books, 2014.

Wawro, Geoffrey. *Warfare and Society in Europe, 1792–1914*. New York: Routledge, 2000.

CHAPTER 7

The Catastrophe of the Offensive

> Blood red lightning flashes over the walls of the old winged lion, and the sky is a single sea of fire.
>
> From the clouds rush the enemies and pour over the sleeping Austria. And their goal is the old Phaeacian city on the Danube with the golden Stephansdom.
>
> And each one takes a piece of loot, and the House of Habsburg flees lamenting into foreign lands.
>
> That is the end of the proud winged lion. And its inhabitants will mourn lost happiness.
>
> But too late![1]

Thus spoke Cassandra, the cursed priestess of Apollo and prophetess whom no one believed, in Gustav Sieber's 1913 novel *Quo Vadis, Austria?* Sieber's work describes the life and difficulties of a loyal Austro-Hungarian officer true to the emperor and fatherland shortly before the outbreak of World War I. Comparing the Habsburg Empire to ancient Troy, the protagonist laments the poor status of a once powerful state. According to a member of the military chancery of the imperial heir Franz Ferdinand, the primary concern addressed by the author was the

J.A. Dredger, *Tactics and Procurement in the Habsburg Military, 1866–1918*, DOI 10.1007/978-3-319-57678-7_7

weakness of Austria-Hungary's position in foreign politics as a result of the loss of great power status.[2] This concern affected not only lower-ranking officers but also the high command. General Baron Moritz Auffenberg, war minister from 1911 to 1912, expressed the low regard for the Dual Monarchy as a world power among the other nations.[3]

Although Cassandra's prophecy came true by 1918, the Habsburg Empire did not have to suffer military catastrophe in 1914. Using strategy and tactics suitable for the inferior numbers and equipment of the *k.u.k.* army, Austro-Hungarian military leaders could have forged a defensive plan to enable Habsburg forces to fight the two-front war against Russia and Serbia successfully. However, the strategic and tactical offensive *à outrance*, combined with deficiencies in men and weapons because of inept spending decisions, made defeat inevitable for *k.u.k.* armies in Galicia, Bosnia, and Italy.

Prewar Strategy: Austro-Hungarian Offensives and the Schlieffen Plan

Before Austria-Hungary invaded Serbia on 28 July 1914, Conrad von Hötzendorf, as chief of the general staff and de facto head of the *k.u.k.* army, had drawn up a plan to counter the armies of Russia to the northeast and Serbia to the south. Conrad had designed this plan to crush Serbia first and then turn the victorious Habsburg forces to defeat slowly mobilizing Russia. Conrad divided the *k.u.k.* troops into three groups: *Minimalgruppe Balkan* with 8–10 divisions against Serbia, *A-Staffel* with 28–30 divisions against Russia, and *B-Staffel* with 12 divisions to support either of the other groups for offensive operations. Although this arrangement appeared brilliant in theory, Conrad failed to consider the difficulty of transportation using Habsburg railroads, especially the insufficient number of lines and cars between Galicia and Bosnia. Once Conrad committed *B-Staffel* in either direction, long delays would slow the 12 divisions from reversing course if need arose in the other theater.[4] As General Baron Josef von Stürgkh, *k.u.k.* representative at the German headquarters, later wrote, the forces facing Serbia consisted of "too little, as was proven later in so tragic a way, for a success, too much for a merely defensive stance. A half measure, which, as always, can have only an evil result."[5] The troops of *B-Staffel* took little part in the Serbian offensive and arrived in Galicia too late to do anything other than participate in the retreat.[6] The size of the Austro-Hungarian army only contributed to the confusion and difficulty. Without experience in transporting large numbers of troops, the railroads could not handle the requirements of mass army movements.

Another problem with this plan was cooperation with Austria-Hungary's ally Germany. Lieutenant General Helmuth von Moltke, nephew of the famous victor of 1866 and 1870–1871 and chief of the German general staff, remained true to the Schlieffen Plan of his predecessor, Lieutenant General Count Alfred Schlieffen. This plan called for eight-ninths of the German army to deliver a knockout blow against France while a mere 12–14 divisions defended East Prussia against a Russian invasion. Only after victory over France would the bulk of the German army go east to destroy the Russians.[7]

The implications of the Schlieffen Plan for Austria-Hungary meant that the Habsburg army would have to bear the brunt of the Russian offensive with little help from Germany. Moltke not only desired *k.u.k.* forces to help defend East Prussia but also to take the offensive in Galicia and thus divert Russian troops away from German territory. This wish remained almost an impossibility in light of Conrad's plan to invade Serbia. The Habsburg army could not embark upon offensives in both theaters with any hope of success. Thus, the plans of the Central Powers had neither concrete operational coordination nor foundation in the reality of *k.u.k.* abilities.[8] This situation resulted in the need for Germany to support the Dual Monarchy's armies almost continually later in the war.

The Austro-Hungarian chief of the general staff had no intention of remaining on the defensive in any theater. Even though Conrad expressed his conviction that Habsburg forces in Galicia could not take the offensive without the promise of a German attack from East Prussia, he rejected any defensive ideas in a desire to win a purely *k.u.k.* decisive victory.[9] The Austrian wrote to Moltke that, "In my decided aversion against any waiting and in my conviction of the worth of the initiative, I will seize the forward deployment and the fastest offensive possible."[10] This view coincided with the peacetime ideal of seeking a decisive offensive in the style of earlier wars, such as the elder Moltke's victories in 1866 and 1870 that Conrad admired so ardently.[11] Conrad endorsed the Clausewitzian doctrine of annihilation of the enemy as the goal of warfare, or as American historian Isabel Hull called it, "absolute destruction."[12]

Although the requirements of the Schlieffen Plan bound Conrad to attack the more powerful Russian army while simultaneously fighting Serbia, the offensive always suited the plans of the Habsburg general staff chief. As General Anton Pitreich, chief of staff for the Third Army in Galicia, wrote after the war, "Attack had become almost routine."[13] Despite the inferiority of *k.u.k.* troops in numbers and weaponry, Austria-Hungary could have taken no other action without compromising the great power status that Habsburg leaders envisioned for the empire. If *k.u.k.* forces stood on the defensive against Serbia while attacking Russia, there was the possibility of defeat at the hands of the Serbs, as in the minds of the Austro-Hungarian high command only the offensive brought victory. Deploying enough troops to have a decisive advantage against Serbia involved denuding Galicia of sufficient numbers to ward off the Russians. Although prudence dictated the defensive on at least one front, great powers always attacked.

Upholding the alliance with Germany as a great power also necessitated an Austro-Hungarian attack on Russia. The German high command had long held a low opinion of Habsburg military capabilities. Schlieffen considered the *k.u.k.* army inferior to the Russian army in total numbers and in the combat abilities of individual units. Therefore, he regarded Austro-Hungarian assistance in the east as a chimera.[14] The younger Moltke and other high ranking German generals also shared this view of Habsburg unpreparedness.[15] Even the German emperor, Wilhelm II, had inquired on different occasions with some skepticism about the war readiness of Franz Joseph's troops, especially the artillery.[16] The most influential leaders of the Dual Monarchy's army and most of the officer corps regarded the military as the most important bulwark of the great power position of Austria-Hungary.[17] The only way for the *k.u.k.* high command to prove the worth of Habsburg military force was to seize the initiative in all theaters of war.

Disaster in Galicia

Attempting the impossible proved to be exactly the opposite of what Conrad had hoped. The early battles of the First World War turned into a catastrophe of epic proportions for the Habsburg army. According to the official Austrian history of the war, the *k.u.k.* forces in Galicia at the beginning of the 1914 summer campaign amounted to 38.5 infantry and 10 cavalry divisions against 46.5 Russian infantry and 18.5 cavalry divisions.[18] These numbers reveal the great numerical disadvantage of the Habsburg forces but do not disclose the whole situation. The 38.5 infantry divisions included the troops of *B-Staffel* that did not arrive in Galicia until engagements with the Russians had already begun. Moreover, one third of the Austro-Hungarian units consisted of inadequately trained *Landwehr* troops who, like all other *k.u.k.* infantry, used the same 1886 model repeating rifle that had last received an upgrade in 1895, almost 20 years previously.[19]

In addition, according to the twentieth century Austrian historian and archivist Rudolf Jeřábek, each Russian division surpassed the *k.u.k.* units by 60–70% in infantry, 90% in light field artillery, 230% in heavy guns, and 33% in machine guns.[20] Moreover, the quality of most of the Russian artillery far exceeded the Habsburg cannon, which still included 12 obsolete M.99 and M.99/04 howitzers with steel-bronze barrels per division.[21] These howitzers only received 330 rounds per weapon compared with the 500 rounds for the field guns. Furthermore, two-thirds of this ammunition consisted of shrapnel rather than high-explosive shells for destroying fortified positions.[22] The poor financial decisions of the *k.u.k.* high command to spend hundreds of millions of Kronen on Dreadnoughts and permanent fortifications instead of modern artillery now adversely affected the Austro-Hungarian troops on the battlefield. As *FML* Alfred Krauss, former commandant of the *Kriegsschule* and holder of numerous important staff and command positions during the First World War, later wrote, "The infantry had to pay for this mistake in blood, because they had to attack the insufficiently shaken enemy."[23]

A defensive strategy in Galicia would have suited the Habsburg inferiority in men and artillery.[24] Prudent strategy, however, did not suit the ideas of Conrad, who believed in the psychological importance of winning the first battle. The *Drang nach vorwärts* with the accompanying reliance on high morale ruled operational and tactical planning at the cost of the material prerequisites for victory.[25] Despite the grave deficiencies of the *k.u.k.* army, Conrad ordered an offensive against the much stronger Russians because he believed that only attack could achieve success.[26] Such an attack meant that Austro-Hungarian troops had to spread out so that Russian forces would not turn the Habsburg flanks. Unlike the theater of war in the west, where trench lines quickly covered the terrain from the North Sea to Switzerland and limited maneuver while turning the conflict into siege warfare, the eastern front provided vast expanses for large-scale movement. In the rolling plains of Galicia, the *k.u.k.* army groups, advancing to the north, northeast, and east, became more and more separated from each other. Although the troops going north and northeast met roughly equal numbers of Russians and even achieved some tactical success, seven to eight Austro-Hungarian divisions moving east encountered 21 Russian divisions. Without the advantages of the defense, disaster ensued for the Habsburg units. Rushing headlong without sufficient artillery support into a greatly superior enemy, *k.u.k.* troops suffered crushing losses in futile frontal assaults. Nevertheless, Conrad, disconnected from the realities of the battlefield, refused to believe the reports of his generals confirming the overwhelming numerical superiority of the Russians. Instead, Conrad ordered more attacks from the already exhausted Austro-Hungarian troops. The outcome was even worse than the previous assault: more than 20,000 casualties and 70 guns lost.[27] The size of the Habsburg army, much larger than any that Conrad had ever commanded in maneuvers, magnified his mistakes while rendering communications and control more difficult than ever before.

As the official Austrian history, usually favorable to Conrad, later wrote, "The experiences of the first campaign had overturned much of what possessed troops and leaders in peace training."[28] Conrad, nevertheless, thought that the pummeled Habsburg troops still retained the *Wille zum Siege* and could achieve decisive victories regardless of the situation.[29] Hearing reports from captured Russian officers that *k.u.k.* units had attacked with more ferocity than the Japanese had in 1904–1905, Conrad looked for another opportunity for an offensive. After learning of the German victory over Russia at Tannenberg, Conrad desired to restore not only the prestige of the Austro-Hungarian Empire as a great power but also his own reputation as a commander.[30] The defensive nature of the German action in East Prussia did not lessen the humiliation of the *k.u.k.* staff chief from the losses in Galicia.

Conrad ordered yet another offensive to take back the lost ground. Although gaining early tactical successes, the outnumbered Habsburg army could not maintain any advantages. Yet Conrad continued calling for more assaults from all units of the Dual Monarchy army in Galicia against greater enemy numbers and artillery, until finally even the *k.u.k.* chief of the general staff admitted that retreat was the only option.[31] After less than a month of combat, the Austro-Hungarian military had lost most of Galicia as well as 350,000–400,000 men and 300 guns, or almost 50% of the Habsburg forces facing Russia at the beginning of the war.[32] The offensives of Conrad could not have garnered a more abysmal result. General Krauss stated after the war that the chief of the general staff had transgressed the principle of war that the inferior party should repulse the attack of the stronger before assaulting the weaknesses of the enemy.[33] A defensive posture would have held part of Galicia for longer than 3 weeks with fewer casualties. Certainly, the defensive could have brought no worse defeat because strong entrenchments with artillery support would have afforded enough protection for the Habsburg troops to compensate for their inferiority in numbers and material.

In withdrawing from most of Galicia, the *k.u.k.* military also left behind the fortress of Przemyśl with a garrison of 120,000 men. These soldiers now became completely useless to the Austro-Hungarian war effort and the source of more casualties as Conrad focused his next offensive on relieving the fortress. After the debacle of the first Galician campaign, Conrad joined with the victor of Tannenberg, General Erich Ludendorff, to attack the Russians and relieve Przemyśl in late September and October. Once again, the *k.u.k.* offensive met with early success and even rescued the Galician fortress, but Habsburg troops had to retreat in the face of superior Russian numbers. Repeated Austro-Hungarian attempts to cross the San River failed abysmally. With little support from the artillery, which felt lucky to have an average of four rounds per day, the infantry could not break through Russian entrenchments.[34] Conrad next invented a complex plan to lure the Russians forward while withdrawing, and then strike the enemy unexpectedly in the flank. However, the plan backfired. The *k.u.k.* forces, not the Russians, received the flank attack with another 40,000 casualties and withdrew to the relative safety of the Carpathian Mountains.[35] The prewar neglect of artillery in the Habsburg army precluded any small chance of success held by the outnumbered Dual Monarchy troops. Although the Austro-Hungarian artillery branch performed as well as possible, the emphasis on infantry as the only truly important force rendered field guns ineffective.[36]

Once again, Conrad's attacks resulted in heavy losses for the Austro-Hungarians as more of Galicia fell into the hands of the Russians. The *k.u.k.* forces had performed reasonably well, considering the poorly trained *Landsturm* and reserve troops who had filled the ranks of the battered units from the first campaign. Even the Slavic soldiers that

Austro-Hungarian officers had regarded as untrustworthy had fought, in general, as bravely as non-Slavic forces.[37] The leadership of Conrad, however, failed by putting Habsburg soldiers into situations too difficult for inexperienced men. The will for victory could not overcome superior numbers and weaponry. Yet Conrad did not learn from the mistakes of the opening battles and allow the Austro-Hungarian forces to take advantage of field fortifications. Ample use of entrenchments would have allowed decimated units to recuperate and given time for new replacements to acquire some familiarity with the weapons and requirements of modern warfare. Instead, Conrad relied on the *Wille zum Siege* of his subordinates to perform the impossible. The general staff chief expressed this idea, so prominent in his tactical thought, thus: "We must compensate for our paucity of soldiers with activity."[38] However, as Colonel Maximilian von Pitreich, general staff chief of various *k.u.k.* divisions and army groups on the Russian front and son of the former minister of war Heinrich von Pitreich, wrote after the war, "We have learned in war often enough that the concentration of cannon is for the most part more important than the iron will for victory of different leaders."[39]

Cavalry Failure

In the open expanses of Galicia, the Habsburg army could also have used more mobility. The Burstyn tanks that the Technical-Administrative Military Committee of the *k.u.k.* general staff rejected could have helped compensate for the fewer numbers of the Austro-Hungarian military. The hundreds of millions wasted on Dreadnoughts could have procured hundreds of tanks to help fill the gaps in the Habsburg lines or protect their flanks. Poor financial decisions brought catastrophe for the *k.u.k.* military.

Cavalry could also have provided more mobility for Austro-Hungarian forces in Galicia. Although mounted troops provided inviting targets for enemy artillery and machine gun fire, cavalry units could at least have alleviated the difficult communication and coordination problems of the widely separated *k.u.k.* army groups. This possibility never surfaced because Conrad had sent the Habsburg mounted forces on a long reconnaissance ride in the spirit of the Southern cavalry in the American Civil War. The Austro-Hungarian ride extended through an area of Galicia 250 miles wide and 90 miles deep, and achieving success became an almost impossible task. The vastness of the Galician expanse wore out the horses and the *k.u.k.* mounted troops encountered dismounted Russian cavalry and infantry units that inflicted heavy losses on the attacking Habsburg horsemen. Only one engagement between mounted forces took place. This battle at Jaroslavice on 21 August featured saber-wielding cavalry in a traditional mounted encounter. With no decisive result, the outcome had no bearing on the overall campaign, especially when a Russian infantry unit intervened.[40] Although *k.u.k.* officers knew the futility of cavalry attacks on entrenched infantry and that the regulations did not advocate this kind of assault, practical application failed as horsemen full of bravado charged the enemy regardless of the actual situation.[41] The Russians had learned from the experiences of the Russo-Japanese War to dismount and employ fire like infantry, whereas the Habsburg cavalry still sought the traditional mounted encounter, which accomplished little.[42] A last minute attempt to impress upon the *k.u.k.* cavalry the importance of fire tactics did little to change the battle methods of the Austro-Hungarian mounted branch.[43]

The primary result of all this riding and fighting on the part of the Austro-Hungarian cavalry was exhaustion of the men and, more importantly, of most of the available horses. The saddles that had looked so impressive on parade did not prove adequate for long rides in war and rubbed off the horses' skin. Thus, many horsemen returned leading their mounts rather than riding.[44] Only 26,800 cavalrymen remained battle-ready by the beginning of October.[45] Even Conrad admitted that the *k.u.k.* mounted branch failed because of poor training and equipment unsuitable for the modern battlefield.[46] Responsibility for the debacle lay primarily with the chief of the general staff for demanding the impossible. According to one cavalry officer, achieving success on a raid covering too large an area against an enemy superior in numbers, firepower, and tactics proved too much for Habsburg horsemen.[47] With the cavalry out of action, the *k.u.k.* army had insufficient troops for reconnaissance and flank security. Infantry units that could have performed other more important tasks, such as preparing entrenchments for a strong defensive position, now had to compensate for the cavalry without possessing the same mobility.

Once again, the Habsburg military high command displayed a poor sense of how to spend limited funding. Instead of wasting money on unserviceable saddles or even cavalry that most Austro-Hungarian officers realized played a limited role in modern warfare, *k.u.k.* leaders should have developed and procured armored vehicles similar to

Burstyn's tank. These vehicles, after extensive testing and development, could have helped perform the same tasks as cavalry in protecting the army's flanks and providing mobility for faster communications and contact with other units. They also could have eventually taken the offensive role that mounted troops could no longer achieve. Prewar financial decisions created a situation almost impossible for Habsburg victory. Rather than compensating for numerical inferiority with superior equipment and weaponry, the Austro-Hungarian high command exacerbated *k.u.k.* deficiencies with inept spending on useless battleships, poorly-equipped cavalry, and outdated or vulnerable permanent fortresses.

Przemyśl: Permanent Failure

Przemyśl again became the focus of Conrad's attention for the next offen sive in January 1915. After more indecisive sallies from the Carpathians against the Russians in November and December and successful thwarting of the Russian thrust toward Cracow at the battle of Limanowa-Lapanów, the Habsburg chief of the general staff returned to his fixation on relieving the permanent fortress of Przemyśl.[48] Even though Habsburg soldiers had suffered immensely during the campaigns of the summer and fall, Conrad failed to perceive the impossibility of the task he now presented to his men. Conrad's offensive *à outrance* strategy had sacrificed 1,250,000 soldiers with no beneficial result by the end of 1914. In addition, *k.u.k.* soldiers had lost confidence in the abilities of the Habsburg high command.[49] Yet, the official Austrian history of the First World War, written by former general staff officers loyal to Conrad, echoed the staff chief's belief in the unconquerable ability of troops of "unbroken will."[50]

Once more, instead of allowing the battered Austro-Hungarian troops to settle into defensive positions with artillery support, Conrad ordered a series of frontal assaults to push the Russians back beyond Przemyśl. In the bitter cold and frozen mountains, the attacks amounted to suicidal efforts to perform the impossible, although the soldiers fought admirably. The drive to assault the enemy rendered ineffective the little artillery support that the Dual Monarchy troops possessed, just as in the earlier campaigns.[51] Making almost no progress against the well-entrenched enemy from late January through February 1915, Habsburg forces incurred huge losses that the badly-equipped Austro-Hungarian army could ill afford. In addition, the wintry conditions bogged down the offensive and caused even more casualties from frostbite and freezing.[52]

In this situation, surprise, so important to *k.u.k.* offensive theory, proved impossible to obtain.[53] Incapable of learning from past experience, Conrad provided little support in the form of artillery or even hand-grenades for the attacking forces of the Dual Monarchy. Even though the high command realized the grave deficiencies of the Habsburg forces, *k.u.k.* leaders relied upon the soldiers to do the impossible.[54] According to Conrad, spirit and high morale should suffice.[55]

Following the repulse of the first attacks, Conrad responded with the only solution he ever considered, more assaults. By applying a tactical offensive solution to strategic problems, the general staff chief failed to look at the situation from an operational standpoint.[56] The attacks garnered the same fruitless result. For roughly 4 weeks, thousands of *k.u.k.* soldiers hurled themselves against the Russian field fortifications. These insane attacks gained hardly any ground and had no effect on the besieged fortress of Przemyśl. A third wave of assaults produced no effect. Instead of receiving relief from the siege, the commander of the permanent fortress had to surrender on 22 March with 3500 officers and 120,000 men suffering from starvation. This number pales in comparison with the 673,000 soldiers lost during the Carpathian winter campaigns to relieve Przemyśl.[57] The permanent fortress that cost at least 52,500,000 Kronen before the war provided no advantage during the campaigns.[58] On the contrary, Przemyśl consumed not only the 120,000 soldiers of the garrison, who had to surrender and hardly affected the war in any way, but also the 673,000 casualties lost in the attempts to relieve the fortress. Almost 800,000 Austro-Hungarian men sacrificed themselves for no gain whatsoever. By the end of these vain offensives, according to the official Austrian history of the war, the *k.u.k.* military resembled "a *Landsturm* and militia army," rather than the force of a great power.[59]

Even if Conrad had succeeded in regaining Przemyśl, he would not have made proper use of the fortress. Despite the efforts of Habsburg officers to stress the offensive capabilities of permanent fortifications, the primary benefit of Przemyśl, or any other fortress, was in bolstering a strong defense as the anchor for the position. A defensive stance along the San and Dniester rivers in Galicia would have used the advantages that Przemyśl offered. Conrad never considered this option seriously, because he viewed the defense as the choice of the weak. The strong only attacked and, as a great power, Austria-Hungary must attack as well. Any other strategy would show weakness, loss of prestige, and the sunken status of a second-rate power.

Even though the Russians had resumed the offensive, pushing Habsburg forces farther back over the Carpathians into Hungary and threatening the important passes over the mountains, Conrad chose to attack once again. Far from the battlefields where Austro-Hungarian units suffered immeasurably from cold and malnutrition, Conrad never realized the realities of the winter campaigns and visited the troops only three times in 3 years.[60] Instead of attempting to understand the horrific conditions of the modern battlefield, Conrad chose to spend long hours writing to his mistress, Gina von Reininghaus, and mope about his personal life.[61] While persistently advocating willpower as the solution to *k.u.k.* problems, Conrad's own will for victory flagged. As Colonel Pitreich said, "If the conditions for victory are not created, the strongest will is worth nothing."[62] Thus, the same results stemmed from the same causes: frontal attacks against a numerically superior enemy in strongly entrenched positions with artillery support brought more heavy losses.

Gorlice-Tarnów: German Support and Success

The campaign continued in the same fruitless manner until German reinforcements arrived to steady the *k.u.k.* front and launch a counter-attack. This combined German-Austro-Hungarian Gorlice-Tarnów offensive had good results because the Germans provided the necessary artillery and numbers for such an operation to succeed. Beginning in early May, the Central Powers drove back the Russians and recovered not only the fortress of Przemyśl but also almost all of Galicia by the end of June.[63]

The successful Gorlice-Tarnów campaign restored some of the *k.u.k.* confidence and prestige lost during the earlier disastrous offensives. The Germans, however, took the larger share of credit for the victory, even though the Habsburg army provided more troops for the attacks. Without German support, especially in artillery, the Austro-Hungarian military would never have proved capable of pushing the Russians out of Galicia.[64] *FML* Arthur Baron Arz von Straussenburg, corps commander and future chief of the general staff, remarked, "Under the thundering noise we had the impression of having a Vulcan working before us; this was still new for us Austrians with our artillery so weak in number and for the most part suffering from deficiency in ammunition."[65] The Habsburg decision-makers had determined Dreadnoughts and permanent fortresses more important than modern field guns. With the money spent on battleships and Przemyśl, the *k.u.k.* army could have procured sufficient artillery and shells to rival the other armies of Europe.

Naval Weakness

While Austro-Hungarian units suffered catastrophic losses in Galicia, the Habsburg navy accomplished little in the Adriatic Sea. As on land, *k.u.k.* forces met numerical superiority at sea. In May 1914, Austria-Hungary possessed only 105 ships in comparison to the 166 of the Entente powers in the Adriatic and near vicinity. The Entente preponderance of cruisers, destroyers, torpedo craft, and submarines made the Habsburg disadvantage even greater.[66] The *k.u.k.* preference for the offensive had also penetrated the navy. Thus, the commander-in-chief of the Austro-Hungarian navy, Grand Admiral Anton Haus, desired a great sea battle that would destroy the enemy fleets, such as Vice Admiral Wilhelm von Tegethoff had won against Italy at Lissa in 1866. The number of French and British ships in the Mediterranean, however, deterred Haus from attempting anything rash. The Habsburg admiral limited naval operations primarily to coastal defense and raiding, mainly using submarines. Although this strategy proved successful in keeping the Entente away from Austro-Hungarian ports, the *k.u.k.* navy had no effect on operations outside the Adriatic.[67] This situation meant that the hundreds of millions of Kronen spent on Dreadnoughts provided no positive results for the Habsburg military because the huge battleships remained idle in port and did not contribute to the defensive. Instead of wasting funding on Dreadnoughts, the *k.u.k.* high command could have constructed 6 scout-cruisers, 20 destroyers, and 35 submarines for the cost of a single Dreadnought.[68] Such procurement decisions would have coincided far better with the defensive and raiding strategy that Haus chose. Using the money to buy more artillery or to develop tanks also would have given the Austro-Hungarians more chances for success in Galicia.

Serbian Campaign: Debacle and Disgrace

Disaster struck for the Austro-Hungarian military not only against the Russians but also against the Serbs, although the latter catastrophe did not have the same dimensions as the former. Nevertheless, the inability to defeat a small Balkan country resounded as an immense loss of prestige. The *k.u.k.* leaders made several mistakes in the Serbian campaign. First, the Habsburg high command underestimated the capabilities of the enemy. Instead of attributing Serbian successes in the Balkan Wars of 1912–1913 to superior leadership and training in the Serbian army, most *k.u.k.* reports concentrated on the ineptitude of the Turks. One Austro-Hungarian officer noted, "The main reasons for recent Serb successes lay in the inferior numbers and general low quality of the Turkish forces in Macedonia. The young Serb army cannot yet be considered the equal of the great power armies."[69] Even the author of a *Kriegsschule* report who praised the courage and *élan* of the Turkish troops focused on the weakness of Turkish artillery training and leadership as the primary cause for Serbian victory.[70]

Rather than a weak, inferior army of a small Balkan nation, the Habsburg military faced a Serbian force filled with high morale, recent experience in modern warfare, and confidence in the excellent leadership of their Serbian commanders. In addition, Serb soldiers possessed greater motivation to fight because of hatred for the Dual Monarchy and a desire to protect their homeland.[71] In comparison, the Austro-Hungarian army contained no members of the rank and file who had participated in combat and few officers of any rank who had actually fought in battle. Those officers who did have combat experience, such as Conrad and *FML* Moritz Baron Auffenberg von Komarów, had experienced war only against irregular troops during the invasion of Bosnia-Hercegovina 36 years earlier in 1878. These conditions did not correspond to the realities of Great War battlefields with greatly advanced weaponry. Thus, the most experienced commanding officer in the Habsburg army possessed less practical knowledge from experience in combat than the lowest-ranking veteran of the Serbian military.

In addition, *k.u.k.* forces did not enjoy numerical or technical superiority over the Serbs. Habsburg troops numbered 282,000 infantry, 10,000 cavalry, and 744 cannon at the outset of the campaign, although only 219,000 foot soldiers, 5100 horsemen, and 522 guns remained after the departure of *B-Staffel* for Galicia. Against these forces, Serbia set 264,000 infantry with 11,000 mounted troops and 828 field pieces.[72] Inadequately trained *Landsturm* units equipped with obsolete Werndl breech-loaders made up more than half of the Dual Monarchy's forces in the Balkans.[73] In addition, the heavy *k.u.k.* field gun could shoot only 5000 meters, far less than the 8000 m range of the enemy guns.[74] Even though some Serbian units did not possess enough weapons for every man, the Serbs compensated with better leadership, experience, and the advantages of defense.[75]

The second mistake of the Austro-Hungarians was constantly taking the offensive. The commanding general, *FZM* Oskar Potiorek, a rival of Conrad, ordered an offensive to knock Serbia out of the war as quickly as possible, in accordance with the ideas of the chief of the general staff.[76] Although this plan suited the political goal of avenging the assassination of the Habsburg heir Franz Ferdinand by young Serbs under the direction of Serbian military intelligence officers, the offensive strategy of Potiorek did not correspond to the military realities of the situation. Without superiority in numbers or weaponry, the *k.u.k.* forces had little hope of gaining a decisive victory over the more experienced Serbian army. However, the desire to prove great power status drove the *k.u.k.* high command to call for an offensive against Serbia. The mood of public opinion within the monarchy pressed for a quick, decisive blow before Russia fully mobilized.[77] As a military power, Austria-Hungary could not allow a small Balkan state to defy the Habsburg Empire and escape unscathed, especially if Serbia dared to invade Bosnia-Hercegovina and capture Sarajevo.[78] As Major-General August von Cramon, the German liaison officer at the *k.u.k.* headquarters, wrote after the war, "If the Danubian Monarchy left the eternally unruly Balkans alone, it would cease to be a great power."[79] Therefore, although a defensive posture would have fit the occasion, the prestige of Austria-Hungary necessitated a punishing attack on a presumably weaker opponent.

Potiorek also had his own reasons for an offensive. As Conrad's rival, the commander of the *k.u.k.* troops facing Serbia needed a victory to bolster his hope of becoming the next chief of the general staff.[80] Conrad himself, despite later protests of innocence for the ensuing events, fully approved of Potiorek's attack, as the original plan of sending *B-Staffel* to the Balkans revealed.[81] Like all the other high-ranking Habsburg officers, Potiorek believed that only the offensive could give decisive results. Before the war, the Balkan army commander wrote that anyone wishing to begin a great war defensively had not recognized the nature of the *k.u.k.* military.[82] Potiorek also considered an offensive as the best means of solving the defensive tasks of guarding the borders of both Bosnia-Hercegovina and Hungary against a Serbian invasion.[83] Therefore, a quick strike into the heart of Serbia was the only strategy to both stop any Serbian attacks and knock the enemy out of the war.

Austro-Hungarian war games earlier in 1914 had predicted defeat against the Serbs.[84] In addition, a general staff study several years before the war had indicated that an invasion of Serbia from Bosnia would invite disaster.[85] Nevertheless, Potiorek, disregarding these accurate predictions as well as the deficiencies in troops and equipment, attempted the impossible just as Conrad had done in Galicia. The Habsburg commander in the Balkans invited disaster by attacking from Bosnia, without enough artillery, over the mountainous ground of western Serbia, which the enemy knew far better than any *k.u.k.* officer.[86] In mid-August 1914, Potiorek waged a campaign using strategy similar to Conrad's first offensive in Galicia and thus committed the same mistakes as the chief of the general staff. The two Austro-Hungarian armies in Bosnia, separated by more than 100 km, had little communication with each other as the advance into Serbia commenced. While driving deeper into enemy territory, contact became even more difficult and thus removed the possibility of mutual support. The gap between the two armies exposed the flanks of the *k.u.k.* forces. Supply became increasingly difficult as Habsburg troops penetrated further into Serbia. The combination of these mistakes with the rough terrain and the advantages of the defense for the Serbs, who knew how to establish strong field fortifications quickly, resulted in defeat after less than 2 weeks.[87] The choice of the offensive to accomplish defensive needs had resulted in frightful losses, not only in men but also in prestige for the Habsburg monarchy, while raising Serbian confidence even higher than before.[88]

Potiorek, just like Conrad, responded to setbacks by planning another offensive. This time, the Serbs attacked first in September. Once again, the offensive party found initial success. Austro-Hungarian troops, using the strength of the defense, halted the Serbian drive and counterattacked, sending the enemy back to Serbia 3 weeks later.[89] Despite minimal defensive training in the Habsburg army, *k.u.k.* forces found victory in a true offensive defense according to the ideas of Clausewitz, who advocated choosing the attack only at the moment when the enemy assault had broken down. However, Potiorek's attempt to invade Serbia a second time to follow up the defensive victory and recover lost prestige, both his own and the Dual Monarchy's, ended in achieving no more than the first abortive effort while adding an additional 40,000 Habsburg casualties to the war losses.[90]

The Austro-Hungarian commander now judged the situation opportune for a renewed offensive against the reeling Serbs. In theory, Potiorek's thinking appeared plausible. In practice, the same reasons as before advised against another invasion of Serbia: mountainous terrain, poor supply and communications, insufficient number of troops and weaponry, and an enemy superior in fighting ability and morale. In addition, the offensive did not begin until November when the weather had started to deteriorate with rain and snow, which rendered movement even more difficult. None of these concerns hindered Potiorek from seeking a decisive victory over the Serbs. After 4 weeks of combat, the Austro-Hungarians had succeeded in pushing the Serbian army farther into Serbia, but at the cost of half the *k.u.k.* forces. Now overextended and out of supplies, Habsburg troops presented a prime target for counterattack. From 2–15 December, the Serbs drove Potiorek's men back over the Bosnian border and ended the *k.u.k.* attempt to knock Serbia out of the war.[91]

The outcome of the Serbian campaign amounted to a military stalemate. By mid-December, neither army had the ability to mount another offensive. Even though inflicting 273,804 casualties on the Habsburg army, the Serbs had barely forced the Austro-Hungarian troops out of Serbia and could not continue the advantage with 132,000 casualties of their own.[92] Considering the differences in training, experience, and leadership between the two armies, Habsburg troops had fought remarkably well under difficult conditions, despite the ineptitude of *k.u.k.* leadership.

Politically, the Serbian campaign was a resounding defeat for Austria-Hungary, which lost its former great power status in the Balkans.[93] The official Austrian history, authored by former general staff officers, called the outcome "politically a grave loss in prestige and validity for the Danubian Monarchy."[94] As a great power confronting a smaller state, the Habsburg government and military high command had expected an easy victory, avenging the assassination of Franz Ferdinand and maintaining great power status. When the fighting ended without success, no one could regard the Dual Monarchy as being on the same level as the other European first-rate powers, who considered the Habsburg Empire almost dead.[95] Germany urged Austria-Hungary to restore lost prestige by yet another offensive against Serbia.[96] By the end of December 1914, Conrad had other ideas: the relief of Przemyśl and the ensuing winter debacle in the Carpathians.

Another invasion of Serbia would have suited the capabilities of the *k.u.k.* army far better than an offensive against the entrenched Russians. Although Potiorek had failed to crush Serbia, the Serbs had exhausted their military abilities. One more strong push, from the north rather than through the rugged western Serbian terrain, would have finished the Balkan state. This option would have required transferring troops from the Russian front and taking a completely defensive stance in Galicia, a choice that Conrad would never have made. Great powers never defended. The Balkan campaign should have achieved a very different result. If Conrad had allowed *B-Staffel* to stay in the Balkans and invade Serbia, instead of only arriving in Galicia in time to participate in the disaster, the extra Habsburg troops driving into Serbia from the north would have provided the opportunity to take the enemy in the flank. Even though a campaign of envelopment would have taken longer than the *k.u.k.* high command desired because of conditions in Serbia, the numerical superiority would have given a chance of crushing the Serbian army. Conrad could not allow this plan because such a choice did not correspond to the need for Austro-Hungarian offensives on all fronts.

The Results of Catastrophe

This infatuation with the offensive caused catastrophic losses and destruction of the Habsburg army. In less than 1 year, *k.u.k.* forces suffered over 2 million casualties. The 1914 campaigns in Galicia resulted in 979,000 men lost out of 2,232,000. The Carpathian winter war claimed another 793,000 with the fall of Przemyśl. Even the victorious Gorlice-Tarnów campaign in 1915 lost 500,000 soldiers. These offensives, combined with the Serbian invasions, resulted in 2,546,000 casualties, almost a million more than the total number of men in the Austro-Hungarian army at the beginning of the First World War.[97] Thus, with the majority of trained fighters out of commission, the Habsburg military became a militia relying on partially trained or untrained men who would not have met the service qualifications at the start of the conflict. As Edmund von Glaise-Horstenau, an Austro-Hungarian staff officer, wrote after the war, "These workers and farmers clad in field gray uniforms were cannon fodder far more than conscious warriors."[98]

Similarly, the *k.u.k.* officer corps suffered immense losses. By the end of 1914, almost half of the career and reserve officers, 22,310 men, counted among the casualties. The high number resulted from the practice of officers leading assaults in front of the troops. Just as with the rank and file, the Habsburg high command had to rely on young officers who had little training and in some cases had not qualified for officer status before the war.[99] In the officer corps, inexperience in combat and unfamiliarity with the men reigned. This situation only exacerbated the insufficient training and fitness of the replacement forces that the officers had to lead and greatly impaired the combat effectiveness of the Austro-Hungarian army as a whole.

Nevertheless, the *k.u.k.* army showed amazing resilience. Despite the disastrous losses from the campaigns of 1914 and 1915, the officers as well as the rank and file, whether trained veterans or inexperienced replacements, attacked over and over again in the seemingly endless offensives of Conrad. One tsarist general remarked that the ability of the *k.u.k.* army, which the Russians considered completely defeated, to mount repeated attacks surprised Russian leaders.[100] Although exceptions occurred, most Habsburg troops fought admirably under extremely difficult conditions, especially when under capable officers.[101] These men, who obeyed commands and charged headlong toward the enemy, shared no part of the blame for Austro-Hungarian defeats.[102] The narrow-minded offensive strategy and tactics of Conrad and the rest of the high-ranking *k.u.k.* officers, together with imprudent spending decisions, led to the catastrophic Habsburg losses of the First World War.

More Offensives

Despite the weak state of the *k.u.k.* military, which cried out for a prudent defensive stance in Galicia, Conrad decided on yet another offensive against the Russians in the late summer and fall of 1915. This attack, the so-called *schwarzgelbe* or black and yellow offensive, took place without German support because the *k.u.k.* chief of the general staff wanted to restore the prestige and self-confidence of the Austro-Hungarian army. The opposite happened, resulting in 230,000 casualties and no gains from 26 August to 15 October.[103] Conrad proved once again that devotion to the offensive, no matter the situation, brought only disaster and loss of morale, not the spoils of victory.

The troops that futilely charged Russian entrenchments from August to October 1915 should have invaded Serbia for more probable success. The German high command had advised Conrad to attack the Serbs in December 1914 and ever more pressingly since March 1915, but to no avail. Conrad always refused because of offensives in Galicia. Moreover, without Bulgarian participation in an offensive against Serbia, the Austro-Hungarian commander-in-chief would not consider another invasion. Yet Conrad planned offensive operations against Russia and even Italy, which had recently entered the war against the Central Powers during the spring of 1915.[104] An attack on severely weakened Serbia had greater possibilities for victory than any offensives against the numerically superior Russians and Italians. A strong *k.u.k.* proposal for a knockout blow on the small Balkan state would have forced Bulgaria to join Austria-Hungary earlier so that they would not lose the opportunity of reaping part of Serbia as spoils of war.

By the time an invasion of Serbia finally took place on 5 October 1915, the failed offensive in Galicia had dragged on for 6 weeks before ending in defeat 9 days later. The Habsburg military supplied only one army against Serbia, while Germany devoted one and Bulgaria two. Instead of sending a larger *k.u.k.* force to attack the Serbs, Conrad's main concern was to put an Austro-Hungarian general in charge of the operation. Always focused on maintaining the prestige of the Habsburg Empire, Conrad fought over command with the Germans and caused strained relations between the Central Powers.[105] The invading armies easily defeated the Serbs within 6 weeks because of numerical superiority, especially in artillery.[106] Rather than worrying about command relationships, Conrad should have assigned a much larger contingent of *k.u.k.* soldiers to the Serbian campaign. Demands for control over the offensive would then have held more weight, in conformity with the number of troops involved. Thus, Conrad could have conquered Serbia in a predominantly Habsburg invasion and restored some belief in Austro-Hungarian military abilities. With only one *k.u.k.* army group participating, no one could fail to realize the secondary role that Austria-Hungary played in the Central Powers.

The Italian Menace

At the same time as the offensives against Russia and Serbia, the Dual Monarchy also had to form a front against its former ally Italy, which declared war on the Habsburg Empire on 23 May 1915. In this theater, Conrad had to remain on the defensive. Now fighting a three-front war against Russia, Serbia, and Italy, the *k.u.k.* military did not have the manpower to wage offensive campaigns. Nevertheless, the Austro-Hungarian general staff chief devised a plan for luring the Italians over the mountains and then falling upon the unsuspecting enemy.[107] This strategy, although not the offensive *à outrance* of previous Habsburg campaigns and thus more realistic for the situation, still employed surprise and assault according to Conrad's tactical ideas. However, Conrad's idea was impractical because of the great numerical superiority of the Italians with 460,000 men and 1810 field pieces as opposed to 228,000 *k.u.k.* soldiers and 640 guns.[108] When the German high command heard of the plan, General Erich von Falkenhayn, chief of the German general staff, refused to send any troops to support such insanity. Against his will, Conrad had to use the excellent defensive positions that the Alps offered, instead of any preferred offensive actions.[109]

This strategy proved highly beneficial for the outnumbered Austro-Hungarians along the Italian frontier. The Italian army assaulted the strong defensive positions of the Habsburg military eleven times between the summers of 1915 and 1917. Eleven times, *k.u.k.* troops easily repulsed the attacks while inflicting heavy casualties on the Italians.[110] Austro-Hungarian forces had wisely reinforced the mountainous terrain with field fortifications and rendered the frontal assaults of the Italians suicidal.[111] Permanent fortresses along the Italian border had little effect on the battles because the majority could not withstand heavy shelling or guarded areas of lesser strategic importance.[112] The millions spent on these fortifications provided little for *k.u.k.* soldiers. Field fortifications gave far more advantages than their permanent counterparts. The money wasted on fortresses should have gone to more and better artillery, which would have strengthened Habsburg positions and compensated for inferiority in the number of men on the Italian front.

The entry of Italy into the war against the Dual Monarchy also worsened the position of the *k.u.k.* navy. The Italian fleet added another 137 ships to the Entente powers in the Mediterranean and thus increased the unlikeliness of any Austro-Hungarian offensive actions at sea. Apart from a partially successful raid on the undefended Italian coast with almost all of the Habsburg fleet before the Italian navy arrived from the south, Haus adhered to coastal defense and submarine attacks on the enemy. This strategy remained the most effective stance for the *k.u.k.* fleet, which inflicted a loss of 33 Entente ships while losing only nine Habsburg boats. The battleships, the supposed offensive part of the Austro-Hungarian navy, played no role whatsoever in *k.u.k.* operations in the Adriatic.[113] Thus, the hundreds of millions of Kronen granted for modern Dreadnought battleships floated in the port of Pola instead of procuring vital field pieces for the Russian, Serbian, and Italian fronts.

Technical and Tactical Progress: Artillery and Cavalry

As the war continued, the Austro-Hungarian artillery branch greatly improved in number and quality. Industrial production rose as factories produced more modern field guns, such as the 15 cm M.14 field guns,

15 cm M.15 howitzers, 24 and 38 cm M.16 howitzers, and 42 cm M.16 and M.17 howitzers. These larger and more powerful weapons no longer used steel-bronze barrels and thus replaced the old M.99 and M.99/04 models as well as the M.5 guns that the Habsburg high command finally realized could not perform the tasks of modern artillery on First World War battlefields. The Germans and Turks even adopted the new *k.u.k.* 7.5 cm M.15 mountain artillery during the war, and the Italians continued to use these guns after the war ended. With the new cannon, each *k.u.k.* division had 68 guns and rivalled the artillery of the other powers in quantity and quality. The Habsburg army also developed better mortars and flamethrowers as well as new machine guns and hand weapons. Each battalion had eight machine guns, twice as many as at the beginning of the conflict. This increase signified great progress for the Dual Monarchy. However, despite the better and more numerous field pieces, the Austro-Hungarian army could not supply *k.u.k.* units with a sufficient number of light machine guns and handguns until the last stage of the war.[114] Habsburg industry also had difficulty in compensating for the initial shell shortage, which became a chronic problem.[115] Even with more and better artillery, the firepower of Austro-Hungarian field pieces could not equal the other major military powers because of the deficiency in ammunition, an even worse problem for the Dual Monarchy than for the other main belligerents.

By March 1917, the *k.u.k.* military had 5700 field and mountain cannon and 1530 heavy pieces, but only 7000 machine guns, 2100 mortars, 1100 grenade launchers, 664 infantry cannon, and 320 trench mortars. Nevertheless, by the end of the war, the *k.u.k.* artillery had increased from 369 light, 28 heavy, and 74 mountain batteries to 864 light, 328 heavy, and 324 mountain formations. However, the *k.u.k.* military never developed any tanks, despite the continued presence of Burstyn within the army. General Arz von Straussenberg, who became general staff chief in 1917, later mentioned only *Honvéd* Colonel Benesch's tank, which the war ministry received in 1915, but not Burstyn's model. Because of deficiencies in material and time, and the judgment that tanks had limited usefulness for mountain warfare, the Habsburg high command decided against the development of this new weapon.[116] The Austro-Hungarian army missed the opportunity to take advantage of the technological expertise of an officer who had invented a working model of a decisive means of war.

Although the Austro-Hungarian military made great strides in artillery, there remained problems inherent in issuing new weaponry to troops with little training. Even at the beginning of the war, reserve troops had no idea how to use much of the issued equipment.[117] This situation worsened during the war as new troops rushed to the front without adequate training, especially for the more technical weapons such as artillery. Experienced soldiers, who had never fired the M.15, M.16, and M.17 field guns and howitzers, had to learn how to operate the new weapons on the battlefield. Some weapons, such as grenade launchers, required improvisations to suit the battlefield, especially in the mountains along the Italian front.[118] Although the Habsburg army equaled the other military powers in cannon per division and in the quality of individual guns, the *k.u.k.* artillerists did not possess the same proficiency as the soldiers of other nations.

The cavalry of the Dual Monarchy also progressed during World War I by putting into practice the idea of horsemen as mounted infantry, as envisioned by Habsburg officers before the conflict. By 1917, only one division remained as a traditional cavalry unit. The rest of the mounted branch fought on foot, with the result that little difference remained between infantry and cavalry.[119] As the official Austrian history of the war said, "Machine guns, carbines, and spades had become their most trusted weapons."[120] Learning the lessons of war in practice, Austro-Hungarian military leaders realized that horses had little place on the modern battlefield. In addition, the *k.u.k.* army had great difficulty replacing the animals lost in the August 1914 Galicia raid and in finding enough provisions for new horses. Therefore, the Habsburg high command determined that units that could perform both infantry and cavalry tasks gave greater advantages than troops fighting only while mounted.

As the war progressed, Austro-Hungarian officers also realized the importance of the defense and entrenching. Technical troops took on a greater role in both attack and defense. Soldiers learned to use the terrain and dig in, even while assaulting, as Habsburg military leaders tried to adapt to the realities of the modern battlefield.[121] Although Dual Monarchy forces did not achieve the proficiency of the Germans in storming enemy positions, Austro-Hungarian officers and troops showed a willingness to learn from experience and put into practice the lessons of previous First World War campaigns.

Failure in Italy and Galicia

While the *k.u.k.* army continued to recover from early reverses and make progress in artillery, cavalry, and technical troops, Conrad merely saw more resources and opportunities for offensives. The chief of the Habsburg general staff desired to punish the perfidious Italians for betraying the alliance with the Central Powers and saw a chance to raise Habsburg prestige by victory over another military power. Rejecting Falkenhayn's suggestion of continuing the purely defensive strategy against Italy and Russia, Conrad concocted a grand plan of envelopment in the style of the elder Moltke.[122] As usual, Conrad failed to take into account the realities of mountain warfare, especially in winter. The 2 month delay in starting the assault, as well as the concentration of large numbers of men and field pieces for the attack, lost any chance of surprise. The offensive began on 15 May 1916 but was complicated by difficult terrain and became bogged down shortly after small successes. Conrad, believing the enemy had won only because of greater morale and the *Wille zum Siege*, insisted on driving *k.u.k.* troops forward until 17 June and amassing more casualties. By that point, continuation of the offensive had become not only a waste of manpower and resources but also impossible because of the Russian Brusilov offensive in Galicia.[123]

This attack on Habsburg forces had great success, primarily because Conrad had denuded the *k.u.k.* defenses against Russia to bolster the fruitless assault on the Italians.[124] The removal of nine divisions, including most of the *k.u.k.* army's best troops, along with a large number of field guns, machine guns, and ammunition, exposed the entrenched Austro-Hungarians to the Russian offensive.[125] General Alexei Alexandrovich Brusilov easily broke through the weakened *k.u.k.* positions on 4 June, the first day of the attack and 13 days before Conrad finally admitted that the offensive against Italy had failed. Sending only five divisions back to Galicia, despite knowing Russian plans well before the assault, Conrad had to call upon Germany yet again to compensate for the Austro-Hungarian inability to cope with the Russians. Falkenhayn sent troops from the German reserve and the western front to halt the Russian advance. The Brusilov offensive ended by the end of September, but only after taking most of Galicia and causing another 613,587 casualties for the *k.u.k.* army.[126]

Because of Conrad's perpetual insistence on offensive operations on at least one front, in this case against Italy, the Habsburg military suffered another catastrophic defeat. Although *k.u.k.* troops had established strong entrenchments opposite the Russians, the Austro-Hungarian leadership proved deficient as soldiers did not train enough, learned little about defensive fighting, and continued to practice assault techniques.[127] Adequate defense both in Galicia and along the Alps would have enabled the Austro-Hungarians to continue building military resources while conserving manpower. As Colonel Pitreich wrote later, "It was precisely the sickness of our time that it wished to know nothing of the defensive and that it considered defense only as an evil, which could not be overcome quickly enough."[128] Over half a million casualties meant that inexperienced and poorly trained replacement troops filled the ranks of the Habsburg army and further eroded any Austro-Hungarian pretensions of great power status.

Secondary Status

For the rest of the war, the Dual Monarchy's military rarely waged any campaign without German support. When Rumania joined the Entente nations on 27 August 1916 near the end of the Brusilov offensive, the Central Powers formed the Danube Army, a combination of Germans, Austro-Hungarians, Bulgarians, and Turks. In a campaign that lasted from early September 1916 until early January 1917, the Central Powers launched a two-pronged invasion of Rumania. Taking the capital Bucharest and most of Rumania, the Danube Army easily and effectively knocked Rumania out of the war.[129] Although Habsburg troops had fought well during the campaign and formed a large part of the invading forces, German commanders led the combined army and reaped praise for the victory.[130] No doubt existed about the subordinate role of the Dual Monarchy with regard to the war effort.

The Central Powers agreed on a unified command on 13 September 1916, just as the Rumanian campaign started. This arrangement stipulated that the German emperor Wilhelm II would serve as supreme commander, with Hindenburg and Ludendorff in actual control of military operations. Although Austro-Hungarian officers, especially Conrad, complained about the new structure because of the ensuing loss of prestige for the Dual Monarchy, the events of the first 2 years of the war had illustrated the ineffectiveness of the *k.u.k.* army when fighting alone. Continually requiring German help, Habsburg military leaders had already suffered the humiliation of having to work under German commanders or German chiefs of staff. The September 1916 command arrangement merely confirmed the predominant role that Germany played in the Central Powers.[131] Although the world power status of Austria-Hungary suffered greatly, the military situation demanded that considerations of prestige no longer control Habsburg thinking.[132]

German officers had no delusions about the great power status of the Dual Monarchy. The German Major General Hans von Seeckt, who served as chief of staff for Archduke Charles, heir to the Habsburg throne, held an extremely negative view of Austro-Hungarian commanders. According to Seeckt, only German leadership could produce victory on the eastern front because *k.u.k.* leaders displayed little initiative, knowledge of the troops, responsibility, training, or prestige.[133] Ludendorff compared Austria-Hungary to Bulgaria and Turkey because of the need for German support and wrote of the First World War as a struggle of "Germany and its allies against the great European military powers."[134] Obviously, the Dual Monarchy did not rank as one of the major powers but merely as an ally of Germany.

The New Emperor and the Army

During the Rumanian campaign, Emperor Franz Joseph died at the age of 87 after 68 years of rule. His heir Charles assumed supreme command over the army and made all operational decisions, while the chief of the general staff took on a subordinate position. Several months later, on 1 March 1917, Charles dismissed Conrad as chief of the general staff because of Conrad's continuous defeats, refusal to take a lesser role, and desire to continue the war. The former chief of the general staff became the commander of a k.uk. army group on the Italian front and General Arz von Straussenburg, who had performed well in the field and showed himself willing to take a position subordinate to the new emperor, assumed direction of the general staff.[135] Charles had finally replaced the incompetent Conrad, but far too late to save the weakened Habsburg military. Even if the removal of Conrad had taken place earlier in the war, doubt remains as to whether another high-ranking officer would have rejected the desire for more offensives and developed a more defensive strategy. Conrad's ideas had disseminated throughout the *k.u.k.* officer corps and his former students at the *Kriegsschule* filled 49 of the highest Austro-Hungarian military positions by 1917.[136] These men agreed with Conrad's offensive doctrine. Other high-ranking officers, such as Auffenberg, maintained that Conrad grasped the right principles of war but exaggerated the offensive in practice. Thus, despite Conrad's great intelligence and dedication, superficial tactics that emphasized the offensive at all costs entered into maneuvers that did not correspond to correct theory.[137] One of the greatest critics of Conrad, *FML* Alfred Krauss of the general staff, concluded that Conrad's greatest mistake was the failure to implement effective strategy and operations rather than a mistaken insistence on the tactical offensive.[138] A large number of prominent Habsburg officers did not learn the primary lesson of the Great War, the supremacy of the defense.

Charles, like most members of the royal family, had little military training, although the new emperor had gained experience from commanding army groups on the Italian front during the war. Charles devoted great energy to restoring humaneness to the battlefield and improving the conditions of the *k.u.k.* soldiers.[139] The emperor outlawed physical punishments and executions in the field, as well as duels. In addition, the Habsburg army could no longer engage in strategic bombing that might harm civilians or use gas without Charles's approval. Some officers disapproved of these reforms because of the fear of losing troop discipline.[140] These measures, however, marked an improvement in the treatment of the rank and file, and no reports emerged concerning a decrease in discipline or willingness to fight.

On the contrary, Austro-Hungarian forces responded to the call for another offensive against Italy and performed their duty as usual. With the exception of some Slavic troops, especially Czechs, desertions did not cause excessive problems for the multinational Habsburg army until the very end of the war.[141] During the July 1917 Kerensky offensive, which the Russians launched at the command of Alexander Kerensky, the second prime minister of the Russian Provisional Government after the fall of the tsar in the previous spring, the Czechoslovak Brigade, predominantly containing former *k.u.k.* soldiers, joined in the attack. The Russian offensive stalled after some initial success and Czech propagandists later exaggerated the effect of this unit on Habsburg forces. With German help, Austro-Hungarian troops counterattacked, regaining the lost ground and driving the enemy even farther back than before.[142] Again, the *k.u.k.* army required German support to withstand another Russian assault. The new Habsburg high command now knew better than to order another fruitless offensive in Galicia. By remaining on the defensive, Austro-Hungarian forces had the chance to recover and push back the Russians while cooperating with German troops.

The success of the Central Powers on the eastern front revived Habsburg hope for a victorious offensive against Italy. Charles desired no German help for this endeavor. Instead, the new emperor wanted to employ only Austro-Hungarian forces in an attempt to revive the prestige of the Dual Monarchy with a victory over Italy, a hereditary enemy. The presence of German troops would harm the spirit of Habsburg units.[143] This proposal did not please Ludendorff, who held little trust in the battle-worthiness and leadership abilities of the *k.u.k.* army. The German general sent seven divisions to support the offensive. Under the direction of German commanders, who made all the important decisions, the assault troops gained great success. During the battle of Karfreit (Caporetto), beginning on 24 October 1917, Habsburg and German forces pushed the Italians back 70 miles. Using the new German tactics of sudden saturation bombardment and infiltration, rather than the long cannonades and frontal charges of previous years, the attack units inflicted over 300,000 casualties on the Italian military. As in most Great War offensives, the successful troops outdistanced the supply lines and had to halt. By mid-November, the Italians had established a new line along the Piave River and thus ended the offensive.[144] Although Habsburg soldiers had supplied most of the troops for this endeavor, German leadership and tactics had created the victory. Charles's wish for a solely *k.u.k.* triumph was not fulfilled. No one failed to see the Germans as the power responsible for such great success rather than Austria-Hungary, which *FML* Krauss later called a "dying" state.[145]

Progress and Reform

Before the war ended, the *k.u.k.* high command tried to implement reforms stemming from the lessons of the modern battlefield. In March 1915, Conrad developed a plan for reorganizing the army after the war ended. This plan emphasized creation of a reserve army.[146] Charles and Arz, realizing that peacetime never offered the best opportunity for instituting such measures, decided to draw up a new program and begin reforming the army during the war. Based on experiences from Great War campaigns, the reform plan called for a peacetime army of 594,000 with a permanent supreme command structure. This much larger military would consist of 60 infantry divisions and ten cavalry, with 72 light field pieces and 24 heavy per division, as well as a mortar battery and anti-aircraft battery. The presence of more technical troops, including sapper and communications units, in addition to a much larger air branch showed recognition of the importance of technology in modern warfare. In addition, each division would have a special assault battalion to employ the new German infiltration tactics. Officers had to master the art of both the attack and the defense and study the methods of other armies.[147]

Although the determination to keep ten cavalry divisions revealed a certain persistence in retaining formations that no longer had much use on the battlefield, there were fewer mounted units than in Conrad's plan. Charles and Arz stressed the need for cavalry to fight in the style of infantry by increasing the number of machine guns per unit and relying on firepower rather than shock tactics. The emperor and his chief of staff also determined to employ artillery in mobile units rather than stationing cannon in fortresses.[148] The new program definitely emphasized the roles of infantry, artillery, and technical troops while lessening the importance of cavalry and permanent fortifications. The *k.u.k.* leaders again proved the ability to learn from experience, although this reform program came too late to save the Dual Monarchy.

As in the past, practical application also presented difficulties for the Habsburg military. Reorganizing the army in the midst of a war entailed numerous troop transfers and much marching, which did little to enhance the morale of the rank and file. Several officers objected to the confusion and fatigue that the men experienced during the reforming of units.[149] Certainly, the Austro-Hungarian army needed reorganization, especially with the high casualties and ensuing haphazard replacement arrangements that produced provisional units of varying strengths. Although the First World War ended in defeat for the *k.u.k.* military and dismantling of the Habsburg Empire, Charles's reform program would have set the framework for modernization of the Austro-Hungarian army during peacetime.

The Last Offensives and Final Defeat

The *k.u.k.* forces had sustained vast losses in both men and material by the beginning of 1918. Yet, with the support of German forces, the Habsburg military gained victories against external enemies Serbia, Russia, Rumania, and Italy, while achieving some stability through reorganization. The Austro-Hungarian army proved incapable, however, of solving the internal issue of supply. Shortages of coal and food became more problematic than producing sufficient weapons and ammunition. This difficulty applied not only to the military but also to industrial workers, many of whom went on strike. To relieve this situation, the army sent rations to the workers and thus rendered the *k.u.k.* supply predicament desperate.[150]

Nevertheless, the Habsburg high command regarded another offensive against Italy as the best means for the Dual Monarchy to proceed. Even though the Austro-Hungarians had gained success in the previous assault on Italian positions, the present difficulties made an attack inadvisable. Still looking for a knockout blow against Italy and under the influence of German prodding, Charles ordered the offensive, which began on 6 June 1918. Facing a numerically superior enemy that had French and British support, especially in air and armor, the Habsburg offensive had no chance for victory. Within 2 weeks of almost fruitless assaults costing another 142,500 casualties, Charles signaled a retreat.[151] The last Austro-Hungarian offensive failed, just as every other solely *k.u.k.* offensive during the war. For an army with so many inexperienced and poorly trained troops suffering from malnutrition, inadequate supplies, and lack of ammunition, the attack amounted to insanity. The temptation to emulate German successes and eliminate Italy without relying on German intervention had become too great for a high command desiring to restore the former prestige of the Habsburg military.

Similarly, the *k.u.k.* navy attempted an offensive action against Entente ships in the Adriatic in the spring of 1918. This sortie marked the first and only time during the First World War that the whole Habsburg fleet, including the four Dreadnoughts, attacked enemy vessels. The new fleet commander, Rear Admiral Miklós Horthy de Nagybánya, felt that a major action would raise morale, which had fallen because of low rations and inactivity. The sortie, however, had the opposite result. An Italian torpedo boat surprised the newest Austro-Hungarian Dreadnought, the *Szent István*, and sank the battleship with two hits. Horthy then called off the attack and returned to port after rescuing most of the Dreadnought's crew.[152] The most modern Dreadnought that the Dual Monarchy produced went to the bottom of the Adriatic Sea without firing a shot. This ship, as well as the three other Dreadnoughts, accomplished nothing throughout the whole war. Instead of wasting hundreds of millions of Kronen on useless battleships that did not even participate in a major sea battle during the Great War, the *k.u.k.* high command should have employed the funding to procure modern artillery or develop tanks that would have benefitted the army in Italy far more than four anchored Dreadnoughts.

The combination of defeat with supply difficulties, which reduced *k.u.k.* troops to starvation rations, as well as nationalistic sentiments within the Habsburg Empire resulted in an increasing number of desertions.[153] Almost 250,000 soldiers deserted in the early part of 1918, in addition to mutinies in other units. The Austro-Hungarian army continued to defend the lines against Italy until the end of the war. For 2 days, 24–25 October, *k.u.k.* forces withstood the attacks of Italian and French troops. With little food and other provisions, Habsburg units began to mutiny as the Austro-Hungarian military crumbled. On 3 November, the *k.u.k.* high command ordered the remaining troops to cease firing.[154] Out of 8,000,000 men, the Habsburg army suffered 2,707,200 casualties, mostly in offensive actions.[155] Another 1,943,000 counted among the wounded.[156] The percentage losses for Austro-Hungarian troops surpassed that of any of the other major combatants.[157] Surely, defensive positions with strong entrenchments and adequate artillery support would have limited the immense numbers of deaths, wounds, and captures.

Conclusion

The First World War resulted in the death of the Habsburg Empire, just as Sieber's Cassandra had foretold. The *k.u.k.* military also ceased to exist when the Entente powers divided the Dual Monarchy into smaller states. The German liaison officer Cramon contended after the war that Habsburg military power might have sufficed to defeat Serbia alone.[158] Entering the war on two fronts against enemies superior in numbers and weaponry, the Austro-Hungarian high command needed a strategy that suited the disadvantageous position of the Habsburg army. Austria-Hungary's only ally, Germany, sent most of the German army into an enveloping maneuver against France according to the Schlieffen Plan; Conrad's troops faced the forces of Russia in Galicia with little support. The obvious strategy, despite Germany's prodding, was a defensive stance along the San and Dniester rivers that could have taken advantage of the expensive fortress of Przemyśl. At the same time, defense against Serbia would have afforded *k.u.k.* soldiers the opportunity to train with new weapons and given time for the Dual Monarchy's industry to produce the artillery that the high command had ordered before the war.

Entrenched positions with the support of field guns on both fronts would have given the Habsburg army the chance to survive the initial campaigns of World War I until German units arrived from the failed campaign on the western front.

Such prudent ideas, however, did not correspond with the offensive strategy and tactics of Conrad and the *k.u.k.* infantry regulations. Conrad possessed only one solution to every military problem, the offensive *à outrance*. As General Baron Josef Stürgkh, the Austro-Hungarian representative at the German headquarters, noted, Conrad "was considered erroneously as the right man for chief of the general staff." Although regarded as an expert in tactics and troop leadership, Conrad failed in every solely Habsburg offensive.[159] Despite the Austro-Hungarian inferiority in men and weaponry, Conrad believed that the *Wille zum Siege* would give Habsburg troops higher morale than the enemy and thus the ability to overcome the numerical superiority of Russia. This attitude imbued the whole Austro-Hungarian officer corps, especially the highest ranks, which were filled by Conrad's former students at the war college. One officer, over 40 years after the war, attributed one of the *k.u.k.* military's victories over Russia to the "unshakeable will for attack" of Habsburg forces.[160] Yet General Pitreich wrote after the First World War, "The morale of these troops who had to experience such an especially heavy baptism of fire was worth much too little."[161]

In addition, concern for the great power status of the Dual Monarchy committed the *k.u.k.* high command to an aggressive approach to war. According to Habsburg military theorists, only attacking strategy and tactics, such as the enveloping battles of the elder Moltke in 1866 and 1870, brought victory. Great military powers always attacked. Therefore, Austria-Hungary had to employ offensive strategy and tactics to achieve success and prove its rank among the European states. In particular, the *k.u.k.* army needed a quick knockout blow against Serbia, a second-rate military nation, to show the world how a great power deals with smaller foes.

The offensive *à outrance* was not the only error of the Habsburg military. Imprudent prewar spending decisions compounded the mistake of assaulting more numerous enemies. Rather than focusing procurement decisions on upgrading the artillery branch by purchasing more modern field pieces and mortars, the Austro-Hungarian high command poured immense sums into permanent fortifications and Dreadnoughts. Raising the number of cannon per infantry division to equal or even exceed the allotments of enemy formations would have accomplished far more than spending millions to build and upgrade fortresses and battleships that did not provide much help during the war.

The combination of offensive strategy and tactics with poor spending decisions resulted in catastrophe for the *k.u.k.* military. The numerically inferior Habsburg army entered the First World War without adequate field pieces and ammunition. Even after disaster struck in the opening campaigns in Galicia and Serbia, Conrad insisted on more offensives, even in the bitter winter of the Carpathian Mountains with poorly trained replacement troops. Only when German forces arrived to support Austro-Hungarian units did the Dual Monarchy achieve victory. Yet Conrad continued to try to mount offensives to restore the sinking prestige of the *k.u.k.* army, without success.

After the new emperor, Charles, dismissed Conrad, the offensive doctrine remained, as shown by the two assaults on Italy in the last years of the war. Charles did begin a program of reforms to raise the fighting capabilities of the Austro-Hungarian army. These reforms came too late to rescue the disintegrating Dual Monarchy. Suffering from malnutrition, inadequate supplies, and demoralization, *k.u.k.* troops began to mutiny and surrender to the enemy. Although resilient throughout the war, the army could no longer exist in the political and social turmoil at the end of the conflict. Under the conditions of 1918, defeat had become inevitable for the Habsburg military. The Austro-Hungarian army, however, did not have to endure early and repeated disasters. The mistake of undertaking offensive strategy and tactics that did not fit the abilities of *k.u.k.* forces and weaponry, combined with imprudent spending on permanent fortresses and battleships, ensured catastrophe for the Dual Monarchy.

Notes

1. Gustav Sieber, *Quo Vadis, Austria? Ein Roman der Resignation* (Berlin: "Vita" Deutsches Verlagshaus, 1913): IX–X.
2. 6 Untertänigste Meldung betr. den Militärroman "Quo Vadis, Austria?—ein Roman der Resignation von einem österreichischen Offizier" 27.09.1913, KA MKFF, Karton Nr. 208, Nichtprotokollierte Stücke 1898–1914.
3. Moritz Auffenberg-Komarów, *Aus Österreich-Ungarns Teilnahme am Weltkriege* (Wien: Ullstein & Co., 1920), 35.

4. Gunther E. Rothenberg, *The Army of Francis Joseph* (West Lafayette, IN: Purdue University Press, 1976), 159; Norman Stone, "Moltke-Conrad: Relations between the Austro-Hungarian and German General Staffs, 1909–1914," *The Historical Journal* IX, 2 (1966): 205.
5. Josef Stürgkh, *Politische und militärische Erinnerungen* (Leipzig: Paul List Verlag, 1922), 287.
6. General der Infanterie Alfred Krauß, *Die Ursachen unserer Niederlage: Erinnerungen und Urteile aus dem Weltkrieg* (München: J.F. Lehmanns Verlag, 1921), 135.
7. Graydon A. Tunstall, *Planning for War against Russia and Serbia: Austro-Hungarian and German Military Strategies, 1871–1914* (New York: Columbia University Press, 1993), 261–262; Stone, "Moltke-Conrad: Relations between the Austro-Hungarian and German General Staffs, 1909–1914," 206; Geoffrey Wawro, *A Mad Catastrophe: The Outbreak of World War I and the Collapse of the Habsburg Empire* (New York: Basic Books, 2014), 65, 96, 122, 270.
8. Generalleutnant Ernst Kabisch, *Streitfragen des Weltkrieges 1914–1918* (Stuttgart: Bergers Literarisches Büro und Verlagsanstalt, 1924), 21; Holger H. Herwig, "Disjointed Allies: Coalition Wafare in Berlin and Vienna, 1914," *The Journal of Military History* 54, 3 (July 1990): 274–276; Tunstall, *Planning for War against Russia and Serbia*, 264.
9. Kabisch, *Streitfragen des Weltkrieges 1914–1918*, 23–24, 104.
10. FML Franz Graf Conrad von Hötzendorf, *Aus Meiner Dienstzeit 1906–1918* (Wien: Rikola Verlag, 1921), 1: 399.
11. Oberst Maximilian Freiherr von Pitreich, *1914: Die Militärischen Probleme unseres Kriegsbeginnes, Ideen, Gründe, und Zusammenhänge* (Wien: Selbstverlag, 1934), 5.
12. Isabel V. Hull, *Absolute Destruction: Military Culture and the Practices of War in Imperial Germany* (Ithaca: Cornell University Press, 2005), 2–3.
13. General Anton Pitreich, *Der österreichisch-ungarische Bundesgenosse im Sperrfeuer* (Klagenfurt: Artur Kollitsch, 1930), 82.
14. Herwig, "Disjointed Allies: Coalition Wafare in Berlin and Vienna, 1914," 272–273.
15. John R. Schindler, *Fall of the Double Eagle: The Battle for Galicia and the Demise of Austria-Hungary* (Lincoln, Nebraska: Potomac Books, 2015), 154.
16. Rothenberg, *The Army of Francis Joseph*, 127.
17. Edmund Glaise-Horstenau, Josef Brauner, Eduard Czegka, Jaromir Diakow, Friedrich Franek, Walther Heydendorff, Rudolf Kiszling, Franz Mühlhofer, Ernst Wisshaupt und Georg Zobi, *Österreich-Ungarns letzter Krieg 1914–1918* (*ÖULK*) (Wien: Verlag der Militärwissenschaftlichen Mitteilungen, 1930–1938) 1: 40.

18. *ÖULK*, 1: 158, 175–177.
19. Kabisch, *Streitfragen des Weltkrieges 1914–1918*, 23; Auffenberg, *Aus Österreich-Ungarns Teilnahme am Weltkriege*, 39–40.
20. Rudolf Jeřábek, "The Eastern Front," in *The Last Years of Austria-Hungary: A Multi-National Experiment in Early Twentieth-Century Europe* (Exeter: University of Exeter Press, 1990), 153.
21. Erich Gabriel, "Die wichtigsten Waffen der Österreichisch-ungarischen Armee 1918," *Österreichische Militärische Zeitschrift* (*ÖMZ*) 6 (1968): 436–438.
22. A. Pitreich, *Der österreichisch-ungarische Bundesgenosse im Sperrfeuer*, 78–79; Krauß, *Die Ursachen unserer Niederlage: Erinnerungen und Urteile aus dem Weltkrieg*, 94–95.
23. Krauß, *Die Ursachen unserer Niederlage: Erinnerungen und Urteile aus dem Weltkrieg*, 95.
24. Auffenberg, *Aus Österreich-Ungarns Teilnahme am Weltkriege*, 87; Kabisch, *Streitfragen des Weltkrieges 1914–1918*, 58–60.
25. M. Pitreich, *1914: Die Militärischen Probleme unseres Kriegsbeginnes, Ideen, Gründe, und Zusammenhänge*, 229.
26. *ÖULK*, 1: 155.
27. Auffenberg, *Aus Österreich-Ungarns Teilnahme am Weltkriege*, 147–257; *ÖULK*, 1: 155–258; Manfried Rauchensteiner, *Der Tod des Doppeladlers: Österreich-Ungarn und der Erste Weltkrieg* (Graz: Verlag Styria, 1993), 128–136; Norman Stone, *The Eastern Front 1914–1917* (London: Hodder and Stoughton, 1975), 81–89; Lawrence Sondhaus, *Franz Conrad von Hötzendorf: Architect of the Apocalypse* (Boston: Humanities Press, Inc., 2000), 154; Graydon A. Tunstall, *Blood on the Snow: The Carpathian Winter War of 1915* (Lawrence: University Press of Kansas, 2010), 15–16; Dieter Hackl, "Der Offensivgeist des Conrad von Hötzendorf," (Mag. Phil. Diplomarbeit, Universität Wien, 2009), 67–73; Jeřábek, "The Eastern Front," 154–155; Johann Christoph Allmayer-Beck, "Der Sommerfeldzug von 1914 gegen Rußland," *ÖMZ* Sonderheft I (1965): 34–39; Rothenberg, *The Army of Francis Joseph*, 180; Kabisch, *Streitfragen des Weltkrieges 1914–1918*, 91–97; Wawro, *A Mad Catastrophe*, 169–252; Schindler, *Fall of the Double Eagle*, 149–244.
28. *ÖULK*, 1: 449.
29. Kabisch, *Streitfragen des Weltkrieges 1914–1918*, 105.
30. Oberst Maximilian Freiherr von Pitreich, *Lemberg 1914* (Wien: Adolf Holzhausens Nachfolger, 1929), 26–113; Sondhaus, *Franz Conrad von Hötzendorf: Architect of the Apocalypse*, 154; Stone, *The Eastern Front 1914–1917*, 89; Hackl, "Der Offensivgeist des Conrad von Hötzendorf," 73.

31. Auffenberg, *Aus Österreich-Ungarns Teilnahme am Weltkriege*, 272–392; *ÖULK*, 1: 259–338; A. Pitreich, *Der österreichisch-ungarische Bundesgenosse im Sperrfeuer*, 130; Stone, *The Eastern Front 1914–1917*, 89–90.
32. A. Pitreich, *Der österreichisch-ungarische Bundesgenosse im Sperrfeuer*, 130–131; Rothenberg, *The Army of Francis Joseph*, 180; Stone, *The Eastern Front 1914–1917*, 91; Sondhaus, *Franz Conrad von Hötzendorf: Architect of the Apocalypse*, 158.
33. Krauß, *Die Ursachen unserer Niederlage: Erinnerungen und Urteile aus dem Weltkrieg*, 138–139.
34. A. Pitreich, *Der österreichisch-ungarische Bundesgenosse im Sperrfeuer*, 138–139; *ÖULK*, 1: 356–513; Wawro, *A Mad Catastrophe*, 269–289.
35. Rothenberg, *The Army of Francis Joseph*, 181; Stone, *The Eastern Front 1914–1917*, 96–97, 99–100; Sondhaus, *Franz Conrad von Hötzendorf: Architect of the Apocalypse*, 159; Franz Forstner, *Przemyśl: Österreich-Ungarns bedeutendste Festung* (Wien: Österreichischer Bundesverlag, 1987), 164–195.
36. A. Pitreich, *Der österreichisch-ungarische Bundesgenosse im Sperrfeuer*, 82–83.
37. Schindler, *Fall of the Double Eagle*, 257, 271–272, 274–275.
38. Gustav Stöckelle, "Der Feldzug von Limanova-Lapanów 1.–20. Dezember 1914," *ÖMZ* Sonderheft I (1965): 39.
39. M. Pitreich, *Lemberg 1914*, 155.
40. Rauchensteiner, *Der Tod des Doppeladlers: Österreich-Ungarn und der Erste Weltkrieg*, 125–127; Rothenberg, *The Army of Francis Joseph*, 180; Stone, *The Eastern Front 1914–1917*, 80.
41. A. Pitreich, *Der österreichisch-ungarische Bundesgenosse im Sperrfeuer*, 83; Auffenberg, *Aus Österreich-Ungarns Teilnahme am Weltkriege*, 41; Sondhaus, *Franz Conrad von Hötzendorf: Architect of the Apocalypse*, 152–153.
42. FML Josef Metzger, "Der Krieg 1914 gegen Rußland," in *Der große Krieg 1914–1918*, ed. Max Schwarte (Leipzig: Johann Ambrosius Barth, 1922), 5: 26.
43. Heinrich Mast, "Die Aufklärungstätigkeit der österr.-ung. Kavallerie bei Kriegsbeginn 1914," *ÖMZ* Sonderheft I (1965): 9–10.
44. Stone, *The Eastern Front 1914–1917*, 80; Wawro, *A Mad Catastrophe*, 176.
45. *ÖULK*, 1: 357.
46. Conrad, *Aus meiner Dienstzeit*, 4: 877.
47. Mast, "Die Aufklärungstätigkeit der österr.-ung. Kavallerie bei Kriegsbeginn 1914," 15–17.
48. *ÖULK*, 1: 563–600, 765–812.

49. Tunstall, *Blood on the Snow*, 12.
50. *ÖULK*, 1: 600.
51. A. Pitreich, *Der österreichisch-ungarische Bundesgenosse im Sperrfeuer*, 191–192.
52. August von Cramon, *Unser Österreich-Ungarischer Bundesgenosse im Weltkriege: Erinnerungen aus meiner vierjährigen Tätigkeit als bevollmächtiger deutscher General beim k.u.k. Armeeoberkommando* (Berlin: Ernst Siegfried Mittler und Sohn, 1920), 7–8; *ÖULK* 2: 94–179; Tunstall, *Blood on the* Snow, 66–113; Rothenberg, *The Army of Francis Joseph*, 184; Stone, *The Eastern Front 1914–1917*, 113; Sondhaus, *Franz Conrad von Hötzendorf: Architect of the Apocalypse*, 163, 165; Jeřábek, "The Eastern Front," 156; Hackl, "Der Offensivgeist des Conrad von Hötzendorf," 90; Wawro, *A Mad Catastrophe*, 341–360.
53. Tunstall, *Blood on the* Snow, 3.
54. A. Pitreich, *Der österreichisch-ungarische Bundesgenosse im Sperrfeuer*, 200.
55. A. Pitreich, *Der österreichisch-ungarische Bundesgenosse im Sperrfeuer*, 81–82.
56. Krauß, *Die Ursachen unserer Niederlage: Erinnerungen und Urteile aus dem Weltkrieg*, 99–100.
57. *ÖULK* 2: 180–224; Cramon, *Unser Österreich-Ungarischer Bundesgenosse im Weltkriege*, 8–9; Tunstall, *Blood on the Snow*, 212; Rothenberg, *The Army of Francis Joseph*, 185; Stone, *The Eastern Front 1914–1917*, 114–116; Edmund von Glaise-Horstenau, *Die Katastrophe: Die Zertrümmerung Österreich-Ungarns und das Werden der Nachfolgestaaten* (Wien: Amalthea Verlag, 1929), 42; Rauchensteiner, *Der Tod des Doppeladlers: Österreich-Ungarn und der Erste Weltkrieg*, 203–208; Hackl, "Der Offensivgeist des Conrad von Hötzendorf," 90–91.
58. Forstner, *Przemyśl: Österreich-Ungarns bedeutendste Festung*, 121.
59. *ÖULK*, 2: 271.
60. *ÖULK*, 1: 58; Cramon, *Unser Österreich-Ungarischer Bundesgenosse im Weltkriege*, 101–102; Tunstall, *Blood on the Snow*, 11; Rothenberg, *The Army of Francis Joseph*, 177.
61. Wawro, *A Mad Catastrophe*, 202, 238.
62. M. Pitreich, *Lemberg 1914*, 155.
63. Arthur Albert Arz von Straussenburg, *Zur Geschichte des großen Krieges 1914–1918* (Graz: Akademische Druck-u. Verlangsanstalt, 1969), 57–92; *ÖULK* 2: 315–504; Cramon, *Unser Österreich-Ungarischer Bundesgenosse im Weltkriege*, 11–19; Tunstall, *Blood on the Snow*, 163–208; Rothenberg, *The Army of Francis Joseph*, 185–186; Stone, *The Eastern Front 1914–1917*, 120–143; Sondhaus, *Franz Conrad von Hötzendorf: Architect of the Apocalypse*, 173–175; Jeřábek, "The Eastern

Front," 157; Forstner, *Przemyśl: Österreich-Ungarns bedeutendste Festung*, 264–275; Rauchensteiner, *Der Tod des Doppeladlers: Österreich-Ungarn und der Erste Weltkrieg*, 211–214; Hackl, "Der Offensivgeist des Conrad von Hötzendorf," 92–94.

64. A. Pitreich, *Der österreichisch-ungarische Bundesgenosse im Sperrfeuer*, 198–199.
65. Arz, *Zur Geschichte des großen Krieges 1914–1918*, 60.
66. Milan N. Vego, *Austro-Hungarian Naval Policy 1904–1914* (Portland, OR: Frank Cass, 1996), 178.
67. Lawrence Sondhaus, *The Naval Policy of Austria-Hungary, 1867–1918: Navalism, Industrial Development, and the Politics of Dualism* (West Lafayette, IN: Purdue University Press, 1994), 251, 256–270.
68. Vego, *Austro-Hungarian Naval Policy 1904–1914*, 194–195.
69. Quoted in Rothenberg, *The Army of Francis Joseph*, 182.
70. K.u.k. KS 1912/13 Die Schlacht von Kumanova am 23ten und 24ten Oktober 1912, KA Militärschulen, KS Karton Nr. 67, Studienbehelfe: 1912/14.
71. Kurt Peball, "Der Feldzug gegen Serbien und Montenegro im Jahre 1914," *ÖMZ* Sonderheft I (1965): 21.
72. Rudolf Jeřábek, *Potiorek: General im Schatten von Sarajevo* (Graz: Verlag Styria, 1991), 108. Rothenberg, drawing from A. Pitreich and the *ÖULK* for the Austro-Hungarian statistics, sets the total amount of Habsburg troops throughout the Serbian campaign at 460,000 and the Serbian number at 450,000, *The Army of Francis Joseph*, 182.
73. A. Pitreich, *Der Österreichisch-ungarische Bundesgenosse im Sperrfeuer*, 108.
74. Krauß, *Die Ursachen unserer Niederlage: Erinnerungen und Urteile aus dem Weltkrieg*, 94.
75. Stone, *The Eastern Front 1914–1917*, 79.
76. Rothenberg, *The Army of Francis Joseph*, 182; Stone, *The Eastern Front 1914–1917*, 75; Peball, "Der Feldzug gegen Serbien und Montenegro im Jahre 1914," 26.
77. M. Pitreich, *1914: Die Militärischen Probleme unseres Kriegsbeginnes, Ideen, Gründe, und Zusammenhänge*, 90.
78. Allmayer-Beck, "Der Sommerfeldzug von 1914 gegen Rußland," 32.
79. Cramon, *Unser Österreich-Ungarischer Bundesgenosse im Weltkriege*, 200.
80. Sondhaus, *Franz Conrad von Hötzendorf: Architect of the Apocalypse*, 161; Peball, "Der Feldzug gegen Serbien und Montenegro im Jahre 1914," 25.
81. Stürgkh, *Politische und militärische Erinnerungen*, 288; Rothenberg, *The Army of Francis Joseph*, 183; Stone, *The Eastern Front 1914–1917*, 79; Sondhaus, *Franz Conrad von Hötzendorf: Architect of the Apocalypse*, 162.

82. M. Pitreich, *1914: Die Militärischen Probleme unseres Kriegsbeginnes, Ideen, Gründe, und Zusammenhänge*, 92.
83. M. Pitreich, *1914: Die Militärischen Probleme unseres Kriegsbeginnes, Ideen, Gründe, und Zusammenhänge*, 93–94; Allmayer-Beck, "Der Sommerfeldzug von 1914 gegen Rußland," 33; Peball, "Der Feldzug gegen Serbien und Montenegro im Jahre 1914," 22.
84. Jeřábek, "The Eastern Front," 153; Peball, "Der Feldzug gegen Serbien und Montenegro im Jahre 1914," 24–26.
85. Stürgkh, *Politische und militärische Erinnerungen*, 288.
86. Krauß, *Die Ursachen unserer Niederlage: Erinnerungen und Urteile aus dem Weltkrieg*, 149.
87. *ÖULK*, 1: 102–152; Gunther E. Rothenberg, "The Austro-Hungarian Campaign Against Serbia in 1914," *The Journal of Military History* 53, 2 (April 1989): 137–138; Jeřábek, *Potiorek*, 118–132; Jonathan E. Gumz, *The Resurrection and Collapse of Empire in Habsburg Serbia, 1914–1918* (New York: Cambridge University Press, 2009), 44–61; Wawro, *A Mad Catastrophe*, 146–168; Schindler, *Fall of the Double Eagle*, 118–148.
88. Kabisch, *Streitfragen des Weltkrieges 1914–1918*, 90.
89. Kabisch, *Streitfragen des Weltkrieges 1914–1918*, 138–139; *ÖULK*, 1: 603–647; Peball, "Der Feldzug gegen Serbien und Montenegro im Jahre 1914," 27–28; Jeřábek, *Potiorek*, 143–148.
90. Wawro, *A Mad Catastrophe*, 253–268.
91. *ÖULK*, 1: 651–762; Rothenberg, "The Austro-Hungarian Campaign Against Serbia in 1914," 141–143; Peball, "Der Feldzug gegen Serbien und Montenegro im Jahre 1914," 28–30; Jeřábek, *Potiorek*, 166–193; Rauchensteiner, *Der Tod des Doppeladlers: Österreich-Ungarn und der Erste Weltkrieg*, 184–188; Hackl, "Der Offensivgeist des Conrad von Hötzendorf," 91–92; Wawro, *A Mad Catastrophe*, 315–339.
92. *ÖULK*, 1: 759, 762; A. Pitreich, *Der Österreichisch-ungarische Bundesgenosse im Sperrfeuer*, 108–109. The *ÖULK* figures include sick and missing as well as dead, wounded, and prisoners.
93. Glaise-Horstenau, *Die Katastrophe: Die Zertrümmerung Österreich-Ungarns und das Werden der Nachfolgestaaten*, 38.
94. *ÖULK*, 1: 762.
95. Krauß, *Die Ursachen unserer Niederlage: Erinnerungen und Urteile aus dem Weltkrieg*, 166.
96. Tunstall, *Blood on the Snow*, 24.
97. *ÖULK*, 2: 118, 141, 270, 279, supplement, Beilage 1; Jeřábek, "The Eastern Front," 157–158.
98. Glaise-Horstenau, *Die Katastrophe: Die Zertrümmerung Österreich-Ungarns und das Werden der Nachfolgestaaten*, 64.

99. István Deák, *Beyond Nationalism: A Social and Political History of the Habsburg Officer Corps, 1848–1918* (New York: Oxford University Press, 1992), 194; Glaise-Horstenau, *Die Katastrophe: Die Zertrümmerung Österreich-Ungarns und das Werden der Nachfolgestaaten*, 39.
100. Stöckelle, "Der Feldzug von Limanova-Lapanów 1–20. Dezember 1914," 46.
101. *ÖULK*, 1: 42–47; A. Pitreich, *Der Österreichisch-ungarische Bundesgenosse im Sperrfeuer*, 192; Rothenberg, *The Army of Francis Joseph*, 185, 187, 192; Krauß, *Die Ursachen unserer Niederlage: Erinnerungen und Urteile aus dem Weltkrieg*, 71–72.
102. Krauß, *Die Ursachen unserer Niederlage: Erinnerungen und Urteile aus dem Weltkrieg*, 98.
103. *ÖULK*, 3: 51–175; Cramon, *Unser Österreich-Ungarischer Bundesgenosse im Weltkriege*, 27–30; Jeřábek, "The Eastern Front," 157; Rauchensteiner, *Der Tod des Doppeladlers: Österreich-Ungarn und der Erste Weltkrieg*, 287–296.
104. Rothenberg, *The Army of Francis Joseph*, 189–191.
105. Cramon, *Unser Österreich-Ungarischer Bundesgenosse im Weltkriege*, 32.
106. Cramon, *Unser Österreich-Ungarischer Bundesgenosse im Weltkriege*, 34–35; *ÖULK*, 3: 187–336; Rothenberg, *The Army of Francis Joseph*, 191; Rauchensteiner, *Der Tod des Doppeladlers: Österreich-Ungarn und der Erste Weltkrieg*, 297–301.
107. General Erich von Falkenhayn, *The German General Staff and its Decisions, 1914–1916* (New York: Dodd, Mead and Company, 1920), 102.
108. Rothenberg, *The Army of Francis Joseph*, 190.
109. Falkenhayn, *The German General Staff and its Decisions, 1914–1916*, 103.
110. *ÖULK*, 2: 733–792, 3: 345–520, 4: 667–706, 5: 21–108, 631–683, 6: 133–184, 431–487.
111. Glaise-Horstenau, *Die Katastrophe: Die Zertrümmerung Österreich-Ungarns und das Werden der Nachfolgestaaten*, 53.
112. Rothenberg, *The Army of Francis Joseph*, 188.
113. Sondhaus, *The Naval Policy of Austria-Hungary, 1867–1918: Navalism, Industrial Development, and the Politics of Dualism*, 273–295.
114. Gabriel, "Die wichtigsten Waffen der österreichisch-ungarischen Armee 1918," 436–439; A. Pitreich, *Der Österreichisch-ungarische Bundesgenosse im Sperrfeuer*, 312–314.
115. Krauß, *Die Ursachen unserer Niederlage: Erinnerungen und Urteile aus dem Weltkrieg*, 95.
116. Arz, *Zur Geschichte des großen Krieges 1914–1918*, 142, 259–260.
117. Josef Neumair, *Im Serbischen Feldzug 1914: Erlebnisse und Stimmungen eines Landsturm Offiziers* (Innsbruck: Verlagsanstalt Tyrolia, 1917), 34–35.

118. A. Pitreich, *Der Österreichisch-ungarische Bundesgenosse im Sperrfeuer*, 313–314.
119. Auffenberg, *Aus Österreich-Ungarns Teilnahme am Weltkriege*, 41; Rothenberg, *The Army of Francis Joseph*, 194.
120. *ÖULK*, 4: 122.
121. *ÖULK*, 4: 102–103, 116–131.
122. Glaise-Horstenau, *Die Katastrophe: Die Zertrümmerung Österreich-Ungarns und das Werden der Nachfolgestaaten*, 55–56.
123. Glaise-Horstenau, *Die Katastrophe: Die Zertrümmerung Österreich-Ungarns und das Werden der Nachfolgestaaten*, 194–195; *ÖULK*, 4: 253–356; Cramon, *Unser Österreich-Ungarischer Bundesgenosse im Weltkriege*, 53–66; Stone, *The Eastern Front 1914–1917*, 245–246; Sondhaus, *Franz Conrad von Hötzendorf: Architect of the Apocalypse*, 183–187; Rauchensteiner, *Der Tod des Doppeladlers: Österreich-Ungarn und der Erste Weltkrieg*, 339–343.
124. Stürgkh, *Politische und militärische Erinnerungen*, 288; A. Pitreich, *Der Österreichisch-ungarische Bundesgenosse im Sperrfeuer*, 275.
125. Jeřábek, "The Eastern Front," 159; Glaise-Horstenau, *Die Katastrophe: Die Zertrümmerung Österreich-Ungarns und das Werden der Nachfolgestaaten*, 57; Cramon, *Unser Österreich-Ungarischer Bundesgenosse im Weltkriege*, 64.
126. *ÖULK*, 4: 359–664, 5: 117–220; Rauchensteiner, *Der Tod des Doppeladlers: Österreich-Ungarn und der Erste Weltkrieg*, 345–352; Rothenberg, *The Army of Francis Joseph*, 196–197; Stone, *The Eastern Front 1914–1917*, 246–263; Sondhaus, *Franz Conrad von Hötzendorf: Architect of the Apocalypse*, 188–189.
127. *ÖULK*, 4: 373–374; Jeřábek, "The Eastern Front," 158–159.
128. M. Pitreich, *Lemberg 1914*, 168.
129. *ÖULK*, 5: 223–358, 449–628; Cramon, *Unser Österreich-Ungarischer Bundesgenosse im Weltkriege*, 80–85; Rauchensteiner, *Der Tod des Doppeladlers: Österreich-Ungarn und der Erste Weltkrieg*, 414–417; Rothenberg, *The Army of Francis Joseph*, 197; Stone, *The Eastern Front 1914–1917*, 264–281.
130. Arz, *Zur Geschichte des großen Krieges 1914–1918*, 102–120; Sondhaus, *Franz Conrad von Hötzendorf: Architect of the Apocalypse*, 192.
131. Cramon, *Unser Österreich-Ungarischer Bundesgenosse im Weltkriege*, 66–73; Rothenberg, *The Army of Francis Joseph*, 198–199; Stone, *The Eastern Front 1914–1917*, 268–269.
132. Glaise-Horstenau, *Die Katastrophe: Die Zertrümmerung Österreich-Ungarns und das Werden der Nachfolgestaaten*, 58.
133. Rothenberg, *The Army of Francis Joseph*, 198, 206.

134. Erich Ludendorff, *Meine Kriegserinnerungen 1914–1918* (Berlin: Ernst Siegfried Mittler und Sohn, 1921), 66.
135. *ÖULK*, 6: 68–72; Cramon, *Unser Österreich-Ungarischer Bundesgenosse im Weltkriege*, 100; Rothenberg, *The Army of Francis Joseph*, 202–203.
136. Sondhaus, *Franz Conrad von Hötzendorf: Architect of the Apocalypse*, 198–199.
137. Moritz Freiherr von Auffenberg-Komarów, *Aus Österreichs Höhe und Niedergang: Eine Lebensschilderung* (München: Drei Masken Verlag, 1921), 173.
138. Sondhaus, *Franz Conrad von Hötzendorf: Architect of the Apocalypse*, 162.
139. Krauß, *Die Ursachen unserer Niederlage: Erinnerungen und Urteile aus dem Weltkrieg*, 198–202.
140. Arz, *Zur Geschichte des großen Krieges 1914–1918*, 134–136; Cramon, *Unser Österreich-Ungarischer Bundesgenosse im Weltkriege*, 95.
141. A. Pitreich, *Der Österreichisch-ungarische Bundesgenosse im Sperrfeuer*, 390–391; Rothenberg, *The Army of Francis Joseph*, 187; Deák, *Beyond Nationalism*, 197–198.
142. *ÖULK*, 6: 213–336; Arz, *Zur Geschichte des großen Krieges 1914–1918*, 159–162; Jeřábek, "The Eastern Front," 160.
143. Arz, *Zur Geschichte des großen Krieges 1914–1918*, 171; Cramon, *Unser Österreich-Ungarischer Bundesgenosse im Weltkriege*, 126–127.
144. *ÖULK*, 6: 493–669; Arz, *Zur Geschichte des großen Krieges 1914–1918*, 174–185; Krauß, *Die Ursachen unserer Niederlage: Erinnerungen und Urteile aus dem Weltkrieg*, 217–252; Rauchensteiner, *Der Tod des Doppeladlers: Österreich-Ungarn und der Erste Weltkrieg*, 501–509.
145. Krauß, *Die Ursachen unserer Niederlage: Erinnerungen und Urteile aus dem Weltkrieg*, 301.
146. Johann Christoph Allmayer–Beck, "Heeresorganisation vor 50 Jahren: Planungen und Maßnahmen für den Friedensausbau der k.u.k. Wehrmacht nach beendigtem Kriege," *ÖMZ* Sonderheft (1967): 18.
147. Arz, *Zur Geschichte des großen Krieges 1914–1918*, 257–259.
148. Allmayer-Beck, "Heeresorganisation vor 50 Jahren: Planungen und Maßnahmen für den Friedensausbau der k.u.k. Wehrmacht nach beendigtem Kriege," 22–24.
149. Glaise-Horstenau, *Die Katastrophe: Die Zertrümmerung Österreich-Ungarns und das Werden der Nachfolgestaaten*, 248; Krauß, *Die Ursachen unserer Niederlage: Erinnerungen und Urteile aus dem Weltkrieg*, 247; *ÖULK*, 7: 55.
150. Rothenberg, *The Army of Francis Joseph*, 210–211.
151. *ÖULK*, 7: 207–359; Arz, *Zur Geschichte des großen Krieges 1914–1918*, 262–273; Cramon, *Unser Österreich-Ungarischer Bundesgenosse*

im Weltkriege, 164–173; Rauchensteiner, *Der Tod des Doppeladlers: Österreich-Ungarn und der Erste Weltkrieg*, 570–579.

152. Sondhaus, *The Naval Policy of Austria-Hungary, 1867–1918: Navalism, Industrial Development, and the Politics of Dualism*, 334–336.
153. Glaise-Horstenau, *Die Katastrophe: Die Zertrümmerung Österreich-Ungarns und das Werden der Nachfolgestaaten*, 332–335.
154. *ÖULK*, 7: 565–757; Arz, *Zur Geschichte des großen Krieges 1914–1918*, 333–338, 356–378; A. Pitreich, *Der Österreichisch-ungarische Bundesgenosse im Sperrfeuer*, 390–395; Cramon, *Unser Österreich-Ungarischer Bundesgenosse im Weltkriege*, 191–197; Rauchensteiner, *Der Tod des Doppeladlers: Österreich-Ungarn und der Erste Weltkrieg*, 613–616; Rothenberg, *The Army of Francis Joseph*, 216–218.
155. *ÖULK*, 7, supplement 1, Beilage 37.
156. Rothenberg, *The Army of Francis Joseph*, 218.
157. Susan Everett, *History of World War I* (New York: Simon and Schuster, 1982), 248.
158. Cramon, *Unser Österreich-Ungarischer Bundesgenosse im Weltkriege*, 200.
159. Stürgkh, *Politische und militärische Erinnerungen*, 288–289.
160. Stöckelle, "Der Feldzug von Limanova-Lapanów 1–20. Dezember 1914," 46.
161. A. Pitreich, *Der Österreichisch-ungarische Bundesgenosse im Sperrfeuer*, 82.

Bibliography

Unpublished Documents

Kriegsarchiv (KA), Vienna.
Allerhöchster Oberbefehl (AhOB).
Militärkanzlei Seiner Majestät des Kaisers (MKSM) Sonderreihe 1866–1918.
Militärkanzlei des Generalinspektors der gesamten bewaffneten Macht Erzherzog Franz.
Ferdinand (MKFF) 1898–1914.
Chef des Generalstabs (GSt) Operationsbüro 1866–1918.
Zentralstellen.
Kriegsministerium (KM) Präsidialbüro (Präsidium) 1866–1918.
Militärerziehungs- und Bildungsanstalten (MEB).
Kriegsschule Wien 1867–1914.

Published Primary Sources

Arz von Straussenburg, Arthur Albert. *Zur Geschichte des großen Krieges 1914–1918*. Graz: Akademische Druck-u. Verlangsanstalt, 1969.

Auffenberg-Komarów, Moritz. *Aus Österreich-Ungarns Teilnahme am Weltkriege.* Wien: Ullstein & Co., 1920.

Auffenberg-Komarów, Moritz Freiherr von. *Aus Österreichs Höhe und Niedergang - eine Lebensschilderung.* Munich: Drei Masken Verlag, 1921.

Conrad von Hötzendorf, FML Franz Graf. *Aus Meiner Dienstzeit 1906–1918.* Wien: Rikola Verlag, 1921.

Cramon, August von. *Unser Österreich-Ungarischer Bundesgenosse im Weltkriege: Erinnerungen aus meiner vierjährigen Tätigkeit als bevollmächtiger deutscher General beim k.u.k. Armeeoberkommando.* Berlin: Ernst Siegfried Mittler und Sohn, 1920.

Everett, Susan. *History of World War I.* New York: Simon and Schuster, 1982.

Falkenhayn, General Erich von. *The German General Staff and its Decisions, 1914–1916.* New York: Dodd, Mead and Company, 1920.

Glaise-Horstenau, Edmund, Josef Brauner, Eduard Czegka, Jaromir Diakow, Friedrich Franek, Walther Heydendorff, Rudolf Kiszling, Franz Mühlhofer, Ernst Wisshaupt und Georg Zobi, *Österreich-Ungarns letzter Krieg 1914–1918* (*ÖULK*). Wien: Verlag der Militärwissenschaftlichen Mitteilungen, 1930–1938.

Kabisch, Generalleutnant Ernst. *Streitfragen des Weltkrieges 1914–1918.* Stuttgart: Bergers Literarisches Büro und Verlagsanstalt, 1924.

Krauß, General der Infanterie Alfred. *Die Ursachen unserer Niederlage: Erinnerungen und Urteile aus dem Weltkrieg.* München: J.F. Lehmanns Verlag, 1921.

Ludendorff, Erich. *Meine Kriegserinnerungen 1914–1918.* Berlin: Ernst Siegfried Mittler und Sohn, 1921.

Metzger, FML Josef. "Der Krieg 1914 gegen Rußland." in *Der große Krieg 1914–1918*, edited by Max Schwarte. Leipzig: Johann Ambrosius Barth, 1922.

Neumair, Josef. *Im Serbischen Feldzug 1914: Erlebnisse und Stimmungen eines Landsturm Offiziers.* Innsbruck: Verlagsanstalt Tyrolia, 1917.

Pitreich, General Anton. *Der österreichisch-ungarische Bundesgenosse im Sperrfeuer.* Klagenfurt: Artur Kollitsch, 1930.

Pitreich, Oberst Maximilian Freiherr von. *Lemberg 1914.* Wien: Adolf Holzhausens Nachfolger, 1929.

Pitreich, Oberst Maximilian Freiherr von. *1914: Die Militärischen Probleme unseres Kriegsbeginnes, Ideen, Gründe, und Zusammenhänge.* Wien: Selbstverlag, 1934.

Sieber, Gustav. *Quo Vadis, Austria? Ein Roman der Resignation.* Berlin: "Vita" Deutsches Verlagshaus, 1913.

Stürgkh, Josef Maria Aloysius Graf von. *Politische und militärische Erinnerungen.* Leipzig: Paul List Verlag, 1922.

Secondary Sources

Allmayer-Beck, Johann Christoph. "Der Sommerfeldzug von 1914 gegen Rußland." *ÖMZ* Sonderheft I (1965): 31–39.

Allmayer-Beck, Johann Christoph. "Heeresorganisation vor 50 Jahren: Planungen und Maßnahmen für den Friedensausbau der k.u.k. Wehrmacht nach beendigtem Kriege." *ÖMZ* Sonderheft (1967): 18–27.

Deák, István. *Beyond Nationalism: A Social and Political History of the Habsburg Officer Corps, 1848–1918.* New York: Oxford University Press, 1992.

Forstner, Franz. *Przemyśl: Österreich-Ungarns bedeutendste Festung.* Wien: Österreichischer Bundesverlag, 1987.

Gabriel, Erich. "Die wichtigsten Waffen der österreichisch-ungarischen Armee 1918." *ÖMZ* 6 (1968): 436–439.

Glaise-Horstenau, Edmund von. *Die Katastrophe: Die Zertrümmerung Österreich-Ungarns und das Werden der Nachfolgestaaten.* Wien: Amalthea Verlag, 1929.

Gumz, Jonathan E. *The Resurrection and Collapse of Empire in Habsburg Serbia, 1914–1918.* New York: Cambridge University Press, 2009.

Hackl, Dieter. "Der Offensivgeist des Conrad von Hötzendorf." Mag. Phil. Diplomarbeit, Universität Wien, 2009.

Herwig, Holger H. "Disjointed Allies: Coalition Wafare in Berlin and Vienna, 1914." *The Journal of Military History* 54, 3 (July 1990): 265–280.

Hull, Isabel V. *Absolute Destruction: Military Culture and the Practices of War in Imperial Germany.* Ithaca: Cornell University Press, 2005.

Jeřábek, Rudolf. *Potiorek: General im Schatten von Sarajevo.* Graz: Verlag Styria, 1991.

Jeřábek, Rudolf. "The Eastern Front." in *The Last Years of Austria-Hungary: A Multi-National Experiment in Early Twentieth-Century Europe.* Exeter: University of Exeter Press, 1990.

Mast, Heinrich. "Die Aufklärungstätigkeit der österr-ung. Kavallerie bei Kriegsbeginn 1914," *ÖMZ* Sonderheft I (1965): 8–17.

Peball, Kurt. "Der Feldzug gegen Serbien und Montenegro im Jahre 1914." *ÖMZ* Sonderheft I (1965): 18–30.

Rauchensteiner, Manfried. *Der Tod des Doppeladlers: Österreich-Ungarn und der Erste Weltkrieg.* Graz: Verlag Styria, 1993.

Rothenberg, Gunther E. *The Army of Francis Joseph.* West Lafayette, Indiana: Purdue University Press, 1976.

Rothenberg, Gunther E. "The Austro-Hungarian Campaign Against Serbia in 1914," *The Journal of Military History* 53, 2 (April 1989): 127–146.

Schindler, John R. *Fall of the Double Eagle: The Battle for Galicia and the Demise of Austria-Hungary.* Lincoln, Nebraska: Potomac Books, 2015.

Sondhaus, Lawrence. *Franz Conrad von Hötzendorf: Architect of the Apocalypse*. Boston: Humanities Press, Inc., 2000.

Sondhaus, Lawrence. *The Naval Policy of Austria-Hungary, 1867–1918: Navalism, Industrial Development, and the Politics of Dualism*. West Lafayette, IN: Purdue University Press, 1994.

Stöckelle, Gustav. "Der Feldzug von Limanova-Lapanów 1–20. Dezember 1914." *ÖMZ* Sonderheft I (1965): 39–46.

Stone, Norman. *The Eastern Front 1914–1917*. London: Hodder and Stoughton, 1975.

Stone, Norman. "Moltke-Conrad: Relations between the Austro-Hungarian and German General Staffs, 1909–1914." *The Historical Journal* IX, 2 (1966): 201–228.

Tunstall, Graydon A. *Blood on the Snow: The Carpathian Winter War of 1915*. Lawrence: University Press of Kansas, 2010.

Tunstall, Graydon A. *Planning for War against Russia and Serbia: Austro-Hungarian and German Military Strategies, 1871–1914*. New York: Columbia University Press, 1993.

Vego, Milan N. *Austro-Hungarian Naval Policy 1904–1914*. Portland, OR: Frank Cass, 1996.

Wawro, Geoffrey. *A Mad Catastrophe: The Outbreak of World War I and the Collapse of the Habsburg Empire*. New York: Basic Books, 2014.

CHAPTER 8

Conclusion

"A great general does not need to hold on to prevailing theory; others cling only to secondary greatness. While the latter are ruled by theory, the born general—and there is only such—rules theory and art."[1] In this way General Alfred Krauss wrote of the difference between Moltke and Benedek 35 years after the Austro-Prussian War. Krauss also applied this distinction to leaders of the First World War, but claimed that the Dual Monarchy possessed no men of greatness to display "the hard, inflexible will, the will for action, for battle, for victory."[2]

This analysis has merit in that Conrad and the majority of high-ranking *k.u.k.* officers during World War I adhered staunchly to the doctrine of the offensive in the face of mounting casualties and catastrophic defeats. Instead of adapting military doctrine to the realities of the battlefield, Conrad and his followers futilely attempted to force Habsburg soldiers to do the impossible—frontal assaults without artillery support against numerically and materially superior defenders in entrenched positions. Similarly, without sufficient artillery preparation, Benedek ordered Austro-Hungarian troops to assault Prussian infantry firing needle guns in 1866. Much like Benedek's attacks, Conrad's tactics removed any chances of victory for the Austro-Hungarian army in the Great War.

Krauss's words, however, fail to deliver a complete picture of the causes for Habsburg defeat in both 1866 and 1914–1918. Krauss not only omitted the problem of imprudent spending decisions on the part of the Austro-Hungarian high command, but also stressed the *Wille zur Siege* far too much. Military success does not depend solely on the

J.A. Dredger, *Tactics and Procurement in the Habsburg Military, 1866–1918*, DOI 10.1007/978-3-319-57678-7_8

will of leaders for victory, as all leaders desire to win. If that idea were valid, then the Dual Monarchy should have achieved more success during both the Austro-Prussian War and the Great War. Benedek, though pessimistic, certainly wished to win a great victory in 1866 but relied too much on *élan*. Conrad, with his constant offensives and desire to restore the fallen prestige of the Habsburg Empire and army, maintained the will to win. The tenacious will of a leader far from the battlefield, however, cannot compensate for grossly inferior numerical and material deficiencies. Therein lay the causes of the military demise of *k.u.k.* forces.

The words of Krauss also fail to take into account the ability of leaders to learn from mistakes and form new ideas. The Habsburg military high command displayed this ability throughout the years between 1866 and 1918. Following the disaster against Prussia during the Austro-Prussian War, the new high command (Archduke Albrecht, Beck, and John) realized the tactical errors committed by Benedek in Bohemia. Immediately, these men started to reform the Austro-Hungarian army in an effort to restore lost prestige for the Dual Monarchy and maintain the Habsburg Empire as a great power. The new leadership forbade frontal assaults against enemies wielding breech-loading rifles and determined to procure breech-loaders for Habsburg soldiers. The new war minister Kuhn also attempted to reform military education by implementing tests for promotions and emphasizing intellectual training of the officer corps. Rivalry between Albrecht and Kuhn, who disagreed about the best methods of reform, slowed the reforms until Kuhn's dismissal in 1874.

Despite this delay, the Austro-Hungarian army made great progress in fighting methods and weaponry during the years following 1866. Finding an opportunity to display these improvements, the Habsburg military welcomed the mandate of the Congress of Berlin to invade Bosnia-Hercegovina in 1878. Although the mostly irregular enemy forces in the Balkans did not constitute an opponent worthy of great power status, the Habsburg victory in Bosnia-Hercegovina restored the confidence of the Dual Monarchy's population in Austro-Hungarian military ability. More importantly, representatives of the Delegations, which determined funding for the Habsburg army, softened their view of military appropriations and began to agree more willingly to the army's budgetary requests. War Minister Bylandt-Rheidt promoted good relations with delegates by proving fiscal responsibility in the Habsburg military and thereby convincing delegates to fund the purchase of repeating rifles in the 1880s.

However, problems still occurred within the Dual Monarchy high command in the 1870s and 1880s. The two main issues were tactics and spending decisions. Despite the move toward less offensive tactics and the insistence on using terrain and artillery to support infantry, the reforms stayed more within the realm of theory than practice. On the exercise field and during maneuvers, contrary to the instructions of the regulations, Austro-Hungarian officers instilled attacking methods into the men and paid little attention to defensive principles. This spirit of the offensive continued among certain members of the Habsburg officer corps, especially in the cavalry. Mounted officers, decrying the smaller role that horsemen would play in future wars, attempted to maintain the offensive power of cavalry in charging infantry. Nevertheless, The Dual Monarchy's military high command became one of the first European powers to eliminate the lance from mounted units and stress the importance of firepower for all branches.

The other major problem for the Austro-Hungarian high command involved procurement decisions. With far less funding than the rest of the great military powers, Habsburg leaders had to make wise spending choices to keep pace with other European armies. The Dual Monarchy's military leadership, however, did not make prudent use of funds. Instead of ensuring that the Austro-Hungarian artillery, the strongest branch of the Habsburg army in 1866, maintained the same quantity of field pieces per division as other militaries, the *k.k.* high command decided that upgrading and building permanent fortresses offered greater advantages for defending the borders of the empire. Compounding this problem, Austro-Hungarian military leaders decided to produce artillery using inferior Uchatius steel-bronze barrels from the Viennese arsenal rather than purchase from foreign firms such as Krupp in Germany. This foolish decision wasted vital funds on poor weaponry that weighed more and shot a smaller distance than the lighter steel barrels. Thus, the *k.k.* artillery became the worst equipped of the major European states.

Imprudent spending decisions and insufficient practical application of theoretical tactical reforms stymied the progress that the Habsburg army had made during the 1870s and 1880s. Despite great interest and debates about new technology and methods of war, the Austro-Hungarian military continued to lag behind the other armies of Europe. This situation worsened dramatically during the 1890s, when two events reversed the improvements made by the Dual Monarchy's army. First, Conrad von Hötzendorf became tactical instructor at the *Kriegsschule* from 1888–1892. Second, Archduke Albrecht died in 1895.

With the rise of Hötzendorf to the most important position in the Habsburg war college, an obsession with the offensive, especially the victories of Moltke in 1866 and 1870, permeated the staff officers who studied under Conrad. These men held most of the high-ranking positions during the First World War and promoted the offensive *à outrance* according to the instructions received at the *Kriegsschule*. The death of Albrecht removed the most influential voice of reason concerning the tactics that would suit the ever-increasing firepower of both infantry and artillery with the advent of repeating rifles and more destructive field guns. Though Albrecht had advocated greater use of cavalry and permanent fortresses, the archduke wisely opposed useless frontal assaults against well-trained and equipped soldiers. After his death, few officers dared resist the reversion to the offensive tactics so vehemently endorsed by Conrad.

By the time Conrad was appointed chief of the general staff in 1906, no more discussions on the correct form of tactics ensued. The new regulations of the 20 years before the Great War focused more and more on assault methods and emphasized the role and importance of the bayonet, especially for morale. To compensate for numerical and material inferiority, Conrad and most of the *k.u.k.* officer corps looked to the *Wille zur Siege* to provide the advantage. During the years preceding World War I, Conrad and his subordinates adhered more strenuously than ever to the dictates of the offensive. Instead of learning the lessons of recent wars, Austro-Hungarian officers interpreted the events of the Boer War, the Russo-Japanese War, and the Balkan Wars to fit preconceived notions of the supremacy of the offense, higher morale, and will-power of the attacker over the passivity of the defense that the conflicts of 1866 and 1870 had supposedly proven. Interpreting the victory of the smaller Japanese army over the Russians in 1905 to be the result of superior will and offensive ability, Habsburg officers took morale and attack as the secrets of success against a likely future opponent. Although seeing the devastating effect of artillery fire with explosive shells, shrapnel, and grenades, *k.u.k.* writers chose to leave the true lessons of modern warfare as theory rather than translate these ideas to the battlefield. After all, the offensive side always won.

At the same time, Conrad and the rest of the Dual Monarchy's high command realized the grave deficiencies in Austro-Hungarian artillery. In a desperate attempt to rectify this situation, the war ministers appealed to the Delegations for extraordinary funding. The parliamentary delegates approved most of the *k.u.k.* requests, but the Habsburg army could not procure enough new cannon and ammunition nor sufficiently modern field pieces to equal the artillery of the enemy in the First World War. In addition, the Austro-Hungarian military decision-makers chose to spend immense sums of money on permanent fortresses and Dreadnoughts rather than on modern field guns and tanks. Great power status played a major role in the high regard for battleships. The delegates who approved funding for superfluous naval projects echoed the Habsburg military's refrain of needing Dreadnoughts to maintain the Dual Monarchy's place among the great powers and to foster overseas business ventures. The latter consideration appealed strongly to parliamentary delegates who represented business interests within the Austro-Hungarian Empire. Thus, the *k.u.k.* army obtained approval from the majority of delegates to spend hundreds of millions of Kronen on useless fortresses and battleships, rather than providing Habsburg soldiers with the necessary material and technology for victory.

Entering World War I with fewer soldiers and inferior weaponry, especially artillery, than the Entente powers, Austria-Hungary required strategy and tactics that give a chance for success. The offensive *à outrance* approach of the de facto commander-in-chief Conrad provided the opposite. During the opening campaigns in Galicia and Serbia, only the defensive in at least one theater could have afforded the possibility of victory for *k.u.k.* forces. Instead, Conrad ordered attacks against superior opponents. These mindless assaults resulted in catastrophe, destroying a major percentage of trained Habsburg fighters and transforming the Dual Monarchy's military into a militia of poorly equipped reserves. Although Austro-Hungarian troops showed amazing resiliency and the *k.u.k.* army strove vigorously to adapt to the realities of the modern battlefield, particularly in upgrading the artillery branch, the Habsburg high command merely saw more occasions for offensives. Every solely Dual Monarchy offensive ended in defeat and added to the disastrous losses of the army. Austria-Hungary only achieved success when employing the defensive or attacking with the support of Germany. Rather than restoring the great power status of the Habsburg Empire, the offensive strategy and tactics of *k.u.k.* leaders culminated in destruction of the Dual

Monarchy's army and the empire it tried to defend. The combination of imprudent prewar spending decisions and obsession with the offensive eliminated any hope of a Habsburg victory in the First World War.

During the Great War, primarily after the dismissal of Conrad as chief of the general staff, the Austro-Hungarian high command showed the ability to learn from battlefield experiences. The reforms that Emperor Charles and his chief of staff Arz implemented and proposed revealed that these men realized the need to possess excellent artillery in sufficient numbers and the waning importance of cavalry. In addition, *k.u.k.* leaders recognized that permanent fortresses played little part in the outcome of campaigns, whereas tanks held a decisive role. At the same time, no one mentioned the waste of money on Dreadnoughts that mainly sat in port for most of the war. The reform program required officers to gain proficiency in both attack and defense tactics. Although officers such as Krauss still maintained the necessity of the *Wille zur Siege*, the new Austro-Hungarian military leadership appeared to have formulated a plan for future success based on the experiences of the First World War and would adapt strategy and tactics to the conditions of future battlefields.

Whether this plan would have succeeded remains unknown. With the fall of the Habsburg monarchy and the splitting of the Austro-Hungarian Empire into multiple smaller states, the *k.u.k.* high command never had the opportunity to test the reform program completely. Habsburg officers of the First World War recognized most of the problems that had caused the catastrophe, just as after the disaster of 1866. The practical application of theory, however, had never been a strength of the *k.u.k.* high command. Although new formations and an improvement in the quantity and quality of artillery were practical accomplishments, the introduction of new tactics was a different question. Training officers and soldiers to fight according to new styles of warfare required great patience and time on the exercise field. Spending decisions also remained a difficult issue, although Charles and Arz had already started well by procuring modern field guns and wanted to acquire tanks rather than upgrade permanent fortresses. The ultimate outcome of the new reform program remains, however, at best an intriguing counterfactual.

Notes

1. General der Infanterie Alfred Krauß, *Moltke, Benedek und Napoleon* (Wien: L.W. Seidel & Sohn, 1901), quoted in Johann Christoph Allmayer-Beck, "Heeresorganisation vor 50 Jahren: Planungen und Maßnahmen für den Friedensausbau der k.u.k. Wehrmacht nach beendigtem Kriege," *ÖMZ* Sonderheft (1967): 27.
2. General der Infanterie Alfred Krauß, *Die Ursachen unserer Niederlage: Erinnerungen und Urteile aus dem Weltkrieg* (München: J.F. Lehmanns Verlag, 1921), 301–302.

Bibliography

Published Primary Sources

Krauß, General der Infanterie Alfred. *Die Ursachen unserer Niederlage: Erinnerungen und Urteile aus dem Weltkrieg.* München: J.F. Lehmanns Verlag, 1921.

Secondary Sources

Allmayer-Beck, Johann Christoph. "Heeresorganisation vor 50 Jahren: Planungen und Maßnahmen für den Friedensausbau der k.u.k. Wehrmacht nach beendigtem Kriege." *ÖMZ* Sonderheft (1967): 18–27.

Bibliography

Unpublished Documents

Kriegsarchiv (KA), Vienna.
Allerhöchster Oberbefehl (AhOB).
Militärkanzlei Seiner Majestät des Kaisers (MKSM) Sonderreihe 1866–1918.
Militärkanzlei des Generalinspektors der gesamten bewaffneten Macht Erzherzog Franz Ferdinand (MKFF) 1898–1914.
Chef des Generalstabs (GSt) Operationsbüro 1866–1918.
Zentralstellen.
Kriegsministerium (KM) Präsidialbüro (Präsidium) 1866–1918.
Militärerziehungs- und Bildungsanstalten (MEB).
Kriegsschule Wien 1867–1914.

Published Primary Sources

Albrecht (anonymously). *Das Jahr 1870 und die Wehrkraft der Monarchie* Vienna: Faesy & Frick, 1870.

Arz von Straussenburg, Arthur Albert. *Zur Geschichte des großen Krieges 1914–1918*. Graz: Akademische Druck- u. Verlangsanstalt, 1969.

Auffenberg-Komarów, Moritz. *Aus Österreich-Ungarns Teilnahme am Weltkriege*. Wien: Ullstein & Co., 1920.

Auffenberg-Komarów, Moritz Freiherr von. *Aus Österreichs Höhe und Niedergang - eine Lebensschilderung*. Munich: Drei Masken Verlag, 1921.

Bartels, Eduard. *Kritische Beiträge zur Geschichte des Krieges im Jahre 1866*. Zurich: Cäsar Schmidt, 1901.

Bartels, Eduard. *Österreich und sein Heer*. Leipzig: Otto Wigand, 1866.

J.A. Dredger, *Tactics and Procurement in the Habsburg Military, 1866–1918*, DOI 10.1007/978-3-319-57678-7

Benedek, Ludwig August Ritter von, and Heinrich Friedjung, *Benedeks nachgelassene Papiere*. Leipzig: Grübel & Sommerlatte, 1901.

Berndt, Hauptmann Otto. *Die Zahl im Kriege. Statistische Daten aus der neueren Kriegsgeschichte in graphischer Darstellung*. Wien: G. Freytag & Berndt, 1897.

B.P.S., "Unsere Aufgabe," *ÖMZ* 4 (1866): 34–46, 140–155.

Chamberlain, Houston Stewart. *Der Wille zum Sieg und andere Aufsätze*. München: Hugo Bruckmann, 1918.

Conrad von Hötzendorf, FML Franz Graf. *Aus Meiner Dienstzeit 1906–1918*. Wien: Rikola Verlag, 1921.

Conrad von Hötzendorf, Franz. *Infanterische Fragen und die Erscheinungen des Boerenkrieges*. Wien: Seidel & Sohn, 1903.

Conrad von Hötzendorf, Franz Graf *Mein Anfang: Kriegserinnerungen aus der Jugendzeit 1878–1882*. Berlin: Verlag für Kulturpolitik, 1925.

Conrad von Hötzendorf, Franz. *Zum Studium der Taktik*. Vienna: L.W. Seidel & Sohn, 1891.

Cramon, August von. *Unser Österreich-Ungarischer Bundesgenosse im Weltkriege: Erinnerungen aus meiner vierjährigen Tätigkeit als bevollmächtiger deutscher General beim k.u.k. Armeeoberkommando*. Berlin: Ernst Siegfried Mittler und Sohn, 1920.

Die Occupation Bosniens und der Hercegovina durch k.k. Truppen im Jahre 1878. Vienna: k.k. Generalstab and L.W. Seidel & Sohn, 1879.

Exerzierreglement für die k.u.k. Fußtruppen. Wien: k.k. Hof- und Staatsdruckerei, 1911.

Falkenhayn, General Erich von. *The German General Staff and its Decisions, 1914–1916*. New York: Dodd, Mead and Company, 1920.

Friedjung, Heinrich. *Der Kampf um die Vorherrschaft in Deutschland 1859 bis 1866*, 2 vols. Stuttgart: J.G. Cotta, 1900.

Glaise-Horstenau, Edmund, Josef Brauner, Eduard Czegka, Jaromir Diakow, Friedrich Franek, Walther Heydendorff, Rudolf Kiszling, Franz Mühlhofer, Ernst Wisshaupt und Georg Zobi, *Österreich-Ungarns letzter Krieg 1914–1918* (*ÖULK*). Wien: Verlag der Militärwissenschaftlichen Mitteilungen, 1930–1938.

Goltz, Wilhelm Leopold Colmar Freiherr von der. *Das Volk in Waffen. Ein Buch über Heerwesen und Kriegführung unserer Zeit*. Berlin: R. v. Decker's Verlag, 1883.

Hess, FML Heinrich Freiherr von. "Strategische Grundsätze über die Verteidigung der österreichischen Monarchie," in *Schriften aus dem militärwissenschaftlichen Nachlass*, ed. Manfried Rauchensteiner. Osnäbruck: Biblio Verlag, 1975.

Holtz, Georg Freiherr von. *Von Brod bis Sarajevo*. Vienna, Leipzig: Stern, 1907.

John, FML Franz Freiherr von. "Allerunterthänigster Vortrag des Kriegsministers," *Wiener Zeitung*, Nr. 317, 31 December 1866.

Jomini, Antoine Henri. *The Art of War*. Westport, CT: Greenwood Press, 1862.

Jurnitschek, Dr. Alfred. *Die Wehr-Reform in Österreich-ungarn von 1866 bis 1873*. Vienna: Carl Gerold's Sohn, 1873.

Kabisch, Generalleutnant Ernst. *Streitfragen des Weltkrieges 1914–1918*. Stuttgart: Bergers Literarisches Büro und Verlagsanstalt, 1924.

Keltie, J. Scott, ed. *The Statesman's Yearbook: Statistical and Historical Annual of the States of the World for the Year 1891*. London: Macmillan and Co., 1891.

Kerchnawe, Hugo. *Die Vorgeschichte von 1866 und 19??* Wien: C.W. Stern Verlag, 1909.

K.k. Generalstabs-Bureau für Kriegsgeschichte. *Österreichs Kämpfe im Jahre 1866*. Wien: R.v. Waldheim, 1867–1869, vol. 1–5.

Krauß, General der Infanterie Alfred. *Die Ursachen unserer Niederlage: Erinnerungen und Urteile aus dem Weltkrieg*. München: J.F. Lehmanns Verlag, 1921.

Ludendorff, Erich. *Meine Kriegserinnerungen 1914–1918*. Berlin: Ernst Siegfried Mittler und Sohn, 1921.

Martin, Frederick. *The Statesman's Year-Book: Statistical and Historical Annual of the States of the Civilised World for the Year 1878*. London: Macmillan and Co., 1878.

Martin, Frederick, Sir John Scott Keltie, Isaac Parker Anderson Renwick, Mortimer Epstein, Sigfrid Henry Steinberg, and John Paxton, *The Statesman's Year-Book: Statistical and Historical Annual of the States of the Civilised World for the Year 1889*. London: Macmillan and Co., 1889.

Martin, Frederick, Sir John Scott Keltie, Isaac Parker Anderson Renwick, Mortimer Epstein, Sigfrid Henry Steinberg, and John Paxton, *The Statesman's Year-Book: Statistical and Historical Annual of the States of the Civilised World for the Year 1902*. London: Macmillan and Co., 1902.

Metzger, FML Josef. "Der Krieg 1914 gegen Rußland." in *Der große Krieg 1914–1918*, edited by Max Schwarte. Leipzig: Johann Ambrosius Barth, 1922.

Militär-statistisches Jahrbuch für das Jahr 1870. Vienna: Kaiserlich-Königlich Hof- und Staatsdruckerei, 1871.

Mollinary, FZM Anton Freiherr von. *Sechsundvierzig Jahre im österreich-ungarischen Heere, 1833–1879*, 2 vols. Zurich: Art. Institut Orell Füssli, 1905.

Mollinary, Anton von. *Studien über die Operationen und Tactique der Franzosen im Feldzuge 1859 in Italien*. Wien: Wilhelm Braumüller, 1864.

Neumair, Josef. *Im Serbischen Feldzug 1914: Erlebnisse und Stimmungen eines Landsturm Offiziers*. Innsbruck: Verlagsanstalt Tyrolia, 1917.

Organ der militärwissenschaftlichen Vereine (*O.*), 1867–1906.

Österreichische Militärische Zeitschrift (*ÖMZ*), 1866–1914.

Ostrymiecz, August Urbański von. *Conrad von Hötzendorf*. Graz-Leipzig-Vienna: Ulrich Mosers Verlag, 1938.

Ottenfeld, Rudolf Ritter Otto von. *Ein Ruhmesblatt der österreichischen Artillerie. Die Armeegeschützreserve nach der Schlacht bei Königgrätz am 3. Juli 1866*, oil on canvas, Heeresgeschichtliches Museum, Vienna, 1897.

Pitreich, General Anton. *Der österreichisch-ungarische Bundesgenosse im Sperrfeuer*. Klagenfurt: Artur Kollitsch, 1930.

Pitreich, Oberst Maximilian Freiherr von. *Lemberg 1914*. Wien: Adolf Holzhausens Nachfolger, 1929.

Pitreich, Oberst Maximilian Freiherr von. *1914: Die Militärischen Probleme unseres Kriegsbeginnes, Ideen, Gründe, und Zusammenhänge*. Wien: Selbstverlag, 1934.

Poten, Bernhard von. *Geschichte des Militär- Erziehungs- und Bildungswesens in Österreich-Ungarn*. Berlin: A. Hoffman & Comp., 1893.

Przibram, Ludwig Ritter von. *Erinnerungen eines alten Österreichers*. Stuttgart-Leipzig: Deutsche Verlags-Anstalt, 1912.

Rechkron, Josef Ritter Rechberger von. *Das Bildungswesen im österreichischen Heere vom dreissigjährigen Kriege bis zur Gegenwart*. Vienna: R. v. Waldheim, 1878.

Reinländer, Oberst Wilhelm. *Vorträge über die Taktik*. Vienna: L.W. Seidel & Son, 1870–1871.

Salis-Soglio, FZM Daniel Freiherr von. *Mein Leben und was ich davon erzählen will, kann und darf*. Stuttgart and Leipzig: Deutsche Verlags-Anstalt, 1908.

Sammlung der Armeebefehle und speziellen Anordnungen des k.k. Feldzeugmeisters Benedek, Kommandanten der k.k. Nordarmee vom Jahre 1866. Vienna: k.k. Staatsdruckerei, 1866.

Schnitzler, Arthur. *Leutnant Gustl*. Berlin: S. Fischer, 1901.

Sechzig Jahre Wehrmacht 1848–1908. Vienna: k.u.k. Kriegsarchiv, 1908.

Sochor, Vaclav. *The Battery of the Dead*, oil on canvas, Heeresgeschichtliches Museum, Vienna, 1901/7.

Sieber, Gustav. *Quo Vadis, Austria? Ein Roman der Resignation*. Berlin: "Vita" Deutsches Verlagshaus, 1913.

Statistisches Jahrbuch für das Jahr 1870. Vienna: Kaiserlich-Königlich Hof- und Staatsdruckerei, 1872.

Statistisches Jahrbuch für das Jahr 1877. Vienna: Kaiserlich-Königlich Hof- und Staatsdruckerei, 1880.

Stenographische Protokolle des Hauses der Abgeordneten des Reichsrathes. Vienna: k.k. Hof- und Staatsdruckerei, 1863–1871.

Stenographische Sitzungs-Protokolle der Delegation des Reichsrathes. Vienna: k.k. Hof- und Staatsdruckerei, 1869–1911.

Stürgkh, Josef Maria Aloysius Graf von. *Politische und militärische Erinnerungen*. Leipzig: Paul List Verlag, 1922.

Trotha, Thilo von. “Tactical Studies on the Battles around Plevna,” translated by First Lieutenant Carl Reichmann U.S. Army. Kansas City, MO: Hudson-Kimberley Publishing Co., 1896.

Wertheimer, Eduard von. *Graf Julius Andrássy, sein Leben und seine Zeit.* Stuttgart: Deutsche Verlags-Anstalt, 1913.

Zitterhofer, Oberleutnant [Karl]. *Streffleurs Militärische Zeitschrift 1808–1908: Eine Geschichte dieser Zeitschrift anlässlich ihres 100jährigen Bestehens.* Vienna: L.W. Siedel & Sohn, 1908.

Secondary Sources

Albrecht, Walther. *Gunther Burstyn (1879–1945) und die Entwicklung der Panzerwaffe.* Osnabrück: Biblio Verlag, 1973.

Allmayer-Beck, Johann Christoph. “Der Feldzug der österreichischen Nordarmee nach Königgrätz,” in *Entscheidung 1866: Der Krieg zwischen Österreich und Preußen*, eds. Wolfgang v. Groote and Ursula v. Gersdorff. Stuttgart: Deutsche Verlags-Anstalt, 1966.

Allmayer-Beck, Johann Christoph. “Der Sommerfeldzug von 1914 gegen Rußland.” *ÖMZ* Sonderheft I (1965): 31–39.

Allmayer-Beck, Johann Christoph. “Die Bewaffnete Macht in Staat und Gesellschaft.” in *Die Habsburgermonarchie 1848–1918*, Vol. 5 *Die Bewaffnete Macht.* Vienna: Verlag der Österreichischen Akademie der Wissenschaften, 1987.

Allmayer-Beck, Johann Christoph. “Heeresorganisation vor 50 Jahren: Planungen und Maßnahmen für den Friedensausbau der k.u.k. Wehrmacht nach beendigtem Kriege.” *ÖMZ* Sonderheft (1967): 18–27.

Angetter, Daniela and Ewald. *Gunther Burstyn (1879–1945): Sein 'Panzer' - eine bahnbrechende Erfindung zur falschen Zeit am falschen Ort.* Wien: Verlag der Österreichischen Akademie der Wissenschaften, 2008.

Beller, Steven. *Francis Joseph.* New York: Longman, 1996.

Clausewitz, Carl von. *On War.* Edited and translated by Michael Howard and Peter Paret. Princeton, New Jersey: Princeton University Press, 1976.

Craig, Gordon. *The Battle of Königgrätz.* Philadelphia: Lippincott Co., 1964.

Crankshaw, Edward. *The Fall of the House of Habsburg.* New York: The Viking Press, 1963.

Deák, István. *Beyond Nationalism: A Social and Political History of the Habsburg Officer Corps, 1848–1918.* New York: Oxford University Press, 1992.

DiNardo, R.L., and Austin Bay, “The First Modern Tank: Gunther Burstyn and His Motorgeschütz.” *Military Affairs* Vol. 50, No. 1 (Jan. 1986): 12–15.

Everett, Susan. *History of World War I.* New York: Simon and Schuster, 1982.

Förster, Rolf. "Die Leistungsfähigkeit der bayrischen Armee im Feldzuge 1866: Dargestellt an der militärische Ausbildung vor dem Krieg." Ph.D. dissertation, Munich, 1987.

Forstner, Franz. *Przemyśl: Österreich-Ungarns bedeutendste Festung*. Wien: Österreichischer Bundesverlag, 1987.

Frankl, Viktor E. *Man's Search for Meaning*. Boston: Beacon Press, 1959.

Franzel, Emil. *1866. Il Mondo Casca. Das Ende des alten Europa*. Vienna: Verlag Herold, 1968.

Gabriel, Erich. "Die wichtigsten Waffen der österreichisch-ungarischen Armee 1918." *ÖMZ* 6 (1968): 436–439.

Gat, Azar. *A History of Military Thought: From the Enlightenment to the Cold War*. New York: Oxford University Press, 2001.

Glaise-Horstenau, Edmund von. *Die Katastrophe: Die Zertrümmerung Österreich-Ungarns und das Werden der Nachfolgestaaten*. Wien: Amalthea Verlag, 1929.

Glaise-Horstenau, Edmund von. *Franz Josephs Weggefährte*. Wien: Amalthea Verlag, 1930.

Good, David. *The Economic Rise of the Habsburg Empire, 1750–1914*. Berkeley: University of California Press, 1984.

Gumz, Jonathan E. *The Resurrection and Collapse of Empire in Habsburg Serbia, 1914–1918*. New York: Cambridge University Press, 2009.

Hackl, Dieter. "Der Offensivgeist des Conrad von Hötzendorf." Mag. Phil. Diplomarbeit, Universität Wien, 2009.

Herwig, Holger H. "Disjointed Allies: Coalition Warfare in Berlin and Vienna, 1914." *The Journal of Military History* 54, 3 (July 1990): 265–280.

Höbelt, Lothar. "Die Marine." in *Die Habsburgermonarchie 1848–1918*, Vol. 5 *Die Bewaffnete Macht*. Vienna: Verlag der Österreichischen Akademie der Wissenschaften, 1987.

Holtman, Robert. *The Napoleonic Revolution*. New York: J.B. Lippincott, 1967.

Hull, Isabel V. *Absolute Destruction: Military Culture and the Practices of War in Imperial Germany*. Ithaca: Cornell University Press, 2005.

Inventar des Kriegsarchiv Wien, I. Band. Wien: Ferdinand Berger, 1953.

Jelavich, Barbara. *The Habsburg Empire in European Affairs, 1814–1918*. Chicago: Rand McNally & Co., 1969.

Jelavich, Charles. "The Revolt in Bosnia-Hercegovina, 1881–2." *The Slavonic and East European Review* 31, No. 77 (June 1953): 420–436.

Jeřábek, Rudolf. *Potiorek: General im Schatten von Sarajevo*. Graz: Verlag Styria, 1991.

Jeřábek, Rudolf. "The Eastern Front." in *The Last Years of Austria-Hungary: A Multi-National Experiment in Early Twentieth-Century Europe*. Exeter: University of Exeter Press, 1990.

Kiszling, Rudolf. *Erzherzog Franz Ferdinand von Österreich-Este: Leben, Pläne und Wirken am Schicksalsweg der Donaumonarchie*. Graz: Hermann Böhlaus Nachf., 1953.

Kronenbitter, Günther. *"Krieg im Frieden." Die Führung der k.u.k. Armee und die Großmachtpolitik Österreich-Ungarns 1906–1914*. Munich: Oldenbourg, 2003.

Lackey, Scott. *The Rebirth of the Habsburg Army: Friedrich Beck and the Rise of the General Staff*. Westport, CT: Greenwood Press, 1995.

Macartney, C.A. *The Habsburg Empire 1790–1918*. London: Weidenfeld and Nicolson, 1969.

Mast, Heinrich. "Die Aufklärungstätigkeit der österr.-ung. Kavallerie bei Kriegsbeginn 1914," *ÖMZ* Sonderheft I (1965): 8–17.

Menning, Bruce W. *Bayonets before Bullets: The Imperial Russian Army, 1861–1914*. Bloomington & Indianapolis: Indiana University Press, 1992.

Österreichisches Biographisches Lexikon 1815–1950 Vol. 1. Vienna: Verlag der Österreichischen Akademie der Wissenschaften, 1957.

Peball, Kurt. "Der Feldzug gegen Serbien und Montenegro im Jahre 1914." *ÖMZ* Sonderheft I (1965): 18–30.

Rauchensteiner, Manfried. *Der Tod des Doppeladlers: Österreich-Ungarn und der Erste Weltkrieg*. Graz: Verlag Styria, 1993.

Rauchensteiner, Manfried. *Heeresgeschichtliches Museum Vienna*. Vienna: Styria Verlag, 2000.

Regele, Oskar. *Feldmarschall Conrad*. Wien: Verlag Herold, 1955.

Regele, Oskar. *Feldzeugmeister Benedek und der Weg nach Königgrätz*. Wien: Verlag Herold, 1960.

Regele, Oskar. "Staatspolitische Geschichtsschreibung: erläutert an Königgrätz 1866." *Mitteilungen des österreichischen Staatsarchivs (MÖSA)* 3 (1950).

Reti, Steven P. *Silver and Gold: The Political Economy of International Monetary Conferences, 1867–1892*. Westport, CT: Greenwood Press, 1998.

Ritter, Gerhard. *Staatskunst und Kriegshandwerk*, München: R. Oldenbourg, 1954–1968.

Rothenberg, Gunther E. *The Army of Francis Joseph*. West Lafayette, IN: Purdue University Press, 1976.

Rothenberg, Gunther E. *The Art of Warfare in the Age of Napoleon*. Bloomington, IN: Indiana University Press, 1980.

Rothenberg, Gunther E. "The Austro-Hungarian Campaign Against Serbia in 1914," *The Journal of Military History* 53, 2 (April 1989): 127–146.

Schindler, John R. *Fall of the Double Eagle: The Battle for Galicia and the Demise of Austria-Hungary*. Lincoln, NE: Potomac Books, 2015.

Schmidt-Brentano, Antonio. *Die Armee in Österreich: Militär, Staat und Gesellschaft 1848–1867*. Boppard am Rhein: Harald Boldt, 1975.

Showalter, Dennis E. *Railroads and Rifles: Soldiers, Technology, and the Unification of Germany*. Hamden, CT: Archon Books, 1975.

Sked, Alan. *The Decline and Fall of the Habsburg Empire, 1815–1918*. London: Longman, 1989.

Sondhaus, Lawrence. *Franz Conrad von Hötzendorf: Architect of the Apocalypse*. Boston: Humanities Press, 2000.

Sondhaus, Lawrence. *The Naval Policy of Austria-Hungary, 1867–1918: Navalism, Industrial Development, and the Politics of Dualism*. West Lafayette, IN: Purdue University Press, 1994.

Srbik, Heinrich von. *Aus Österreichs Vergangenheit*. Salzburg: O. Müller, 1949.

Stöckelle, Gustav. "Der Feldzug von Limanova-Lapanów 1.-20. Dezember 1914." *ÖMZ* Sonderheft I (1965): 39–46.

Stone, Norman. *The Eastern Front 1914–1917*. London: Hodder and Stoughton, 1975.

Stone, Norman. "Moltke-Conrad: Relations between the Austro-Hungarian and German General Staffs, 1909–1914." *The Historical Journal* IX, 2 (1966): 201–228.

Taylor, A.J.P. *The Habsburg Monarchy 1809–1918*. London: Hamish Hamilton, 1948.

Thiel, Major Joshua. "COIN Manpower Ratios: Debunking the 10 to 1 Ratio and Surges." *Small Wars Journal* (Jan. 15, 2011), http://smallwarsjournal.com/jrnl/art/coin-manpower-ratios-debunking-the-10-to-1-ratio-and-surges (accessed 2 May 2017).

Tunstall, Graydon A. *Blood on the Snow: The Carpathian Winter War of 1915*. Lawrence: University Press of Kansas, 2010.

Tunstall, Graydon A. *Planning for War against Russia and Serbia: Austro-Hungarian and German Military Strategies, 1871–1914*. New York: Columbia University Press, 1993.

Vego, Milan N. *Austro-Hungarian Naval Policy 1904–1914*. Portland, OR: Frank Cass, 1996.

Vego, Milan N. *Joint Operational Warfare: Theory and Practice*. Newport, Rhode Island: Naval War College, 2009.

Wagner, Walter. "Die k.(u.)k. Armee - Gliederung und Aufgabenstellung." in *Die Habsburgermonarchie 1848–1918*, Vol. 5 *Die Bewaffnete Macht*. Vienna: Verlag der Österreichischen Akademie der Wissenschaften, 1987.

Wagner, Walter. *Geschichte des K. K. Kriegsministeriums, II. Band 1866–1888*. Wien-Köln-Graz: Hermann Böhlaus: 1971.

Walter, John. *The Rifle Story*. London: Greenhill Books, 2006.

Wandruszka, Adam. *Schicksalsjahr 1866*. Vienna: Styria Verlag, 1966.

Wawro, Geoffrey. *A Mad Catastrophe: The Outbreak of World War I and the Collapse of the Habsburg Empire*. New York: Basic Books, 2014.

Wawro, Geoffrey. "An 'Army of Pigs': The Technical, Social, and Political Bases of Austrian Shock Tactics, 1859–1866." *The Journal of Military History* Vol. 59, No. 3 (July 1995): 407–433.

Wawro, Geoffrey. *The Austro-Prussian War: Austria's War with Prussia and Italy in 1866*. Cambridge: Cambridge University Press, 1996.

Wawro, Geoffrey. "The Austro-Prussian War: Politics, Strategy and War in the Habsburg Monarchy, 1859–1866." Ph.D. dissertation, Yale University, 1992.

Wawro, Geoffrey. *Warfare and Society in Europe, 1792–1914*. New York: Routledge, 2000.

Index

A

Albrecht, 5, 8, 16, 19, 23, 29, 31, 35, 50, 51, 57–60, 64–66, 68, 70, 73–75, 77, 79, 85, 103, 115, 134, 136, 142, 152, 160, 161, 163, 181, 206, 207

Andrássy, 65, 83, 85, 104, 113, 119

Artillery, 2, 3, 5, 6, 8, 9, 14, 15, 17, 19, 21, 22, 24, 25, 36, 50, 54–56, 59, 62, 74, 82, 83, 87, 101, 104, 107–112, 116, 121, 133, 148, 151–153, 155–157, 160–163, 176, 178, 182, 185, 189–200, 203–205, 207, 209, 238–242, 244–248, 250, 254–258, 263, 265

Arz, 6, 246, 256, 260, 262, 263

Auffenberg, 6, 114, 115, 182, 197, 198, 206, 207, 236, 248, 260

Ausgleich, 68, 85

Austria-Hungary, 2–4, 8, 9, 82–84, 103, 120, 121, 137, 139, 144, 150, 153, 154, 157, 158, 160, 175, 176, 178, 182, 188, 194–196, 200, 203, 206, 209, 236–238, 245, 247, 249, 251, 254, 260, 262, 265, 266

Austro-Prussian war, 1, 2, 5–8, 14, 15, 20, 24, 26, 35, 50, 53, 55, 56, 58, 64, 67, 79, 82, 85, 113, 139, 155, 179, 183, 200

B

Balkan wars, 8, 190, 193, 247

Bartels, 1, 26–28, 30, 31, 68

Bauer, 157, 160, 163, 206

Bayonet, 21, 23, 24, 37, 54, 55, 57–59, 86, 100, 108, 122, 137–140, 144, 145, 162, 180, 182–184, 186, 188–190

Beck, 2, 3, 17–19, 24–26, 29–31, 50–52, 64–66, 70, 77, 79, 81, 82, 85, 86, 103, 114–116, 138, 142, 156, 159, 160, 163, 206, 207

Benedek, 2, 6, 7, 13, 15–20, 22–26, 28–30, 37, 49–51, 79

Boer war, 8, 183, 184, 192, 199, 207

J.A. Dredger, *Tactics and Procurement in the Habsburg Military, 1866–1918*, DOI 10.1007/978-3-319-57678-7

Bosnia-Hercegovina, 8, 99, 102, 104–108, 110, 112, 118, 158, 248, 249
Britain, 3, 104, 120, 158, 195, 201–203
Budget, 2, 6, 32–35, 37, 52, 61, 63, 70, 71, 111, 117, 118, 120, 121, 135, 148, 153, 197, 198, 200–204, 206
Burstyn, 204, 205, 208, 242, 256
Bylandt-Rheidt, 110, 118, 121, 122, 141, 157–161, 163, 204, 206

C
Cavalry, 5, 13, 17, 30, 56–59, 62–64, 74, 83, 86, 101, 108, 109, 121, 122, 133, 134, 139, 146–152, 157, 161, 183, 191, 192, 207, 239, 242–244, 248, 257, 258, 263
Chamberlain, 187
Charles, 22, 261–263
Clausewitz, 21, 22, 27, 56, 140, 184, 250
Conrad, 2, 7, 8, 56, 115, 133, 134, 137–140, 142–146, 150, 162, 163, 177–181, 183–186, 188, 189, 191, 193, 196, 198–201, 206–208, 236–246, 248–251, 253, 254, 258–261, 263, 265–267
Custozza, 5, 8, 13, 50, 146

D
Defensive, 5, 8, 9, 22–24, 26–28, 37, 50, 55–58, 102, 107, 137, 139, 140, 145, 146, 149, 151, 154, 155, 162, 176, 178, 182, 184, 186, 199, 236–241, 244, 245, 247, 249–251, 254, 255, 259–261, 265
Delegations, 6, 52, 63, 69, 87, 113, 117, 118, 120, 134, 156, 158, 159, 200, 204–206
Dreadnoughts, 3, 9, 202–205, 239, 242, 246, 247, 255, 264, 266
Dreyse, 1, 19, 20, 23–25, 37, 52

F
Falkenhayn, 254, 258
Fischer, 15, 20, 56, 59
France, 3, 35, 36, 62, 69, 73, 83, 100, 101, 118–120, 134, 139, 144, 150, 153, 155, 158, 163, 175, 177, 180, 193–196, 201–203, 237, 265
Franco-Prussian war, 57, 61, 83, 86, 102, 110, 139, 147, 154, 179, 180, 191, 192
Franz Ferdinand, 183, 189, 190, 201, 206, 207, 236, 249, 251
Franz Joseph, 16, 17, 25, 30, 49–52, 58, 59, 64, 65, 67–70, 72, 83, 85, 99, 114, 120, 135, 159, 160, 206, 208, 238, 260
Funding, 3, 4, 7, 8, 15, 20, 34, 36, 51, 52, 61–64, 72, 113, 117, 120, 133, 153, 157, 158, 195, 197, 201–204, 209, 247, 264

G
Galicia, 2, 27, 103, 119, 154–156, 159, 163, 199, 236–242, 245–254, 257–259, 261, 265, 267
General staff, 5, 6, 8, 37, 50, 51, 53, 54, 56, 57, 61, 64, 65, 67, 75, 77, 79, 81, 82, 85, 86, 101–103, 108, 114, 115, 119, 136, 137, 139, 141, 142, 144, 148,

156, 159, 163, 177–179, 182, 190, 193, 197, 200, 206, 208, 236–238, 240, 242–246, 249, 251, 254, 258, 260, 261
Germany, 3, 7, 9, 27, 69, 74, 101, 103, 106, 118–120, 141, 144, 153, 155, 158, 160, 163, 175, 177, 191, 194–196, 200, 203, 237, 238, 251, 254, 258, 260, 265
Giskra, 33–36, 61, 62
Great power, 1, 4, 7, 8, 49, 84, 86, 119, 158, 160, 176, 177, 196, 202, 203, 205, 206, 209, 236, 238, 240, 245, 249, 251, 260, 266

H
Henikstein, 29, 30, 37, 51, 79
Hess, 27, 59
Honvéd, 69, 71, 101, 118, 142, 144, 256
Horsetzky, 145

I
Infantry regulations, 137, 146, 155, 162, 177, 183–190, 193, 196, 266
Italy, 7, 8, 17, 20, 22, 26, 27, 30, 37, 100, 120, 121, 144, 154, 158, 175, 194, 196, 198, 200–203, 236, 247, 253–255, 258, 261–265, 267

J
John, 2, 24, 35, 50–52, 55, 56, 59, 61, 64, 65, 70, 72, 74, 76, 80, 81, 86
Jomini, 21, 25, 27

K
Koller, 81, 85, 141
Königgrätz, 1, 2, 13–16, 18–20, 25, 26, 28, 31, 37, 49, 50, 52, 79, 86, 102, 145
Krauss, 181, 239, 241, 261
Krieghammer, 160, 161, 163, 204–206
Kriegsschule, 6, 53, 56, 108, 137, 138, 141, 142, 145, 151, 154, 163, 177–179, 181, 190, 193, 208, 239, 248, 260
Krismanić, 18, 19, 29–31, 51, 52
Krobatin, 206
Krupp, 110–112, 121, 152, 153, 194, 195
Kuhn, 53, 61, 62, 65–67, 70, 74, 76, 77, 80–86, 103, 116, 141, 160, 161, 163

L
Landwehr, 60, 68, 69, 71, 72, 74, 102, 117, 118, 139, 142, 144, 152, 177, 239
Lang, 182
Lorenz, 14, 18, 20–22, 24, 37, 52
Ludendorff, 241, 259, 260, 262

M
Mannlicher, 135, 138, 139, 159, 160, 162, 198
Moltke, 23, 58, 107, 134, 141, 150, 179–181, 185, 237, 238, 258, 266

N
Navy, 6, 8, 99, 120, 135, 158, 200–204, 207, 247, 264
Nietzsche, 187

O
Offensive, 1, 5–9, 21–24, 26–28, 37, 55, 57, 58, 86, 102, 106–109, 134, 137–148, 151, 154, 155, 160, 162–164, 176–190, 193, 196, 199–201, 203, 204, 207–209, 236–238, 240, 241, 244–247, 249–255, 258–262, 264, 266, 267
Organ der militärwissenschaftlichen Vereine, 5, 71, 75, 76, 135
Österreichische Militärische Zeitschrift, 5, 18, 135, 176

P
Parliamentary stinginess, 2, 4, 9, 13, 36, 113, 159, 204
Pensions, 33–35, 80, 117, 118
Permanent fortifications, 3, 8, 26–28, 36, 59–61, 74, 87, 101, 112, 122, 133, 153–158, 163, 197–200, 239, 245, 263, 266
Philippović, 104, 113, 115
Pitreich, 6, 148, 203, 206, 238, 242, 246, 259, 266
Plevna, 100, 102, 122, 152, 155
Potiorek, 190, 248–251
Prestige, 1, 4, 6, 7, 9, 59, 178, 202, 240, 245–247, 249–251, 253, 254, 259, 260, 262, 267
Procurement, 17, 19, 36, 37, 51, 83, 87, 110, 118, 121, 123, 133, 135, 158, 159, 161, 176, 195–198, 204, 207, 247, 266
Prussia, 7, 15, 16, 26, 27, 32, 35, 37, 62, 70, 82, 83, 99, 118, 139, 177, 237, 240
Przemyśl, 60, 61, 102, 119, 153, 156, 161, 199, 241, 244–246, 251, 252, 265

R
Radetzky, 13, 21, 22, 49, 116, 143
Ratzenhofer, 57, 136, 137, 141, 183
Reichsrat, 2, 15, 20, 32, 33, 38, 62, 66, 71
Rumania, 68, 195, 259, 263
Russia, 3, 61, 62, 68, 69, 74, 83, 100, 101, 103, 120, 144, 153–156, 160, 162, 163, 175, 186, 188, 191, 194–196, 203, 208, 236, 238, 240, 241, 253, 254, 258, 263, 265, 266
Russo-Japanese war, 8, 179, 185, 186, 188, 191–193, 199, 203, 207, 208, 243
Russo-Turkish war, 100–103, 122, 139, 150, 179

S
Salis-Soglio, 6, 104, 110, 111
Schemua, 197, 206
Schlieffen plan, 237, 238, 265
Schönaich, 203, 206
Schönfeld, 156
Serbia, 2, 4, 68, 190, 191, 194, 236–238, 248–251, 253, 254, 263, 265–267
Social Darwinism, 115, 140, 178
Spending, 1, 3, 4, 6–9, 14, 20, 32, 33, 36, 62, 64, 100, 111, 117, 122, 133, 152, 157, 158, 163, 197, 198, 200, 204, 209, 244, 253, 266, 267
Strategy, 5–9, 19, 25–28, 30, 37, 38, 49, 59, 61, 75–77, 100, 102, 107, 140, 142, 144, 148, 161, 181, 182, 236, 239, 244, 245, 247, 249, 250, 255, 258, 261, 265, 267
Streffleur, 66, 76, 77, 82

T

Tactics, 1, 5–9, 13, 18–25, 29, 32, 37, 38, 49, 52–56, 58, 59, 74–77, 84–86, 100, 102, 105–108, 122, 134, 136–139, 142–144, 146, 150, 162, 163, 176, 178, 179, 181–186, 191, 193, 196, 208, 243, 261–263, 266, 267

Technology, 1, 2, 5, 6, 28, 38, 53, 55, 60, 63, 76, 77, 86, 109, 112, 133, 145, 151, 156, 159, 187, 191, 207, 208, 263

U

Uchatius, 8, 110, 111, 152, 163, 194, 197, 198

W

Waldstätten, 23, 56, 109, 115

War ministry, 6, 8, 18, 20, 32, 34, 63–65, 67, 74, 82, 85, 86, 110, 114, 120, 134, 157–160, 163, 198, 205, 206, 256

Werndl, 52, 53, 63, 83–85, 107, 111, 121, 135, 198, 248

Wuich, 145, 146

CPSIA information can be obtained
at www.ICGtesting.com
Printed in the USA
LVHW041842011219
639064LV00013B/817/P

9 783319 576770